# How the Jesuits Settled in New York

D1214253

# HOW THE JESUITS SETTLED IN NEW YORK

## A Documentary Account

by Thomas C. Hennessy, S.J.

SOMETHING MORE PUBLICATIONS

DISTRIBUTED BY FORDHAM UNIVERSITY PRESS

<u>COVER</u>

Jesuits would take a steamboat like this one from Manhattan to Blackwells Island for their ministries there; a great improvement over being rowed out.

The St. John's College, Fordham, church before the 1929 renovations.

The Fordham Jesuit cemetery today.

Rev. John Larkin, second Jesuit President of St. John's College, Fordham, and founder of St. Francis Xavier College.

The back cover has snippets from the early New York Jesuits' letters.

© Copyright 2003 by Thomas C. Hennessy

All rights reserved. No part of this publication may be reproduced or transmitted in any form or by any means, electronic or mechanical, including photocopy, recording, or information or retrieval system, without permission in writing from the publisher.

This book is being distributed by the Fordham University Press

Library of Congress Control Number 2003105126
ISBN 0-9622889-7-7

Layout, design and cover by George McCauley

This book especially honors

Rev. Joseph A. O'Hare, S.J.

for his nineteen years

of  dedicated service

as President of Fordham University

and for his interest in all its activities

past and present.

# CONTENTS

**FOREWORD**    *Rev. Joseph A. O'Hare, S.J.*                                    *p. ii*

**INTRODUCTION** *Rev. Thomas C. Hennessy, S.J.*                                 *p. iv*

**PROLOGUE**    *Rev. John W. O'Malley, S.J.*                                     *p. ix*

**PART I**    **How the French Jesuits Came to Settle "Near New York"**

   CHAPTER 1   Rev. Clément Boulanger, S.J.                         *p. 2*

   CHAPTER 2   Fr. Minister's Diary, St. Mary's College, KY,           *p. 5*

   CHAPTER 3   Fr. Boulanger's Correspondence, 1845-1847                *p. 12*

**PART II**    **St. John's College, Fordham**

   CHAPTER 4   Rev. August Thébaud, S.J.                              *p. 48*

   CHAPTER 5   Fr. Minister's Diary, St. John's College                 *p. 52*

   CHAPTER 6   The *Annual Letters* to Rome                            *p. 65*

**PART III**    **The College and Parish of St. Francis Xavier**

   CHAPTER 7   Rev. John Larkin, S.J.                               *p. 113*

   CHAPTER 8   The Early Years                                        *p. 117*

   CHAPTER 9   The *Annual Letters* to Rome                            *p. 122*

**PART IV**    **The Fordham Cemetery: New York and Beyond**

   CHAPTER 10 The Cemetery History                                    *p. 155*

   CHAPTER 11 What Documents Can Tell Us                              *p. 161*

   CHAPTER 12 Biographical Profiles                                   *p. 169*

**EPILOGUE**    *Rev. Gerald A. McCool, S.J.*                                    *p. 245*
              *Rev. Gerald R. Blaszczak, S.J.*

**ENDNOTES**                                                          *p. 255*

**APPENDIX I**   The *Liber Defunctorum* on Moving the Cemetery       *p. 259*

**APPENDIX II**  The Honored Dead                                     *p. 264*

**APPENDIX III**  Martyrs of Charity                                  *p. 269*

**APPENDIX IV**  Fr. Mulledy's Last Days                              *p. 273*

**SELECTED REFERENCES**                                               *p. 275*

**INDEX**                                                             *p. 277*

# FOREWORD

Like the other 27 Jesuit Colleges and Universities and 47 high schools in the United States, Fordham University's distinctive history and continuing identity are rooted in the convergence of two stories: the 450 year tradition of Jesuit education and the history of the particular community in which the institution was founded and continues to exist, whether this be large cities like Boston and San Francisco or smaller communities like Worcester and Wheeling. Thus, the history of Fordham and Xavier is inextricably tied to the history of New York City, from its origins as a port of entry for immigrants from other lands to its present status as one of the two or three world cities of the 21st century.

When the Jesuits came to New York in the mid 19th century, they were known as "the French Fathers" because of their leadership and province of origin but, in fact, they were a diverse group with many different national and linguistic roots. They had come to the New World as missionaries, pioneers of the Faith, first to places like Louisiana and Kentucky, and then, at the invitation of the pioneer Archbishop of New York, John Hughes, to New York City. The historical records in this volume, which have been so lovingly recovered and restored for contemporary readers and scholars, are testimony to a remarkable encounter between sons of the Old World and the first generations of the New World that occurred in a city that has from its beginning been a beacon of hope for refugees from other lands and from various forms of repression.

My own experience at Fordham University bears out this dynamic of an educational institution that reflects important characteristics of the city in which it was founded. Because New York City is still at the center of an international network, Fordham University has increasingly become international in its outlook, with programs in places like Beijing and Oxford and students and faculty from many different waves of new Americans who came to these shores in search of freedom and opportunity, today Fordham continues to offer educational opportunities at all three of its campuses to students from families of modest means who seek an entrance into academic, professional and corporate roles of leadership in the service of others.

For their historic interest alone the documents contained in this volume represent an important source of institutional memory for Fordham University, Xavier High School and the 33 other Jesuit apostolic centers in New York and New Jersey (parishes, schools, retreat houses and residences). The experiences of those first Jesuits find a contemporary echo in the commitment to the service of the poor that has become a more deliberate and self-conscious emphasis of our contemporary Jesuits wherever they work. As the documents in this book attest, in the language and idiom of another time, the Jesuits in New York, at Fordham and Xavier and at other apostolates, had a special concern for the poor and the marginalized.

Their commitment to those left behind and left out of the growing prosperity of the new nation received a new articulation in the second half of the twentieth century in the affirmation of the Jesuit mission as service of faith and promotion of justice. The classic Christian humanism that has been at the center of the Jesuit educational tradition now includes an explicit recognition that a constitutive dimension of this tradition must be a responsibility for others. The documentation in this volume provides evidence that their mission to the poor and the marginalized has been a mark of the Jesuit apostolate in New York from its earliest origins.

Similarly, as we move into the first years of the third millennium, we recognize that the opportunities and challenges of the inexorable tide of globalization demand that the education of men and women include an appreciation of intercultural differences and a capacity for conversation across those differences, particularly in the complex dialogue that must take place between the great religious traditions of our world - Christians, Muslims and Jews - and their encounter with modernity. This kind of dialogue the early Jesuits who "settled in New York" could not have imagined or fully appreciated, since most of them were victims of the destructive religious conflicts of Europe and had experienced the destructive purposes to which religious passion can be converted and betrayed.

The restoration of important historical documentation that we see in the following pages allows us to catch a glimpse of the evangelical spirit of an earlier generation of Jesuits in New York, a spirit that can instruct and inspire the response of the sons of Ignatius and their associates of another time, this new millennium, different in so many ways from the decades of the 19th century to which these records attest, but still a time for pioneers who are unafraid, as those first New York Jesuits were, to explore a new world and journey into uncharted territory.

In responding to the needs of this time, with a sense of an international community and a commitment to justice, the Jesuits of this generation will be most faithful to the memory of past generations not by seeking to repeat their history (if that were even possible), but by renewing in creative fashion the tradition that gave their history its meaning.

Joseph A. O'Hare, S.J.
President, Fordham University
February 5, 2003

# INTRODUCTION

This book is the result of treasure-hunting among documents in archives, chiefly the archives of Fordham University — faded documents, with torn edges, of different shapes and sizes, in different languages, with quaint scripts, some with scribbling in the margins, others punctilious to a fault But if the book borrows from these documents, its main focus is its stories about people — great Jesuits who "left all things" to follow Jesus and make his mission their own. They left their native lands — most were French — some moving from a cultured, sophisticated background to the relative wilderness of Kentucky and then onward to a still pioneer-style of living near New York. As the title of this book indicates, they were not the first Jesuits to serve in New York. French-born St. Isaac Jogues passed through in the Fall of 1603, after being rescued by the Dutch from captivity among the Iroquois. A group from the English Province led by Thomas Harvey with two other priests and two brothers ran a Latin School from 1684 to 1687 in the governorship of Col. Thomas Dongan. After the Revolution, the noted German-born Ferdinand Farmer made flying visits from his parish in Philadelphia to numerous New Jersey and New York State areas, including New York City where he founded its first parish, St. Peter's, in 1785. Alsace-born Anthony Kohlmann came to the New York in 1808 as administrator of the diocese; he brought four Jesuits with him to start a college, the New York Literary Institute, which prospered but lasted only until 1815 when all the Jesuits were recalled to Maryland.

But if these men weren't in New York long enough to settle in, those who came to Rose Hill in 1846 from Kentucky and many other climes were more numerous than the others and were better prepared to seize the opportunity for permanent educational and religious service to a city characterized at the time as a dynamic hub of manufacturing, steel industries, ship-building, retailing, newspaper and literary activities, banking, and other money-making sources. Still, they fully appreciated that their primary goal was missionary: spreading the Gospel of Jesus. To do this they became men of their time and place. That meant learning languages and unfamiliar customs. It meant making decisions about where and to whom they would make themselves available. America was then a vast refuge for political and economic refugees from the same Old World they had come from. Anti-Catholicism often greeted them at the dock. America's towns were becoming cities and its cities becoming experiments in modernity. Civil War was in the air, yet the idea of a land of opportunity was fast taking root.

The Jesuit priests spread the Gospel in schools, often most effectively outside the classroom through devotional groups like the Sodalities. The Jesuits brothers saw their missionary task as enabling schools or parishes to run smoothly. Their common mission, before it was all over, took them not only to Kentucky and New York but far and wide — to St. Louis, Indiana and numerous cities and towns in eastern and central Canada. Some names will sound familiar, like Fordham, Xavier, St. Ignatius Parish, St. Peter's College, the islands in the East River, prisons like the Tombs and Sing Sing, Holy Cross, Troy, Boston College, Georgetown. Others will hardly register, like La Prairie, Sandwich, Grand Couteau, Manitouline.

These Jesuits were men of St. Ignatius' *Spiritual Exercises*, preaching love for Jesus in the manner of St. Paul. Their ministry, even those serving in schools, was at heart sacramental — reconciling sinners, caring for the sick and dying, leading people to the Eucharist to hear God's Word and celebrate God's presence. It is such men as these that the time-worn documents in this book attempt to bring to life.

The book is divided into four parts. The opening chapter of each part introduces some significant person or persons central to the action of the book. The two following chapters zero on the documents that illuminate in greater detail the events surrounding that person or persons.

Thus, in Part I, Chapter 1 introduces Fr. Clément Boulanger, an engaging, impressive figure empowered by his Jesuit superiors in Rome to determine the fate of the Jesuit community at St. Mary's College in Kentucky. Chapter 2 presents selections from a diary kept at St. Mary's College's during the time Boulanger was engaged in his difficult task. Chapter 3 contains the trenchant, telling summaries Boulanger wrote of his own correspondence during the same hectic period and after.

Part II repeats the same pattern in this way: Chapter 4 profiles Fr. August Thébaud, the first Jesuit president of St. John's College, Fordham. There follows (Chapter 5) documentation from the early diary kept at St. John's College, near New York. The *Annual Letters* to Rome from St. John's College (Chapter 6) is a veritable treasure-trove of documentation on the inner workings and thinking of those first pioneers. Up to a point, that is. Historians will look in vain for specific details of why the diocesan seminary left Fordham, or why all the comings and goings of the Jesuit scholasticate and novitiate there, or, most intriguingly, why the quarrel (which was studied eventually by the late Fr. Francis X. Curran, S.J.) between Archbishop Hughes and the Jesuits goes largely unmentioned in the diaries and letters cited in these chapters.

Part III begins in Chapter 7 with the story of Fr. John Larkin, founder of the College of St. Francis Xavier. In Chapter 8, a document entitled *Historia Domus* (A History of the House) touches on facets of the Jesuit enterprise on 15th Street. Finally (Chapter 9), there are *Annual Letters* to Rome describing the different ministries of both the College and Parish of St. Francis Xavier.

In Part IV, the significant persons introduced are the dead resting in the Fordham University Jesuit cemetery, which today occupies a small, almost hidden, space between Faber Hall and the University Church. The cemetery contains the remains of seventy percent of the 1846 pioneer Jesuits at Fordham. Chapter 10 describes the history of the cemetery and its relocation from a hilltop that once belonged to Fordham but now is part of the New York Botanical Gardens. Chapter 11 relies on archival sources to unravel certain historical conundra about the cemetery as well as to dispel certain myths. Chapter 12 ranges farther afield with the help of archival and other Jesuit biographical sources to bring to life the individual stories of these honored dead.

Part IV is the nearest thing we have to a definitive history of the cemetery itself, but it serves here as well to illuminate the expanding work of Jesuits in the New York region during the latter half of the nineteenth century.

Working with documents written at such a distance has its own set of problems. Many were written in French or Latin, and I will describe shortly the contribution of our many generous translators to break down the long Ciceronian writing style of that period into something more manageable for today. For my part, I have sometimes added headings and section titles to orient the reader. Where documents expressed things somewhat elliptically, I have added — always in square brackets — the relevant information. I have retained in the text many Latin words and phrases I thought contained some special flavor that would be hard to capture in translation. In the *Annual Letters*, I dropped the dry statistical summary that would normally be appended at the end of each letter.

For some terms I thought we needed, so to speak, a translation of the translation, since the terms would be unfamiliar to the modern ear. Who would know that 'Ours' meant Jesuits? Or that 'externs' meant anyone who wasn't a Jesuit? Or that 'province' could mean both an administrative division of the Society of Jesus and a State, as in United States? Who would casually accept 'heretic' when speaking of non-Catholics or Protestants? Who would know how far a 'league' is (three miles)? Or what a 'franc' was worth in those days (20 cents)? Who would know that a 'gymnasium' or 'college' of that era would include elements of our present day elementary, high school, college *and* university?

Even alumni of institutions I have been associated with like Fordham Prep would be surprised to learn that, from Fordham's foundation, up to and even after World War I, the 'college' was divided into three sections: The First Division, which included the last three years of what now call college; the Second Division, often called the Humanities, which covered today's high school years and the first year of our college; and the Third Division, which included our upper elementary grades and, in some 'colleges' back then, even our middle elementary grades. Thus, Fordham Prep, as I tell alumni, in many ways corresponds to the Second Division of years ago and the history of Fordham College is also the history of Fordham Prep. In any case, we will call the reader's attention to language shifts like these frequently in this book.

Acknowledgments

I must express my gratitude to very many who contributed their knowledge and time towards this labor of love. Most of the documents in the archives were in Latin or French — a fact that partially explains why they have remained for some time hidden treasures! Fortunately, the Jesuits I live with not only share the same religious and educational ideals as I do, but also have skills in Latin and other languages. Many very generously agreed to help, thereby enabling the work to be completed. I therefore thank for their enormous contribution the following Jesuits: Thomas V. Bermingham+, Gerald Blaszczak, Vincent Butler, W. Norris Clarke, William B. Cogan, Frederick Dillemuth, G. Richard Dimler, Joseph V. Dolan, Garrett J. Fitzgerald, Daniel J. Fitzpatrick, Charles H. Giblin+, L. Augustine Grady, Edward F.X. Kennedy, Albert J. Loomie+, George McCauley, Gerald A. McCool, James H. Reid, Richard J. Regan, William L. Reilly, James A. Sadowsky and Robert J. Sealy. A lay teacher at Xavier High

School, Dr. Philip Caliendo, also helped in the translation project. Special gratitude is due Frs. William Cogan and Robert J. Sealy for their generosity and patience in unraveling Latin and French puzzles respectively.

Most of the documents used in this book are housed in the Fordham University archives, The New York Province of the Society of Jesus archives and in the archives of the Province of France. So I wish to acknowledge the help I received from Ms. Patrice Kane and Ms. Vivian Shen, Director and Assistant Director respectively, of the Fordham University Archives, who, besides providing numerous manuscripts related to St. Mary's and St. John's colleges, gave frequent, exact and cheerful assistance.

Rev. Frederick J. O'Brien, the New York Province archivist, provided me with Fr. Boulanger's letter-summaries and assisted in many other ways. Rev. Robert Bonfils, archivist of the Province of France, contributed a complete set of the pertinent *Annual Letters*, and, in an extraordinary act of kindness, not only typed the hand-written summaries but filled out abbreviated words and translated older French words to their modern equivalent. Many other archivists in provinces and colleges also were helpful in providing information and photographs; for want of space I hope they will be satisfied with a general thank-you.

Another excellent contribution came from Rev. Daniel J. Gatti, President of Xavier High School, who provided copies of documents and photographs and other materials about his predecessors and their associates.

Authors of the separate essays found in this book also merit special recognition. The Foreword was written by Rev. Joseph A. O'Hare, S.J., who is now completing his 19th and final year as President of Fordham University. On another page we express gratitude for his many contributions to the university and for his assistance to efforts such as this one to increase an understanding and appreciation of the institution's Jesuit heritage. Rev. John W. O'Malley's studies of church and Jesuit documents have made him a recognized leader among historians. In the Prologue he gives us a foretaste of what to expect in the book as he reflects on the people who wrote the documents at the heart of this book and gives us some highlights of what he read.

Two others essays are found in the Epilogue, the first by Rev. Gerald A. McCool, a distinguished philosophy professor and author of many books on philosophy and theology. He shows us how the pioneer New York Jesuits successfully implanted academic traditions built on a solid philosophical/theological basis that are retained to this day. The final essay is by Rev. Gerald R. Blaszczak, the Fordham University Chaplain, whose reflection on the cemetery leads him to ponder what sort of ministries Jesuits should be involved in today in order to be truly "men for others."

And how do I adequately thank my durable editor, publisher and friend, Fr. George McCauley, who generously took on this task in the midst of numerous other commitments? I could not have done it without him.

Firnally, I wish to thank Rev. Vincent J. Duminuco, Rector of the Jesuits of Fordham, for facilitating the speedy printing of the book, and Mr. Saverio Procario and the Fordham University Press for handling its distribution and sale.

Thomas C. Hennessy, S.J.

# PROLOGUE

The documents in this collection have a significance that might escape the casual reader. In the first place they provide the essential building blocks for constructing the early history of two important institutions in the history of New York City — Fordham University, and the St. Francis Xavier complex of school, parish, and other ministries located at Sixteenth Street in Manhattan. Beyond that they provide the basic information for constructing the early history of the institution behind those institutions, the New York Province of the Society of Jesus. Even if these were the only purposes served by publishing the collection, the effort would be well worth it.

The documents provide, however, windows onto other worlds as well. They open our eyes to important aspects of the social history of Catholicism in New York just as it was becoming a force to be reckoned with. I was particularly struck by the several times the plight and the importance of the "Irish maids" was described. Like many others, I have often heard how American Catholicism was founded on the pennies of the poor, but I have seldom had the reality brought home to me so pointedly. Although the documents indicate, sometimes only obliquely, how many immigrants for one reason or another gave up their Catholic faith, or at least its practice, they also confirm the great sacrifices many of them made simply to assist at Mass on Sunday and, perhaps more remarkable, the time and effort they expended to receive the sacrament of Penance.

This was not the passive Catholicism of the pre-Vatican II stereotype. The men and women in question would probably have been shocked to have themselves described as performing a ministry of the church, but in actual fact that is what some of them did when they undertook teaching catechism, often seemingly with little direct supervision. Of special importance for giving them a sense of cohesion and direction was membership in the Sodality of Our Lady, also known as the Marian Congregation. That organization, founded in Rome in 1564, was the Jesuit adaptation of the "confraternities" that flourished in Catholic Europe from about the fourteenth century well into the twentieth. In these voluntary, usually self-determining organizations, Catholics of all social classes joined together to foster their religious devotion and to undertake on a corporate basis some activity that today we would term a "social ministry." As the scholarship of the past twenty years has shown, it would be difficult to exaggerate the importance of such institutions in the daily lives of the members. What emerges from the pages of this collection of documents especially as related to the Xavier complex, in any case, is the image of a people, weary and oppressed though they often were, filled with an energy and optimism that sprang to a large extent from their Catholic faith.

The many pages concerning the students at Fordham reveal another side of the Catholic experience. Here are young men, surely from modest backgrounds, pursuing a course of studies comparable at least in its structure with that pursued by their surely more affluent and well born counterparts in Europe. For those pursuing the "liberal" program, the curriculum is roughly the same as it had been since the Renaissance, which itself built on the directions left by Cicero and Quintilian. That curriculum, with its underlying philosophy, had been adopted by the Jesuits. It had been adopted in fact by most serious educators engaged in what we now call primary and secondary schooling. The aim was to produce the well-spoken gentleman with all the skills necessary to assume his responsibilities to family, city, and church. Underlying the program, therefore, was a philosophy of education that had a strong ethical component.

Between the lines, that is what we read in the pages describing the main-line education at Fordham. You will note that theology was not taught, and practically no mention is made of religion playing any direct or important role in the curriculum. Catholicism had not yet entered into the highly doctrinalized stage in which we find it today. The belief of the students in the basic truths of the faith was assumed. What was important was to inspire a deeper appreciation of them through example, ritual, and similar means, and, even more important, to inspire the boys through the general orientation of the curriculum to ideals of service, self-sacrifice, and justice. This was not simply the Jesuit ideal, though it had particular manifestations in the Jesuit milieu, but an ideal that for the most part was taken for granted by educators from all traditions. It created an international bond of civility and mutual understanding that was activated anywhere in the world upon contact with one another of one graduates from this *paideia*.

Some particulars at Fordham deserve special mention, such as the importance given to games and sports, a tradition in humanistic education the Jesuits did much to advance. The games were for recreation, but, as the documents hint or state, they also fit into the broadly moral framework that underlay the whole educational enterprise. The integral part played by music in church and in academic celebrations was an especially important Jesuit tradition, contrary to what we have often been told. Also worthy of note is how "business" courses were present from the beginning, a reminder that for all the idealism of the undertaking a certain responsiveness to the needs and wants of prospective students was likewise operative.

It was Jesuits of course who wrote the letters and about whom they for the most part were written. What is the image of them that emerges? Perhaps the first thing that struck me, as it has struck me so often in dealing with Jesuit documents from earlier eras, is how honest the discourse seems to be. Issues are laid out in a clear and un-adorned fashion. The letters are circumspect in that they avoid being specific when discussing a Jesuit's failures or problems, but otherwise they are straightforward and even blunt. The letters to the Father General state unambiguously the conflicting claims, for instance, of the Jesuits from the Missouri region and those from the East Coast, with the perennial problem of the equitable distribution of manpower at the center of the agitation.

Like similar Jesuit documents from earlier eras, however, the letters, for all their obvious intent of making honest reports, sometimes read like victory bulletins. Discerning historians need therefore to approach them not unarmed with the hermeneutics of suspicion. The glowing terms in which the harmony of the communities is reported, for instance, hardly seems to correspond to the difficulties one would expect, even with the best of will of the part of everybody concerned. As the reports indicate, the size of the Fordham community fluctuated considerably, almost from year to year, with notable admixture of ages and status in the Society. Even more problematic, I venture, would be the pooling together of adult males from such a variety ol national backgrounds, some of whom were refugees fresh off the boat from Europe. I an not challenging the basic veracity of the reports in this regard, please understand, but only suggesting that human interaction tends to be more complex than these, admittedly brief, reports seem to suggest.

Also noteworthy about them is how relatively little notice is taken in them of the great events taking place in the wider world, such as the "Revolutions of 1848" in Europe and the Civil War in America. Mention is of course made of both these events, but not much more. The former, for all the upheaval it caused for the Catholic church in Europe, had a seemingly beneficial effect in North America, where many priests and religious took refuge. The American Civil War gets even less mention, although it was much closer to home. The basic reason for this inattention of course is the literary genre we are dealing with, internal reports on basically internal matters. In that regard, once again, the letters are similar to their counterparts from earlier times.

For that matter, the format of the reports follows a pattern that was established at the very origins of the Society of Jesus in the sixteenth century, principally under the example and directives emanating from the brilliant first Secretary of the Society, Juan Alfonso de Polanco. These official reports to the Father General tended to have three distinct parts. The first was the simple statement of the basic statistics about the community-how many members, their status, etc. This was followed by a narrative on the various ministries in which members of the community were engaged, beginning with the major institutions operated by the Society. The narrative could take different forms and the focus might shift from year to year, but noteworthy happenings, whether for good or ill, were to be described, and problems as well as opportunities reported clearly. The third element consisted in anecdotes or specific incidents that illustrated some larger truth and that reduced a generality of the narrative to its human dimension.

For me the human dimension pervades the documents, and nowhere more tellingly than in the image of the Jesuit personality that emerges. Do you not get the impression that they were kind men? The letters cannot say enough good about the students at Fordham. The boys are praised for their intelligence, for their diligence in their studies, for their religious devotion, for their sense of responsibility, for their respect for their teachers, for their care for one another. If we were investigating the social reality of the students, perhaps here too a little hermeneutics of suspicion would be in order. That hermeneutics would be directed towards the students, however, not toward the attitude of the writer of the report, which is clear enough.

We know that in schools of the nineteenth century strict discipline was enforced, to a degree inconceivable in the twenty-first century. Our documents occasionally betray suggestions that at Fordham an upright regime was taken for granted and deviations not tolerated. Nonetheless, within that framework of expectations shared by parents, faculty, and even students, the atmosphere seems to have been congenial and respectfully familiar. There is, to put it negatively, no hint of the Jesuit as martinet or of the school as a boot camp in discipline.

The same positive assessment of the people to whom the Jesuits ministered is evinced also in the reports from Xavier on the parish, the school, and the Sodalities. Given the historical context, the concern at Xavier for the black population further reinforces this impression, as does the perceptive observation by the Jesuit writer of the report that the liberators of the slaves wanted to have nothing to do with them once liberated. It would be interesting to know more in detail what further measures, if any, were taken for the black population. In this instance as in so many others, the documents provide pointers to historians for possibly rewarding research.

According to these reports, as is true throughout the history of the Jesuits, people flocked to hear Jesuit sermons and in many instances preferred them to the preaching of other priests. This impression recurs in the documentation about Jesuits buried in the cemetery at Fordham which offers a panoramic view of Jesuit work in the New York region in the second half of the 19th century. Make allowances here for exaggeration, but do not out of hand dismiss the claim. Was there something special about their preaching? If so, what? Even more intriguing is the persistent claim throughout the history of the Jesuits, made several times in our documents, that people sought out Jesuit confessors above others and found themselves more comforted by them. True? If so, why? These are questions too big to be addressed here. I will simply say that for my part I suspect that the compassion that these documents manifest when telling of those to whom the Jesuits minister might help explain the phenomenon. In these documents I read nothing of scolding or of God's anger. I read much of desire to help others and to make their burdens lighter. No small legacy that.

John W. O'Malley, S.J.

PART I

"Near New York"

How the French Jesuits Came to Settle There

# CHAPTER 1

## REV. CLÉMENT BOULANGER, S.J.

### A Man of Many Parts Who Chose New York over Kentucky

Jesuits had been passing through New York on the way elsewhere for over two hundred years. The first one was St. Isaac Jogues who visited in 1643 as he escaped from his Indian captors on the route back to France. It had been the entry point for many a Jesuit missionary heading for the wilds of Maryland or St. Louis or Trois Rivières. And it had been the temporary residence for two groups who began short-lived schools there.

But it was Clément Boulanger who made New York the site of two permanent Jesuit educational institutions. He was the son of Pierre Boulanger, a blacksmith (maréchal-ferrant), and Marguerite Receveur, born October 30, 1790, at St. Clément, France. He entered the Jesuits as a diocesan priest and a theology professor in 1823. After only one year of noviceship, he made additional theological studies and taught theology at St. Acheul (near Amiens), and at Madrid from 1830 to 1833. From 1833 to 1841 he twice held the office of rector, first at the Vals-près-Le Puy Seminary and later at the Paris Seminary. He became Provincial Superior of the Jesuit province of France from February 4, 1842 to March 16, 1845. As Provincial, he was responsible for making numerous difficult and critical decisions in France and in the New World. One of his decisions was to return the Jesuits to Canada through the on-site leadership of the local mission Superior, Fr. Peter Chazelle. And a few years later he would make the critical decisions regarding the future activities of the Jesuits who had struggled for more than a dozen years at St. Mary's College in Marion County, Kentucky.

On April 1, 1845, at age 55 and shortly after completing his term as Provincial, Boulanger was appointed official Visitor to the French province's missions in the new world with authority to make important decisions on his own. The official appointment and the authority to act came from Fr. Jan Roothaan, the Jesuit General in Rome.

On his way to Kentucky, he stayed in New York for a few days, and made two courtesy calls on Bishop Hughes. During those visits he surely must have recalled that when he was Provincial he had informed Hughes that he just didn't have the manpower to accept the college at Rose Hill. He was also aware of extensive correspondence, beginning in 1839, between Fr. General Roothaan, Fr. De Smet, and others regarding Hughes' hope that the Jesuits have his new college. Yet when the bishop and he met twice that spring of 1845, neither made any reference to the college, as is the way of experienced bargainers which they both were. Boulanger wrote to Rome that it would not help his cause to give "the air of wanting it [the college], of looking for it." Likewise, when the bishop decided to renew his offer in writing, he did not do it directly to the Visitor but wrote on October 8, 1845 to Fr. Larkin and suggested that he could show the letter to the Visitor.

On June 14, 1845, Boulanger arrived as Visitor at St. Mary's, Kentucky, and immediately began an on-site evaluation regarding the future of the college. By June 28 he made the final decision to refuse the oft-repeated offer from the diocese there to take over St. Joseph's College in Bardstown. While he was weighing various other options for St. Mary's, the letter arrived from Bishop John Hughes renewing his earlier invitations to the Kentucky Jesuits to move to Rose Hill, near New York City. On November 10, he left Kentucky for New York to discuss details of the invitation. An agreement was made rapidly because the bishop was leaving shortly for Rome. So, on November 24, 1845, documents to transfer the Rose Hill property were signed by the Visitor and the bishop. In following decades some Jesuits blamed him for rushing into the vaguely worded agreement on which he could do little consultation and had no legal advice.

On March 26, 1846, the Jesuit General modified Boulanger's appointment by making him the Superior of the Kentucky and Canada Mission (which shortly was renamed, the New York-Canada Mission) with headquarters at Fordham. He continued in that assignment until November 17, 1855. The task of a Visitor is temporary; the Mission Superior usually stays in that position for years if his health and other conditions warrant it.

At Fordham Boulanger accepted an additional position, that of professor of Moral Theology; an honored teaching post similar to that usually held by college Presidents of his day in American colleges; they usually taught Ethics (Moral Philosophy) courses to seniors.

One of the disappointments of his term of office must have been the increasing tensions between the Jesuits and Archbishop Hughes. Tensions centered around the administration and faculty of the seminary; the seminary grounds, and other issues which escalated to crisis proportions during the term of office of his successor, Rev. John-Baptist Hus. On the other hand, he must have felt a sense of satisfaction at the growth of manpower in the missions: in 1842 the Canada and Kentucky Jesuit personnel totaled 39 but in 1855 the mission numbers mounted to 180.

After completing his term as Mission Superior, Boulanger became spiritual father for one year at College Ste.-Marie, Montreal. He then returned to France to be Superior of the new Jesuit residence at Nancy, in the diocese where he was born. From 1862 to 1864, he was Rector of the Jesuit College at Laval, France. His final assignment during 1865-68 was again at Nancy, where he was spiritual father. He died on June 12, 1868 at Issenheim, France.

During his nine-year term as Mission Superior, in addition to bringing the Jesuits to Fordham, he shared in credit for founding the following institutions: the College and parish of St. Francis Xavier in New York City (1847), College Ste.-Marie in Montreal (1848), and Maison St. Joseph, Sault-au-Récollet in Montreal (1853). In addition, he encouraged new missionary and educational activities in numerous sites among the Canadian Indians.

Fr. Boulanger was regarded by most of his contemporaries as an exceptional administrator. He was seen as an affable person, an outstanding counselor, a man well qualified to solve skillfully the difficult problems he faced both in France and in the new world. As is seen in the following chapters, his solutions to these problems showed his initiative and vision in entering into new situations and recognizing possibilities for development, and at the same time they demonstrated his zeal to share his Christian and Ignatian worldview with people in the new world. His writings reflect his deep concern for the spiritual progress of his fellow Jesuits and their students, as well as his love for the Church and for the Society of Jesus.

Fr. Boulanger was a critically important figure in the history of the Jesuits of the New York Jesuit province. As official Visitor to the Mission from the Province of France (1845), he rejected other attractive invitations, and decided to remove the Jesuits from Kentucky in favor of Bishop Hughes' offer to purchase and staff his struggling St. John's College at Rose Hill which the bishop began in 1841. The Rose Hill location was for many years the site of the Mission Superior's headquarters, the novitiate and scholasticate, and thus the birthplace of what later became the New York Jesuit province.

As Superior of the Mission, Fr. Boulanger assigned and recruited the new faculty and administration of the college at Rose Hill and at other foundations such as the College of St. Francis Xavier. Better than many of his contemporaries, he recognized that the New York area was an important locale for Jesuit apostolates in both educational and pastoral ministries. For his vision of New York as an important site for future Jesuit ministry, for making the decisions to move there, and for translating those decisions into actuality, this writer believes that Fr. Clément Boulanger should be honored as the "Father of the New York Province of the Society of Jesus."

CHAPTER 2

"A refusal pure and simple"

## THE JESUIT DIARY, ST. MARY'S COLLEGE, 1845-46

The end of the Jesuit mission in Kentucky was the beginning of its work New York. A fuller account of that transition will be found in Fr. Boulanger's correspondence in Chapter Three. But we do have a record of the last days at St. Mary's College in Kentucky, a diary kept by the Fr. Minister of the Jesuit Community there and written in French. We see in this translation the bare outlines of what must have been a painful disengagement for all concerned: the closing of a recently begun college in Louisville and several important chaplaincies, arrangements made for the continuance of St. Mary's college under new, non-Jesuit management, and the pure and simple refusal to make any future commitments in the region such as taking charge of St. Joseph's College in Bardstown.

In some ways the account below, beginning with June, 1845, reads like the business-as-usual doings of any Jesuit college of those days: students studying, praying, recreating, graduating; Jesuits coming and going or making their retreats or being assigned different roles in the Jesuit community (probably with an eye to New York). In these brief pages, the figure of Fr. Clément Boulanger, the official Visitor (in the diary he is at times identified by name, and at other times by his office), may at first seem muted, almost marginal. But he was making all the important decisions, so we may assume much more was afoot.

JUNE, 1845

8, Sunday: We receive the good news that the Visitor, Rev. Father Clément Boulanger and his Socius, will arrive soon.

A long awaited box from France has arrived.

13, Fri.: Fr. Petit returned after having given many missions or retreats in Scott County and in neighboring places. Rev. Mr. McMahon came with him.

Fr. De Luynes went to Lebanon to meet Rev. Fr. Visitor.

14, Sat.: Rev. Fr. Boulanger and Fr. Hus arrived early at St. Mary's. The issue that led them here was the oft repeated offer, earnestly reinforced by the bishops and numerous leading Bardstown citizens, that the Society take charge of St. Joseph's College in Bardstown.

In the afternoon a letter arrived from Rev. Fr. Boulanger, dated March 16. It informed us that Very Rev. Fr. General has appointed the Rev. Fr. Ambrose Rabillon to be his successor as Provincial of the French province.

21, Sat.: One of our students, William James Seto, 16 or 17 years of age, was baptized in the Sodality chapel. Rev. Fr. Visitor and Fr. Hus were present.

22, Sun.: Feast of St. Aloysius Gonzaga (and of our) Sodality. 6 A.M. Mass; Communion with choir; Rev. Fr. Boulanger was celebrant. Eleven students made their First

Communion; Benediction of the Blessed Sacrament in the evening, preceded by a short exhortation from Rev. Fr. Rector.

24, Tues.: At 11:00 and at 5:45 Rev. Fr. Visitor assembled all the Fathers.

25, Wed.: Rev. Fr. Visitor, accompanied by Fathers Murphy and Hus, left for Bardstown to see [St. Joseph's] College and come to a decision about the offer made by the bishop and several of the local citizens. During the last few days there was a meeting of all the Fathers to discuss the question.

28, Sat.: Rev. Fr. Visitor returned from Bardstown with the two Fathers who went with him. Bishop Flaget with Fr. Martin Spalding, the Vicar General, met with them there. The definitive reply about accepting the college in Bardstown was a refusal, pure and simple.

29, Sun.: Feast of Saints Peter and Paul. Renovation of vows after the usual triduum. Those who renewed their vows were Fathers Thébaud, Driscol and De Luynes, and Brothers Lacoste and Callaghan.

JULY, 1845

3, Thu.: Rev. Fr. Visitor and Fr. John Hus, his Socius, left for Louisville and Canada.

4, Fri.: Independence Day, celebrated as usual: speeches, etc.

5, Sat.: A student, John Sellers, 15 or 16 years of age, was baptized.

6, Sun.: Three First Communions. ...

16, Tues.: Exhibition. Everything was going smoothly when toward one o'clock, a heavy downpour scattered the crowd, estimated at 5,000 people. The barn and the residence, everything, was occupied by the crowd looking for shelter. No further disorder except what the situation made inevitable. After an hour and a half the weather improved and the game began. Then the distribution of medals and the conferring of degrees followed on the terrace of the college, witnessed by a small number of spectators. There were students in seven grades and the public retired satisfied.

17, Thurs.: Fr. Larkin arrived this evening from Louisville.

20, Sun.: Fr. Larkin preached at St. Charles and began his retreat that evening along with Fr. Gilles.

22, Tu.: Several of the Fathers went to Loretto and to Holy Mary to help in the students' examinations which will take place tomorrow.

30, Wed.: Fr. Driscol and Br. Gockeln returned from a visit to Nazareth and to St. Thomas.

AUGUST, 1845

2, Sat.: Fr. Larkin went to St. Rose to preach there on Monday, the feast of St Dominic. From there he returned to Louisville.

Rev. Mr. Quinn (a scholastic) and a seminarian from St. Thomas spent the night.

3, Sun.: Brs. Ryan and Gockeln went to St. Rose for the feast of St. Dominic.

6, Wed.: This evening the retreat for Loretto and its environs began. Three of our

Fathers were there to give the retreat and hear confessions of about 70 religious on the final day of the retreat.

14: Fr. Driscol returned from Cincinnati.

15: Rev. Fr. Rector left for Louisville and Cincinnati.

16: Brothers Ryan, Gockeln and Hennen began their retreat at the novitiate.

17, Sun.: This evening Fr. Verdin (a Belgian of the Missouri province, here a few days), Fr. Du Merle, and Brothers Maréchal and Séné began their retreat at the novitiate.

25, Mon.: Brothers Gockeln, Ryan and Hennen returned to Louisville.

27, Wed.: A circular letter from Fr. Provincial to the superiors of our missions: With the approval of the Holy See (not an order to do so), Rev. Father General has taken several measures that should make for changes in several of our houses. For a long time the existence of these houses had been threatened. And lately the French government entered into the subject on the side of the enemies of the Society and sent a diplomat to Rome to get the Holy See to intervene. The negotiation did not obtain what it sought. But Rev. Fr. General, understanding the considerations that should have an influence on his judgment and on his conscience, decided under the circumstances to yield somewhat. The house in Paris will be dispersed as well as the one in Lyons on Sala Street. If there are other modifications they will be made later on.

This is a crisis for our province and for the Society. It is a cause of profound affliction for its members and devoted friends.[1]

29, Fri.: Fr. Rector returned from Louisville and Cincinnati. Fr. Du Merle and Br. Maréchal left this evening for Louisville.

## SEPTEMBER, 1845

1, Mon.: At the invitation of Fr. Young of St. Rose, Fr. De Luynes went to Menton to preach on the occasion of the laying of the corner- stone of the new church.

4, Thurs.: Today, as we learned later, V. Rev. Peter Chazelle, first superior of St. Mary's and of the Kentucky Mission, died in Green Bay, Wisconsin. For several years he had been the superior of the Canada Mission at Sandwich.

He had been on his way for Sault Sainte Marie where he had thought he would set up a house. But at Machinaw he was obliged to stop over and wait for a ship; he profited from the few days' delay to visit Green Bay, where our Fathers long ago had a mission. He wanted to acquire certain information there. But hardly had he arrived than he was taken with a violent fever which at the end of two weeks carried him to the grave.

He had been received by Madame Gaignon, a respectable Catholic of the region. Two other missionaries who were in the region attended to him. A newspaper of Wisconsin spoke of the event in a manner that honored the memory of the deceased. His patience and resignation had singularly edified those who saw him during his illness. Mme. Gaignon and the newspaper said the same thing: the whole city gathered together to accompany the priest, a stranger, to the grave. R.I.P.

5, Fri.: Fr. Thébaud began his retreat this evening.

8, Mon.: Feast of the Nativity of Our Lady. The students return today.

9, Tues.: Around 9 o'clock this morning the bell rang calling the students to study.

14, Sun.: Students' Mass at 8:15, as at other years. Rev. Fr. Rector said the Mass and preached. During the Mass, the *Veni Creator* was sung. Each priest was required to say Mass for heaven's blessings on this year.

18, Thurs.: A young Irishman, Mr. O'Regan, sent from Canada by Rev. Fr. Visitor, arrived; he wished to be a teacher.

OCTOBER, 1845

2, Thurs.: The Fathers and Brothers have been invited to commend our college to the protection of the Holy Angels that it please God to preserve us from contagious diseases and from all accidents.

10, Fri.: Feast of St. Francis Borgia. Rev. Fr. Visitor (Fr. Clément Boulanger) returned from his trip to Canada. Fr. John Hus, his Socius, is to return a month later.

16, Mon.: Domestic exhortation by Rev. Fr. Visitor.

19, Sun.: Fr. Driscol and Br. Ledoré began their retreat this evening.

NOVEMBER, 1845

1, Sat.: Feast of All Saints. Mass at the college church at the usual time, 8:15. At 6:30 P.M., Rev. Fr. Thébaud preached and the sermon was followed by Benediction of the Blessed Sacrament. Supper after the Benediction, about 7:30. For several days now, supper has been served on Sundays and on holidays at 7:30 as on other days.

Our Fathers and Brothers enter the refectory as they leave Litanies. Thus the students have had a longer study period on this day. Supper on Sunday and on holidays is a half-hour later than at other times. On these days, as on the other days, the students are given a light collation. This they take at the end of their three o'clock study period.

At dinner today the college appointments were read: Rev. Fr. August Thébaud Rector beginning Feb. 1, 1845, Fr. Simon Fouché, Minister, etc. The latter will cease being confessor at Loretto since his work at the college will not permit him to continue there any longer. For eight years he has exercised that ministry with the sisters through a special permission given by V. Rev. Fr. General at the request of Bishop Flaget. Also at the request of the Bishop Fr. Fouché reviewed and corrected their old rules. The new rules have been sent to Rome for definitive approval. Until that arrives, the new rules are being observed almost in their entirety. (Look elsewhere for what has been said on this subject.)

Fr. Fouché will be in charge of the writing of the house Diary

3, Mon.: The cleaning of the rooms, particularly recommended by Rev. Fr. Visitor has begun. The work will continue during the following days.

8, Wed.: Rev. Fr. Boulanger departed for New York.

11: Fr. Petit left for Loretto to begin tomorrow his ministry as ordinary confessor.

21: Fr. Lebreton began his retreat which will end on December 4, the feast St. Francis Xavier.

DECEMBER, 1845

23: Fr. Fouché began his retreat to end on the vigil of the feast of the Circumcision, Dec. 31.

JANUARY, 1846

3: Fr. Murphy had to go this evening to Loretto to say Mass there the next day.

6: Feast of the Epiphany. Low Mass at which Rev. Fr. Murphy preached. In the evening the Benediction of the Blessed Sacrament was attended by the students.

10: Fr. Murphy began his retreat this morning to end it next Saturday evening.

FEBRUARY, 1846

9: Fr. Legoüais began his retreat this morning.

16: The house in Louisville was dissolved. The members who composed it were reassigned except Fr. Larkin and Br. Hennen . . . . They arrived [here] today.

25: Ash Wednesday. Ashes were blessed in the domestic chapel at 5:15 A. M. and distributed to our community immediately after. The young ones received theirs after an instruction given by Fr. Rector who also said the Mass. Classes as usual.

MARCH, 1846

9: Fr. Hus has been called to France by the Fr. Provincial. He left today.

18: Fr. Hus set sail today on the steamboat *Le Havre*.

22?: Mr. Delaune, a priest from Indiana, arrived with proposals in the name of the Brothers of St. Joseph. They will continue our school after our departure and will open a primary school. If the project succeeds, they agree to pay 2,500 pounds for the major part of our movable effects in accordance with the bill of intent which Mr. Delaune has in hand.

APRIL, 1846

9, Holy Thursday: Fr. Thébaud sang the Mass at 6 o'clock and the students attended. The Blessed Sacrament was exposed in the domestic chapel. A priest, a scholastic, or a brother, and some young persons were assigned for each hour to remain in adoration up till 9 o'clock in the evening.

10, Good Friday: The liturgy was said by Fr. Fouché. There was no singing except during the adoration of the cross. The celebrant offered reflections which preceded the ceremony. The students attended the whole liturgy which began at 6 o'clock in the afternoon.

The evening sermon on the passion by the Fr. Rector Several stanzas of the *Stabat Mater* were sung. All the Jesuits were present.

11, Holy Saturday: Mass was sung at 6:00 A.M. by Fr. Rector for our community only. The students at that time were studying during these three days with classes held as usual.

Fr. Larkin arrived.

12, Easter: High Mass was sung by Fr. Larkin. In the afternoon he also preached. Then Benediction was given by Fr. Gilles.

19, Sunday: Fr. Rector started out for New York with Fr. Murphy.

Fr. Larkin was named interim president and Fr. Fouché Minister, Superior and Vice-Rector.

*[The Diary of St. Mary's College, which was written in French, ended at this point. The Diary of St. John's College, Fordham, began in Latin. Because the story of St. Mary's wasn't completed until its staff arrived in New York, I have placed here from the Fordham diary more extensively reported in Chapter 5 the entries from April 19 until August 9 that describe the scene 'near New York' when most of the Kentucky contingent had come to their new home. Of course, the new community received others who arrived later from all directions.]*

April 19: Rev. Fr. Rector [Thébaud] and Fr. [William Stack] Murphy set out for the new headquarters and new labors with the joyful songs of those who remain here. And on April 28 they were kindly received by the president and professors of the New York college.

July 1: This year the report of the celebration of graduation, public prizes and promotions at St. Mary's College, KY, was a sad one: speeches were not welcomed as formerly with applause but with groans and tears. Fr. Larkin escaped this sad scene rapidly and arrived at the New York college on July 18.

July 20: Today Rev. Fr. Visitor warned the Fathers and Brothers that they be prepared to undertake their journey within a few days. He divided all into four distinct groups and gave each group a leader, the first one named in the list:

1. Rev. Fr. Visitor [Boulanger], Frs. [Michael] Driscol and [Peter] Lebreton, Brothers [Alexander] Chauvet, [Patrick] Crow, and [James] Séné.

2. Frs. [Nicholas] Petit and [Vitalis] Gilles, Brothers [Wilhelm] Gockeln, [Philip] Corne, [Michael] Jarry and [Philip] Ledoré.

3. Frs. [Charles] DeLuynes and [Henry] Du Merle, Brothers [James] Graves and [Xavier] Maréchal, [Peter] Constance and [Adrian] Lacoste.

4. Fr. [John] Ryan, Brothers [Henry] Hudon and [Michael] Nash, [John] Callaghan, [Jeremiah] Garvey and [Wilhelm] Hennen).

It was considered necessary that Fathers [Simon] Fouché and [Thomas] Legoüais remain in Kentucky a little longer.

July 21: Today the first group set out. It arrived safely on July 29th. The other bands left at other times, namely, the second group on the 23rd, the 3rd group on the 29th, the 4th, finally, on the 31st.

July 31: Once all domestic details were settled, Frs. Fouché and Legoüais moved from St. Mary's to an inn in Louisville, and from there they set out again on August 10 and arrived in the New York college on August 22.

August 2: Frs. Petit and Gilles, Br. Gockeln, and Brs. Come, Jarry and Ledoré arrived [at Rose Hill].

August 9: Added to the above were Frs. DeLuynes and Du Merle, Brs. Graves and Maréchal, Constance and Lacosta, and Fr. Ryan with his group.

This chapter ends fittingly with a picture of the likely route the Jesuits took from St. Mary's to St. John's, based on the recollections of Fr. M. Nash.[2]
  • From St. Mary's to Loretto to Bardstown [probably by private stage]. 20.5 miles.
  • From Bardstown to Louisville, KY. By stage. 35 miles.
  • From Louisville to Cincinnati, Ohio, Aug. 2. By mail boat. 150 miles.
  • From Cincinnati towards Pittsburgh. By steamer. But they did not get to Pittsburgh; the steamer ran aground close to Wheeling, WV. 450 miles.
  • From Wheeling to Cumberland, MD. By stage. 110 miles.
  • From Cumberland to NYC, crossing the Potomac at Harper's Ferry. By the B&O Railroad via Baltimore, Philadephia, and Jersey City; by ferry across the Hudson to NYC. About 320 miles.
  • In NYC near City Hall they boarded the NY & Harlem RR; arrived at Fordham station (for a time the northern terminus of the line) in 2 hours. Their vehicle was drawn first by horse to 4th Ave. and 32nd St. and thence by steam engine. 12 miles

They started their trip on July 31and arrived on August 9.

But arrived where? The political designation of the Rose Hill campus varied over the years. The first printed St. John's College catalogue, 1849-1850, states that the college was situated "about eleven miles from the City of New York and three from Harlem." It was "near" the village of Fordham in the town of West Farms. All these places were in Westchester County until 1874, the year the towns of the "West Bronx" were incorporated into New York City and County. Incorporation happened to the "East Bronx" in 1895. When Queens, Staten Island and Brooklyn were consolidated into New York City in 1898, the Bronx area was designated a borough of the city. In 1914, it became the 32nd and last county in New York State.

# CHAPTER 3

## "I am neither subtle nor political."

## FR. BOULANGER'S CORRESPONDENCE, 1845-1847

If Boulanger's nine years of leadership of French Jesuits were to have an impact on the future of the Society of Jesus in New York, he would certainly face numerous challenges to his judgment and to his physical stamina. Assigned as Visitor by the Fr. General in Rome and later as its Mission Superior General by the Provincial of the Province of France, even his routine duties were mind-boggling. Geographically, his purview at first included Canada and Kentucky, each of which had a Mission Superior. In Canada alone, missions stretched from Montreal to places like Sandwich (near modern day Windsor, Ontario) to Walpole Island in Lake St. Lucy to Manitoulin Island at the top of Lake Huron, La Prairie and Trois Rivieres. But individual Province of France Jesuits also worked in Louisiana and Missouri. As will appear, this latter dispersion was one of Boulanger's biggest headaches. Travel in those times was rugged and utterly dependent on the weather, not to mention complications caused by, say, a war with Mexico. The mails were also irregular, to put it mildly.

In all the places mentioned, the relationship of the Jesuits and all religious orders to the local bishops was very important since some were friendly and some were not. However, at a time of huge expansion of the church on the American continent, it seemed that all of them were hungry for Jesuit services (a school, a parish, a chaplaincy to nuns, a teaching post in a seminary or a diocesan post like rural dean); some were annoyed when their own priests joined the Jesuits or ex-Jesuits tried to join their dioceses. In one and the same region where Jesuits worked, there might even be more than bishop to deal with. Working through the details of transferring a bishop's college and seminary to Jesuit ownership would be a special challenge.

Boulanger also had to relate some of his projects with other American Jesuit provinces, Maryland and Missouri, and that a time when the boundaries of these provinces were quite fluid. Missouri was thinking of opening an operation as far east as Pittsburgh and indeed it took over the responsibility for St. Joseph's College in Kentucky a few years after the French Jesuits turned it down. The Maryland Province had conducted its Literary Institute in New York from 1809 to 1815 and had already established Holy Cross College in Massachusetts; some in that province were surprised that they were not invited to accept the bishop's college in New York.

The ebb and flow of missionary work also required him to be on good terms with other religious groups, especially when negotiating with them to take over schools like St. Mary's in Kentucky and La Prairie in Canada that the Jesuits were leaving behind.

Manpower and personnel were uppermost in Boulanger's mind as it must be for any religious leader. He juggled postings to meet the urgent needs of this or that mission. Sometimes Jesuits proved incompatible with another, requiring more shifting around. He dunned Europe for more Jesuits, but asked that they be smart, flexible and secure about their vocation. Health considerations kept intruding themselves. Many men were sick, which was not surprising in their circumstances. From his letters, it is clear that Jesuit Brothers were often the backbone of the missionary effort. With two of them, he tells a missionary at one point, "you should be able to start your college." Much of his time, we mentioned earlier, was spent trying to recapture some Province of France Jesuits from American Provinces unwilling to give them up. Sometimes the men were so happy where they were they were unwilling to give themselves up!

A final challenge was that all his works required financing, so there is much in his letters about where the money is going to come from, the sale and acquisition of property, fiscal planning, belt-tightening and even fund-raising.

Boulanger was also in frequent contact with the Provincial in Paris and with the Fr. General in Rome, with whom he had to clear important decisions and from whom he had to beg personnel, influence and money.

Boulanger's letters reveal a man of decisiveness and compassion, of attention to both detail and to long-term vision, of practical expediency and principled spirituality. They give a flavor of his times and of the man.

## INTRODUCTION TO THE LETTER-SUMMARIES (1845-1847)

For his records, Boulanger made summaries of his official correspondence. The manuscript of these letter-summaries is in the Archives of the New York Province of the Society of Jesus. Certain difficulties with the abbreviations used in them and at times the handwriting were soon detected. Fortunately, Rev. Robert Bonfils, S.J., the present Archivist of the Jesuit Province of France, filled out the abbreviations, typed the pages, and modified some of the French of that early time to French 2002. Rev. Robert J. Sealy, S.J., a Fordham University Professor Emeritus of French, was the other major generous contributor to this project. He translated the entire manuscript into English, in spite of his own current visual challenges.

I have removed some repetitions, technical terms and obscure or unclear phrases and sentences, and have added — in square brackets as I do elsewhere in this book — some explanatory information and dates.

Names and titles that occur frequently in the letter-summaries include:

The Jesuit General in Rome, who at the time was Very Rev. Jan Roothaan (1785–1853), General from July 9, 1829 to May 8, 1853. He is often referred to as 'the General' and at times more formally as 'His Paternity'.

The Jesuit Provincial in Paris, who was Rev. Ambrose Rubillon (1804-1888), Provincial of the Province of France, from March 16, 1845 to March 19, 1851. In the letters he is often referred to as 'the Provincial'. Rev. Peter Fournier (1802-1855) was the Socius or First Assistant to the Jesuit Provincial of the Province of France from 1842 to 1851. Rev. Eugene Coué (1803–1878) was the Treasurer of the Province of France (1845-1851).

Fr. Felix Martin (1804–1886), who was the Superior of the Jesuits in Canada and as such a subject of the overall Mission Superior, Fr. Boulanger.

Fr. James Van De Velde (1795-1855), who was the Superior of the Mission and later Vice-Province of Missouri, headquartered in St. Louis; in 1849 he became the second bishop of Chicago.

Besides these, the following are frequently mentioned in his correspondence: Dominique and Henry du Ranquet, John Peter Choné, John Larkin, Nicolas Point, William Stack Murphy and August Thébaud. Choné, Dominique du Ranquet and Point were in the Indian missions in Canada. Larkin, Murphy and Thébaud were leaders in St. John's College, Fordham. Henry du Ranquet (brother of Dominique) was one of several members of the French province whom Boulanger strove persistently to recall from the vice-province of Missouri because of the increasing needs of the New York-Canada mission.

## FR. BOULANGER'S ACCOUNT

### 14 June 1845 to Fr. General:
Arrived at St. Mary's, Kentucky. Details of trip. Met Fr. Verhagen in Philadelphia. Br. Kohler left at Georgetown for his theology.

In New York two visits to the bishop [John Hughes]: not a word about his plan to entrust his school to the Society.

Saw Bishop Flaget in Louisville: his strong preference for Bardstown. I replied I came to see and decide all. This satisfied him.

St. Mary's: charming spot, but very hard to get to. All Fathers are in good health.

Start Visitation tomorrow. We will discuss the difficult question of Bardstown. Letter from Paris to Fr. Soller; scheduled to come here from New Orleans.

Fr. Larkin is going to build his college in Louisville. Very good choice, but difficulties ahead if we refuse Bardstown. Perhaps matters will take so long that Fr. Hus, my socius, and I must spend the winter in Canada.

### 21 June 1845 to Bishop Flaget:
Allow me to propose, both to you and to Msgr. Spalding, the most favorable conditions you could possibly grant. I see immense difficulties in taking on St. Joseph's, Bardstown, and I cannot deliberately plunge us into a bottomless morass.

### 23 June 1845 to Fr. Martin in Montreal:
As of now, send Fr. Hanipaux to Sandwich. I hope to be in Sandwich during the first half of July. Fr. Pédelupé will be ordained early so that he might go to Sandwich before the bad weather.

### 23 June 1845 to Fr. Chazelle:
Want very much to see Fr. Choné at Sandwich, if not at Montreal. So much the more as he has been all alone for a long time. So write and tell him to come. Fr. Hanipaux would be at Sandwich, had I not thought, that, according to your letters, Fr. Point had already left for Manitouline at the beginning of spring. You alone are the cause of the delay. Superiors are to be spoken to clearly. Besides, had I known that Fr.

Choné was alone, you would have received the order to send Fr. Point to him immediately. I am writing to Fr. Martin to send Fr. Hanipaux to Sandwich. Hope of arrival during first half of July.

*28 June 1845, To Fr. General:*

Today I returned from Bardstown where I had gone with Fr. Murphy. Bishop Flaget had gone there with Msgr. Spalding, his Vicar General, to discuss the matter of St. Joseph's school. Both before and after my arrival in the States, I studied the pros and cons. I asked both in person and by letter the considered opinions of all the Fathers. Then I called them all together to discuss the same subject several days before I left for Bardstown. The result was the resolution to refuse. Here are the principal reasons:

1. After 14 years of struggle, St. Mary's is beginning to breathe. Together with Kentucky, it still owes 30,000 francs in France.

2. The college at Louisville already begun. Land bought for 30,000 francs. In order to build, it must assume still more debts. St. Mary's will be able to help up to 5000, perhaps, 10,000 francs. This would allow Fr. Larkin to pay the interest.

3. Accepting Bardstown means leaving St. Mary's, leaving the certain for the uncertain. France will lose her credibility [*son credit*] and Louisville its hope.

4. Success at Bardstown is most uncertain, and, even were it to be a success, it would still be encumbered for some 10 to 15 years. In Maryland and in Missouri our Fathers are hard pressed. Boarding schools, especially in cities, are very difficult to manage.

These are the more important reasons presented to the bishop. Others were kept secret:

1. The impossibility of protecting ourselves from those who held our notes: they would make their claims known the minute we took possession.

2. The need to abandon certain ministries which we had allowed ourselves to provide and whose suppression would be odious to the Americans. The need to change from teaching ministry, plus extensive material repairs: the entire framework of the church and the poor condition of the school itself since the fire, and the impossibility of keeping St. Mary's open, even as a primary school, especially the first year.

My determination pained the bishop. Less so the laymen. One of them told me they would indeed find a way to shoulder the debts. I received the impression that they want to frighten the bishop in order to get from him certain large sums given to him for that purpose but which he would have put to other works. Promise to write after visit to St. Mary's.

*5 July 1845 from Louisville to Fr. Provincial:*

Left St. Mary's before the end of the Visitation to meet Fr. Van de Velde in Louisville. Received your letter of May 13 announcing new storm: the refusal of Bardstown, principal reasons. To Fr. General giving reasons for giving up St.Mary's. Must discuss with Rev. Fr. Van de Velde the return of our subjects, and also perhaps, of a still graver matter.

Probably in Canada for feast of St. Louis. The little time given to St. Mary's and Louisville will necessitate further discussion. Probably I shall spend the winter there. Plan to go by way of Pittsburgh to see Bishop O'Connor. But he is going to France. If you see him, and if he asks, we can promise him two Brothers for the end of 1846. What they would be doing there. If the bishop goes to Rome, suggest you write to the General about the matter.

Absolute need for help here in 1846. Fr. Thébaud wants to return to France. If he doesn't change his mind, he will have to be replaced.

Possible return from Canada to St. Mary's through Pittsburgh.

Our young men must learn English: so also our novices. The men sent must leave at the beginning of May to be here at the beginning of July.

*27 July 1845 to the French Provincial:.*
From Sandwich for Fr. Soller.

Only Fr. Choné absent, replacing Fr. du Ranquet, who is still sick, for Sunday. It was a great sacrifice for Fr. Soller: He needs encouragement. A word about the exchange project .... Fr. Hanipaux, who arrived several days ago, will go to Manitouline Island with Fr. Choné. Fr. Pédelupé will go later in September to rejoin Fr. du Ranquet on Walpole Island.

Saw Fr. Van de Velde, the Provincial of Missouri. I got nowhere regarding the return of our subjects. The whole affair had been submitted to the General, who, according to Fr. Van de Velde, has not written a single word on the subject. I am going to write to His Paternity. You would do well to write to him yourself and ask Fr. Mallard to do the same and ask that Fathers Abbadie and Chauvet be returned to his jurisdiction. He would leave them here in America. Two reasons to insist upon this restitution:

1. According to Fr. Van de Velde both Fathers and Brothers are very indignant: they will be returned to us when they shall have become useless.

2. In Louisville there is only one Brother. Fr. Chauvet would be very useful there during the construction of the school. In two months several of our Fathers in Missouri will be in a deplorable state while our houses in Kentucky suffer from the great lack of personnel.

A word about the heat, about the rapidity of travel by steam, and the slowness of travel by coach. Request to be informed of matters in France, about the number of novices, about a Brother for Sandwich and another for Manitouline.

*27 July 1845 to the General:*
Arrival in Sandwich. Joy of Frs. du Ranquet and Choné. Fr. Hanipaux, having come from Montreal, will leave with Fr. Choné for Manitouline after the visitation. Fr. Pédelupé, ordained July 6, will rejoin Fr. du Ranquet at Walpole in September and thus our Fathers will no longer be isolated, at least, except for the periods of their trips.

Details of the interview with Fr. Van de Velde who assured me that since his becoming provincial His Paternity had written not a single word concerning that institution. Taking his silence for permission, Fr. Van de Velde writes that he has power to retain members of our province indefinitely. Not only has he been unwilling to return anyone, but he has made no promise of doing so. Nonetheless, the matter is urgent because:

1. Several of Ours have conscience problems: their vocation is gravely compromised. Fr. Van de Velde admits he is aware of their desire to return.

2. Louisville needs them.

3. A Father coming from France would be useless until he learned English. Fr. Chauvet, who is physically very strong, would be most useful there.

But these reasons made no impression on Fr. Van de Velde. Fr. Soller was returned because they did not know what else to do with him. It will be the same with others. Nor was an exchange acceptable. Fr. Soller could not stay alone in New Orleans. He believes he can do good only in this spot in America and he wants no more either of Canada or Kentucky. The twin fire in Quebec will impede the projected work in Montreal.

*19 August 1845 from Montreal to the General:*

I wrote to you from Sandwich but brought the letter with me to catch the mail from Montreal which leaves in two weeks.

Had to moderate the zeal of our missionaries, not stir it up. Health of Fr. du Ranquet, his departure for his island. Fr. Choné is well in Manitouline. His mission there will take on new developments with Fr. Hanipaux's help.

The mission of Sandwich numbers Frs. Chazelle, Point, Jaffré, Choné, du Ranquet, Hannipaux and Pédelupé who will leave Montreal for Walpole in September. Only two Brothers for that entire mission, Tupin at Sandwich, Jennessaux at Walpole. Br. Tupin being sick, Fr. Point has taken charge of all household duties: kitchen, cow, horse. Dire need for two brothers. Also at Manitouline there is need of a strong, capable brother. At Sandwich servants simply cannot be found. Frs. Point and Jaffré stationed at Sandwich have much to do there as well as among the surrounding Christians who have no priests.

Fr. Point does very well at Sandwich, but his health is not good. That is why his request to work among the natives has not been granted. At Sandwich there are approximately 200 Protestant converts, the rest, Catholic and Canadian, speak mostly French. French Canadians live on both sides of the river and of Lakes St. Clare and Huron, all the way up to Sault Sainte Marie, which is itself a French settlement.

Finished Visitation of Sandwich on August 8 in order to catch the steam-boat. Twice this year this boat makes the trip from Detroit to Sault Sainte-Marie. Since it stops at Manitouline, our Fathers have profited, getting in their winter provisions. Manitouline is 100 leagues straight north above Sandwich. A little to the north-west of the island is Sault Sainte Marie at the mouth of Lake Superior.

At the repeated request of the bishop of Detroit, it has been decided that Fr. Chazelle will leave with the missionaries of Manitouline for Sault Sainte Marie. He will conduct a mission there and he will also determine whether it would be feasible to set up a mission station there, beginning next summer, 1846. The mission would serve the Indian nations inhabiting the region to the north and to the west. To begin, Sault Sainte Marie would need at least two Fathers and one or two coadjutors.

On his island Fr. D. du Ranquet has already formed a small Christian community of some 30 or 40 Indians. He has already baptized some one hundred of them. While most had come to him from the mainland, the rest he had sought out himself.

Fr. Choné, helped by Fr. Hanipaux, will be able to visit some mainland tribes who had asked him for instruction. I have requested these Fathers to write to Your Paternity so that you might assure them of the great concern you have for their mission endeavors. I hope they will do so. I will send to Your Paternity the advice and instructions which I left with Fr. Chazelle and the missionaries of Manitouline and Walpole.

As to the Superior General of all our houses in America, Fr. Chazelle would be the best choice. But how will he get along with the bishops of Kentucky and even of Montreal? He is too abrupt, decisive, little circumspect or prudent in speech, and he has difficulty in recognizing in himself these faults.

Novitiates joined: easier to send the Americans to Canada than vice-versa. It will be easier to send the scholastics from Canada to Kentucky, but both trips are both long and expensive. From Montreal to St. Mary's is at least 400 leagues. From Sandwich to Montreal is the same distance as from Paris to Rome, some 300 leagues. It is true these trips are now faster, almost always by steam.

Arrived in Montreal a bit under the weather. Briefly saw the bishop. Apparently the opening of the school has again been put off.

Another letter from Fr. Chauvet in Grand Couteau. I sympathize with his troubles as well as his great wish to return to Kentucky. I do not really think Ours should be pushed so far when there is no need. Some will become completely discouraged and even, perhaps, give up. Fr. Van de Velde knows in part their situation. I had avoided replying to the first two letters of Fr. Chauvet sending only a few words of encouragement for Fr. du Ranquet. Barbarous to refuse him ... In his own words: "I do not think it was the intention of my superiors, either in Europe or in Canada, to leave me in this almost continual [unreadable because of ink spot] state of distrust, incertitude, hurt." Once again, Most Reverend Father, it is high time that this come to an end for the large part of those of Ours who are in Missouri.

In Sandwich. During early August I learned from the American newspapers of the sad events in France. Not a single word has yet come directly to us. Saw several issues of *L'Ami de La Religion* which confirm what other newspapers reported as extracted from the *Moniteur,* from *Le Messager* and others. The order/invitation, addressed by Your Paternity to all our houses comes from higher up, and that, in my opinion, is most unfortunate. What is going to become of our good young people? Does God want to shield us from events and save us? Is this not also an invitation of Divine Providence to send more missionaries into these vast territories of North America? I am writing in this vein to Fr. Provincial.

Belgium and Piedmont are temporary asylums. What will become of Rome if France should again bestir herself? I want very much to be brought up to date, either by Your Paternity or Fr. Rubillon. For some six weeks news has been circulating in America, but not a single word from our Jesuit brethren.

I await an end to my incertitude in order to propose to Your Paternity an idea concerning our American houses which has been with me for a long time. I submit to

Your Paternity the decision agreed upon by Fr. Murphy and myself. Priests and other ecclesiastics from Kentucky who wish to enter the Society in the United States *are not to be received, especially now*, without the permission of their bishop. Those from other dioceses are to be received with or without the permission of their bishop. The reason for the second part of this decision is that is how the Fathers of the Missouri province receive them. Fr. Murphy had told a priest of the Vincennes, Indiana, diocese that he needed permission. The bishop refused. So the priest took himself to the St. Louis province and he was received.

Here we await a fifth scholastic novice. There are three coadjutor novices.

*19 August 1845 to Fr. Chauvet. in response to his letter of July 13:*
If it had depended upon me, you would long since have been in Kentucky or Canada. Finally, once again, tried unsuccessfully to move Fr. Van de Velde. Nothing comes of writing to him. As soon as possible write the same thing to Fr. General. Tell Fr. Abbadie from me to write also; so too Fr. du Ranquet. Let the three of you write, and also for Br. Alsberg. While waiting, profit from these trials.

*22 August 1845 to Fr. Guidée, Rector, Paris seminary:*
I ask him to speak or write to the Provincial to promise a beginning of our enterprise to the Bishop of Pittsburgh if the latter goes to Paris. But if he decides to go directly to Rome, to write about this to the General. This is the only way to link Kentucky to Canada. The bishop has already spoken to our Fathers in Missouri about establishing themselves in Pittsburgh.

*24 August 1845 to Fr. Abbadie in Grand Couteau in reply to his letter of June 26:*
This was a futile attempt on my part to have him and the others returned to our province. I begged him to write to the General, to whom I have already written about this, and to Fr. Provincial.

*28 August 1845 to Fr. Murphy:*
I assure him of the receipt of his letter of August 10, 1845. Mr. Ryan is carrying this letter.

*28 August 1845 to Fr. Larkin:*
In addition to Brs. Graves and Nash can a novice from Montreal be received at Louisville and make his second and rhetoric years there? Wrote to the Rector of Georgetown for Br. Régnier and to the Provincial of Maryland for Fr. Tellier at Boston.

*12 September 1845 to Fr. Provincial à propos of Mme. B.:*
A word about the prudence and devotion of this good woman in the service of the Society especially in difficult circumstances. Reminded him of all the letters sent to him since July 5.

*19 September 1845 to Fr. Point at Sandwich:*

He has been named superior of the house in Sandwich and of the Walpole and Manitoutine missions. He should inform our Fathers of this. He must read the Memorial left for Fr. Chazelle and communicate it to his consultors. Also to Fr. Jaffré, and to Fr. du Ranquet. Repeated to good Fr. du Ranquet the instructions he had been given for his health.

Left to the bishop of Toronto what to do about the remains of Fr. Chazelle.

News from Paris with addresses. Announced our leaving for Kentucky.

*21 Sept. 1845 to Provincial:*

Told him of Fr. Chazelles' death.

Du Ranquet still sick at Sandwich. Thanks for the news from France.

Reply to the plan for Pennsylvania: The Maryland Fathers will staff four undertakings. It seems impossible for us to take part there. Pittsburgh would not provide *any* physical basis for unity, but from Louisville by way of the Ohio only three days to Pittsburgh, then one day to Lake Erie, then another day to Sandwich and from Sandwich to Montreal, three days. The Missouri Provincial has to cover much longer distances; these cannot be avoided in America.

Too bad for New York. In his instructions, Fr. General says that if Bardstown is not taken, Louisville must be kept. Which would be impossible if Bardstown were accepted. The Missouri Fathers will work on the General in order to get Kentucky.

I believe we should strongly resist any proposal to give up Kentucky, at least until we are firmly settled in some other location more profitable AMDG. And this will not be very soon. We will be seeing the Bishop of New York. Will he be making some new proposals?

On Sept. 22 left Montreal with Fr. Tellier who will be spending 4 or 5 months at Georgetown learning English. Prairie will be administered by Frs. Mainguy and Saché.

Br. Regnier is making his theology at Georgetown with Mr. Kohler.

Mr. Hudon does his rhetoric at Louisville or St. Mary's. Fr. General commissioned me to set up an important school in Canada so I am working on that. It is possible that the land shall have been purchased before I leave and bids for the construction drawn up. If that goes through, we shall most definitely have to send teachers. But the whole project could not get started before the 5th. Let's hope Canada will provide students.

The *Status*: Br. Roy will be sent to Louisville for the kitchen. I am going to ask the General to allow me to stay in America with Fr. Hus so that I can take care of our Fathers and Brothers in Missouri. If His Paternity recalls me, either immediately or through you, I will return, even during the winter.

Everything will be finished in Louisville in a month or six weeks. The American novices will go to Montreal: the American and Canadian scholastics will study either in Louisville or St. Mary's.

*21 Sept. 1845 from Montreal to Fr. General:*

Notice of the death of Fr. Chazelle at Green Bay on Sept 4. Appointed Fr. Point Superior of our missions in Upper Canada. Outlined for the General my idea for America, and will await his orders at St. Mary's. State of our house in Montreal. Fr. Tellier and Mr. Régnier at Georgetown, Mr. Hudon at Louisville.

Land for the Montreal school on the point of being bought. The offer of the Sulpicians was refused because the land was too far away. The laws forbidding mortgages cause problems for the purchase.

Impossible to think of any other spot for us to settle in Pennsylvania, except Pittsburgh.

When I pass through New York I will stop and see the bishop. Future novitiate for U.S. and Canada at Montreal, but scholasticate for both at Louisville or St. Mary's.

A word about affairs in France. The Catholics in America, just as those in France, condemn concessions from whatever side they may come.

*21 Sept. 1845 from Montreal:*
Wrote to Fr. du Ranquet and Fr. Pédelupé to encourage them and to tell Fr. duRanquet to take better care of his health.

*14 October 1845 from St. Mary's:*
Sent the *Status* to Louisville: you can print it as it stands here in St. Mary's. Letter from Fr. Fournier of June 27 and one from Fr. Guidée of July 9, both received here.

News from Fr. Larkin about his college in Louisville: foundations laid.

Our allocation for Kentucky to Louisville: asked His Paternity to make this assignment as strong as possible.

A word about the need to accept Pittsburgh as soon as possible. Missouri has promised to take it within two years and will keep us informed.

I await word from the General to stay on in America or to return home.

Send some scholastics to America to stay for two or three years.

News from St. Mary's: A word about Fr. Thébaud and his sermons.

*21 October 1845, St. Mary's, to Father General:*
Essence of my letter of 21 September: new Superior at St. Mary's is Fr. Thébaud, reasons for nomination, prayers for confirmation. Fr. Fouché, minister, will no longer go to Loretto convent at Mt. Loretto, Kentucky.

The bishop of New York offers his school in a letter. I replied favorably. I will go to New York to further discuss the matter if he wishes it. The Montreal affair is still not concluded.

If New York is accepted, there will be a complete abandonment of Kentucky, and there will no longer be any question of taking Pittsburgh. We will need more personnel: we will require Frs. Mignard, Abbadie and Chauvet.

*21 October 1845, St. Mary's, to Fr. Martin:*
Don't send Brother Roy to make his novitiate at La Prairie unless there is no suitable school in Montreal. Write every two weeks.

*21 October 1845, St. Mary's, to Provincial:*
New superior at St. Mary's. Please collect new and old *informationes* on Fr. Thébaud, if they exist.

Announcement of the offer by the bishop of New York of his school. I will probably go to New York to discuss the matter further.

Fr. General's letter orders me to stay in America for the winter.

*21 October 1845, St. Mary's, to Fr. Larkin in Louisville:*
Until you receive further orders stop all support, subscriptions or bequests for our new college; Kentucky will be abandoned if New York is accepted.

*21 October 1845, St. Mary's, to Fr. Hus in Montreal:*
Leave on November 10; in New York ask the bishop if I may or should come to New York and then wait for me.

*21 October 1845, St. Mary's, to the Bishop of New York:*
I am totally disposed to both discuss and accept the school. I asked him if he thought it appropriate for me to come to New York to discuss the matter. Best to come as soon as possible because we have many other like offers on our plate.

*22 October 1845, St. Mary's, to Bishop Chabrat, Louisville:* Fr. Fouché, having been assigned to our school at St. Mary's will no longer be able to care for the religious of Loretto as he did in the past. I do not plan to replace Fr. Fouché at the convent of Loretto, especially as you might have decided to appoint another priest of your choice to direct the convent. That I would view with great pleasure. Otherwise, if you approve, Fr. Petit will succeed Fr. Fouché.

*22 October 1845, St. Mary's, to Fr. Larkin in Louisville:*
Stop all trips, purchase of material for the new school until the New York affair has been concluded. No word from the two bishops who have refused their help.

*23 October 1845, St. Mary's, to Bishop Hughes of New York in Cincinnati:*
Sorry that my letter of Oct. 21 could not reach him in New York; learned that he was coming to Cincinnati for the dedication of the cathedral. Offered to meet bishop in Cincinnati to discuss matters, but this did not seem a favorable time to do so. I could, however, meet him in Cincinnati and return with him to New York.

*29 October 1845, St. Mary's, To Father Larkin:*
It was wrong of him to write to our Fathers in Cincinnati to find out whether the bishop of New York was coming for the consecration of the cathedral.

*1 November 1845, St. Mary's, to Fr. Point at Sandwich:*
Reply to his letter of October 15. Fr. Jaffré is in all matters and for all matters

subject to the superior. He is to do nothing except under his direction. He is to go no place except where you shall send him.

A word about the death of Mr. Boué who had been recommended to our prayers here. To the best of your ability settle the affairs of Mr. Boué as he asked us to do, provided there is no litigation involved.

Send on what I have written to Walpole and Manitouline. You will have help, but have a little patience. What was the result of your drive for the church?

Disposition and Instructions to Fr. Chazelle: did you find them as well as the Memorial? Tell us if the Provincial is willing to follow the direction suggested by Fr. du Ranquet. Bits of news.

*2 November 1845, St. Mary's, to Fr. Jaffré at Sandwich:*
I am assigning you to go wherever Fr. Point will send you. You are a child under obedience. When I was at Sandwich, you did not have any consultors. Why? You are a Consultor and in that capacity you must write to me all the time I am in America.

*6 November 1845, St. Mary's. to Frs. Kohler and Régnier at Georgetown:*
Encouragement.

[*At this point the summary of letters skips to Feb. 28, 1846. Pages were removed from the manuscript booklet; when, how or why we know not. These were important times, when the details of the move to New York were being negotiated.*]

*28 February 1846, St. Mary's, to Fr. General in Rome:*
We solemnly assure you that we have neglected nothing in our effort to keep the Society in Kentucky. I put aside for the most part, however, the case of Bishop Flaget. He is no more [active?]. As to Bishop Chabrat, with everybody else, I think his problem is his judgment, not his heart, and that he can cause a great deal of trouble.

To conclude, I repeat to Your Paternity what I have already written: neither would I, nor should I, discuss business verbally with their Excellencies. And, it takes me days to find the correct ways of expressing myself in my letters to them. Each case of complete withdrawal would not be as advanced as it is except that, since Bishop Chabrat's return from France it would have been necessary to pose and examine seriously the question as to whether we should stay in Kentucky.

Your Paternity will kindly allow me to bring to his attention, now, this observation. If you have received some letters from Maryland, all is to be explained with this simple observation: our Fathers in Maryland have been the cause for the Bishop of New York's extending his feelings of distaste and estrangement to the whole Society, and without reason.

All our Fathers and Brothers from Louisville are here, with the exception of Fr. Larkin who is giving a retreat to the people in our church in St. Louis.

*5 March 1846, Reply to General's letter of January 15:*
Informed the General of Fr. Hus' return to France. He must go on to Rome to explain certain matters: the New York school, the seminary, the novitiate and the scholasticate; an explanation is impossible otherwise.

We are leaving six or seven Fathers in Kentucky as I explained in my letter to Fr. Verhagen. Begged General to take no decision until he has heard Fr. Hus.

*5 March 1846, St. Mary's, to Provincial:*
The return of Fr. Hus to France and his trip to Rome are essential if the General's intentions remain the same. Referred to my letters to him of 5 and 19 January, and of my letter of February 18 to Fr. Coué. Sent copies of the two latest letters from Kentucky to New York.

*7 March 1846, St. Mary's, to Fr. Martin in Montreal:*
Have my letters of 14 and 25 January been received? Those of 6 and 18 February are on their way. Votes for Frs. Pernot, Grimot, and Br. Rouillé. Protest that he does not inform me more precisely of their reception.

*8 March 1846, to Fr. Larkin in Saint Louis:*
Return here at the latest by Palm Sunday. When you pass through Louisville take effective measures to sell the land, even though it means the loss of several thousand francs. If possible have the buyer pay some of the price in cash.

*8 March 1846, to Fr. Point, Sandwich:* Announcement of Fr. N. Point's destination for the missions of Upper Canada, the departure of Fr. Hus, and of my continuing stay in America.

*11 March 1846, to Fr. Van de Velde, St. Louis:*
Fr. Chauvet arrived on March 9. Fr. Hus has left for France and Rome. I recommended to our Fathers to direct their students to our school in St. Louis; hope that it holds up well. Fr. Larkin should be here by Palm Sunday.

*11 March 1846, to Fr. Martin in Montreal:*
I fear either that my letters have gone astray, that they have not been read with sufficient attention, or that he does not weigh what he writes to me.

There is no question about the ordination of Br. Ouellet. Let Br. Doucet prepare what he has seen; his examination will take place in New York. As for Fr. Nicolas Point, I doubt that the General has written to him by any other route than Montreal. It matters little whether the Bishop buys in his own name and rents to us with a mutually binding (*amphytétique*) lease. If we would voluntarily withdraw, we should always have to leave both land and building to the bishop or to the city, except for the indemnity we would receive for what we had contributed to the purchase of the land and the construction.

When you have to write to His Paternity on business always tell him if you have spoken to me and what I replied.

Very briefly, let Fr. Baré use his income for his support and pension in the novitiate.

Some details about New York. If Fr. Tellier cannot arrive there during the coming autumn, he will go there a little later; this I promised him.

*16 March 1846 to the General:*
I sent him a long letter from Fr. Choné. Also extracts from two letters: one from Fr. Larkin, the other from Fr. Hus concerning the placement of our Fathers for New York and for Kentucky.

*23 March 1846 to Fr. Martin:*
For the ordination of Ours, no dimissorial letters are required from bishops of the place of birth; this is non-canonical. ...

I authorize Fr. Martin to sign a contract with the publisher for the present case.

Must we invite the bishop to receive the final vows of Br. Rouillé (Cong 8: 34)? ...

*27 March 1846 to the General:*
The Brothers of St. Joseph will replace us here with a primary school. The negotiations with them having been started by our Fathers before they received my letter of February 26! Your Paternity can now be perfectly content with our complete withdrawal from Kentucky. Everything is taken care of according to the good pleasure of our Fathers.

*29 March 1846 to the Provincial:*
Told him of the arrangement for Saint Mary's with the Brothers of St. Joseph. The Fathers had begun negotiations on February 22, so *before* my definitive reply dated February 26. ...

*1 April 1846, to Bishop Flaget in Louisville:*
Since Your Grace has begun and already almost completed the transfer of Saint Mary's to the Brothers of St. Joseph, you undoubtedly wish to have in your hand the act by which our Board transfers the property to Your Grace. I come now to ask you to be so kind as to send us an example of that act of retrocession. The current proprietors will sign the act and I will see that it be returned as soon as possible to Your Grace.

Mr. Delaune surely shall have told you how happy we are and pleased to be replaced at Saint Mary's by such an excellent and edifying community. It is destined to achieve great good, not only in Kentucky but also in the whole United States. Thus, God in his goodness, seems to dispose all things for the best and wishes to receive glory not only from what has been done but also from what is being prepared.[3]

*5 April 1846, to Coadjutor Bishop of New York:*

Frs. Thébaud and Murphy will leave for New York on April 19 or 20. Thanks for his letter of March 26.

*6 April 1846, to the Provincial:*

Received his letter of February 16, long after that of the 26th. Thanks for the arrival of Br. Craigie in New York. It would be very desirable to have a good subject among the future Americans.

Announced the Bill of Incorporation of Rose Hill passed the Lower House unanimously, except for three votes. Frs. Murphy and Thébaud leave for New York on April 19 or 20. I repeated that the new-comers cannot be used as prefects for at least three months, and as teachers for six.

Will we have a Spanish Father? Which one would he be? Fr. Hus will speak to you about Fr. Meyffret for our Scholastics. Did he succeed with Ours in Brugelette?

Well-founded core of three novices starting in New York.

*10 April 1846, to the General:*

Reasons for the custom I introduced of serving a little wine at dinner only, two-thirds of a glass: climate, poor food, debilitated health and strength of many. Wine is served in the two other provinces of America. One vineyard in Georgetown, other near Saint Mary's was planted by the Dominican Fathers, themselves great promoters of total abstinence. However, done only after certain precautions in order not to offend the sensibilities of those who live in the country. Improved the diet: they were eating practically nothing but pork. Living like this in a disgusting state of uncleanliness is called the "American way of life." (Thus falling even below the peasants of Kentucky.)

Will His Paternity authorize the payment of the board of the novices and scholastics of New York from the money allocated to the missionaries of Canada? The names of the scholastics in studies, and only for these, unless necessity should require the money be spent for the school. The board is some 600 francs a person.

There is hope of beginning in New York with three or four novices. No good news about Br. Kohler — his health, his temperament. He is not on the list.

The deplorable state of studies in America. We have not done as much as we might have to enrich the course of studies for those who entered Saint Mary's.

Frs. Thébaud and Murphy will leave on April 19 or 20 for New York.

Copy of the letter sent to Bishop Flaget on April 1 asking him to send us an example of the act of retrocession to His grace for the property of Saint Mary's. Sold the furnishings of Saint Mary's to the Brothers of St. Joseph for 2,500 piasters with the exception of the library, the pharmacy and the altar vessels.

The bill for the incorporation of our school in New York has been passed by the House of Representatives of the State of New York. It has been sent to the Senate; hope it will pass there as well. In obtaining the bill, the reason for secrecy about the school was incorporated.

As to the personnel for the school, only the *informationes* which Frs. Thébaud and Murphy will send me will enable me to draw up the list. According to their plan, Fr.

*Fouché* will be the Superior of the Jesuits, Fr. Larkin, Vice-Superior, and Fr. Driscol will have charge of the young children. Asked His Paternity to confirm Fr. Thébaud as Rector. Difficulty quickly understandable from the list of all our people which I am sending to His Paternity.

As to Montreal alone, if a school be possible, must we wait for several more years before starting it? To transfer [the personnel] of the house at La Prairie to Montreal is very serious and can only be discussed with the bishop *viva voce*. Asked Fr. General to tell me how large is the yearly allotment to Canada because that is the only means of support fot the house in Montreal. Difficulties of the plan explained. Because of all that has to be done in New York, asked the General for permission to visit only Montreal this year.

Regarding tertianship: needed for Fr. Larkin that he may become a good superior. How can we allow Frs. Driscol and Ryan to make their tertianship? Would His Paternity judge it à propos to send them to the novitiate in Maryland? This would be one way of maintaining and cementing the bond of religious brotherhood between us and our Fathers in Maryland.

*10 April 1846 to Fr. Point, Sandwich:*
He's to ask Fr. du Ranquet for his considered judgment as to whether the mission was fruitful and of sufficient use to be continued. I have no firm opinion on the subject. I recommended to Fr. Point that he consult the General.

Response to my letter to Bishop Flaget of April 1. Monsignor Spaulding wrote for the bishop. His reply is correct, with an additional word about the affair.

*10 April 1846, to Provincial:*
List of Greek books that Brugelette can send by the scholastics who will be coming to New York. Let those who come stop only in New York. Reasons for being told the date of their departure from Le Havre, and also the name of the ship and why they must leave during the first half of June.

My last letter to Bishop Flaget and his correct response. Bishop Chabrat fears that some of our fathers will remain in Kentucky!

*11 April 1846, to Fr. Point in Sandwich:*
Received his letter of February 23.
Consultors' meetings must be held regularly. Do you have the letter from Fr. Oliva? Keep your consultors correctly informed of expenses.

Cleanliness of the house. Have you put into effect the means suggested of using our Fathers?

In so far as I am able, I continue you in the authority you had previously received.

*11 April 1846 to Fr. Jaffré:*
Thanks for the Consultors' letter as well as that of Fr. Menet, to whom I shall write.
Cleanliness of the house: cannot the Fathers themselves once or twice a week work in the house? Br. Tupin has too much to do.

*18 April 1846 to the Bishop of New York carried by Frs. Thébaud and Murphy:*

They cannot be given any administrative posts before the vacations. It is quite probable that we will be able to staff the church, which His Grace has kindly promised, with two Fathers.

I am staying in America for an indefinite period. For which I am glad, for that affords me the opportunity to work for His Grace in opening a class for the seminarians. Asked for prayers for the project; respects to the bishop.

*19 April 1846, to Rev. Fr. Verhagen, Georgetown:*

Why did our sister Maryland not take over the opportunity [of New York?]. We would certainly have viewed this with the greatest pleasure, recognizing that she would have accomplished as much and more than we would have been able to do ourselves.

Once again recommended Br. Kohler to his paternal charity. For his exams, I have sent him back to his superiors at Georgetown. He will not be a burden much longer.

Told of the departure of Frs. Murphy and Thébaud for New York. The others will follow in the months of July and August.

*19 April 1846, to Fr. Martin, Montreal:*

Before promotion to the priesthood, there is always the examination of the *ordinandus* as prescribed in *Constitutions* VII. 6. 4.

Fr. Ouellet in New York: he is to learn English and we are to prepare teachers for the future school in Montreal. Tell this to [your] bishop and to those who may ask about the sending of our young people to New York.

Replacement for Fr. Tellier: it is necessary that I know long in advance the founding and duration of the Canadian missions so that I can dispose of a Father from New York. I will do what will be possible.

For spiritual reading use our Rules, from the Master of Novices, *ordinat. général* and *Instructio Institutis.* Probably I will visit you during the month of August.

Departure of Frs. Thébaud and Murphy for New York.

*1 May 1846, to Frs. Choné and Hanipaux in Manitouline.*

The matter of the mill cannot be decided without Fr. Point. Our reasons seem good to me but there is a debt of 6000 francs to be paid to Detroit as well as 5000 francs from this year's budget to go to Montreal. If the mill is bought this year, what will remain to be lived on?

To Fr. Hanipaux. Reply to his letter: encouragements.

*2 May 1846, to P. Coué in Paris:*

I sent him a list of books required for New York but he should send only those marked with + . Some examples of the theology of Bailly or Janvier.

*2 May 1846 to Fr. Pillon in Brugelette:*

Thanks for the Classics offered to New York. Asked for copies of the philosophy of Lyon or Bouvier.

*3 May 1846 to Mgr. Spalding, vicar general of Louisville:*
Replied his letter of April 5 and sent deed of retrocession of St. Mary's to Bishop Flaget.

*3 May 1846 to Fr. Tellier at La Prairie:*
Repeated my promise that he will go to New York, but an understanding must be reached with Fr. Martin. Strongly recommended silence on the Maryland [proposal?] which the bishop rejects (*sur le Maryland que l'éveque repouse*).

*3 May 1846, to Mr. Delaune, in Madison:*
Informed him of the dispatch of the deed of retrocession to Bishop Flaget and of our change of dates for vacation from July 7 to July 1.

Asked him to come several days before July 1 to deal with our affairs and to speak to the bishop about the bill of incorporation. I would like to know with certainty if the bishop accepts our handing over the property to the Brothers of St. Joseph. I do not want to do anything that might offend His Grace.

*6 May 1846 to Fr. Martin:*
Br. Roy is to take care of the kitchen.

Br. Doucet is to retake his math exam without more preparation and spend the best part of his time on Latin. ...

Property of Br. Roy: fine, if the bishop agrees as well as those who subscribed, and it is not too far away for our ministries.

Bull of Leo XII, a case, and recourse to the bishop.

For the *Annals of the Propagation of the Faith*: write about the country of the Jesuit Mission, Province of France, in North America.

Speak to all our Fathers about our school in New York and try to send some students.

*11 May 1846 to Fr. Thébaud, Rose Hill:*
Promise no one a reduction of the boarding fee.

Send here the address of a modest hotel near the railroad where Ours could go and stay when needed.

*14 May 1846 to the Provincial:*
We will have a complete course of theology if you send us teachers. Fr. Daubresse and I are not enough. Gave the names of Ours who will take the course in theology, unless some of them are needed to teach.

The course in philosophy is filled. Neither logic nor metaphysics can be taught in Latin to the students. Latin will be given to Jesuit students during repetitions.

Repeated prayer that he think of the future.

A word about the Irish.

The bishop does not seem to think that we attribute to him our leaving. On the contrary, he approves the decision we have made. ...

Received Fr. Fournier's letter of March 12 and the copy of the General's letter.

*14 May 1846, to Fr. Thébaud at St. John's, New York:*

Let's be prepared for difficulties. Prayer and confidence in God. The General entirely approves. On July 1 eight or nine scholastics and priests will be sent from France. You can retain Mr. Palko and Mr. Stratch, for Spanish and German. But let them be told, if need be, that they will not take their recreation periods with us. Their rooms are not in the main building where we live.

Fr. Hus has arrived.

*17 May 1846 to Fr. Thébaud in New York:*

Fr. Larkin will give the priests' retreat in New York. Inform me of the dates.

I am sending you both the address and the markings on the cases we are sending through Ohio because we fear Mexican bandits.

I am writing to Fr. Provincial to have him send the backup on July 1. Ask Fr. Murphy to write to me and to Fr. Fouché about the arrangements made with Mr. Queen.

*17 May 1846 to Provincial in Paris:*

I have kept your letter of March 30 for Fr. Hus.

Again asked for "smart men." Be so kind as to embark our reenforcements by July 1 but on a French or English ship, not American. The war with Mexico. Pirates will be swarming.

*21 May 1846 to Fr. Thébaud in New York:*

Agreed to the retention of lay teachers in Math, Physics and Chemistry; for drawing; for music; for Spanish; "of Mr. Ausley" [?]. But make no promise of another year. They will not live with the community.

Fr. Murphy will teach Greek.

Asked for further information. Will you be able to do without Fr. Gockeln? What is the time for the vacation period? When will the seminarians and students return?

Author of *Moral and Dogmatic Theology*, taught at St. John's.

A note in the papers reassuring parents concerning the care of the young children, using what they do in France as an example, would be useful.

*21 May 1846 to Fr. Point at Sandwich:*

Replied to his letter of May 7. Agreed to Fr. Choné's mill. He has gone too far for us to pull back.

Let our missionary Fathers put in their letters, from time to time, some word concerning the work of the Propagation. Thanks. Encouragement. Everything, however, is to be sent directly to the Provincial. Fr. du Ranquet is to put in writing seriously his work with the Indians.

*24 May 1846 to Father General:*

A word about the arrangement made concerning the children after they had seen and met Frs. Thébaud and Murphy.

Address of Saint John's. Five lay professors retained.

Second important observation: at Saint Mary's, letting it go its own way has brought about a weakening of the idea and feel for authority. Need to prepare superiors from other nations. Among the future arrivals from France, there is not a single one who you hope might be able to become a superior some day. I wrote about this to the Provincial, but it is worthy of the particular concern of Fr. General. There lies the future of the French mission.

The wish of Fr. Martin for a change in the *Annals de La Propagation de La Foi*, i.e., the entry *Missions of the Society of Jesus in Canada* to read *in North America* rather than *in Canada*. Reasons for the change.

Two candidates for the Society have presented themselves to Fr. Murphy.

*26 May 1846 to Fr. Thébaud, St. John's:*
Seriously examine the affair of the linen-room.

Think of the future: let us not do anything which we may have occasion to regret in the future. Seriously try to find some way of effecting a change in both classes and studies without saying a word about it either now or later.

*29 May 1846 to Fr. Hanipaux, Manitouline:*
1. Perfect obedience to Superiors: defects in that area in France, Montréal and Sandwich.
2. Respect for Superiors.

*31 May 1846 to Fr. Thébaud, New York:*
Do not go back on the approved acceptance of the young man who was admitted with reduced board. Only be careful not to grant such reductions easily: we have not yet reached the state of being generous: we will be able to do that later. Once again approved the admission of the young business man.

Let's see if Fr. de Luynes will be able, without harm to the school, to go and give the retreat asked by Msgr. Stack d' lstia. During the retreat speak to him about it, and beforehand to the bishop.

Tell Mr. Lasalle not to send to Kentucky a carton of books which Fr. Coué wrote to me had been addressed to him.

*31 May 1846 to Fr. Martin, Montreal:* Isn't the bishop asking for one of Ours for the priests' retreat? Delay in our correspondence.
Result of the journey to Quebec? Do you have any scholastic novices?

*1 June 1846 to Rev. Fr. Van de Velde in St. Louis:*
Invited him to spend several days with us here at St. Mary's. Address of St. John's.

*1 June 1846 to Fr. Martin:*
Have Brs. Sauvé and Gauthier make their long retreat.
Fr. Tellier is not to leave before he receives word from me.

I am inclined to accept the school which the Sulpicians are offering us, provided the conditions are favorable to us. ...

*5 June 1846 to Fr. Thébaud in New York:*

It is impossible for me to comply with your request to admit day-students until you let me know the exact number of Ours needed to teach at St. John's, their names and the classes they will teach. Reread my Memorial.

Remember that I had not recommended anything for you to attend to but only to be more expeditious.

*6 June 1846 to Father General:* The bishop of New York has explained to our Fathers in Georgetown his request that our Fathers in Kentucky go to St. John's. The bishop, therefore, has exonerated us of any responsibility.

What Bishop Hughes said to Fr. Thébaud concerning Bishop Chabrat.

The bishops' committee thought we had very good reasons to leave Kentucky.

Bishop Chabrat has gone back to Louisville as coadjutor after being commended by the committee on his resignation.

The American government had summoned the bishop of New York to Washington to ask him to supply chaplains for the Catholics in the army in Texas. The Minister of the Army also asked him for priests to serve on warships.

*6 June 1846 to Fr. Provincial:*

I gave him the same news I had given to the General asking him to have the newspapers carry the request of the American government for chaplains. Frs. Roy and McElroy left for Texas on May 26. For the entire length of the campaign, the government gives them a very acceptable salary.

*14 June 1846 to Fr. Martin:* Make sure that Brother Roy leaves in time to arrive at St. John's by July 30, the vigil of the feast of Saint lgnatius.

Absolutely no news about the school at Kingstown. If they write to us about it, do not give them any hope at all.

*22 June 1846 to Fr. Provincial:*

Replied to his letter of May 3. Yes, send us Fr. Schneider to act as Master of Novices in Montreal: he will do very well. We still need one in New York.

*27 June 1846 to Fr. Martin, Montreal:*

Make certain that Fr. Tellier and Fr. Vachon arrive at St. John's not earlier than August 7 or 8. Fr. Petit would be arriving the following week. Br. Roy is not to leave except with Fr. Tellier.

*29 June 1846 to Fr. Point, Sandwich:*

No promises made to the bishop of Detroit to settle in his diocese. All things being equal, Canadian territory is to be preferred. Having refused Maiden as a parish, give it as many services as possible.

*29 June 1846 to Fr. [Thomas] Mulledy, Rector of Georgetown:*
Sorry we could not come through Georgetown. Hope to arrange something later. Thanks for all the kindnesses shown to Brothers Kohler and Régnier. I asked to have them leave for New York on Monday, August 10. They will not stay in New York. Give my respects to your Fr. Provincial.

*1 July 1846, to Bishop of New York by Fr. Larkin:*
Hope of success of the retreat given according to the direction of the bishop. We will discuss both the church and the boarding school when I shall be at St. John's in August.

*8 July 1846 to Fr. Martin, in Montreal:*
Send off Brothers Ouellet and Doucet on August 17.
As long as there is no obstacle, Br. Ouellet is to pronounce his vows on the feast of the Assumption.

*14 July 1846 to Fr. Provincial:*
Reason for sending only men who will remain [in the Society]: the Bishop of New York demands a written statement that he will not be obliged to receive even a single one of those who might leave.
I spoke once again of correct personnel to be sent and of someone capable of becoming a superior. ...
Passed on small news items: a church promised in New York; ... moratorium on debts, which is one more reason to put off occupancy and opening of the boarding school [in Montreal] until next year. Recommend this undertaking to prayers.

*31 July, 1846 from St. John's, July 31, to Fr. Martin:*
Authorized Fr. Martin to sign, in his own name, the contract to buy Mr. Donigani's property, to accept the seller's conditions for the sale and as they are found in Fr. Martin's letter of July 13.

*1 August 1846 to the General:*
Sent him the conditions mentioned above for the purchase of the Donigani property and my authorization to sign the contract in his own name and to accept the conditions of the sale with the assurance of acceptance by Your Paternity.
A word about my visit to Bishop Flaget while passing through Louisville.

*1 August 1846 to Fr. Martin in Montreal:* Asked him not to proceed further in giving up St. Patrice. Held to the acquisition of Donigani's property.
Replied to his letter of July 27: will be in Montreal on the Assumption, if possible.

*2 August 1846 to the Provincial:*
Sent him, as I had done to the General, the conditions of the purchase of Mr.

Donigani's property in Montreal. Far better for us to take on this debt rather than get involved in I-know-not-what commitment in accepting St. Patrice.

Asked him to send still more scholastics in 1847. We cannot delay longer than that the opening of our first boarding school in New York.

*3 August 1846 to Fr. Point in Sandwich:*
Informed him, following the receipt of a letter from the Provincial, of the probable arrival, at the beginning of winter, of 4 Fathers assigned to Canada, 2 or 3 of whom would be for the missions. ...

Since Fr. Choné is in Manitouline, Fr. Hannipaux will be able to come and help Fr. du Ranquet, if that be necessary. Once again asked for stricter keeping of financial records.

*7 August 1846 to Fr. Maillard, Lyons Province:*
Gave good reasons why Fr. Gilles not go to Mobile and we be left [without a Master of Novices]. His poor health, different climate, voyage of some 1000 to 1200 leagues, and so forth.

Much gratitude if you could let Fr. Chauvet stay with us.

*7 August 1846 to Fr. Provincial, Paris:* The departure of Fr. Gilles would be very difficult for us. No longer any Master of Novices. Reasons why you should strongly insist with Fr. General that he return to us.

*9 August 1846 to the General:*
Once again, Fr. Maillard asks the return of Fr. Gilles and Br. Chauvet. No longer any Master of Novices here: difficulties which will follow from this. They say that Fr. Abbadie is going to be returned very soon and none of Ours has, up to the present, been returned to his province. Fr. Soller cannot be regarded as having been returned.

Request to his Paternity to have Fr. Maillard and Br. Alsberg returned to us this year. Our missions in Upper-Canada are in extreme need of coadjutor brothers. Fr. Provincial can send only one coadjutor brother, while I have absolutely none to give up.

*9 August 1846 to Fr. Martin in Montreal:*
There can no longer be any question of Fr. Tellier coming here: the calamity at La Prairie demands his presence. Fr. Petit will not go to Montreal.

*10 August 1846 to Fr. Point, Sandwich:* Our Brothers may not teach both boys and girls.

*24 August 1846, from Montreal, to the General:*
Informed him of the latest requirements of Mr. Donigani.
Future house planned for Sault Sainte Marie on the American side.
Please have the Bishop of Toronto accept our reasons for doing so.

*29 August 1846 to Rev. Fr. Maillard, Lyons:*
On August 31, Fr. Gilles and Br. Chauvet left for Mobile. Fr. Gilles will draw up and send you the details.

*31 August 1846 to Fr. Provincial:*
The Fathers of Grand Coteau to the Fathers in Lyons: once again pressed Fr. General to allow Ours to be returned to us. I also wrote about this to Fr. Maillard.
Let Fr. Cagnard speak to Mr. de Talence about his interview with Bishop Chabrat.
New restrictions on the purchase of property for the school in Montreal. There will be no chapel for the Fathers who are to come. There are 4 or 5 chalices for missionaries here. ...

*3 Sept. 1846 to the General:*
A word of explanation on the letter of our Fr. Assistant to Fr. Rubillon regarding the examinations of Jesuit seminarians and teachers in the seminary and of the scholastics.
Grand Coteau to Lyons: the sending back of our French Fathers. A word on Mobile. The return of Fr. Gilles and Br. Chauvert to this city at the request of Fr. Maillard was a bit precipitous.
Walpole: another decree from the Government of Canada ordering the expulsion of our missionaries. Fr. Choné will probably be sent to Sault Sainte Marie.
State of our purchase in Montreal.

*17 Sept. 1846 to Fr. Point in Sandwich:*
Your accounts to Province Procurator. If there is an error, write to him. Very sorry for your trouble: however, don't lose confidence. Many extraordinary expenses this year have been paid from the money assigned to Canada.
Next year there won't be so many of them.

*30 Sept. 1846 to Fr. Coué, Procurator, Paris:*
Do not fulfill any request for books or anything else for St. John's or Canada without my approval.
Send by the Fathers who are coming here, or by some other quick route, all monies that may remain from the reserve assigned to Sandwich by the Fr. Visitor. ...

*1 October 1846 to the General:*
Replied to all the observations of the Consultors.
News of St. John's school.
Retreats begin in New York given by the cathedral.
Asked advice on the scholastics recreating with the students.

*9 October 1846, to Fr. Martin, Montreal:*
All borrowing [for the new building] is forbidden. No purchase is to be made nor

work ordered unless you can certainly count on having the necessary money when they have to be paid for.

*9 October 1846 to Fr. Point, Sandwich:*
I approve the arrangement made for Sault Sainte Marie and for Manitouline: ... Fr. Menet to Sault before Fr. Pédulupé who will winter in Manitouline, and Fr. Hanipaux to Sault.

*10 October 1846 to Fr. Provincial in Paris:*
... Gave the names and number of our scholastics who will not be employed at St. John's. Asked for the first trimester of their board as soon as money has been allocated. These are: Brothers Maréchal, Hollinger, Pernot, Desjacques, Tissot, Ouellet amd Hudon, with three novices, Bidwell, Hampston and Adams.

*10 October 1846 to Fr. Gilles, in Mobile:*
I regret but it is impossible to send either Fr. Driscol or Fr. Murphy. News of the school, made the assignments.

*20 October 1846 to Fr. Fournier in Paris. Province Socius:*
Fr. Martin is here.
A word about our affairs in Montreal. Arrangements set by the Fathers of St. Sulpice.

*27 October 1846 to Fr. D. du Ranquet, Walpole:*
Write to your father, to the Provincial and to the General, but not to me.

*28 October 1846 to Father General:*
Requested dispensation for the ordination of Brs. Kohler, Régnier, Ouellet and Maréchal.
Furnished a run-down of the requirements of the Sulpicians of Montreal and the reason why, in spite of all this, we should not back off, according to the opinion of the Consultors.
Nonetheless, Fr. Martin has been told to move slowly as he prepares the reconstruction, not to borrow, to commit his own funds only to the extent of 8 or 10 thousand francs, to announce to the people of Montreal that by reason of the extent of the undertaking he will not be able to seriously pursue the work until he has received pledges covering two-thirds of the expense which will amount to 150 or 200 thousand and without having in hand some 60 or 70 thousand francs.
State of the four missions of Upper Canada. The arrival here of Fr. Maurice and Br. Veronau for these missions. They leave today and I am giving them Br. Lacoste for Sault Sainte Marie, to the great discomfort of St. John's.

*8 November 1846 to the Provincial, by Fr. Sarrando:*
I send the notes of Br. Dealy intended for Fr. Fournier. We have 4 scholastic novices and Montreal has 5 or 6.

Asked him to hold fast and keep me informed of the requirements of the Sulpicians in regard of the school in Montreal.

Fr. Henri du Ranquet and Br. Alsberg have been returned. [*His hope! It happened later. See following entries.*] I wrote this to Fr. Jordan whose letter of Sept.18 I just received.

*8 November 1846 to Fr. Jordan in Lyons:*
Replied to his letter of September 18. Fr. Gilles and Br. Chauver left for Mobile on August 31.

I pressed him to please send back Br. Alsberg and Fr. Henri du Ranquet.

*8 Nov. 1846 Fr. Gargain in Laval:*
Sent two newspaper articles on M. Gallitzin and his two works: *A Defence* and *On Scriptures.*

*8 Nov. 1846 to Fr. Choné, Manitouline:*
Recommended "motherly care" for Br. Veronau. In your letter give me the consolation of knowing you have succeeded. ...

*15 November 1846 to Fr. Gilles in Mobile:*
It is impossible, in spite of the best will, to send Fr. Gockeln to become Vice-President.

*15 November 1846 to Fr. H. du Ranquet in Grand Coteau:*
I am forwarding to him a letter of Fr. Dominique [his brother].
Re St. John's: 118 in the community, including novices & students. ...

*17 November 1846 to Fr. Martin in Montreal:*
... Observations of the General, in his letter of October 1, concerning one article in our agreement with Mr. Donigani. It is up to you when and how you are going to take this up with Mr. Donigani and obtain from him the necessary rectifications. Offer him everything on our property.

*17 November 1846 to Fr. Van de Velde in St. Louis:*
I am sending him a summary of the letter of the Archbishop of Oregon (Ltr. from Fr. Martin of Nov.10).

Complained he suspected me of being involved in the matter of Grand Coteau. I am neither subtle nor political.

A word about the return of Fr. Mignaud. You would be exceedingly kind if you returned him to us. About Fr. Verheyden: I am always ready to receive him.

*26 Nov. 1846 to Fr. [Thomas] Mulledy, Georgetown:*
Recommended Fr. Thébaud who will bring you information on the system of studies and so forth.

*26 Nov. 1846 to the Provincial:*

Brothers Lacoste and Veronau arrived at Sandwich too late. Boat travel to Sault and Manitouline already ended. Fr. Point has no idea how they will get to their postings. Hence, for the future, make certain that they arrive at the latest by Oct. 15.

The moment we have a school in Montreal, La Prairie will be abandoned.

*3 December 1846 to Fr. Martin, Montreal:*

Send Fr. Tellier as soon as he can make the trip. Good Br. Roy or Jennesseaux would be able to help you. Remind me of that when spring comes.

*3 Dec. 1846 to the General:*

Fr. Martin will adjust, I hope, with Mr. Donigani those details of our agreement which Your Paternity criticized in his letter to me.

A word about my too subtle finesse in the delicate matter of Grand Coteau.

Fr. Soderini ill here & other Fathers still more sick. Fr. Thébaud will write to you about this.

Expressed my opinion of the harshness of the government in Missouri.

Fr. Verheyden is not coming. I only accepted him to please your Paternity and the Fathers of Missouri.

*5 Dec. 1846 to Fr. Fournier in Paris:*

Asked the provincial to set aside a reserve fund for me this year in such wise that, having deducted the expense of those who will be coming, I may know by April or May how much will be left to me. More complaints of Fr. Coué.

The novices began their long retreat on December 3, feast of St. Francis Xavier.

I insisted that those who are destined for Upper Canada leave New York in the month of September. Navigation on lake already dangerous in October. Sinking on Lake Erie during last November; 18 bodies washed up on shore. This was at the time Br. Veronau was to leave to go from Sandwich to Toronto in order to get to Manitouline, were it possible.

*10 Dec. 1846 to Fr. Martin in Montreal:*

I am waiting for a copy of the Instruction on the ["*Casuel*".]

*11 Dec. 1846 to Fr. Point:*

Refuse politely but firmly the offer of the Rural Dean and the Vicar for the Clergy. Insist with the Bishop on your involvement.

Spoke of the schools for boys and for girls. He might express generic hopes for the future. The nuns would not stay there if we were to leave. I want very much to know how the bishop responds to our refusal. I fear that this is already part of a first attempt at an already determined plan. We'll see.

*15 Dec. 1846 to Fr. Coué, Paris:*

Fr. Maldonado arrived Dec. 14, 8 days after Fr. Schiansky.

Each one of those coming to America must bring 12 shirts, at least two pairs of trousers, 12 good handkerchiefs. Overcoats and trousers must be of black cloth, or approximating the same, for the priests and the scholastics. The coadjutor brothers are not to wear clerical dress. Overcoats must not be too short.

A Jesuit soutane of suitable material costs here about 100 francs. If they are less expensive in Paris, you must give one to each one who is coming.

Thank you for the gift of the pictures.

Subscribed to the daily *Quotidien* and to the *Correspondant*. Stopped *Villes et Campagnes* as well as *Annales de philosophie*. Asked the price of the *Complementary Course of Theology and S. Scripture*.

*17 Dec. 1846 to the Provincial in Paris:*

On December 14 Fr. Maldonado arrived after 56 days on the sea.

On December 17 Br. Férard had his second exam in *De Universa morali*. Four affirmative ballots. He will be ordained a priest at the first ordination ceremony. Br. Schiansky will receive tonsure and Minor Orders.

Br. Hollinger is on retreat before his first vows to be taken on Christmas Day.

Asked for reserve fund, for example, 3000 francs for the Superior General which would always be at my disposal.

I will visit St. John's. Br. Crowe will pronounce his vows on January 17.

Spoke of the schools for boys and those for girls sought by both Fr. Choné and Fr. Point in Sandwich. It would be desirable to have the boys' schools run by our Coadjutor Brothers. For the schools for girls, Fr. Point wants to take what is needed from Mme. de Saisseval. Please speak to him about this.

*28 Dec. 1846 to Fr. Henri du Ranquet, Grand Coteau:*

Fr. Provincial Rubillon informed me that Fr. Jordan, provincial of Lyons, wrote to Grand Coteau that you were to be returned. Fr. Jordan has just written to me himself and he tells me that "Fr. H. du Ranquet and Br. Alsberg will be returned to you, once our Fathers shall have arrived in Grand Coteau." As a result, my dear Father, let you and Br. Alsberg prepare to leave for St. John's College. You may stay for two weeks or so with the Fathers from Lyons after their arrival if that is necessary or useful to introduce them to this country which is new to them.

It is certainly not necessary, my dear Father, to tell you that both provincials were in total agreement as to what I have ordered in this letter to you. By that very fact you are immediately under my jurisdiction, and only an order from the General can retain you any longer in Grand Coteau.

*29 Dec. 1846 to the General:*

General observations about Ours.

Dispensation because of age for Br. Garvey.

The Sulpicians gave a gift of 3600 francs for our college in Montreal.

Fr. Van de Velde was astonished by what he read in the extract from the Memorandum of the Archbishop of Oregon. He mentioned even greater difficulties concerning the return to us of our Fathers.

*29 Dec. 1846 to the Provincial:*
A note about my visit: the spirit, the good disposition; two anecdotes about one person; Fr. Hollinger's vows on Christmas Day, Fr. Legoüais was the celebrant. ...

Letter from Fr. Van de Velde on December 14, concerning my letter to Fr. Henri du Ranquet. I asked the provincial himself to send him orders as well as to Br. Alsberg. A delay can once again put into question the return to us of our Fathers. Don't forget that we immediately returned to them Frs. Gilles and Chauvet and that we gave them Fr. Soller.

We are having trouble here with our laundry: with women who do the work. ...

*1 Jan. 1847 to Fr. Martin, Montreal:*
... Why not a word about the request of 2000 francs for Sandwich?
Please warn us in time of the arrival of Fr. Tellier so that we can put him up.

*11 Jan. 1847 to the Provincial:*
Asked for the pension of 10 of our scholastics. Concerning this, I cited the letter of His Paternity of June 1, 1846. ...
Supplied some details about several people in the house. ...

*13 Jan. 1847 to Fr. Luiset, Montreal:*
Advice for coadjutor novices. ...

*17 Jan. 1847 to Fr. Jordan, Provincial, Lyons:*
... Dismay over our lack of personnel.
Thanks for the promise of the return of Fr. H. du Racquet and Br. Alsberg to us with the arrival at Grand Coteau of the Fathers from Lyons.

*20 Jan. 1847 to Fr. Martin in Montreal:*
You have permission to do everything necessary for the construction, purchase of construction materials, and the sale of whatever in your block-purchases is not needed.

You may not sell the pictures made by you or for you. See Decree 84 of the 7th G.C.

Take care that the scholastics taking Logic speak only Latin.
Fr. Tellier has arrived.

*20 Jan. 1847 to Fr. Provincial, carried by the Bishop of Toronto:*
It has been proposed that New York [Fordham] also take non-resident students. However that is inconceivable without the addition of three or four additional Jesuits who, after a short period, would be able to teach or to prefect. If possible they should be started on English immediately.

Concerning the post of responsibility for all clergy as Rural Dean and as Vicar for Personnel given by the bishop in an open letter to Fr. Point: the answer is No and neither ask for nor await his consent. I had written to Fr. Point to refuse politely but firmly. Fr. Choné also was appointed to the same position.

*22 Jan. 1847 to Fr. Point, Sandwich:*
Concerning the post of Rural Dean. I discussed with the Bishop of Toronto:
• You and our Fathers take great care to exercise the ordinary ministries of the Society to the extent of the jurisdiction granted *ad hoc* by the bishop, taking great pains, more so than before, to do nothing except what is agreeable to the parish priests.
• You will accept no report about anyone outside [the Society]. If you observe something important by yourself or through our Fathers, you will never take any direct action. You will bring the affair to the attention of the Bishop of Detroit, the vicar general of the Bishop of Toronto.
• I am adding a formal prohibition for you and our Fathers to ever write anything about any ecclesiastical matter which would be in the slightest way disagreeable to the Bishop of Detroit or elsewhere. All matters of this sort are to be done viva voce, and in no other way.
• Let it be known, when you can, to the priests of the diocese that the bishop appointed you Rural Dean only to facilitate the exercise of your ministries.

*25 Jan. 1847 to the Provincial by the bishop of Toronto:*
I communicated the rules sent to Fr. Point and Fr. Choné concerning the Rural Deanship. The bishop showed himself very well disposed.

*1 February 1847 to Fr. Choné:*
Sent him the letters of Fr. General for him and for Fr. Hanipaux. Encouragements.

*7 Feb. 1847 to the General:*
... A few words about Fr. Soderini.
Told Fr. H. du Ranquet there seems to be absolutely no problem about his rejoining us with Br. Alsberg.
I will leave in mid-July to visit Upper Canada. ...
Both Frs. Point and Choné are Rural Deans: short history about that; discussion with the Bishop of Toronto; rules they are to follow sent to the Fathers.
Included letters of Oct. 28 and Dec. 28 for which I await a reply.
The ordinations were done by the coadjutor: Fr. Férard ordained priest, the others received tonsure and minor orders.
Only one Father, as far as I know, does not approve of our mission to the Indians. A long time ago I wrote to him on this subject.

*7 Feb, 1847 to Fr. Point, Sandwich:*
Replied to his letter of Jan 21. Mentioned that of Jan 22. Send your letter to Fr. Nicole Point not by Fr. de Smet, but by Bishop Blanchet of Montreal.

Had you known about the bad news at Sault? Did you hear from Fr. Menet? Please reply to these two questions. I asked the exact date when the water route to Sault will open.

Small portable grill for confessions. How did you distribute your funds? Please tell me.

*7 Feb. 1847 to Br. Lacoste at Sault Sainte Marie:*
In reply to his letter of January, I sent encouragements. Write to Fr. Point in order that he send you books from Detroit. First Mass of Fr. Férard.

*13 Feb. 1847 to Fr. Martin, Montreal:*
I am sending Fr. Férard to help at LaPrairie.

*13 Feb. 1847 to Fr. Nicole Point, :*
For a long time the General has arranged for you to return to our province in Upper Canada. The present provincial wants me to send you the order to return as soon as you can. Bishop Blanchet is kindly bringing you this letter. ...

*13 Feb. 1847 to Fr. Jaffré, Sandwich:*
... Encouragements.
Small items about St. John's.
Fr. Férard is at La Prairie.

*20 Feb. 1847 to Fr. Vespre, Georgetown:*
... I am sending him a letter for Fr. Murphy, to whom I am recommending Mr. Farstall of New Orleans.
I invited him to come and visit us.

*3 March 1847 to the Provincial:*
Financial run-down on St. John's. Impossible to continue there if you pay stipends for only three out of ten scholastics.
News of Brs. Desjardins and Hollings.

*3 March 1847 to Fr. Coué:*
... Demanded the clear and well-defined separation of the accounts of St. John's and those of the missions:
• Send the reserve of 3,000 and what you also owe for the upkeep of the scholastics, according to the decision of Fr. General.
• No longer fit out with short jackets those who are coming but give them long overcoats.

*7 March 1847 to the Provincial:*
... Please give exact details and justification for the jobs, whether prefects or teachers, of the scholastics, Brs. Graves, Nash, Gockeln, Régnier, Maréchal, Kohler, Hudon,

Ouellet and Doucet. Need only 4 or 5 prefects, rotated so that all of them would have time to do their own work. Must all nine be assigned to the college? There still remain Brs. Schiansky, Hollinger, Pernot, Desjacques, Tissot, as well as the novices Bidwell, Dealy and Hampston, all of whom are *ZERO* for the college.

Hampston while still in the house, *dismissus* on March 8 by reason of health. Another scholastic novice will replace him immediately. A new coadjutor postulant.

Frs. Mignard, H. du Ranquet, Verheyden and Br. Alsberg have arrived.

News from Fr. Point about Sault Sainte Marie. I sent by Br. Lacoste the order to close the girls' school in Sault which Fr. Point can do when the water is navigable. ...

Fr. Maurice is to pronounce his vows on February 21.

*7 March 1847 to Fr. Point, Sandwich:*
Replied to his letter of Feb. 24. He is to write to Fr. Provincial and tell him what I told him to do. Noted his error in regard to the allocation in the account sent by Fr. Coué.

*9 March 1847 to Fr. Martin in Montreal:*
Replied to his letters of Feb. 3 and 23.

As soon as Br. Rouillé's health, and the time, permit, send the good Brother here to restore his health. ...

*23 March 1847 to the Provincial:*
... Walpole and Sault, now isolated.

From here only Fr. Kohler could replace the two who are leaving!

We need to send to America only those men who are certain and solid, who do not need to be tested.

Work of our Fathers in New York preparing for the jubilee.

*23 March 1847 to Fr. Point, Sandwich:*
Replied to his letter of March 10. Recalled the content of my letter of March 7 and urged the execution of my instructions regarding Sault.

Very probable that I will bring along with me a Father from here destined for Sault.

*28 March 1847 to Fr. Martin, Montreal:*
Replied to his letter of March 15. He may send to St. John's the two novices, Sépial and Boisvert. You will pay for their trip. ... Br. Constance will go to Walpole to replace Br. Jennesseaux who will help you in Montreal. Please notify me 15 days before the departure of these two novices for St. John's.

Jubilee in Canada. You will certainly receive Fr. Mignard but he is not very robust. He must not be sent to a mission to preach and hear confessions. ... Using the two coadjutor brothers, you will be able ... to set up the college.

Please take great care that the two novice brothers at La Prairie ... have a conference and catechism every week. ...

*30 March 1847 to Fr. Martin, Montreal:*

With Fr. Mignard, you will have Fr. du Ranquet to celebrate the jubilee in Canada, and always, probably, Fr. Petit.

The first two should return here in mid-July and Fr. Férard as soon as they shall have arrived in Montreal.

A way [suggested] to make use of these Fathers according to their strong points.

*1 April 1847, to the General:*

Two of our Protestant students have been baptized.

Gave a run-down of what our Fathers in New York and the vicinity did to celebrate the jubilee. Fr. Larkin is in Troy where the pastor has offered us a house for boarders. We will look this over.

What Fr. S. has acquired since he left the Rocky Mountains until he arrived here. May he be kept in New York or should he be returned to Cincinnati under the hypothesis that the Father will renew his vows and re-enter the Society? It would do this poor Father a great deal of good to receive a word from Your Paternity. We have reason to be pleased with him up till now.

*1 April 1847 to the Provincial:*

Fr. Abbadie once again is asking for Br. Corne. Will you come to an understanding with Fr. Jordan? I will not give up this brother until you shall have written to me: *Give him up!*

Fr. Soler, a donné, doesn't he deserve two coadjutor brothers? I told you of this request in my letter of the end of December.

I am going to send Br. Constance to Walpole in the place of Br. Jennesseaux who is needed by Fr. Martin.

Br. Brenans is no longer at La Prairie. Fr. Mainguy finds him incompatible. We need to send two novices there. Just as we need you to send us several good brothers.

*18 April 1847 to the Provincial, carried by Fr. de Smet:*

First and second catalogues for the College.

Sheets concerning suitability *ad gubernandum* for Frs. Thébaud, Larkin, Murphy, Lebreton, Tellier.

Two copies of the formula for final vows and for the renunciation of possessions for Fr.H.du Ranquet.

My observations on these *informationes*.

Reasons not to accept the church in New York which the bishop wanted to offer to us and to buy another church less restricted [Universalist] for 18 thousand piasters.

Chouvy is here as well as the box of books. Thanks for everything. Asked for unbound copies of the *Proper of the Society*.

Recommended Mr. Donegan.

*26 April 1847 to the Provincial in reply to his letter of March 1:*

Reasons why it would be extremely difficult or impossible to do without Fr. Larkin in 1847-1848: the church is on the point of being finished; the college; there is no other superior except him, even for the residence, if, in the first place, we want a residence. ...

*27 April 1847 to Fr. Point at Sandwich:*
I hope to be in Sandwich on July18.

*29 April 1847 to Fr. Choné:*
Replied to his March letter. Lest there be any difficulties for the final vows of Fr. Hanipaux on the feast of the Assumption, let him pronounce them on Pentecost, or Trinity Sunday, or Corpus Christi. You will receive them. Tell Father all he must do.

*30 April 1847 to Fr. Menet, Sault Sainte Marie:*
Repeated the main things to be done: suppression of the school for girls; ditto for the boys' school unless the numbers increase; use Brothers for the care of the house and the mission.

*30 April 1847 to Fr. Abbadie in Grand Coteau:*
Replied to his letter of the 15th: I will send you Br. Corne when the 2 provincials (Paris, Lyons) tell me to do so. That is the routine followed up till now for the return of Fr. Gilles, Br. Chauvet, Fr. H.duRanquet and Br. Alsberg. ...

*9 May 1847 to the Provincial:*
Replied to his letter of April 16 and to that of Fr. Fournier of the 12th. I asked him to read the letter for the General. ...

*11 May 1847 to Fr. Martin, Montreal:*
*Informationes ad gubernandum* concerning Fr. Pedro Point. Announced the arrival of Fr. Murphy with the bishop.

11 May 1847 to Frs. Luiset and Saché:
*Informations ad gubernandum* about Fr. Felix Martin. Tell all to send them directly to the provincial. ...

*26 May 1847 to the General:*
Replied to his letter of April 2. Many details about people and affairs, for the past & the present.
Purchase of the church, renting of house in New York. ...

*1 June 1847 to Fr. Martin, Montreal:*
Since the need to send Br. Jennesseaux to you no longer exists, as you have two good older brothers, Fr. Point will keep him at Walpole. This I wrote to him. ...
I beg you to see to it that Fr. Férard and Brs. Baxter and Glackmeyer are here July 3.

*1 June 1847 to the Provincial:*

On April 12, I sent you, according to the instruction of the Socius, all *informationes* and all the *status temporalium*.

Trouble also in New York. The contract for the church is to be signed today by Frs. Thébaud and Larkin who are in New York.

An idea about some economies already made and to be made.

Two coadjutor novices have arrived here from Montreal.

*8 June 1847 to the Provincial :*

... Sent him the *status domorum, historia domus*.

Details about the establishment in New York: several gifts, the borrowing of 6500 piasters.

Asked Fr. Coué for partially-bound edition of Migne's *Complete Course of Theology and Scripture*.

*11 June 1847 to Fr Martin, Montreal:*

Fr. Férard and Brs. Baxter and Glackmeyer should be here on July 3. You will probably have Fr. Tellier for Trois Riviêres.

Reply concerning the purchase of adjacent property: details required.

The promised boarding facility is hardly to my liking.

No news from His Paternity.

*24 June 1847 to the Provincial:*

Reasons to send Br. Kohler: otherwise Fr. Menet would be all alone.

Incertitude as to whether Fr. Nicolas Point will arrive and when he will arrive.

Reasons for the need for prefects of the day-students in New York.

Charlestown is impossible; an English Father for Mobile, impossible.

Br. Gockeln is leaving soon for France.

Fear of discord in the new Swiss-German mission.

Part II

"To break for them the bread of knowledge and devotion."

St. John's College, Rose Hill

# CHAPTER 4

## REV. AUGUSTUS J. THÉBAUD, S.J.

### Priest, Scientist, Friend, Writer, Breton

When at age 39, Fr. Thébaud was appointed the fourth president of St. John's College, he became in effect the first Jesuit president of Fordham and also one of the youngest to hold that position. Later he would become one of the few presidents who left that post [1846-1851] and then would hold it a second time [1860-1863].

Born in Nantes, Brittany, and educated in a local seminary, he was ordained on Oct. 17, 1831 for his local diocese and spent three years doing parochial duties at his own parish church, St. Clement, Nantes. He later decided to become a foreign missionary and, after a protracted interview in Rome with Fr. Jan Roothaan, the Jesuit General, he became one of the four priest-novices at San Andrea on Nov. 27, 1835. After the noviceship, he spent a year at the Jesuits' Gregorian University where he did a private review of theology and attended some classes as an auditor. Next he went to the Sorbonne in Paris and spent a year studying chemistry and other sciences under Ampère and others to prepare for college work in the American missions.

Fr. Thébaud arrived at St. Mary's College, Marion County, Kentucky, on January 14, 1839. Focusing first on improving his English, he demonstrated his humility by attending for six months a class where the elements of English were taught. Soon he became the teacher of chemistry and physics and biology, and later dean of the college. Then on Nov. 1, 1845, he was appointed president and thus became the last Jesuit president at St. Mary's College until he took up his role at Rose Hill.[4]

During his first term as president, his major challenge was the lack of an organized curriculum for the college; students' programs were based on individual needs without an academic model on which to make academic judgments. So he devoted himself specially on a revision of the college's curriculum and visited Georgetown College to learn how they adapted the structures of the Jesuit *Ratio Studiorum* to the American scene. He must have been impressed by what he saw there because he adopted the Georgetown curriculum with only minor modifications. Classes were divided into grammar, humanities [Thébaud used the term *belles-lettres* instead of humanities], rhetoric and philosophy to designate the main areas for study during each of their college years. In local terminology, the grammar classes were called the Third Division, humanities and rhetoric classes, the Second Division, and the philosophy classes, the First Division. Grammar was similar to twenty-first century upper elementary school, humanities/belle letters/rhetoric similar to high school and first year of college, and philosophy similar to the other years of college.

Once the curriculum was stabilized he established a students' library.[5] Furthermore, he had a three-story building erected for additional classrooms. During his first presidency he was also superior of the diocesan seminary at Rose Hill. He continued to teach during his presidency; in his first year he taught French and in his last three years he was also professor of botany. After the conclusion of his presidency, he remained at the college for a year to be of service to his successor in the role of vice-president. In that year he also taught physics and mathematics.

During his second term as president (1861-64), he was also dean of the college. In addition, he planned out the main campus roads, improved the overall campus landscape, and introduced a university-level program in graduate philosophy. An important purchase was made in those years, as described by Fr. T. J. Campbell in his biographical sketch of Fr. Thébaud: "the seminary portion of the college, ... about eight acres, passed into the hands of the fathers, the purchase-price being $45,000, the other section having been transferred when the Society first took possession in 1846 for $40,000." The seminary portion

of the college included St. John's Hall, the university church and the Rodrigue cottage. During that second term the college also purchased the Powell farm which adjoined the southern border of the campus.

Between his two terms as president he was pastor of St. Joseph's in Troy, NY, for eight years, At the completion of his second presidency he returned there for five years as superior. At Troy he clashed with the Nativitists and the Know-nothing party in the city. It was powerful locally and had elected its candidate to the mayoral office; threats were made to prosecute "foreigners." Fr. Thébaud wrote a series of four articles in the *Troy Times* to show that the fears of foreigners as portrayed by some papers were without foundation and unworthy of sensible people. Though the opposition was inclined to physically attack those who opposed them Father wrote: "I had nothing to fear from Know-nothing attacks. I was surrounded by an army of Irishmen. ... [The Know-nothings] would not have dared to attack me in my fortress" (*Forty Years*, p. 251).

In 1869 he returned to Fordham as spiritual father to the community; he taught history, philosophy and rhetoric, and as well was moderator of the college's St. John's Historical Society. In 1874 he was again at Fordham but this time at age 67 he must have felt a lessening of energy since his assignment was limited to spiritual activities. Between these major multi-year assignments he also did pastoral work for shorter periods at churches such as St. Mary's in Montreal, St. Lawrence O'Toole's in New York City and St. Joseph's in Hudson City, NJ.

In 1875 until shortly before his death he was at the College and parish of St. Francis Xavier in New York City. There, besides pastoral work, he taught history, philosophy and rhetoric, and was librarian, writer and house consultor.

He died at Fordham on Dec. 17, 1885 at 10:40 A.M. The Minister's diary noted that he had been anointed on Dec. 8 at 9:45 P.M. by Fr. Campbell. His death certificate gave the cause of death as diabetes mellitus and exhaustion. The Office of the Dead was recited at 6:00 P.M. on Dec. 18. Next day the Requiem Mass was said in the university church at 9:A.M. The diary noted that in attendance besides the community were the provincial, V. Rev. Robert Fulton, Fr. John Murphy, president of Gonzaga College in Washington, D.C., and old friends Fathers Daubresse and Ronayne. Burial was in the Fordham cemetery.

Fr. Thébaud wrote a glowing tribute to his friend Archbishop John Hughes long after the archbishop's death. He claimed that Hughes' personality was dominated by a quality that was not recognized by others who wrote about him: "extraordinary prudence." It was displayed especially in the way he met with his opposition, both within and outside the Church. Fr. Thébaud wrote that the Archbishop knew when to push forward and when to be patient, and always showed charity towards opponents. These laudatory traits he perceived in the Archbishop others saw in Fr. Thébaud.

Thébaud's friendship with the Archbishop was facilitated no doubt by the fact that the Rodrigue family lived for many years in a cottage on the seminary property that adjoined the college. Mrs. Margaret Rodrigue was one of the Archbishop's sisters; her husband was the archbishop's architect. It is likely that the rector-president was an honored guest when their main guest was the archbishop. Thus during both presidencies of Fr. Thébaud, relationships between the college and the archbishop were cordial, but reached crisis proportions between the two presidencies. He was socially oriented and enjoyed visiting and being visited. Even the index to his memoirs testified to the number and varied social status of his many friendships.

As the author of numerous books and journal articles, he was undoubtedly the most published writer among the Fordham faculty or administrators in the nineteenth century. He was a recognized contributor on current issues to Catholic journals such as *The American Catholic Quarterly Review* (15 articles) and *the Catholic World*. Another publication to which he contributed was *The Month* of London; to it he contributed a series of twelve long articles regarding The Native Tribes of North America and the Catholic Missions.

The themes of his books demonstrate the wide range and depth of his interests and encyclopedic knowledge. Two of the books are specifically on religious topics: *Gentilism: Religion previous to Christianity* (1876); and *The Church and the Moral World: Considerations on the Holiness of the Church* (1881, 2 volumes). The books provide sweeping histories and analyses of religious thinking before and after the life of Jesus Christ. The historical analysis of holiness in the Church even in times of corruption and scandal merits attention in every age.

His first published book was *The Irish Race in the Past and in the Present* (1873). That was followed by *Ireland, Past and Present* (1878). Furthermore, the real heroes in his novel, *Louisa Kirkbride*, were an Irish-American couple who edify their employer by their life styles despite their moral environment. These books on Ireland (and numerous positive references to the Irish in other writings) were written by a man born in France, and an observer might ask, "How come?" I am convinced that the key to his empathy with the Irish was his recognition that they and he shared a special common heritage because he identified himself as a Breton (he referred to a Jesuit brother as "a Breton like myself") and the Breton people, of course, are one of the branches of the Celts as are the Irish. Both peoples also shared a deep and historic faith in Roman Catholicism. The general poverty and antagonism to the Irish immigrants in America shown by the Nativists and others must have made him resolve to help them if he could and he did so in his writings.

Orestes Brownson, the prominent convert, columnist, and editor who clashed with Thébaud publicly in some issues, wrote a 20 page essay on Thébaud's book on the Irish race in his Oct., 1873 *Quarterly Review*. He began the review by calling it "solid and erudite, really profound and instructive" which has "given us the key to Irish history." He said it caused him to esteem the Irish race more highly. His summary view was that the book does "credit to the illustrious society of which he is a distinguished member. He has made a most valuable contribution to American literature."

Publication of Thébaud's writings did not stop with his death. Almost twenty years later, a close friend and noted historian, Charles G. Herbermann, began editing three volumes of Fr. Thébaud's reminiscences from his surving manuscripts. The first two volumes were about modern times and the church in Italy and in France. The third volume, a retrospect, written from documents and memory, *Forty Years in the United States of America* (1839-1885) is important to historians, particularly the last two chapters that describe the Catholic church and the education scene of his times.

His contemporaries attested to the high esteem they felt for Fr. Thébaud. A Kentucky historian, Benjamin Webb, wrote that his writings "are no less full of the fire of intellect than they are pervaded by the spirit of religion." Fr. Thomas Campbell, who at one time was his Provincial, wrote of Fr. Thébaud: "He was a quick and eager observer, and his eagerness made him ready to maintain his view of a disputed question without, however, being contentious or disputatious. ... He was a high-souled French gentleman ... of exquisitely tender sensibility, of lofty motives, of large and generous views." An anonymous writer of his obituary at the College of St. Francis Xavier summarized his views thus: "he was venerable in appearance, urbane, very prudent, and very zealous for the glory of our faith."

The June, 1892, *Fordham Monthly*, reported that John A. Mooney made this suggestion to the St. John's Historical Society, which was founded in 1862, during Thébaud's second presidential term: "Reverend Augustus J. Thébaud deserves that the memory of his learning, scholarship, and zeal, should be kept alive. . . . Here where he labored so long, so modestly, so wholeheartedly, so successfully, it were only fitting that he should be honored, and that his memory and the memory of his interest in sound historical study should be kept alive." Some forty years after Mooney's plea, when campus buildings were renamed to honor individuals, the Science Building on the Rose Hill campus was renamed Thébaud Hall as a well-deserved permanent memorial to the achievements of Fordham's first Jesuit President/rector. But surely there are other ways of honoring him such as researching his work and influence in depth. A minimum honor for him would be that each Fordham student and graduate recognized him as Fordham's fourth president and the First Jesuit president.

# CHAPTER 5

## FR. MINISTER'S DIARY, ST. JOHN'S COLLEGE, ROSE HILL

We have already seen selections from this diary in Chapter 2, selections relevant to the move from St. Mary's to New York. Now we take a closer look at it to get a sense of what Fr. Thébaud faced those first months at St. John's. Curiously, little emerges from the diary about the academic side of things. The focus instead is on the Jesuit community life as it was lived under his direction. We get a picture of these Jesuits that has them wedded to a regular routine of religious practices: benedictions, spiritual exhortations, abstinence, processions, self-accusation penances at table, retreats, the College patronal day (John the Baptist), vow days, ordinations and so forth. Time seems measured by intervals between feast days. Customary Jesuit practices like *Toni* and Cases of Conscience recurred on a firm schedule. The former, *Toni* (from the Latin, *tonus*, meaning tones), was an elocution or speech exercise for correct public reading and speaking, ' in the great Jesuit tradition of *eloquentia perfecta*. The latter were gatherings (for those who had already studied moral theology) in which difficult moral cases were presented and a solution offered with an opportunity for discussion of the issues involved. The ministries to which each person was assigned were listed once a year on what was called the Status.

Pastoral work by the Jesuits at the College is mentioned frequently, although not in the detail we will see in the Chapter 6. Some of it is local, some 'in the city', some across the river, and some upstate or even in Canada. Many visitors, including prelates, pass through their doors.

Basically, though, "all is usual."

### AUGUST, 1846

11. Brs. [Augustus] Kohler and [Augustine] Régnier, Scholastics from Georgetown College in Maryland, came to us.

12. Since the death of Rev. Dr. [Benedict] Fenwick, bishop of Boston, had been announced, Fr. Larkin set out for Boston to be at his exsequies; he also gave the Spiritual Exercises there at that time.

14. Rev. Fr. Visitor gave an exhortation to very many of Ours who were working at St. John's College. He strongly urged one and all to put themselves, their work and the whole house under the tutelage of the Blessed Virgin Mary and that they very fervently continue that devotion to the Lord's Mother (*omnes et singulos admonet ut se suosque labores, ac domum integram sub tutela B.M.V. collocent, atque eidem beneginissae Parenti devotissime conservant*).

15. Feast of the Assumption of the B.V.M. The house status was read at table: Very Rev. Fr. Thébaud, Rector, beginning Nov. 1, 1845, Fr. Peter Lebreton, Minister, etc.

19. Very Rev. Fr. Visitor went to Canada.

20. Brothers [Edward] Doucet and [Thomas] Ouellet, scholastics from the Canadian novitiate, arrived to do their studies.

25. Fr. DeLuynes headed for Utica to give the mission exercises to the people.

26. Fr. [Isidore] Daubresse and Brs. [Martin] Desjacques, [Martin] Férard, [Anthony] Hollinger, [Claude] Pernot and [Peter] Tissot came from France [and they reported they were] driven by favorable winds.

28. Rev. Fr. Visitor returned from Canada.

30. Fr. Petit set out for Utica to hear confessions. Br. Doucet began to devote himself to the customary Spiritual Exercises.

31. Fr. Gilles set out for his own province [Missouri] with Br. Chauvet, both about to be added to the lists of the Jesuits in Alabama.

SEPTEMBER, 1846

3. Brs. Desjacques and Tissot began their annual retreat.

4. Rev. Fr. Visitor gave a domestic exhortation.

5. Fr. Legoüais made Spiritual Director [*Prof. spir.*]

6. Talking from dinner [midday] to supper must be done in English. [*A prandio et cena confabulantes anglice loqui jubentur.*]

7. Br. Doucet, having finished his novitiate, pronounced his first vows.

8. Br. [Francis] Vachon, novice Brother, came to us from the Canadian novitiate.

12. Frs. DeLuynes and Petit, having finished giving Spiritual Exercises at Utica, returned home.

14. Fr. Joseph Irisarri, a Spaniard, who is returning to Europe from the Missouri mission, visited us and tomorrow will set out again.

15. Fr. Petit began his customary eight day Spiritual Exercises.

A wooden frame house for our workers (*famulis*) was being built.

16. Rev. Jos. Stokes, pastor of the church at Utica, came here to visit (*invisendi gratia*).

19. Today the Most Reverend Bishop of New York was here to deal with Rev. Fr. Superior about the seminary and the seminarians.

25. Rev. B. Cull, associate pastor at Utica, came here to visit.

30. The Most Rev. D. McCloskey, bishop of Albany, came and took dinner with us.

OCTOBER, 1846

2. Rev. Fr. Rector gave a domestic exhortation.

3. A Canadian Sulpician priest, soon to travel to France, visited us.

5. The bishop of Albany, Most Rev. McCloskey, and Bishop Bourget, were here with many others.

7. Rev. Frs. Bailee and Chalbosse, from the Canadian Sulpician community, who are going again to Baltimore, visited us.

8. Fr. Lebreton was made ordinary confessor of the nuns of the Sacred Heart until the return of Fr. D. Lafont, who is their usual confessor.

10. The feast of St. Francis Borja was celebrated in our customary way.

15. Our customary Toni and Cases of Conscience.

16. The Spiritual Father gave a domestic exhortation, as customary.

21. Fr. Felix Martin, the superior of the St. Mary's house in Canada, came to us, and brought with him Br. D. Gauthier, a novice Brother who will be with us.

22. Toni and as usual. Mr. Joseph Adams, a Kentucky priest, came here; soon he is going to enter the novitiate.

23. The following came from France: Fr. Arsenius Havequez who will stay with us; Fr. Louis Maurice and Br. John Veronau, both of whom are heading for the missions near Lake Superior.

27. Fr. Felix Martin returned to Canada.

28. Fr. Louis Maurice, and Brothers Lacoste and Veronau, began their journey to the Canadian missions.

29. Toni and Cases of Conscience as usual.

30. Domestic exhortation. Benediction in honor of Bl. Alphonsus Rodriguez.

31. Today at eventide the novitiate was publicly placed under the auspices of the Blessed Virgin and all the Saints.

NOVEMBER, 1846

1. The Feast of All Saints was solemnly celebrated, as customary.

5. Toni and then Cases of Conscience, as customary.

12. Domestic exhortation.

19. Toni and then Cases of Conscience, as usual.

24. St. Cecilia's day was celebrated as usual with concerts and speeches.

26. Toni and then Cases of Conscience, as usual.

27. Fr. A. O'Brien, a Dominican from Ohio, came to us seeking money for the building of a church.

The Dominican Father left. Domestic exhortation as usual.

28. Fr. Rector left for Georgetown College.

30. Fr. Joseph Adams left the house, though he left the novitiate on Nov. 22.

DECEMBER, 1846

2  Fr. Rector returned from Georgetown. He came with Fr. Tibor Soderini who up to now was in charge of the Vice-province of Missouri.

3  The feast-day of St. Francis Xavier was celebrated as usual.

Today the 30 day retreat was begun by six novices: Brothers Thomas Bidwell, John Hampston, Patrick Dealy, Scholastics, and Felix McParland, Jeremias Garvey and Patrick Crowe, Brothers.

Also today, the visitation of the college by the Mission Superior began.

5  Fr. Ocken [?], S.J., missionary among the Potawatomies, came to us, traveling nearby as he sought help for the Indians.

6  Toni and then Cases of Conscience, as usual.

8  Feast of the Immaculate Conception was celebrated as usual. No classes.

Br. Charles Schianski, a scholastic, came from France to continue his studies.

10   R.I.P.; Rev. D. Harley, who formerly was president of this college, died. Many of our Fathers , seminarians, and former students attended his obsequies.

Visit from Fr. Vincenzo and Mr. Tenaglia, Dominicans, with a Coadjutor Brother of the same order who will remain in our seminary until they proceed to Illinois.

11   Domestic exhortation.

13   Toni and then Cases of Conscience, as usual. Fr. Minister began his annual retreat.

14   Fr. Francis Maldonado arrived here from Naples to teach theology to Jesuit seminarians.

Mr. Belcarique also came here, asking to enter the Society.

19   Visitors: Fathers Francis Xavier Kalcher, Martin Saisl and Br. Jenny, a Dominican scholastic; they are soon to set out for Spring Hill, in Mobile, the college of the Vice-province of Missouri.

20   Toni and then Cases of Conscience, as usual.

21   Scholastics Kolchur and Seisl, and Br. Jenny left us.

22   Academies and a disputation for rhetoricians were held.

The clock [brought from St. Mary's] was placed in the tower erected for it.

25   Christmas was celebrated with a solemn Mass, vespers and benediction of the Blessed Sacrament. Then the great majority of the students will be dispersed in different directions.

No classes from today to January 2.

Rev. Fr. Rector, Fr. Larkin, Brothers Hudon and Kohler began their annual retreat.

26   Today the Most Rev. bishop of New York was with us to visit Superiors and other Jesuits.

27   Refreshments were served for the professors and all the prefects.

28   Fr. Fouché went to the City to give the Spiritual Exercises to the Mercy Sisters.

29   Fr. Superior visited various college rooms with the Minister and Subminister to inspect their situation.

31. Fr. Murphy visited the bishop to offer his best wishes and those of all the Jesuits for the new year.

At the request [*postulanti*] of Fr. Superior, the Fathers and Brothers will not gather to express good wishes to him [on New Year's Day]. That custom [gathering with the Superior and usually heaping high praises on him] seemed to conflict with the customs of the region.

JANUARY, 1847

1. The Circumcision of Our Lord Jesus Christ was celebrated as usual.

3. The coming renovation of vows was announced and the extraordinary confessors named according to the house rules. Toni and then Cases of Conscience.

4. Mr. Balgarigue, a diocesan seminarian entered the novitiate, with the bishop's approval.

5. Rev. Fr. Mission Superior declared that his Visitation of the mission was ended. There was a domestic exhortation in the evening.

Six novices completed their month-long retreat[*Menstrua exercitia*]: Thomas Bidwell, John Hampston, Patrick Dealy, Felix McParland, Jeremiah Garvey and Patrick Crowe.

6. The Epiphany of the Lord was celebrated according to custom.

13. At table the letter from Fr. General Caraffa was read and the spiritual exercises to be performed during the three days before the renovation of vows were prescribed. We had a domestic exhortation in the evening.

16. Self-accusation of defects at table, as customary. In the evening, a domestic exhortation. Abstinence at table.

17. Renovation of vows. Br. Ouellet gave a sermon at table. Reading of scholastics' verses laboriously completed. Today Br. Patrick Crowe made his first vows after his noviceship was correctly completed.

18. Fr. Remigius J. Tellier [later a Fordham president and the last superior of the New York-Canada mission] came here from the Canadian residence of La Prairie to learn English.

20. Most Rev. [Michael] Power, bishop of Toronto, visited us on his way to Europe.

22. Abstinence as usual.

24. Toni and then Cases of Conscience. In the evening Br. Férard began his retreat; he will soon be ordained.

29. Domestic exhortation. Abstinence.

31. Toni as usual, and then Cases of Conscience.


FEBRUARY, 1847

2. Feast of the Purification of the Blessed Virgin Mary. The Sodality of the Purification of the Blessed Virgin Mary was begun for the boarding students.

5. The feast of our Martyrs of Japan was celebrated as customary.

7 Br. Férard was ordained to the priesthood in the Seminary church by Most Rev. John McCloskey, Coadjutor bishop of New York.

12 Domestic exhortation.

13 Fr. Henry Duranquet and Fr. Peter Verheyden came here from the Cincinnati college to stay awhile among their St. John's brethren.

14 Toni as usual, and then Cases of Conscience.

15 The Most Rev. Bishop attended the monthly disputation by the scholastics and seminarians.

17 Lenten fast began. All as usual.

20 Toni as usual, and then Cases of Conscience.

22 Gen. George Washington's birthday was celebrated in the college hall with speeches. Despite a freezing storm, many from the City participated.

26 Domestic exhortation.

28 Toni as usual, and then Cases of Conscience.

MARCH, 1847

2  Fr. Peter DeSmet visited us with Fr. McMullins, a confrere from Philadelphia.

7  Toni as usual, and then Cases of Conscience.

12  Domestic exhortation.

13  Br. Aug. Hampston left the novitiate because of poor health.

Fr. Mignard and Fr. Verheyden went to the City to hear confessions in the cathedral church at the request of the bishop.

14  Toni as usual, and then Cases of Conscience.

16  Fr. De Smet visited us again; soon he will set sail for Europe. Fr. F. Egan finished his retreat.

18  Fr. Larkin gave the Spiritual Exercises to our students so they could gain the plenary indulgence of the Jubilee. Some of the younger boarders were also being prepared to make their First Holy Communion at this time.

21  A General Communion concluded the Spiritual Exercises for the boarders. Some [three or four?] of them did not share in the Sacred Banquet.

Toni and Cases of Conscience.

Many of our Fathers went to the City and to neighboring areas at the invitation of the pastor to help either with the Communions or with hearing confessions at Jubilee time.

25  Feast of the Annunciation of the Blessed Virgin. All as usual.

28  Toni as usual, and then Cases of Conscience.

31  Ceremonies of the Holy Week in which our scholastics and boarders were present. Silence was declared for our Fathers and Brothers in honor of the Passion of our Lord Jesus Christ.

APRIL, 1847

1. Holy Thursday. Everything done according to custom. At 5:30 P. M. our Fathers and Brothers received Communion. At 8 P.M. a solemn Mass was sung.

3. Many of our students went to the City, to return on Wednesday.

4. Easter Sunday, celebrated as usual: solemn Mass, vespers, Benediction.

11. Toni as usual, and then Cases of Conscience.

12. The treasurers made an agreement with a family in Harlem that they do the linen laundry for the college. The women who until now did this at home were informed that there is a new arrangement and that a home would be provided for them. One of them left immediately.

13. Patrick Harney began the Spiritual Exercises, seeking to be admitted as a Brother.

15. Fr. Férard was sent to the LaPrarie district to exercise the sacred ministry.

16. Domestic exhortation. Abstinence.

17. Patrick Egan entered the novitiate as a Brother.

18. Toni as usual, and then Cases of Conscience.

22. Patrick Harney entered the novitiate as a Brother.

25. Toni as usual, and then Cases of Conscience.

29. Domestic exhortation.

30. Abstinence.

MAY, 1847

1. May devotions began ... D. Firtch, a German youth, seeking to enter the Society, began the Spiritual Exercises.

2. Toni as usual, and then Cases of Conscience.

4. Th. Creeden, an Irishman, seeking to enter the Society as a Brother, began the Spiritual Exercises. [Th. for Thomas, *sic.* His Christian name was Joseph.]

5. Mr. Jos. Cull, a priest from the city of Utica, visited us. Novice Brother Felix McParland returned home to provide for his parents' needs.

9. Toni as usual, and then Cases of Conscience.

10. College linens were sent to Harlem for washing.

11. Feast of St. Francis Jerome was celebrated as usual.

12. The women who had done the washing for the college left.

14. Domestic exhortation. Br. Vachon began his eight-day retreat to prepare himself for taking vows.

16. Toni as usual, then Cases of Conscience.

After an eight-day retreat, Br. Creeden was admitted to the noviceship.

17. Fathers Duranquet and Paul Mignard went to Canada to do pastoral work.

18. Mr. Shea, a New York City youth, began the Spiritual Exercises; he asked to enter the Society. Brothers Kohler, Regnier and Schianski began their retreat as they prepared to receive Holy Orders.

19. Mr. Firtch entered the novitiate after completing the Spiritual Exercises.

22. Mr. Brautis, a German, began the Spiritual Exercises.

23. Pentacost Sunday, celebrated as usual.

Br. Vachon took his first vows after finishing his noviceship.

25. Br. Patrick Dealy, novice, visited his relatives to spend some time with his younger brother.

27. Brothers Coté and Sipiot, novices from the Canadian house of probation, visited us.

30. Brothers Kohler, Schianski and Regnier [were ordained] in the Cathedral church.

JUNE, 1847

1. Mr. Brautis left after finishing the Exercises.

2. Br. Patrick Dealy, novice, returned after a brief visit with relatives.

3. The solemnity of Corpus Christi was celebrated with a solemn processions.

5. Fr. Tellier went to Harlem to do parish work for the time being.

6. Toni as usual, and then Cases of Conscience.

7. The coming dates for the renovation of vows were announced and extraordinary confessors named.

9. John [Gilmary] Shea finished the Spiritual Exercises and entered the novitiate.

13. Toni as usual, and then Cases of Conscience.

17. At table the letter of Very Rev. Vincent Caraffa was read; it stated that three-day spiritual exercises should be made before the renovation of vows. In the evening there was a domestic exhortation.

18. The three-day triduum before the renovation of vows.

   Visitors: Fr. Fritchez from the Upper German province and Br. De Pooter from the Belgian province.

19. Fr. Caveng and Fr. Joset, both from the Upper German province, visited us.

20. Domestic exhortation before the renovation.

   Br. Jarry fell dangerously ill. Fr. Tellier was also sick.

21. Vows were renewed. Br. Pernot gave a sermon at table. The scholastics' verses were read.

24. The college's patron feast day was celebrated with both speeches and songs. The Most Rev. Bishop was with us.

26. Fr. Joseph Stokes, priest of the city of Utica, visited us.

27. Fathers Carung and Fritchez set out for the missions in Canada. Br. De Pooter will stay with us.

28. Fr. Stokes left. Novice Brother Creeden fell ill.


JULY, 1847

2. Fr. Férard with Br. Rouillé and two scholastics, Brs. Baxter and Glackmeyer came from the Canadian mission. We had a domestic exhortation.

4. The day when the first declaration and proclamation of the freedom of America was appropriately celebrated.

6. The Rev. Fr. Superior of the American Mission set out to visit the Canadian houses and residences, as per custom. Traveling with him was Fr. Kohler [bound for the] Indian missions.

   Visiting us are Fr. Maisonabes of the province of Lyons with a scholastic. Both are bound for the college in Mobile in the state of Alabama.

7. Left us today: Fr. Maisonabes and his scholastic companion and Br. Corne who has been called back [to his province].

8. Students' exams began.

10. Br. Creeden, novice Brother died today [first Jesuit death at Fordham].

11. Br. Creeden was buried, according to our custom.

15. Solemn distribution of premiums. The bishop and his coadjutor were present. Beginning of the major vacation.

   Fr. John Ryan went into the city commonly called Williamsburg to assist the pastor.

17. Fr. Larkin began his Spiritual Exercises.

19. Fr. Remi J. Tellier returned to Canada with Mr. Ausley.

24. Br. W. Gockeln left for Europe to complete studies in the French province's scholasticate.

   Fr. Legouais began his Spiritual Exercises.

Lawrence O'Connell entered the novitiate after making the spiritual exercises.

26. Fathers du Merle, Férard, Driscol and Schianski traveled to Canada to hear the confessions [of the Irish immigrants] while a contagious disease was raging.

31. The feast of St. Ignatius was celebrated according to custom.

The major vacation has ended and the minor vacations began.

In New York City Coadjutor Bishop McCloskey consecrated our church with the title Holy Name of Jesus.

AUGUST, 1847

1. The scholastics and two Brothers, as well as Fr. Ryan, made their annual retreats.

3. Visitors: Fr. Pinsonneau, priest of the Canadian Sulpicians, who is returning to Canada from Rome and Paris.

5. Brother Jennesseaux came from the Canadian mission to work among us for some time.

6. The scholastics finished their annual retreat.

At table the house status was read: Fr. Thébaud rector, Fr. Paul Mignard Minister, etc. In addition the status for the New York house [just opening] was read: Fr. Larkin Superior, Fr. Lebreton Minister, etc.

25. Rev. Fr. Boulanger returned from his visitation of the Canadian mission. With him came Fathers DuRanquet and Férard, and a certain diocesan priest who wished to join the Society. Fathers DuRanquet and Férard stayed for some days in New York City because of the Canadian contagion.

27. Fr. Grimand and Brothers Baudevain and Thiry, Scholastics, arrived from France. [This item is a footnote added later in the diary.]

28. Fr. Férard returned to the college to continue his task as subminister.

29. Fathers De Villaneuve and de Charbonnel from the Canadian Sulpician community visited the New York community; and with them came Fr. Du Merle but he stayed in the City with Fathers DuRanquet and Férard for the same reason [the contagion].

Fr. Driscol was sick and was detained at a hospital in Montreal.

SEPTEMBER, 1847

1. Fathers Mignard and Schianski returned from the trip to Canada. They stayed for a while in the city of Brooklyn because of the Canadian contagion. Perhaps their tasks in the college were divided up to others.

4. Fr. Mignard returned to the college and immediately did his work as Minister.

6. Fr. Grimaud set out for his mission in Canada. Fr. Schianski returned to the college from the city of Brooklyn.

12. Rev. Fr. Thomas Mulledy, procurator of the province of Maryland, visited the college.

14. Rev. Fr. John Elet, procurator of the vice province of Missouri, visited the college.

OCTOBER, 1847

1. Fr. Driscol returned from the Canadian mission fully recovered from his dangerous illness. After a few days he was actively engaged in his duties as superior of the diocesan seminary and professor in the college.

On the same day Brothers Bidwell and Dealy, and novice Brother Egan began their eight-day retreat. At the same time Brothers Fortich, Shea, Phelan and O'Connell, novice scholastics, and Br. P. Harney, novice brother, began their 30-day retreat, given by Fr. Legouais, Master of Novices.

4. Fr. Petit came from the City to give the Spiritual Exercises to the seminarians.

14. D. Phelan who entered the novitiate on Sept. 5, returned home today.

15. The Most Rev. bishops of New York, Albany and of the new diocese of Buffalo visited the college and seminary. Though everything had been well prepared for dinner and they had agreed upon the time, yet they arrived late for dinner.

17. Mr. O'Connell left the novitiate and became a diocesan seminarian.

19. Fr. Schianski was sent to the Canadian mission.

20. Fr. Sadler and scholastics Pramstaller and Weger with a Brother named Burger came to us from the Austrian province. Fr. Sadler will travel with the Brother next Friday. The scholastics will remain with us so they can do their theological studies.

25. Fr. Tiberius Soderini traveled to New York City; he will remain there.

30. The feast of Bl. Alphonsus was celebrated as customary. Fr. Subminister served at table.

31. Planning to enter the Society, Mr. Matthew Gardiner made the Spiritual Exercises. This evening the novices completed their 30 day retreat.

NOVEMBER, 1847

1. The feast of All Saints was celebrated as usual. Since on the past Sunday the students and the people heard a sermon [on the feast], there was no sermon in the church today.

4. Fr. Blackney and Br. Montillot, a scholastic from France, visited us. Tomorrow morning they head off to the college of the Lyons province called Spring Hill.

5. Rev. Fr. Rector gave us an exhortation. Benediction of the Bl. Sacrament in honor of the Sacred Heart.

7. After he made the Spiritual Exercises, Matthew Gardiner was admitted as a novice and wore the habit.

15. Fr. Frémiot came to us from France. He was scheduled to go to the Canadian mission with a Father who was formerly a Dominican novice and with Br. Martin Barbiana who was accepted as a novice in France and will remain with us.

21. Br. Marin Barbiana began his eight day retreat and on the 29th was admitted to the community dining room.

29. Two employees were dismissed; the two formerly made up the students' dormitory rooms; they were sent to the wash rooms. Two of our Brothers took care of [the rooms] from that day forth.

DECEMBER, 1847

1. Mr. Thomas Fowler came here. He's from New Brunswick, a man 52 years of age, who wished to enter the Society as a brother. His first task was in the clothes room.
5. Brothers Sipiot and Coté began their eight-day retreat this evening. And Br. Chorivi made a 30-day retreat. Mr. Fowler was sent to the kitchen.
6. Novice Bidwell was sent to the City to teach boys in place of Fr. Lebreton, who was having chest pains. On the same day Fr. Soderini was sent to the college.
8. Feast of the Immaculate Conception of the B.V. M. Fr. Murphy said the 8 A.M. Mass in the chapel of the Sacred Heart of Jesus. He gave a sermon about the glorious privileges of the Blessed Virgin. In the evening at 6:30 P.M. a solemn Benediction was held in the same chapel.
14. The Rev. Superior of the Mission began the Visitation of the house. In the evening he gave an exhortation to the community. Each day during the visitation the Veni Creator was recited, as usual.
16. The boys had a literary demonstration. About 30 came from the city and found a meal prepared for them in the students' dining room. Arrangements were made thus: after the students' meal, lunch for the outsiders; at 1:00, the literary demonstration; at 2:30, a small celebration for the students of the literary academy.
17. Mr. McMahon of the Montreal Sulpician community came here desirous to enter the Society.
20. Mr. McMahon began the Spiritual Exercises and afterwards entered the novitiate.
23. Many of our Fathers were sent to different parishes to help the pastors in the festive Christmas season. On the same day Fr. Ryan was sent to Schenectady, a city in this state, to give spiritual exercises to the people.
24. The Christmas vacation began.
25. The Nativity of our Lord Jesus Christ. Solemn Mass and the rest as usual. This evening Fathers Duranquet, Du Merle, Driscol and Férard began their eight day retreat.

JANUARY, 1848

1. The feast of the Circumcision was celebrated as usual.
6. Epiphany of Our Lord Jesus Christ. In the evening vespers were not sung. We had benediction of the Blessed Sacrament in the private chapel.
13. The renovation triduum began.
15. Fr. Mignard went to Tarrytown to the Dominican S.U. [?] to give a mission.
16. The feast of the Holy Name of Jesus. Renovation of vows. One of the Scholastics gave the sermon in the dining room.

17. Today Br. Ouellet was ordained to the priesthood in the New York Cathedral; Mr. McQuaid and Mr. Murphy, graduates of our seminary, were ordained at the same time.

19. The Superior of the Mission ended the Visitation. He had separate conferences with the Fathers and Scholastics about the Institute.

\* \* \* \* \*

In addition to the diary, at the end of this chapter we cite one other document, a *Memoriale*. It was long the Jesuit custom that, after a Provincial's or even a higher superior's Visitation to a community, he would leave behind, beyond whatever praise he might include, a gentle — or sometimes not so gentle — reminder (*Memoriale*) of things the community could and should do to improve itself religiously. This particular *Memoriale*, written by Fr. Clément Boulanger, covers the year 1846-47, modifying slightly the picture of uniform religious piety that is sometimes conveyed above. It reads:

1. Drapes [*tapetes*] are to be removed from all Jesuits' rooms, except the Rector's and the Procurator's.
2. Recommendation to Fr. Minister: that with more vigilance he make sure that silence be better observed by all, especially in the part of the house that is reserved to Jesuits.
3. In the future no one is to have an afternoon cup of wine without permission.
4. Fr. Rector should see to it that, as far as possible, all make their eight-day retreat during the time of 'long vacation'.
5. Everyone should recall Common Rule 32 ["No one should touch another, even in jest, except for the embrace of charity on setting out or returning from a journey"] and 35[Briefly, it urges care in communication and avoiding worldly talk], and let everyone know that no one can enter the infirmary, the kitchen, the linen room, and the tailor's room without the permission of the superior.
6. Our Prefects of Discipline are not allowed to accept and consume any kind of liquor offered by students in their walks.
7. In summer and autumn none of Ours are allowed to take the fruit in the garden and give them to the resident students.
8. Smoking or chewing tobacco is not allowed to anyone without the express permission of the Superior General of the Mission, and in his absence, of Fr. Rector.
9. Let Fr. Rector and Fr. Procurator be especially vigilant about the house treasury. Let them carefully refrain from all expenses that are not absolutely necessary.
10. Let Fr. Rector grant permission to students to go into the city only with difficulty. [The wisdom of this rule for those times is demonstrated in a recent film, *Gangs of New York*.] And then it is very appropriate that the Prefect of Studies, or at least a teacher, be alerted of the absence of the student .... All teachers are also strongly urged to immediately alert the Prefect of Studies or the Prefect of the residence of the absence of their students.

11. Let them, especially teachers and prefects of discipline, frequently recall and regard very seriously Common Rule 34 [Briefly, dealing with others without the superior's approval]. Let them be vigilant about an exact observation of that rule. Fr. Rector should not allow that it be broken without penalty.

12. Let the work of the Prefects of Discipline be so arranged that they have sufficient time for fulfilling their spiritual exercises.

13. Let regulations be drawn up and observed by the students who stay here during the major and minor vacations. Each day there should be a period for study. And each week they should receive religious instruction.

14. In the future: the custom of providing a snack at night time for academics is to be suppressed.

15. Once each month this *Memoriale* is to be read before the consultors.

16. The teachers and prefects of discipline are not to admit students into their rooms without the express permission of the superior for each visit.

In St. John's College, January 14, 1847.
Cl. Boulanger, S.J.

# CHAPTER 6

# THE *ANNUAL LETTERS* TO ROME

INTRODUCTION

A wider picture of the early adventures of the Jesuits at St. John's College can be assembled from the Annual Letters they sent to the Father General in Rome. Such letters were hardly casual. They followed the example of their founder, St. Ignatius Loyola, who urged the members of his "least society" to maintain frequent, good communications with one another. A section in the Jesuit Institute [*Institutum Soc. Iesu*, III, V: *Formula Scribendi*, par. 26-31] is devoted to five long paragraphs on the Annual Letter. In general terms, it urges the selection of material that "encourages and edifies" prospective readers; on the other hand, it urged that care be exercised to omit what could be interpreted as offensive or regarded as secret.

The instruction then becomes more specific. Heading the list for the contents should be the numbers in the house, i.e., the number of priests, scholastics, and brothers, and the general type of work they do — teaching, supervise students' behavior, etc.; changes in personnel from last year's, information about those who died. The special virtues of the deceased and their principal accomplishments should be included in the report. Successful ways that proved helpful in assisting Jesuits in their quest for spiritual progress needed to be reported. Facts about Jesuits' religious ministry towards others — sermons, encouraging spiritual reading, teaching Christian doctrine, giving the Spiritual Exercises, visits to prisons and hospitals, the reconciliation of enemies, Confessions, and other religious practices — were a standard section of the report, as well as benefactions received and the community's charities extended toward others. Also to be mentioned in the Annual Letters, in cases where the local community contained a school, were the number of the students and their educational progress, as well as the Society's local reputation and opposition, if there were any. Following instructions in the *Institutum*, names were carefully avoided in the letters; when an individual's work was described, he was identified only as "one of our Fathers." Of course, if names needed to be known at headquarters, separate letters were sent. However, names were used in the necrology section of the Annual Letters and they were also used whenever the reports contain other references to the deceased.

Reports from missionary lands held a special importance and appeal. They became, for example, the source for the 18th century, 74-volume series, *The Jesuit Relations,* whose descriptions of living conditions, challenges, and at times, successes, presented a new side of Jesuit activities to a European audience who already recognized Jesuit leadership in education, science and scholarship. Moreover, these official routines for annual and even more frequent reporting facilitated the written exchange of experiences and helped contribute to their own group *esprit de corps.* And they provided later generations with perspectives on their history.

Hard though it is today to think of New York as missionary territory, that's what it was back then. The Province of France in 1831 dispatched four of its members to

Kentucky in the New World in response to the saintly Bishop Benedict Joseph Flaget's request for help. With annual recruits from home, that foursome had gradually grown to 30 by 1845 when, as we saw earlier, the decision was made to accept Bishop John Hughes' invitation and purchase — for a $40,000 mortgage — his diocesan college in what was to become known as The Bronx. St. John's College at Rose Hill thus became the newest Jesuit college in America, joining a list that already included Georgetown University (1789), St. Louis University (1818), and the College of the Holy Cross (1843).

Back in Paris, the mother province of St. John's, the Province of France, kept up the ancient tradition of collecting, publishing and circulating among its communities the Annual Letters it received before transmitting them to Rome. This custom continued even after the New York-Canada Mission was transferred to the province of Champagne which was carved out of the Province of France in 1863. Champagne and other new French provinces continued to publish their *Litterae Annuae* until the late 1860's but only a few reports from the New York area are to be found in them. This was perhaps because the newly-created provinces in America began to tell their own stories in the feature articles, obituaries and chronologies in the *Woodstock Letters*, a quarterly journal which was published in the Woodstock, MD, seminary from 1872 to 1969. Those *Woodstock Letters* will figure importantly in Part IV of this book.

Of course, the publishers of the earlier collections had to depend on the cooperation of each of the communities to send in their reports. Some years this very gentle reprimand to a house would be published to remind the remiss: "A report from . . . was very much desired but was not received this year." For instance, in the 19 years that this chapter covers, Fordham reports were not received for seven years (1850-1; 1851-2; 1852-53; 1854-55; 1855-56; 1862-63, and 1863-64). Even the one we cite for 1865-66 (no. XII below) is less a report but a complaint by the mother province about not having received a report and a pale attempt of its own to reconstruct a picture of the year in question. Reports from Xavier might be reasonably expected for at least 17 years, but we have only six in Chapter 8 below. Of course, looking back at the uncertainties of the mails in those days, at least some of the reports were sent but likely lost in transit.

The content of the letters from Rose Hill reflect the changes in the institution's activities. Of the twelve letters reproduced in this chapter (covering roughly the years between 1845 and 1866), Letters I-VII describe five such special activities: the *College* itself, the Jesuit *Community*, the *novitiate*, the *scholasticate* (which trained young Jesuits in philosophy and/or theology), and the diocesan *seminary*. The picture changes in the following letters: by Letter VIII the novitiate will be gone. By Letter X the scholasticate and diocesan seminary will by gone, replaced by a Jesuit retreat house and parish residence.

Fordham Superiors change as well. The Rectors represented in the letters are Fr. Thébaud (1845-1851), Fr. John Larkin (1851-1854), Fr. Remi Tellier (1854-1859), Fr. Thébaud again (1860-1863) and Fr. Eduard Doucet beginning in 1863. St. John's was also the residence of the Superior General of the Mission, a post held by Fr. Boulanger from the St. Mary's days to 1855. That year he was succeeded by Fr. John Hus until

1859. For the following three years Fr. Tellier held both jobs of Rector and Superior General and then stayed on as Superior General until 1866.

The first letter we present is not really about St. John's. Rather, it takes one last look at the events that led to the challenging move from St. Mary's. But then, in the following letters, an optimistic spirit prevails. Students were arriving from Cuba, Porto Rico (*sic*), Jamaica, Guadaloupe, Martinique and every state in the Union. These early St. John's letters were probably written by Fr. Thébaud (although a note in the Fordham copy suggests other hands at work). Bouyed by their initial success, Fr. Thébaud could readily give expression to the enthusiastic mood. But other themes begin to emerge from these letters. Clearly, the ecumenical movement and its implications for all branches of Christianity had clearly not arrived "near New York." The Protestant religions are referred to as sects — heretics weighed down by the error of dissent. Conversions by Catholics to Protestantism are lamented; they must be prevented at all costs. That means stiffening the ranks of Catholics. The College sodality dedicates itself to pray for the conversion of lapsed parents and siblings. College Jesuits throw themselves into a gigantic diocesan Jubilee aimed at the spiritual renewal of Catholics. At the end of the Jubilee there is elation not only for whatever spiritual blessings accrued but for the fact that at last "Protestants take notice of Catholic power." Such sensitivity becomes more understandable when we realize that an administrator of a leading New York City public institution at the time and his wife could refer to Catholic rites as "idolatry." The deathbed often becomes the battleground in these matters. To hear the confession of a dying man over the family's opposition, one Jesuit had to pretend he was an Italian doctor who spoke no English.

When these letters speak, as they do, of the Jesuits' desire "to tell the New Yorkers' story well," they often meant assisting people well down the social ladder, especially the Irish, Italians and other ethnic groups. Mostly French themselves, these Jesuits were impressed by the way the Irish took the advice of their priests. The account of a mission from St. John's to the fever-stricken Irish immigrants in a holding camp outside of Montreal illustrates the point. Fr. Thébaud notes with regret in one letter that such devotion to priests was not always true of the French enclave in New York.

There is a growing sense in the letters that the American setting requires new approaches, both educationally and pastorally, despite the fairly traditional mind-set of the Jesuits in both areas. Yes, there is a tug to put in place time-proven principles of the Jesuit *Ratio Studiorum* at the College or to model the seminary training after, say, Laval University in Canada whose program was brought from the old world. But Jesuits also noticed there was something different about the students they encountered — weak perhaps on the Latin and Greek, but ready to articulate opinions on any given topic, to excel in public speaking, to develop debating teams and generally sound off on their perceptions of their immediate social and political circumstance. Pastorally, there's a difference, too. The Jubilee during which the Jesuits were so effective was not old style endless sermons, no bell ringing or pomp of ceremonies, "no sad or happy hymns." It was down- in-the-trenches confessions, conversations and confrontations.

Most surprising of all, there are but a very few passing references in the letters, either at St. John's or at Xavier in Chapter 9, to the Civil War.

## I. Oct. 1, 1845 to Oct. 1, 1846
### *College, Community, Novitiate, Scholasticate, Seminary*

Our total number [at St. Mary's College, Kentucky] was 29: namely, 14 priests, 3 scholastics, 8 brothers with 2 scholastic novices and 2 novice brothers.

On November 1, 1845, a new Rector was appointed, five years and four months after [his predecessor's appointment]. The new Rector was Rev. Augustus J. Thébaud. [On August 15, 1846, he became the first Jesuit rector at Fordham; his predecessor as rector at St. Mary's was the Rev. William Stack Murphy who was later a vice-president at Fordham.]

In June, 1845, the official Father Visitor arrived at St. Mary's.

After finishing his tour of Canada in July, the Visitor had returned to us and was about to stay for the entire year. His Socius [Rev. John-Baptist Hus] was recalled to France in March, leaving here a fond memory among both Jesuits and others.

After completing their period of training, two scholastic novices [James Graves and Michael Nash] pronounced their first vows at the end of April.

One of our Fathers [probably, Nicholas Petit] has assisted fruitfully in several parishes, while the outstanding [*insignis*] work of another Father [John Larkin] took place in the city of St. Louis, Missouri, to which he was invited by our Fathers there to give the Spiritual Exercises in the church of St. Francis Xavier during the fifteen days before Easter. His sermons, delivered three times a day, despite heavy rain and storms were well attended by a large number of men, including non-Catholics, and his eloquence received high praise in the newspapers. The real benefit was seen in the crowds approaching the altar for Communion, many absent for twenty years or more. By chance a company of soldiers was there; they had been recruited for the Mexican War [1846-48] and many of them were Catholics. Their commander, aware of the impact of the Exercises, begged strongly that the Exercises would be given also to his men. Our Father gladly agreed, should time allow, for it would set a new example unheard of in this region. The bishop, however, was pained that the priest had to leave since he was looking forward to an additional harvest in a larger church, but in vain.

At St. Mary's our number of students, the schedule of subjects and other items of that type are not very different from the reports of last year.

With this report our *Annual Letters* from St. Mary's residence are concluded. The reason is that the Society has completely closed that residence by sending its members elsewhere. The history behind the change of location should at least be indicated here.

From the time when the Society first acquired the residence at St. Mary's the Jesuits living there had different opinions about their future. Some predicted that everything would turn out satisfactorily but others believed the prospects had already reached their highest level, for to them there were several drawbacks. The principal problems were the following:

- It required living almost in the middle of a wilderness.
- The whole state contained numerous Protestant sects but only a few Catholics;

• Most of the inhabitants were poor, with little or no hope of building new homes.

• Our Canadian group [*colonia*] which is also just beginning, added more weight and strength to that viewpoint [that we leave Kentucky]. With such a big distance between Canada and Kentucky, it was difficult for this new family group and us to be united under the governance of the same provincial.

• Furthermore, few novices entered in Kentucky and that situation is not expected to change; novices are needed to provide new brethren to take on new tasks. Accordingly, those of us who looked forward to higher accomplishments believed that, since Protestantism widely flourished here, we ought to stay and try to lead as many as possible of those "living in darkness" and "in the land of the shadow of death" toward the great light. Our Canadian group, separated by such a great distance, did not identify very closely with those who felt that way, for: "We will not always be living in the countryside. Once we are out of the wilderness we will be closer to Canada, increase our numbers and houses, and set our sights higher."

• Meanwhile our confidence began to fade about the college [we founded] at Louisville. After much earnest effort it was hardly flourishing, although the staff had tried with all its strength to make it succeed. Catholics gave support at an unimpressive level and even the bishops gave minimal assistance, although we began the institution at their request. But there were few students, expenditures were higher than income without [prospect of] increases, everything seemed exhausted and frozen.

At this time the presence of the Father Visitor, sent by the Very Reverend Father General, was opportune. As soon as he arrived he had a sufficient grasp of our situation and, though the older and wiser men had not yet abandoned all hope, he decided to dispose of everything as far as time and place allowed. He later declined to take over the college at Bardstown that was offered by the bishops; it was burdened with debt and situated in a small town. He saw that in this region our college could not succeed unless the one in Bardstown, so dear to the bishops, should suffer grave damage. He clearly realized that, in looking out for the good of the Society and of the diocese at the same time, there would be new problems as time went on.

During these difficult times the Bishop of New York requested of us by letter that we assume charge of his St. John's College and that we send the Visitor there as soon as possible. Negotiations had to start at once since the bishop was about to sail to Europe. An agreement was reached by late November and the future looked promising as far as could be seen. The State of New York is adjacent to Canada with a border of a hundred leagues [about 300 miles], while New York City, the greatest and wealthiest in both the American republic and the New World, is an easy two-day journey from Montreal. There are about a hundred thousand Catholics living in the State. Another advantage is that there exists a flourishing, rapid and convenient exchange of commodities and travelers with France such that letters are sent by steamships over and back twice a month. From all these perspectives everyone can see the benefit for us.

Furthermore, within the college both young men and clerics were entrusted to our type of regulations. There would be no fear of what happens elsewhere, where a type of student would be alienated from us by teachers who relish a taste for what is not appropriate in college.

Our numbers here, all together, were hardly enough for this new undertaking, so it was clear that all must leave Kentucky and leave no one behind. To place everything in proper order by the coming summer, we completed all our business here, both private and public. In the meantime it was decided that everyone living in Louisville was to go back to St. Mary's, which was done in March; the bishops were duly notified and did not protest.

However, lay Catholics were deeply disturbed when they learned of our decision, for they insisted that, once we had gone, their children and dependents would never be trained in good conduct. Even non-Catholics took the question seriously by complaining that all hope was gone of retaining a college that was an ornament and benefit to the city. Since the site for a new building at Louisville had been bought at a high price and the foundations had been laid, the people were very puzzled that once we left the city we would return to the wilderness [St. Mary's College]. To prevent it, a petition was circulated and several persons promised money or other support. The New York arrangement had not yet been announced, since we were careful not to spread the word prematurely. Yet reports arose that we were about to leave the whole State. Some began to blame the auxiliary bishop [Bishop Guy Chabrat] since no different reason for our decision was evident. We vainly tried in every way to put a stop to these accusations, which increased day by day. The newspapers wrote about it.

The suitable moment for us to announce the reason had not yet arrived, since it was necessary to relate the full story to the Ordinary, Bishop Benedict Joseph Flaget, before it was revealed accidentally elsewhere. When he heard the news he was deeply disturbed, for it never crossed his mind that we were about to leave both St. Mary's College and the diocese itself.

Immediately the bishop wrote to the Father Visitor at first to insist that everyone stay but, when that was refused [he asked] that at least some Fathers remain who would preach our kind of sermons for the people in the towns and countryside as before. As this request was unavailing, he announced that he would write to Rome. But it is believed that he let the matter drop after he changed his mind.

When arrangements were completed [for the transfer north] we returned the property once given to us, as well as several other buildings for which we had spent a hundred thousand francs. Later we were pleased to welcome the priests of the Holy Cross [*presbyteri, quos Sae. Crucis vocant*; this is the first reference to the Holy Cross fathers. They stayed onlu two years. The college was then continued, first by diocesan priests, and, finally, for a century by the Fathers of the Resurrection.] They were to be given our vacant house by Bishop Chabrat. We are confident that the Lord is sending them here to be "good laborers for his harvest." For we pray constantly that perhaps out of the seeds that we have scattered they will come "with joy carrying their sheaves." We also agreed that they would have our furnishings at a modest price acceptable to them. This was both advantageous to the priests, and diminished due to the bungling of a certain man [Mr. Delaune] sent by them to complete negotiations. Through delays and deceit he almost upset the transaction.

At the end of April, 1846, two of our priests [Frs. Thébaud and William Stack Murphy] were sent ahead to New York at the request of the bishop to live in our future college and be listed among its professors. This plan turned out well and brought peace to students and parents who had been upset by rumors and fears about our reputation.

At St. John's, Fordham, the school vacation began on July 8 after the customary distribution of honors by the bishop. He took advantage of that occasion to announce eloquently that he had entrusted the college to us. In glowing tribute he stated that the reason for his decision and gave generous praise for the Society's men and work.

A remarkable number of [New York] citizens have approved of all of the bishop's tribute, with the exception of the few Spanish, French and Italian individuals who are given to swearing by Voltaire's opinions [about Jesuits].

May God grant that we measure up to these expectations and prayers. May we seek His greater glory with all our means and works in our new center.

It is remarkable that, once the transfer was effected, the New York newspapers were either completely silent about it, or were waiting to see our manner of acting and training, or would hint at agreement with those who regularly express prejudiced opinions about everything we do. However, it must be added that since the New York State Senate a few months earlier had conferred on this college the rights and privileges of a university, that group would seem to have understood that the nation would not be severely threatened by publicly granting to the Jesuits the power to teach.

In August all the Jesuits at last reached New York by various routes out of Kentucky. May these changes be for the greater praise of God and for the advancement of education in letters. May they be profitable for our young men and bring them good fortune [*et adolescentibus faustum felixque sit*].

## II. Oct. 1, 1846 to Oct. 1, 1847
### *College, Community, Novitiate, Scholasticate, Seminary*

In the beginning of this current year the total number of our Community was 42, of whom 16 were priests, 14 were Scholastics, 12 were Brothers. But in the course of time that number varied. Three members were transferred into the American mission of the province of Lyons; likewise, four members were recalled or transferred from the province of Missouri into our province. Others departed into the new College in New York [later known as the College of St. Francis Xavier]. But novices and scholastics came, such that by the end of the year we had 52 members in our Community.

This first year was especially fortunate because in barely two months after the beginning of school the routines and exercises of the new novitiate could begin. In fact, at the end of August there remained 5 scholastic novices and 4 Brother novices.

Among the Brother novices was an excellent young man from Ireland: at age 26, Joseph Creeden, was admitted on May 16. On July 3 God took him from among the living. It seemed that God took him to Heaven for no other reason than to transfer him from the Society of Jesus on earth to the Society of Jesus in heaven.

Already some of the odor of religious observance is diffused among members of the Community and day by day we have increased our love and inclination for the Rules.

Of the 120 college students here only two or three were punished for breaking school rules. You would rightly have looked on the whole group as very well prepared for religious practices and regard them as trusting in the helpfulness of various forms of Christian piety.

Some students have a special devotion to the Blessed Virgin Mary. They practice the devotion regardless of the name of the priest who would be named as their chaplain. On their own they met to make their spontaneous offering to their dear Mother. You would not have expected that. At the same time this observation has to be made: a man was there who deserves credit for cultivating this blessed seed. Our Sodality asked to be aggregated to the *Prima Primaria* Sodality in Rome. That was granted; the Sodality in the College was already a legitimate Marian Sodality.

It will be no surprise that some students' relatives or parents are accounted as either non-Catholics or nominal but not practicing Catholics. Therefore the Sodalists were rightfully told of Rev. Desgemettes' well-known Institute. It usually uses spiritual exercises to suggest prayers for the conversion of sinners to Him who alone is the Way, the Truth, and the Life. What they had eagerly heard was the basis for initiating plans to recommend to individual Sodalists and to the group of 60 members. They urged that they say brief daily prayers to God, novena prayers said by some, frequent Mass by others, and, it seems, Mary was listening to their petitions. It was a mercy that two were converted separately to a better way of life, to the Catholic church, from among the five children or near relatives of students whom they had asked to be included in the prayers for conversion.

It is helpful to select one example among other such examples of piety and happy outcome. A certain boy, concerned for the spiritual safety of his mother, had begun to pray to God for her from the beginning of the year. Once he became a member of the Sodality it seemed that he would leave nothing untried in calling on heaven to answer his prayers and did that with the simplicity and warm spirit of faith that more and more certainly foretold the desired outcome. The boy finally dared to approach his mother by letter about his prayer. And in a few days, lo, here was his father's response:

"I want to inform you, my very dear son, of the happy results of the last letter that you wrote to your mother. I received the letter last February 2, while I was beginning my work in the evening. She was not in good health when she visited the parish priest, gave him your letter, and at the same time opened up to him about how much she desired to become a Catholic. The reverend Father with much care received and questioned her on her faith in all the teachings of the Catholic Church. He asked that she be present on Sunday at the Vespers liturgy. She obeyed that request and received the sacrament of Baptism from him. Following her present intention, she is preparing to visit him on the evening of the following Saturday, and I think, on the following Sunday will receive her First Holy Communion. For my part, my son, I am confident that your mother will be only one of the many for whom your good example, good behavior, and religious conversation will bring spiritual benefit."

At Fordham meanwhile, of the five Protestants in the college, three were eager for adoption as children of God; the three were regenerated in the waters of life. They were the ones whose pious lives and genuine signs of religion proved that they were worthy. Also, nineteen students were given their First Communion after an appropriate preparation, and twenty-two were confirmed.

I have already mentioned briefly some academic issues. We had a development this year that we never had before at this college: we had classes in literature and arts in almost all times of the day, and in turn students were separated into different classes and professors.[5]

Something was also changed from what was usual for the seminary students, though this way of learning is certainly less suitable for students in the college. Indeed, the opportunity provided by time and place was favorable. The plan of their studies which they had begun is by great good fortune what exists for Jesuits at the college at Laval: as much dogmatic theology as can be covered in three years, and in view of the shortage of professors, some courses in Holy Scripture, canon law, or Church History are desired. Disputations, both public and private, are held. At times the bishop of New York deems the public disputations worthy of attending so that his presence provides students with an additional factor for work and motivation. And his presence was an occasion for Jesuits to show examples of their teaching.

At Fordham the customary celebration on July 15 for announcing solemnly the awards of prizes and degrees surpassed the solemn occasions of earlier years. The gathering included very many of the diocesan clergy, a great crowd of Catholics as well as Protestants. Two thousand people enjoyed the music and songs of the hired chorus of a symphony orchestra. Five students gave speeches; they were chosen from many possibilities: the talk in Latin that praised the Latin language was itself most worthy of praise exceeding all expectations. Another talk was on an English theme. Nothing entirely original [the Latin text surprisingly added the same idea in English, but misspelled "nothing"]. Its novelty wounded the sensitive ears of the audience, as it seemed to two editors of a Protestant newspaper that was published the following afternoon.

Two prizes and five baccalaureate degrees were awarded. Then, when earnestly requested, the bishop spoke extemporaneously in a warm and very friendly manner to the orators and the audience. He provided a very happy conclusion to the annual solemnity.

And that was the way things were at the college, and it was similar to the way things went with our work outside the college; no one could have desired a happier year. We are involved with a diocese numbering up to about 400,000 people of whom, according to the current Catholic Almanac, 230,000 are Catholics. They function in 100 congregations; some of them have smaller chapels, 120 have really large ones, as they say, churches with rectories. The total number of priests, diocesan as well as other missionaries is 121. There is no shortage of priests on our campus; if they only call us to share in their work, we do so. This very vast region, white with an excellent crop to be harvested is not neglected altogether, nor is it completely without priests. As soon as we reached the State of New York all kinds of works were proposed from all sides and we honored those requests very generously insofar as we could. In early September the appointment of two of our parish priests for a mission in the city of Utica was announced. At the mission a thousand people came, some from the town, some from the suburbs to hear the sermons.

*The French and Irish in New York*

The same Fathers returned from Utica and were soon assigned to New York City to take the places of two priests of the Congregation of the Mission [Vincentians], one of whom was about to set out for several months in Europe, and the other priest was suffering poor health. The first of these was to say Mass at the church of St. Vincent de Paul [123 W. 23 St.] which was so named by the French. The founder and builder of that church when the area was missionary territory, the Most Rev. Forbin Janson, Bishop of Nancy, had earlier seen to it that the French in this city would have their own church, have sermons in their own language, and all kinds of suitable assistance prepared for their Catholic faith. Likewise, at that time a group of Women Vincentians was started there.

But this difficult thing must be said, that if you except almost fifty families, you will very rightly call the French in New York City both most frigid in piety and even alienated from religion. Though the French here are reckoned at more than 10,000, of that number no more than those who sit in the church benches are known by name by the priest.

The Irish here are by far the greatest part of the Catholic population and, among them as the leader of all, towers the bishop. The religion of this people is clearly known; they kept the faith unscathed everywhere among heretics and infidels; though morality had declined, they maintained reverence toward the Church and its ministers. But here is a special fact, one most worthy of noting, about the Irish housemaids. They gladly grant their money, that is their collected pennies, for the use of religion and the ministers of religion. Through them, Catholic churches, places for sacred gatherings, were begun and kept up, as well as schools for the poor, and finally asylums for the sick and orphans. Through these institutions Catholic interests have been retained and spread in these parts.

The church of the Transfiguration [29 Mott St.] is served by another Jesuit priest. A Spanish priest served there for many years; he is very well known particularly for his zeal and his pious liberality especially to Catholic poor people; of all places in the city those people went to him as long as he was well; people outstanding for their piety flocked to his church which was certainly not foremost among the churches in the area of the city. But when the resources of his congregation declined, the Father approached one of our Jesuits to find someone to relieve his burden and penury. So two Jesuits were appointed to daily and varied works of ministry there. It is reasonable to doubt whether their continual work was less demanding than that of those who lived in the college. Certainly on every Sunday and feast day all English-speaking Fathers were usually invited or sent to churches in the towns or countryside.

Experience has shown how much everyone manifested that, because of their manner of proceeding either in the pulpit or in the confessional, all our men, though they came here from many different places, would invite greater openness from their parishioners; and, the one message of the faithful was: they wanted to hear Jesuits and to confess to them. But let me tell you another, and indeed the principal reason for our outside work. From it our newborn Society seemed to have expressed itself in action. The reason, I say, is the Jubilee, the proof of the unmatched divine goodness towards us. Lest you think when you hear the word 'Jubilee' that that has the same appearance here as it does in Catholic lands: there is no sound of the bell calling both sinners and pious faithful to churches, no continuous series of catechizing or sermons, no sad or happy hymns which may move hearts, finally, no pomp of ceremonies.

In the Jubilee the exhortation in the pulpit of the principal church was given by one of our Fathers; everybody praised it. An exhortation was given on Sunday by another of our Fathers in other places. But elsewhere in other pulpits there is silence; there is no religious fervor, no unusual pomp in the churches. And so the truth of Christ is clear to all: "The spirit moves where it wills and you hear its voice; but you know not whence it comes." That the Jubilee's fruit, its nature, as I might say, might be better recognized, it seems good to lay out a few facts.

All [the priests] who were already here, the new ones who had come from other parts of America, and the volunteer clergy, if they were to be considered such, are given faculties [*permittuntur*] by the bishops for the Jubilee. During the time of the Jubilee they will serve people inside the borders of New York and the surrounding places, about 80,000 people. Shouldn't this least Society of Jesus be congratulated for its part in responding to the invitation to work and thereby help relieve the shortage of spiritual laborers?

If you should ask about the principal and more general though perhaps less conspicuous results of our efforts, the fact that people now find it easier to use the sacraments could surely be considered. There was indeed one biased critic who questioned our approach to penitents, but we had our defenders, too. Some of the clergy sent their penitents to us. The Bishop himself praised and supported us. He was pleased that our moral doctrine reflected the solid teaching in his seminary and he had no problem with our technique. People do not seem to have lost any of their confidence in us.

I believe we are partially responsible for the perceptible progress Catholicism has made in this area. Since we finished the Jubilee effort, the faithful are more aware that their numbers are not small and that they must not be disrespected. They experience less abuse, feel stronger and bolder. Protestants take notice of Catholic power, while a new respect for the word 'Catholic' encourages every believer to take pride in his identity.

So maybe the time was ripe for the Society to implement a plan it had prayed over: to have a Residence, to follow it with a College, then to acquire a Church of our own in that city which ranks first in America and second in the world as a commercial center. However God will have chosen to favor our prayers, He will surely help our Companions in the Lord to tell the New Yorkers' story well.

The list of activities in our annual account is long and edifying but we close it with a surprising mission we undertook at St. Mary's in Canada. Such a memorable experience deserves retelling in depth.

*Six New York Jesuits Minister to Canadian Immigrants.*
At winter's end, there was a massive migration of Irish to America. Driven by famine and its dread aftermath, they fled their blighted homeland by the thousands aboard ships bound for the English colonies in Canada. By their count they departed

British shores in 180 such vessels, but we know now that there were 100, 000 passengers on board. With as many as 700 to 800 in some ships, the crowding of destitute, unwashed, hungry exiles guaranteed an epidemic of some kind in transit. A noxious fever crept randomly through the fleet. Its lethal heat carried off 9,000 at sea, leaving 81,000 to make their way to a large island near Montreal.[6]

Religion and humanity would surely elicit actions that show a compassionate response to the immigrants' plight. Certainly that would be true of any Catholic, but above all from the pastors of this vast flock. And so, up in Canada, there they were, the faithful Sulpician priests, attending the stricken and the dying, challenging disease and death itself. The Bishop, who had himself just returned to his flock from Europe, was a towering model for all. But five of the Sulpicians were already dead; five of the rest were down with disease; only one of the Irish clergy was on his feet.

They finally accept the help that the Superior of the Jesuit house in St. Mary's [in Montreal] had often extended. They ask if Jesuits would be available. A letter is sent [by Fr. Felix Martin, the superior of Jesuits in Canada] to our community at St. John's: would we come to help and support them? In response, besides a missionary priest who was seeking admission to the Society, two of our community who were already at St. Mary's on other business, were applied to this task. Back home, with most of the rest of the community competing to volunteer, four more were assigned. They left on July 26, happy to exchange the customary vacation time for this rewarding sacrificial work.

Try to grasp why people would be so glad to see the arrival of these particular Jesuit workers, few though they were. The Bishop was delighted because he remembered the desperately needed service we had provided for his flock long ago. The Sulpicians warmly welcomed them because they would have as comrades in their pastoral endeavor two of our men whom they had known long ago in France, until they could get set up on their own. Lastly, Catholics in general, both lay and religious, were thrilled and encouraged to see them because our men regularly carry out their mission with dogged persistence.

For sure, from the time of the new arrivals onward many of the clergy noted a change. The spirits of fainting wayfarers seemed to be lifted. Many relief workers found new strength. Thereafter, many found their trials less harsh, their struggle and grief less burdensome. For now there were on hand men busily parceling out the tasks to be covered by two men together down in the huts along the river, out on the city's fringes, in the Foreigners' Hospital, and in the city itself.

The Irish, as is known, have kind of innate veneration for Christ's priests and are known to heed them readily and carefully. A striking example of this trait, one that gained the praise even of the Protestants, was provided when the Canadian Governor came up with a startling proposal. The governor realized that the number of patients was growing and along with it the difficulty of providing all with food, which was principally subsidized by the government. The problem was compounded by the lingering presence of all these people. So he asked the Bishop to step in personally. Would he explain the financial crisis, the risk of famine and disease; would he urge all who were physically able to move on.

Sadly indeed the good Prelate accepted the odious but necessary task. He recruited our Irish Jesuit [Fr. Michael Driscol], a man well known the poor people, who would be able to communicate with them. They make their way down to the shoreline where the huts of the sick and most of the migrants are located. They speak about the constraints of the crisis, the constraints on their beloved Pastor, who has left nothing untried, who has expended his energies and very life for their relief and welfare. They press the proposal, the urgent need to depart.

It is not hard to imagine the grief, the groans, the weeping of all. Many would be leaving a spouse, brothers, children, leaving relatives prostrate and penniless, leaving even the dying. How cruel that departure, for many of them would be, more bitter than famine and death itself. Yet, not a sound of protest, of resistance, not a sound. Rather, amid the tears and wailing, all fall to their knees as one, to praise the Bishop's warm affection, and to express deepest gratitude to the men of God. To these they entrust and commit the full care of their parents and dear ones. With gestures of respect for these spiritual leaders and for the civil officials as well, they ask only for a final blessing as they prepare to depart.

It was time, too, for the return of our brethren to St. John's College since with the beginning of September we would have to start classes. Two by two, they were just about to leave behind them this cherished enterprise when the member of the group who loved the mission most of all fell gravely ill [Fr. Driscol]. He could well have been taken from us, but for the Masses and novena prayers we offered to God, with the plea that none would perish of the little band the heavenly Father had provided to labor in his vineyard.[7]

### III. Oct. 1, 1847 to Oct. 1, 1848
*College, Community, Novitiate, Scholasticate, Seminary*

At the beginning of September [1847], the total number in our Community was 52, of whom 17 were priests, 18 were Scholastics, and 17 were Brothers.

One priest novice, two Scholastic novices and three Brother novices left the novitiate. One other novice was sent to New York to take over the teaching assignment of a Father who had fallen ill. Since three others had already been assigned to studies, only three future Scholastics are left who are following the regular novitiate program. One of these is a Portuguese priest.

One of the Scholastics was ordained to the priesthood on the day of renovation of vows, January 16. On the feast of the Purification of Our Lady, two of our priests pronounced their final vows. One of our Brothers [Michael Jarry] died piously in the Lord.

Regarding the condition of our religious life, it might interest you to know that, at the beginning of this year, the novices moved from the College buildings to a small house about a hundred feet away. The house had formerly been used by the laundresses employed in washing and mending our linen, and it may surprise you to hear that the building served the needs not only of the laundry but also of our clothes room, sewing and tailor shop besides being used by some of our sick. One of the advantages which the novices have gained from the move is that, since they are now more out of sight of others, particularly of the boarders, they can more easily live like novices and more readily follow the practices of religious life.

The Superior of the Mission, Fr. Boulanger, has seen fit to institute a number of conferences on our Jesuit Institute, on religious poverty, and on fraternal charity and extend them over several months. They are given in the place and time assigned for our Cases of Conscience.

No one of Ours can ever esteem the demands of charity and poverty too highly, once he thinks of the storms and disasters which are growing more serious constantly all through Europe, or when he sees so many fellow Jesuits, our own brothers, driven from their homes and leaving every part of the continent to come to America as a very safe haven for their holy vocation and a field open for apostolic work protected from the menace of government interference. We should all share the same sentiment, and it should be a cause of happiness for all that, if the vessel of our flesh is suffering affliction, greater opportunity is being given to us for charity.

The order of the community house remains practically the same as it was last year. There were more than 100 boarding students in the College and 25 in the diocesan seminary. The students can be commended for this that, through their willing acceptance of our rules, the somewhat quarrelsome disposition which they had shown in the past has greatly diminished, indeed almost disappeared. Thus in the past year not a single student was dismissed for disciplinary purposes.

The work which began last year in the College, namely the establishment of the Sodality of the Immaculate Heart of Mary for the Conversion of Sinners has been successfully completed. More than 60 students have been enrolled in it. There were also some good results from the Sodality of Our Lady. But they were not as great as you would have liked to hear because of the illness of the Father assigned to direct that Sodality. For, as his health declined, the progress of the Sodality seemed to decline as well.

However, you will be happy to hear that, this year, we have put in place a program of studies which is in keeping with our rules and is better suited to the intellectual progress of our students. To be more specific, we have put our customary Jesuit curriculum in place. Each subject has been assigned its own proper time and a set of readings has been also required for every course.

We still have a small group of our students who follow no courses in liberal studies; they take only courses related to business and commerce. The other students, however, have taken a wider range of courses and are aware of the greater profit they have derived from them. They approve of the change in our curriculum and have accepted our new method. Even stronger evidence in its favor has come from the success our students in the end of the year examinations and from the improved performance of the students in our public academic exhibitions. Certainly we have received not only approval but even enthusiastic praise from His Excellency, the Bishop, on the successful outcome of the solemn academic exercises which were held last year as usual on the name day of the College. We can now entertain some hope that this University of ours will at last live up to the increasingly high reputation which it enjoys in this country.

We come now to the apostolic work done by our Fathers outside the College. It was not as outstanding as it was last year when New York celebrated its Jubilee or when our Fathers went up to minister to the poor and sick among the immigrants to Canada. On the other hand, it would not be right to consider this work either insignificant or of little apostolic value. The novices went out to the surrounding countryside and gave catechetical instruction to the boys and girls they were able to bring together. In this way they were able to prepare these youngsters for their First Communion and Confirmation. Furthermore, as far as their other duties permitted, the rest of our Fathers went out for apostolic work some in the city, some in the small towns around us, some in the countryside and in other places which were completely devoid of spiritual help.

Coming down to some particulars, we can say that beyond visiting the sick in our neighborhood whom they are regularly called upon to attend, our Fathers quite often went on ministry to places which are 10 or 20 miles away from Fordham. They also worked in the county hospital and the state prison, although both of these institutions are under the supervision and subject to the authority of Protestants. If our Father was not welcomed kindly at the state prison, at least he was treated there in a humane way.

### A Way to Deal with a Hostile Administrator

On more than one of his visits, one of our Fathers was less humanely treated in the hospital. We had occasion to bring this treatment to the attention of the authorities. One of our Fathers was asked by one of our employees to go to the hospital with him and visit one of the employee's sisters who was a patient there. In the part of the hospital in which our Father found her he heard her confession and the confessions of several other female patients. Our Father was then informed that, in another part of the hospital, there was a Catholic man who was gravely ill. Consequently he went to the superintendent of the hospital and asked the latter to have him brought to the sick man. By way of answer our Father had to listen to a series of complaints accompanied by many harsh words. The superintendent made clear that he would have no part in this sort of idolatry. There was no need here for ministry of that sort and no place either for idolatry. Without informing the superintendent, and leaving him unaware of his presence, the Father had already spent two hours in the house and had visited the rooms of women patients. He should show better manners and observe the rules of the hospital, etc., etc. Our Father replied to these remarks and to others like them with proper moderation. After apologizing for his mistake, he continued to ask earnestly for permission to visit the sick man. Finally, it was given but with repeated complaints and more harsh words which continued to be spoken through the administration of the sacraments.

When our Father had finished attending to the sick man, and without visiting other patients whom he knew wanted to receive the sacraments, he left the house. However, in the Father's judgment, and in the judgment of others, this type of response was too dangerous to souls to permit it continue. Yet, a formal complaint should not be lodged until it could be established whether the superintendent had acted in the way he had through some sort of chance or by deliberate purpose.

Therefore, twelve days later, the Father went to the hospital again. The superintendent was absent and our Father was told that he would not return until two hours later. Our Father then asked who was in charge of the hospital in the superintendent's absence. The superintendent's wife appeared without delay, and, when she was told the reason for the Father's visit, she told him out of hand that the rules of the hospital forbade any visits of that kind. Her husband would not permit them. Only ministers of Christian denominations could be admitted. Visits by our Father could be of no use to the patients and, in addition, God's law forbade them. Our Father replied "I will wait for your husband's return for we both agreed that I would see patients provided that the superintendent was informed beforehand."

The superintendent finally returned and was asked whether he would permit the Father to visit the Catholic patients. "No one here, no one at all, " the superintendent replied, "needs your services." "Therefore you are refusing me permission to visit the sick," our Father said, and he got up as though he were about to leave. "Who do you want to visit?" the superintendent then said. The Father gave him the name of the patient and he was immediately brought to visit him.

Meantime, he was informed that, although he could visit the sick, no Catholic rites were to be performed over them. Those rites could do nothing but bring the patients to perdition. They were nothing but mindless idolatry, and there was no warrant for them in Scripture. Our Father replied that the rites which the superintendent was calling idolatrous were referred to in Scripture in the passage in which St. James spoke about Extreme Unction. It would seem then that our Father had the right to visit sick Catholics and minister to them in the same way. "James," the superintendent replied, "was not speaking about that, and you have no right, no right whatsoever, to be in this house." "Since then," our Father said, "you are formally denying me the right to visit the sick, I will completely give up my effort to do so." Then he took leave of the superintendent and left the hospital immediately.

Not only was our right of religious liberty endangered, the salvation of souls was being put at risk as well. On the advice of counsel, we decided to bring the case before the County authorities. When the superintendent of the hospital found that out, he demanded that he should be summoned to the trial also. The specific reason which he gave for his request was that our Father had not visited the women's room to hear confession but for a very different purpose. Both our Father and the superintendent were ordered to appear. At the judges' request, our Father gave an oral exposition of his complaint, with each of the judges given the opportunity to question him about it. The hearing proceeded in a calm and peaceful way, and, immediately after its conclusion, the testimony which had been given was read aloud from the court record. Then suddenly, one of the judges, who had been paging through a Bible that had been brought into the court as the testimony was being read, exclaimed, "James really did mention Extreme Unction," and he read out the relevant verse to all the judges. The judges obviously wanted to hush the matter up.

Some good came from the proceedings nonetheless. It was decided that, in the future, Catholics would no longer be compelled to attend Protestant services. The superintendent was reprimanded and later removed from his position by the council, and, from the beginning of May, our priests who attend the sick have ministered to them in our usual way.[8]

IV. Oct. 1, 1848, to Oct. 1, 1849
*College, Community, Novitiate, Scholasticate, Seminary*

At the beginning of September [1849] there were in our Community 17 priests, 20 Scholastics, and 20 Brothers, 57 in all.

One priest, one scholastic and 2 brothers left the novitiate, and one of our scholastics who had lived five years in the Society, decided to become a secular priest and entered the diocesan seminary.

Our manner of life remains the same as it has been in the past, though it may be worth noting that, because of the increasing number of seminarians, our scholastics were forced to leave the seminary building and find a place in the community house, with all of them lodged together in a single room. They have lived the life of the poor in our house but were happy in their poverty, as members of the Society should be.

Furthermore, the wars and disturbances which are constantly going on in Europe have given us the happy opportunity this year to offer temporary hospitality to a number of our Fathers and Brothers. This was a source of no small profit to us. Those of our number who are still young in the Society drew a good deal of profit from living in the company of superiors and veteran members of the Society. On a number of occasions, members of several Provinces came to our house and gave us a vivid picture of the Society, its spirit, and its way of life, and, thanks to them, this has become more deeply rooted in our hearts.

Our college has never been more flourishing and has never shown greater promise for the future. The increase in number of our students was so great at the beginning of the year that we were forced to build a rather large extension to the college.

The program of studies is thriving here, and it is being carried on in the customary manner of the Society. It has been so successful indeed that our college has become very well known in America, and its reputation is constantly growing. In order to show that his observation has not been made without evidence to support it, let me submit two pieces of such evidence. The first is drawn from the well-known author, [Orestes] Brownson, and the second is taken from one of our daily papers. The quotation from Brownson follows [it is quoted in the letter in French]:

"The Jesuits are a blessing to every place in which they are allowed to establish themselves, and the value of their contribution to our country through their education of its youth is inestimable. It would be very difficult for anyone else to take their place in the work of education. Inspired by the pure love of God, they have founded colleges in every state of our Republic in which our children receive an excellent moral education. Jesuit colleges have a long history behind them. Among their number have been reckoned some of the most famous colleges in the world. In a few years they will raise the level of education in our country to the level of the most favored nations of the old world."

Writing in the same vein, but referring specifically to our own college, one of our daily papers, in its account of the public academic exercises through which our students celebrated Washington's Birthday, wrote in the most laudatory manner about the stage presentation, decorations, and the speeches composed and delivered by our students. To quote the words of the reporter [again in French]:

"It was most interesting to note the progress made by this institution which is so universally known. A large number of young people could be seen who have come from abroad to this classic retreat to draw from the well of its sound teaching. We were reminded of the great days of Salamanca when we saw students from every country and every clime, Peru, Mexico, New Granada, and Canada, and when we looked on the intelligent and happy faces of students from Cuba, Porto Rico, Jamaica, Guadeloupe, and Martinique, and saw as well youngsters who have come to the same college from every state in the Union to vie for the palm of literary excellence."

Indeed, other journals have written in even higher terms when the occasion called for it. A chemical demonstration, in which a number of our students successfully completed all the experiments with great dexterity, has also contributed to the growing reputation of our college.

In order to increase our students' zeal for study and stimulate healthy competition among them in that respect, our Fathers have decided to suppress a long established organization called the Chrestamathanian Society. The nondescript set of rules which that society had were rather outdated and seemed to encourage a spirit of unrestricted freedom. For that reason, these rules did not appear to respond to the needs of our time. So the society was suppressed and replaced, to the satisfaction of all, by a new society whose membership is equally open to all.

Hand in hand with the growth in devotion to study among our students has come an increase in their religious devotion. The Sodality which fell into decline last year, due to the failing health of its director, has come back to life this year after his recovery. This has led to an increase in devotion to Mary. It may well be that the handsome appearance of the Sodality chapel after its renovation has contributed in no small measure to the growth of that devotion. The altar, which has the appearance of being marble, the statues and the pictures with which the chapel is now adorned seem to have finally made it a chapel worthy of bearing Mary's name.

Devotion has also been increased by the divine worship which can now be performed with the majesty and pomp which it did not have in the past. For now our students, properly trained in music by a Jesuit [Br. Macé], have succeeded beyond all our expectations in singing a variety of hymns in a harmonious manner conducive to piety. It is remarkable indeed how prompt and able our students have shown themselves to be both at learning hymns and in taking part in the ceremonies at the altar.

Growing among the students is a certain taste for divine things which God is using to imbue their hearts with an increasing spirit of piety. One day one of these students said to a Jesuit in an open and candid way, "Father, I have received two graces today. I received Holy Communion this morning and I also served Mass." Another student asked one of the Jesuits whether he had done enough to keep the commandment of loving our neighbor. "Let us see what you did." "Mister, to make friends again with one of my fellow students with whom I have not been on good terms for some time I wrote a couple of letters and signed them with my own hand. Then I made sure that both of them were delivered to him, but it did no good. Mister, I would like to know if that is enough. I am going to receive Communion tomorrow and I am afraid of making a sacrilegious Communion."

I could give 600 examples of that sort which would show the same sense of purity and tenderness of conscience, but, in order not to take too long, I will crown my account with the following little story. One day, some of our students were amusing themselves by imitating the different ways in which various types of men handle their canes. They went through almost every sort of man with one exception. Then an adult who was watching them observed that they seemed to have forgotten how old men do it. Immediately one of the smaller boys replied with a very serious face, "Mister, it isn't right to make fun of older people. Decent people wouldn't do that."

The retreat which one of the Jesuits gave the students did a great deal to foster and increase this good disposition of soul, and, since that grace was deferred until the end of the year, it flowed into souls which had long been prepared to receive it and produced greater fruit than ever before.

In fact, this year a very special grace of light came to one of our students. This student was born in Florence of parents who were heretics, or to be more truthful about it, infidels. Then the unfortunate lad was sent to one of those Parisian lycées in which there is little concern for religion. He had reached his twelfth year and he was still not baptized. When his parents came to America and sent him to us to continue his education, grace began to move in his soul. Soon the honest boy, distressed by his spiritual state, asked earnestly to be baptized and received into the Catholic Church. There were of a number of difficulties standing in the way of this, but they were overcome, and so he was baptized in our chapel. I can hardly describe how great was the joy which filled his heart. More worthy of note, however, may be the fact that the young boy's conduct has changed greatly, and he has persevered so constantly in his good resolve that the grace of God seems to be working visibly in him. He has been devoted in the observance of his religious and academic duties, and, although he had previously given the impression of being a thoroughly rude and rebellious boy, he has now become gentle and docile in his behavior. During the holidays when he was living with his parents, more than once he withdrew from the loving companionship of his family to come back to the college so that he could prepare himself to go to confession and receive Communion worthily. His parents are to be commended for leaving him completely free to fulfill his duties. Indeed, during the same vacation, his father went to considerable trouble to make it possible for him to attend Sunday Mass in a church five miles distant from their home.

A no less visible sign of God's grace was seen in His calling an old man to the admirable light of faith a few months before his death. The old man had lived as an infidel until the age of seventy, and, although he called himself a Protestant, it was hard to tell what he believed or what religion he professed. He frequently came to our community house, and was given odd jobs to do to help him support his family. Grace was working in him and he corresponded with it. Doubts has arisen in his mind from time to time, as he later admitted, as to whether or not he was adhering to the right religion. Once he was able to observe Jesuits more closely, grace acted more strongly on him, and, thanks to one of our domestic help, he overcome his infidelity. That lay employee began to speak to him about religion and taught him what the true faith was. A little later when he turned the old man over to one of Jesuits for further instruction, the new convert had already accepted the gift of faith. All that remained to be done was to complete his religious education to the extent to which he was capable of it. A mind filled with false doctrines from childhood, advanced age, and a feeble state of health made him capable of understanding barely more than what was absolutely necessary for him to confess the faith. But, if his intellect was weak, the grace which came to him was very strong. The old man did not know what words to use in order to thank the God who, at the moment of his death, had so kindly called him from the darkness of infidelity to the light of faith, or through which he could express in words his sorrow for the errors and sins of his youth over which he was now shedding tears.

His wife and two sons were Protestant and extremely hostile to Catholicism so that, before his baptism, the new convert scarcely dared to tell them that he was about to become a Catholic, even though they had suspected it and had often complained to him about it. Indeed, even after his baptism, he still remained a hidden disciple "for fear of the Jews." However, immediately after he had been strengthened by the bread of angels for the first time, he lost all fear, revealed what he had done, and at once induced them to give up their erroneous belief. They were all angry at first, but were amazed at the effect which the grace of God was evidently having on the heart of the old man. What more can I say? His wife, drawn one by his example, soon surrendered and yielded to the yoke of Christ. His sons, although they have given unambiguous signs of good will, have not yet been baptized and are still living in infidelity. The old man would surely have brought them to the feet of Christ if he had lived longer. It pleased God, however, to summon him from among the living and place him among His friends forever. He died on the last day of September, the seventh day after his baptism. He received the sacraments of the Church with lively faith and his death was filled with every consolation. He had been reduced to poverty and no one had come to visit him during his illness since all the people in this vicinity are bitterly hostile to our religion. Nevertheless, there was one exception: a man so moved by the change which grace had brought about in the old man that he stayed constantly by his side as he was dying and accompanied him to the cemetery. May God grant that the great charity and moral courage this man showed, in those circumstances and facing opposition from all, may bear fruit sooner or later and that his eyes may be opened to the wonderful light of truth.

It remains for me to say something about our dealings with the secular clergy and the good will which they have shown toward us. But this year in that respect nothing worthy of special note and edification has occurred.

V. Oct. 1, 1849 to Oct. 1, 1850
*College, Community, Novitiate, Scholasticate, Seminary*

This year [as of Sept. 1, 1850] the total number of our community was 62, of whom 23 were priests, 13 were scholastics, and 28 were Brothers.

On the Feast of the Solemnity of the Most Holy Trinity, three of our community, were ordained by the Archbishop of New York [John Hughes], and said their first Masses. Another two bound themselves [to the Society] by final vows, one on February 2, the feast of the Purification of the Blessed Virgin, the other on August 15, the feast of the Assumption. During the course of the year one Scholastic pronounced first vows.

Even though those just mentioned are adding more and more to the Society's numbers, others have withdrawn from her: one Scholastic who had lived among us for seven years, and two novice Brothers.

Among us a careful observance of religious life has continued and even flourished, as well as a union of wills, which had clearly firmed up the "fraternal necessity" among us, many of whom are former members of different provinces. Not the least factor in bringing about this most happy condition were several exhortations which the Father Superior of the Mission gave on fraternal charity and religious life. Drawing on these talks, all certainly were motivated to the perfect and strict observance of our rules.

There are students, only a few, who fail out each year. Such developments are part of the pattern of college work, part of the ever-present sameness of things so that the history of one year also explains the happenings of the following years. Yet we realize that, although the college work is quite difficult, it tends in every way ultimately toward the divine glory. Nevertheless, our hard work brought our brethren some consolation. Indeed, you couldn't have desired a more favorable year, whether you look at the number of students or their proficiency in studies and in piety.

In our last letter, if I remember, we had said that the number of our students had so grown that they had insufficient room and that we had to build an entire section. But even though the College was already large, it was not large enough for this year's crowd of boarders who flocked to it from all directions. Hence, we had to build a large section to include a recreation hall for the students, a dormitory, a clothes room, a library and a room which is commonly called a gymnasium [*cabinet de physique*]. Furthermore, our chapels have been enlarged, and everything so arranged that the College could easily accommodate 200 students. Along with our numerical increase there has been an additional new brilliance here in literary studies, because enthusiasm for solid studies, especially for philosophy, has blossomed. Thus, while younger students were at play, older students could often be seen paging through their books, memorizing lessons, and generally maximizing their time to master the liberal arts. Thus, the hearts of these young men began to blaze so high that throughout the year many studied hard to surpass their fellow students and win prizes. There were also students who were animated by praise, but in tears when they lost. Quintilian would have loved them. Especially at examination time, one could also see several of the older students, motivating and helping the lazy, spending leisure hours with them, explaining problems to them, and by every type of diligence working to save the remiss from every kind of disgrace and other types of penalties hanging over their heads. We were happy that this year the desired outcome crowned such unremitting labor, even surpassing expectations.

In large measure, such progress has been achieved by teachers' zeal for instruction; such zeal has needed to be dampened rather than inflamed, exercised according to the true Ratio Studiorum of the Society [*juxta genuinam Societatis Rationem*], and it has been shown especially by those who evidence outstanding effort and talent.

Concerning religious devotion, it will suffice to say that it has grown along with the number of boarders. Since the students have now been divided into two sections, their devotion has benefited from having religious instructions offered in a manner more suited to their ages; thus, as time goes on, they profit better. In the preceding year, we had been overjoyed to witness the appreciation for devotion and zeal among the students; this year, we have witnessed even stronger virtues. To foster such devotion in the students, strong support was offered by the Sodality of the Blessed Virgin Mary, which has been formed of select students in whose ranks no one would be counted who was not exemplary in his devotion and effort.

Now we turn to the ministry of our men outside the college. First, one must say that we retain the continuing kindness and friendship of the faithful. Hardly a day goes by without one or two people, of the best families, lamenting and complaining about the departure of our men from the city [after they served there]. Nonetheless, in these circumstances, nearly all the avenues for zeal are occupied around the City of New York; that work would demand ten- or a hundredfold increase if our numbers would allow it.

The main force of our effort is always bounded by this double ministry: the ministry of the Word and reconciling people. Each week, as Saturday comes around, you would see a veritable flood of priests who head in different directions and nearly cover the whole city to bury, by word and example, the hostility of Protestants and indifference of Catholics. For Advent, we have been engaged in some parish pulpits, and more for Lent. Moreover, each week, several of our men offer Sunday sermons to the people either in the city or in nearby towns. Especially if we are called, we visit shelters for the homeless, prisons, and the poor. In a word, in every way allowable by the work we have undertaken in the college, we try to make ourselves useful. But, as I wrote earlier, a hundred times our number would hardly suffice to do all the work.

One can hardly believe how many of our Catholics go over to Protestantism or at least they languish in dense, lazy ignorance for merely one reason, that there is no one to break for them the bread of knowledge and devotion or fortify them against the continual attacks of the enemy. How many young people there are, aged 17, 20 or more, who for this reason alone have not yet received First Communion or have received it only once. Besides, since they always live with Protestants, they never hear the name of holy religion or of the Catholic Church except in blasphemy. Moreover, many Protestants are mounting, in every possible manner, a genuine, constant persecution against Catholics. One often hears confessions which maidservants approached secretly, as if fearing to be seen by their masters. They even refrained from any external work of piety for many years, lest they be left without any help and any hope. If any upright Catholic in a rural area made his home available for a priest to celebrate Mass — for there are not many Catholic churches outside the city — sometimes you would see a whole congregation of Protestants, always the greatest part of the population, get to-

gether and act so maliciously towards that Catholic hardly anyone will have anything
to do with him and he is scarcely able to sustain his life and support his family.

Even though almost all the zeal of our men is taken up by the City, nevertheless we
travel far and wide in the county. One of ours, twice a month, and often as other duties
allow, visits the public hospital, and it often happens when he goes there that he finds
many dying, or infants to be washed in the water of rebirth or many others who have
not seen a Catholic priest for many years. Quite often he has secretly baptized the
babies of Protestants who are near death. Indeed, throughout all of Lent he weekly held
a class for boys that he might prepare them for the Sacred Banquet and in anticipation
of their confirmation. He was successful in such labor; indeed it happened that on
Whit Sunday well prepared youths (as one may suppose), 370 of them, made their
First Communion.

In the diocese of Boston, one of our Fathers was invited by the Bishop to give a
Mission in a German Church. In fact throughout Holy Week, he preached to the
people three times a day and in the remaining time he heard confessions. At first their
minds were well disposed enough and they undertook the Mission out of curiosity as
something different, rather than out of piety. However, soon all were moved by grace
and received these chosen words of salvation with utmost devotion. They rushed to
confession in droves, confessed their sins with sorrow and went to the Holy Eucharist.
It happened that many older people who had not been to confession for years laid
down the load of their sins with many tears. Our Father himself marveled and could
not give enough thanks to God, when he saw with what simplicity all confessed all
their sins and with what sorrow they truly detested them. The Bishop himself also was
astounded; on the last day he distributed Communion along with our Father to an
immense multitude and he was not able to refrain from tears when at vespers he heard
all solemnly promise to renounce the devil and to take Christ as Leader and Lord. The
most marvelous thing seen by the bishop and others is that this Mission is an extraordinary event in this area and that its memory will not be quickly wiped out from his
heart and the hearts of all.

### *Dealing with Individual Catholics*

Such were the major activities of our community both in the College and outside
the College. Lest no mention be made of some very edifying facts, we add the following
incidents. One day, one of our Fathers is invited to the Church to marry a man and
woman. The Father goes there; but when he makes the proper inquiries, he soon dis-
covers that the young woman has never abjured the Protestant religion. Nevertheless,
he judges that she was disposed to doing everything that seems necessary to contract
matrimony. In good faith she herself had first seemed to be leading her betrothed to
her own faith. Instead, he prevailed with greater ingenuity, and finally persuaded his
betrothed to abhor totally the Protestant errors. The Father, therefore, asks her why she
would want to become a Catholic. She immediately replied, the Catholic religion, as it
is older than the other, had been handed down by the Apostles; therefore, it is true.
Upon hearing this, the Father baptized her conditionally and united them in marriage.

It is well known to all how true and strong the faith of the Irish is, and in this area we see many cases where many of these people have allowed the faith which they received unspotted from their parents to become soiled. In the darkest night of winter two Irishmen accompanied a Father who had come to visit a dying man. They were scarcely able to proceed because of the darkness of the night. Our Father asked them whether or not they were afraid of falling. One of them immediately answered, "Father, when we are with you, we are safe." "Right, if you say so, but when I shall return to the College, you will be alone." The other man replied, "No, you will bless us before we depart and we will be safe."

Another Irishman, when he was seated at table with some Protestants on Ash Wednesday and was abstaining from the forbidden foods, was soon made fun of by the Protestants and attacked in every way: To him one said: "How absurd the Catholics act! They eat butter and drink milk, but they are not willing to eat the cow." To this the Irishman replied: "How absurd you have acted! You drank the milk from your mother's breast and nevertheless you did not eat her!"

Finally, lest I be longer than is due, let the following little story act as a crown of my report. When he was growing very old and felt that death was near, a certain Italian sent one of his friends to our Fathers asking that a priest come so that he could reconcile him with God. Our Father was warned that he must use the greatest concealment possible because the sick man's mother-in-law and wife (both of whom were completely ignorant of the Italian language) were most hostile to our religion. Our Father, therefore, taking off his clerical garb, as it sometimes fitting, and having put on the clothes that doctors usually wear, goes and asks to see the sick man whom he addresses immediately in Italian. He explained why he was with his friend, as mentioned above. The women (wife and mother-in-law) questioned him more than once about who he was. But he appeared to be totally ignorant of their language and kept replying in Italian. When they saw this, they left him alone with the sick man. Therefore, seizing the opportunity, our Father heard his confession and prepared him to go happily to meet his impending death. Two hours had barely elapsed, when the sick man suddenly almost in a moment lost all his strength and breathed his last.

## VI. Oct. 1, 1852 to Oct. 1, 1853
*College, Community, Novitiate, Scholasticate, Seminary*

This year [1852] our Community numbered 64: 19 priests, 8 teachers, 9 Scholastics studying either philosophy or theology, and 28 Brothers.

On the Solemnity of the Assumption of the Blessed Virgin Mary in 1852, one of the Jesuits took his last vows; in the course of the year several Scholastic novices took their first vows; and at the end of that year two Jesuits were ordained by the Bishop of New York. They offered their first Masses in our chapel.

We note not only the continuation, but even the daily increase in the careful observance of religious life, and fraternal bonding has been solidly grounded by the harmony among the wills of so many members who have been drawn from so many different provinces and live together here. It is noteworthy that in the course of the year all, particularly our younger men, were especially outstanding in displaying a gentle, kindly manner toward their pupils. The unremitting toil of Jesuits has not been without reward, some consolation, and yet the Scholastics have advanced to an almost unbelievable degree in patience and all kinds of grace and self-mastery. Really difficult circumstances do not upset them and even seem to make them joyful. Indeed, every day the pleasing influence of gentleness and joyful kindness in the Lord has been so manifest as to permeate even the boarders. Students often say they cannot sufficiently express the joy and readiness with which their prefects offer themselves for every kind of service.

We will add only a bit more about our students. At the opening of the year after the autumn holidays, we peacefully laid to rest some of our student regulations which seemed too harsh; then, as if they had been cured of an ulcer, the students quickly turned their minds to better pursuits.

The change produced among the students a new brilliance in their pursuit of literature, for so brightly did their enthusiasm shine for mature studies that it was often noted in both older and younger pupils. Even in times when they might be engaged in recreation, some would be paging through books, or memorizing lessons, or even stealing all kinds of time to master the fine arts. Such persevering efforts have brought them appropriate rewards, for one could hardly pray for a more blessed year, if a year were evaluated on the basis of progress in studies. No little contribution toward such studies has been made by the series of examinations set up in such a way that, in any month, the whole class would be publicly tested. At examination time, one could observe several, even among the older boys, urging on the sluggards, spending the hours of recreation by explaining problems to them and giving all possible assistance to snatch the lazy from disgrace and other damage which was threatening them. Nor was their hope unfounded, for this year we were overjoyed at the unexpected outcome of the examinations.

As we turn to the topic of the students' devotion, it will suffice to say truly that, like their academics, it has grown. The Sodality of the Blessed Virgin has deservedly risen in the opinion of all. If it appears not to have increased in numbers, it certainly has in fervor beyond previous years. The Sodality has been the source of the fervor and holy zeal which many have shown toward their fellow students. They have shown the results of their growth by their remarkable kindness and good judgment. Many have devoutly frequented the sacraments, as we see in the twenty or thirty who participate weekly in Sunday Holy Communion. Hence, it is no surprise that some of our young men believe and state that they are called to a higher state of life. Some have already gone to a seminary to undertake service to the Church.

Especially noteworthy is the example of devotion given by the older students. Some days before the feast of the Purification, several of the older students approached their professor to ask to be allowed to begin a public novena in honor of the Blessed Virgin to ask her to preserve their purity of body and soul. Of course, the request was granted and, with deep devotion, all of them completed the exercises of the novena.

But especially among the younger boys, even though they be of a less mature age, we have observed many good developments, some of which we will note. One of the youngest had shamelessly refused to obey his teacher. But soon after, touched by repentance, of his own accord he fell to his knees and tearfully begged forgiveness of his teacher and fellow pupils, asking that a severe punishment be imposed on him so that, according to his abilities, he might atone for his fault.

Students of the same class had often heard their professor state that all those who cherish devotion to the Blessed Virgin can almost certainly count upon their future happiness. As a result, before retiring, everyone turned to prayer, overcoming any type of human respect. This is done, not just once or twice a week, but daily throughout the entire year. This practice has grown so strong, especially among the younger boys, that it seems that no reason justifies its omission. . . .

Some students, of whom we have already written, usually write a pious note at the head of their exercises, e.g., "In honor of the Blessed Virgin Mary," or of St. Francis Xavier, or of any saint whose feast day falls on that or the following day.

The father of one lad had been horribly killed by an enemy a few days before. It is noteworthy that, even before the boy knew of his father's murder, the lad wrote "In honor of St. Francis Xavier, that he may open the gates of heaven to my father." As soon as the boy learned of the death of his father, he tearfully poured out only these words: "God's will be done. God's providence arranges all for our good."

But these signs of heartfelt and tender devotion nowhere shine forth more clearly as they do when all the students of the same class were about to undergo public examination. After all of them had been absolved in the Sacrament of Reconciliation, all received Holy Communion. Thus they trusted that, with God's help, the examination would be successful. To conclude these examples, it will suffice to note that the boys of all ages maintain the custom of gathering flowers in the month of May and of buying everything needed for the proper adornment of her altar.

### Ministries Outside the College

We now turn to our ministries outside the college. Over the course of the year, there has hardly been a parish in the City in which one of our men has not labored to hear confessions, or give a homily, or perform every kind of ministry. God has kindly blessed the zeal of our men, as the following will sufficiently demonstrate.

Each week the parish of St. Brigid welcomes people who do not hesitate to wait their turn to confess from 1:00 PM till 10:00 P.M. There are some who, because of the huge crowds, can approach the sacrament only after three or four weeks of waiting. They think nothing of such an expenditure of time provided that they can reach their priest, as they say, make known their conscience to him, and be freed of the burden of sin as they kneel at the feet of Christ.

It will be useful to narrate some facts. A confessor states that, "Around 7:00 P.M. at the time of Jubilee, an Irish woman approached me, tearfully confessed her sins and, after receiving absolution, asked whether there and then she could receive Holy Communion. I replied: 'My daughter, what are you saying? Do you want to receive Holy Communion and it is already night? Perhaps you do not know that you may not receive Communion unless you have been fasting.'" "I have been fasting," the devout woman replied, "from midnight till now; I have taken nothing, not even a drop of water, and since daybreak I have been in church, awaiting throughout the day for my turn to receive absolution. At last, the long desired moment has finally come. Now that I have regained the grace of God, this is y only prayer: that I be allowed to approach the holy table so that I can regain the Lord Jesus for my soul." Who could hear this and not comply with such justified and holy desires?

The same confessor states that "On another day an Irish woman came to lay down the urden of her sins. After her confession, I asked about her state in life: have you sons and daughters? Why have you come alone? Does your husband not get the benefit of confession?" She replies, "Alas, Father, I have come alone: my husband shuns confession; among my daughters, one is twenty-one, the other is nineteen; the younger made confession once, the other never." I say, "My daughter, you are a Christian mother; you know well the duties of a Christian mother; how then, can you, alone, enjoy the benefits of this holy Jubilee? I suggest something better for you to do: prepare your soul for the sacred absolution, return tomorrow morning, but do not return alone; bring with you your husband and daughters."

The next day, around 8:00 A.M., the woman returned and said in a low voice: "My Father, I have brought all of them with me." Then the husband came and said to me: "Reverend Father, last evening my wife said to us: 'The priest to whom I made confession wants all of you to receive Penance. Do not be afraid. He welcomes all with deep love, for he belongs to the Society of Jesus.' Hence, Father, I was at ease. I thought that the priest of God is calling us. I will be the first to go to him and to give all an example of penance and amendment. I said 'If any of you refuse to come with me, I will immediately expel her from my house.' So here I am, Father, and all of them with me." Thus, with the help of God, the devout woman brought her whole family back from sin to a better, truly Christian life.

### VII. Oct. 1, 1857 to Oct. 1, 1858, *College, Community, Novitiate, Scholasticate*

Since once again the official letter on our men is missing, the province catalog will supply the lack, as far as possible. Thus, at the beginning of 1858, the total number in the St. John's, Fordham, community was 56, of whom 17 were priests, 14 were Scholastics, and 25 were Brothers.

Fourteen of the community were teachers of the various subjects, five or six shared in the work of prefecting students' behavior, four were students' confessors and they also gave homilies to them. Three Sodalities of the Blessed Virgin and two Academies flourished.

The curriculum covered a wide range from the elements of Latin to the peak of dogmatic theology and canon law, including German, English literature, business computation, etc. No fewer than three of our men were specializing in mathematical studies. Four of our Fathers were studying their fourth year of theology; six of our Scholastics studied rhetoric with private tutors, and another was privately reviewing philosophy. We possessed a villa and botanical garden.

Five priests devotedly served off campus: one in Croton Falls, another on Randalls Island, a third in Melrose for the confessions of the Ursulines, two others took care of the exhortations or confessions of the girls and of the religious in Manhattanville, where there is a convent of the Religious of the Sacred Heart and school for girls.

## VIII. Oct. 1, 1858 to Oct. 1, 1859
### College, Community, Scholasticate

This year our Community totaled 45, of whom 13 were priests, 7 Scholastics, and 25 Brothers.

In May, 1859, the Father who was Superior-General of the French province's Mission of New York and Canada [Rev. John-Baptist Hus] for more than three years was called back to Europe. His successor here as Superior General of the New York Mission was a veteran of the Mission [Rev. Remi Tellier] who, however, at the very beginning of the school year combined the duties of teaching with administration.

Brother Francis Fauris, whose age was more than sixty, was sent to us during the month of May from the Troy Residence because of illness; he died shortly afterwards in the same month, as indicated in the necrology.

The number of boarders at the year's beginning was a little over 115; little by little the number increased to more than 130, when others more than filled the gaps of those who graduated. Four or five day students from the neighborhood go to school here.

Concerning our progress of education in the liberal arts, it will be appropriate to mention what most people think about our kind of education. That will provide an understanding of our opposition. Because of the conditions of living here, both private and public, hardly anyone seeks a liberal arts curriculum like ours. The first to excuse themselves from needing our studies are those whose interest is business and that's the largest part of this nation. Those in law, medicine and the other professions don't give any more attention to literary studies than illiterates do. But the educational system which prevails in other colleges is so far removed from our *Ratio Studiorum* that when students transfer to us from other colleges, many of them think our studies too over-burdened with Latin and Greek.

But nevertheless the following facts provided excellent proof that our students grow and make progress in those studies. First, they did extremely well in both the February and July examinations which they faced with singular alacrity. Second, they did the same in the exercises for prizes which were held earlier. And third, they take on voluntary and private academic work over and above ordinary and common tasks. Many students this year spent many hours long into the night reading the Latin and Greek authors; one student, by far more excellent than the others, privately read the entire *Iliad* for the honors exam and responded to the questioners in marvelous fashion and beyond expectations.

The philosophy students also deserve praise. They all devoted themselves to studies for the whole year and also studied till late at night; at the end of the year they were inspired by new concepts, and were an example and a stimulus to many of the other groups.

The Jesuits here take delight that this college has all the privileges of a university; it provides a meeting place for the various levels of the sciences and humanities. So this year eight candidates have been promoted to the B.A. degree, of whom six studied in our college, two studied in New York [Xavier College]; five candidates received the M.A.; the total number of graduates was 14.

But there is something peculiar to this generation. It is not *per se* hostile to scholarly discipline. Our most honored youths are eloquent in arguing in the vernacular about certain things, serious and grave, historical, political, literary, philosophical and so forth, whether after reflection or *ex tempore,* especially if the topic involves senatorial, judicial or electoral controversy. In rhetorical exercises flowing from their own natural talent and from their national customs our students indeed excel and triumph in grand fashion when the college offers them an opportunity to address a more mature audience. If you listened to them in that situation you would not say our students are immature boys, but men of mature age and that some of them are self-reliant and courageous. Beforehand you might also judge some to be rather of mediocre talent with average capacity, but when you hear them speaking forcefully about various issues, you realize they express themselves with amazing grace and proper judgment.

As you might surmise, these are the proper achievements of members of a major academy, composed of rhetoricians and philosophers which is called a Debating Society. Every Sunday they meet with a topic for debate with the assistance of a moderator; they discuss among themselves in the vernacular but in oratorical fashion (just as Cicero tells about himself with his equals Pompey, Crassus, Brutus, Caesar, etc.). These rhetorical exercises are their practice sessions; later they demonstrate their skills before the public in more serious and solemn contests. Those contests take place twice a year in February and June, always with a large and illustrious gathering of citizens, along with a delightful musical and choral presentation. This year, in addition, the presence of the Archbishop of New York and his Vicar General in the audience added additional solemnity to the occasion and motivation for the future.

Though the Archbishop had attended the event formerly, this time he said that he was intrigued by the students' two-hours of original speeches. He was so filled with admiration at both their content and their style that he conceived the idea of starting a new Academy for the youth of the college. At the end of the academic exercise the Archbishop indicated how pleased and moved he was and said that each of the speeches was praiseworthy. Then he made known his suggestion, provided only that the college administrators approve: that a team of four or five members of the philosophy class each year produce a paper [*elogium*] on some celebrated historical layman and that a prize for the best one would be commemorated by a special medal and the manuscript preserved in the archives of the college. If this suggestion were accepted, he promised to provide the first of these medals himself to the value of 50 dollars, one of which will be in metal and the other struck as a coin; and he had no doubt that in future years similar grants to pay for the prizes would be given by wealthy citizens.

His Vicar General was the first one to fulfill the Archbishop's wish when he spoke in a similar congratulatory vein at the next contest, at the beginning of June according to custom, at a time when the Archbishop was absent. In fulfilling his wish without delay, four chosen philosophers, undertook the challenge of treating the life of St. Louis. They did that in private study, so that no regularly assignments would be neglected. On the most solemn day for distributing prizes, with the usual 3,000 good citizens in attendance and music played for the festive audience, the philosophers' original speeches were given; one victor was proclaimed and given the medal with great applause. Newspapers reported the event. It seems that this new kind of activity that successfully motivates college students is firmly established and very suitable.

We owe a great deal of thanks to the Archbishop, the author of the suggestion for the Academy and the medal. He founded this, his own college, a few years ago near New York City, inspired as he was by what he thought were the needs of American education. American education favors both English literature and students' freedom. It is not for us to judge its measure of success.

What we in the college have we have invested to great profit. As clear proof of that, we have noted the enormous rise in morale. Many areas of freedom which thus far had been reserved especially for the older students, this year were finally extended to others to the satisfaction of all. It had come to be recognized that anyone outstanding in conduct and studies should be treated as a man, not as a boy. The American temperament is sufficiently understood; it is very quick to take risks as to surpass even Prometheus; in many instances the risk involves dangers. To face these dangers, we ourselves needed to exercise skills at some times or occasions, at other times we have used the students as administrators, sometimes the very architects of the dangers. Once, when one of the prefects of discipline was hesitating to ban something because of foreseen difficulty, one of the students said: "Don't be afraid. Once Father Prefect has communicated his wish, it will be a law for us."

On certain days, in celebration of national victories and on the feast of St. Patrick, it was the custom for students to have dances and other festivities, not without accompanying perils. Hence, when they requested the customary festivities for St. Patrick's day, the Jesuit replied that "It would be more laudable to dignify the celebrations with oratorical exercises in chapel, even though they were unprepared." So, without objection or murmuring, the older ones began to give speeches. Though they were unprepared, they proceeded with meaning and dignity to compete in praising their country and its heroes, above all, the apostle of the faith of their fathers. No one objected or complained.

Sometimes, without any help from us, they heal their own ailments. For example, the older ones have their own gymnasium and reading room, with a supply of various newspapers. Twice a year, from their own ranks, they elect their judges or prefects. This year the first election mingled good with bad; a second election picked only good students in such a way that progress could already be noted. But anger and discord followed this election, so that, for the sake of reconciliation, they demanded a meeting. Thus, in the presence of all, the newly elected president announced that: "Whatever they would do within the walls of the college would afterwards become public knowledge. The business at hand seems of small moment and unworthy of arousing such anger. But later in life matters of great moment must be dealt with in a calm spirit. Further, this is a school not only for arts and letters, but also for a public life which awaits many. So, by all means this storm must be quelled and, no matter how it came about, the situation must be accepted, seeing that the process was completed following our rules." With one or two exceptions, all agreed with what he said.

Thus far, we have written of the elders. The younger boys also deserve praise, especially for their devotion. There were 26 or 27 boys in the Third Division under the direction of a Jesuit Brother; some of the boys had received their first Communion, but most had not. Each day after dinner, 20 of this class visited the Blessed Sacrament. Even more were judged worthy to be admitted into their Marian Sodality. At night before they retired, all were accustomed to say privately part of the rosary; after retiring, with the rosary about the neck, they finished praying only when they fell asleep. Besides, many added a second rosary of the Immaculate Conception; one of them even said the entire office of the Sacred Heart every day. Moved by outstanding devotion, another founded two associations of the perpetual rosary among his classmates. Eight of them observed the six Sundays in honor of St. Aloysius and this included venerating the sacred reliquary of the saint. From the beginning of May till the end of the year, 15 or 20 made the Way of the Cross each Sunday. They offered all these acts for parents and friends, for the faithful departed, and for the Jesuit Fathers and Brothers.

Should I add that the students are outstanding for obedience, for admirable kindness to one another, for generosity in spreading the faith, and for other virtues? Two of the students, brothers, were called home due to their mother's illness; all the others prayed first for her recovery; then, upon the news of her death, they offered frequent prayers for her release from suffering in Purgatory. Later, when during supper they had heard that the orphans had returned, on their own initiative they agreed not to say anything which might cause them pain, but to welcome the boys back, to invite them to their games, and to lose no chance to alleviate by their sorrow.

A teacher had decided to punish a student, but, by mistake, he had written James instead of Peter on his list. So when James was warned that he should do the punishment, he did not object, but immediately took the penalty. A bit later, upon admitting his mistake to the innocent one, the teacher asked: "Didn't I punish you?" To which the boy replied: "Indeed you did not punish me. But how often, when I deserved it, was I not punished!"

Last year, the Brother who is in charge of the young boys was in danger of death with no hope for recovery. To the surprise of the doctor and all others, he recovered in town. From what we know of the boys' prayerfulness, who would doubt that his recovery was gained as a result of their intercessions?

Some of the boys are indeed non-Catholic in name; yet in desire and spirit they are Catholic; they have a strong desire for baptism, but so far they have not won over their parents; they are the only impediments.

## Our Outside Ministries

Outside the college four Fathers offer continual ministries in two nearby schools and missions; besides, they offer useful assistance at the college on major feasts or for a jubilee or other occasional celebrations. During vacations, the Spiritual Exercises were offered, not indeed in response to every request, but nevertheless in many places. One such place was at Seton Hall, New Jersey, the bishop's college that was mentioned above. The one whom superiors sent [probably Fr. Thomas Legoüais] at the invitation of the bishop exceeded expectations; the bishop had been one of his students in a philosophy class. Though he was not skilled in English, that Father deeply moved the hearts of the young toward receiving the sacraments; some shed tears that expressed their sorrow during confession. At Manhattanville, he and the pastor heard 1,800 confessions during the Jubilee. The parishioners and pastor marveled at the number of communicants and at the number of people who at that time received the sacraments, though they had neglected them for a long time. Elsewhere, on a similar occasion, over eight days, our Father and the pastor spent 12 or 14 hours hearing confessions.

To enable him to recover his health and to give the Spiritual Exercises to Religious of the Sacred Heart, another priest was sent in February to the city of Halifax in Nova Scotia. Though two weeks or so were allowed for the trip, he gathered so rich an unexpected harvest there that he had hardly any time for rest. The nuns and students were separately served, as were the students and alumnae; they received not only exhortations but the sacrament of penance. Next, the pastor of the cathedral called on him to move to his rectory, give talks and direct a retreat to the Sisters of Charity. In the end his health was restored, but he was so busy that he was brought directly from the pulpit to the departing ship. He faced his challenge successfully.

At a time when his students were making their retreat at school, one teacher gave the Spiritual Exercises in a parish where drunkenness was raging like a plague. To hear the sermons every day, many had to make a journey of several leagues at night. On the last day, the day of general Communion, people had been fasting during their long trip; several fainted in the confessional from exhaustion. Thereafter, only one man is said to have yielded to drunkenness, and that only once.

IX.  Oct. 1, 1859 to Oct. 1, 1860
    *College, Community, Scholasticate*

1. *Happy Beginning of the Year* [1859].
This year our Community consisted of 15 Fathers, 8 Scholastics, 24 Brothers, a total of 47.

The year began under happy auspices. The number of students was slightly down but the students were all fine young men and well disposed toward their teachers. The Archbishop, for a while somewhat alienated, now showed himself most friendly to our Fathers. He promised his support in all matters and worked energetically to increase the number of our students. He was not satisfied with mere verbal support. For instance, at the annual distribution of prizes it was the practice of the donor of a gold piece to himself confer it on the student writing the best paper on a proposed philosophical topic. At the end of last year he himself, the "Most Benign Bishop," was the first to make the donation and this year his Vicar General followed his example. So it appeared that the practice once started will go on. This will prove to be of great benefit for the students. Driven by the prospect of attaining honors and all afire with eagerness to outshine, they will strive mightily to get this reward.

*2. The Piety of the Students.*

The course of the year proved equal to its promise. There were not many outstanding events, but about the only unfulfilled wish was for an increase in the number of our students. They proved very teachable, devout and well behaved. Discipline, industry and harmony all flourished. No one was expelled from the college for bad conduct. Few failed to follow the practice of receiving Holy Eucharist once a month. Many approached the sacred tribunal of penance, if not weekly, at least every two weeks. The meetings of the different Sodalities were crowded. And many students here, especially among the younger ones, would come to the altar almost every Sunday.

At the beginning of May, a month observed with great devotion, some of the older students besought not the spiritual Father, but, what is more encouraging, their Prefect of Discipline, asking him to please point out whatever he might have observed in them to be in need of correction. And there are many edifying instances of boys who, to obtain some grace or to honor the Blessed Virgin or the Lord Jesus, take upon themselves some act of self-denial in the matter of food, recreation and the like, or for love of God endure some suffering with admirable patience over a long period of time. But let the mention of such devotions suffice.

However, one general observation seems worth mentioning that may shed light on many points and enable the reader better appreciate the special character of our students and more besides. That is, the students here act freely and spontaneously without any urging by the Jesuits or out of fear or pressure of rule in matters of devotion, in their choice of sports, and in other areas; this is especially true of the older students. And they are not upset by any new proposal provided it appears genuinely useful and proves to promote solid piety.

Thus, very many youths from the First and Second Divisions, drawn by mutual example, visit the most Blessed Sacrament after breakfast, dinner and supper. All the students in the Third Division do so. The past two years the whole Third Division accompanied their prefect in making the Stations of the Cross each Sunday; and, though it is entirely optional, rarely does anyone fail to be present for this devotion.

During Lent the Father giving an exhortation invited all to join in the pious practice of the Stations of the Cross. And, on this and the following day, you could see many students in chapel kneeling before images of the passion. Likewise a year ago they followed the same suggestion of the Father.

They were also invited to assist the Society for the Propagation of the Faith, a work that we seriously began here only recently. The response was swift and unanimous, and many made larger offerings than were asked.

They have very great devotion toward the Blessed Virgin. Some fall asleep at night reciting her rosary, and when they wake up in the morning, you will see the beads dangling from their necks. These practices are done at the prompting, not of their teachers, but of their angels. And although they recite evening prayers together, it is a rare boy who does not pray a while, kneeling at bedside before going to sleep.

Here the question can be raised why such a small group of students join our Society to fight for the salvation of souls under the standard of Holy Father Ignatius. In response it will suffice to cite the large number entering the ecclesiastical seminary each year. Priests scattered across the whole United States, especially in the neighboring New York area, have come from these buildings. They are devout, capable and diligent, working strenuously for the building up and defense of God's church. Thus, last year almost the whole philosophy class chose this state of life. There was one who did not go along with the others. But he had a task to do in his home state. There shortly after he left college a law in own state was abrogated; the law was very burdensome to Catholics, because it restricted Catholic churches from either selling their property holdings or offering them as security without the state's permission. By approaching senators, by urging and persuasion, this fine young man accomplished the undoing of this legislation.

The Third Division, I might say, without prejudice to the others, deserves some special praise here. Under the strict regime of one scholastic, youthful spirits are tightly curbed; the smallest laws are followed with great exactness. In First Division also there are many young men who would scrupulously avoid the least infraction. And in this regard for the rules they are especially served by the harmonious spirit binding all together. You would think them brothers rather than strangers. Thus one young man, recently admitted, wondered aloud: "Who could not be happy here?" Likewise those who have come to our college from other academies will not hesitate to declare openly what a great pleasure it is to be here.

The students participate fiercely in sports; it does them good both for relaxation and for strengthening their bodies; but it is also a help for their piety. Yet they leave their sports rapidly when the bells sound for them to do so. Many of Second Division and all in the Third have small gardens they zealously cultivate. For each division there are gymnasia for all residents' athletic activities. They were built and repaired by the lads themselves with the financial help of the college. So it is that the students enjoy the best of health, grow stronger day by day and by far surpass others of the same age in physical strength. This was made evident to all when students from the College of St. Francis Xavier came here from the city to contend in a championship game with First Division students.

3. *The Natural Qualities of the Student.*
There is no denying that some shortcomings are found in American young men which can be due either to their youth or regional mores and early formation. Yet there is much in their natural endowment to attract an observant and reflective person. And this can be said of the students generally: boyish levity is here and there apparent and lasts until they reach about thirteen. But then, gifted by nature with sharp mental powers and experiencing at an early age that energy of mind which has Americans ever on the go, they turn out sooner than boys of equal age in many parts of Europe to be capable of serious reflection and proper deportment. In a word, they mature more quickly than others.

Some in the lower grades scarcely kept up with their fellow-pupils or gave indication of any particular talent. But with the grammar classes behind them and now in humanities and rhetoric, they are as it were completely transformed into different men in excellent charge of themselves. No better examples of young Americans' precocious capacity for perceptive judgment are seen than their serious bearing during academic disputations, held two or three times yearly, when they speak in public before a good-sized audience.

Quite often this involves some important historical, political or moral issue. A team has two speakers on each side. The student chairman presides and first explains the "state of the question" for the audience. The speeches follow in order; but the attention of the audience is relieved by pleasing presentations of music and songs. Finally, the chairman briefly reviews what was said, weighs reasons pro and con for each case, and gives his own opinion solemnly. Indeed, if you attended to their manly facial appearance, to the fitting and orderly use of their body and voice, to their completely logical method of arguing, and finally, to the deep feeling for the topic which they hold and show, you would judge the speakers serious elders of the state rather than immature boys.

These are their natural gifts; if cultivated they could be and now are great sources of help for making true, brave and faithful ministers of Christ.

### 4. *External Ministries.*

Since there are hardly enough Jesuits here to attend to the work needed within the community, they cannot devote much time to external ministries. Certainly, were they available, there would be no lack of opportunity where there are so many of the faithful and unbelievers steeped in such great misery, strapped by difficulties, exposed to perils every day an with no one to help. For such assistance, if not they themselves, then surely their angels are calling out for apostolic men.

And yet we do work successfully among these souls. For often as though by chance but really by Divine Providence a Father will meet with some sinner whom he does not let go unless he is first washed in the waters of penance or at least truly and sincerely promises to come to the college and be reconciled with God, a promise almost always kept.

There are occasional conversions of Protestants or adult baptisms. This year a certain nineteen year-old woman, born a Protestant and married to a Catholic, was instructed in the true faith here in our college. Although her home was quite distant, she came faithfully, very often in the worst weather, traveling on foot since she was poor, and with her infant at her bosom. Her diligence, zeal and good faith proven, she was admitted to the Sacrament of Regeneration with her husband present. Nor did the pair depart before agreeing to return before long to prepare for the Eucharist.

One of the Fathers makes weekly visits to *Randalls Island* near New York City. On this island are certain public buildings which serve as hospital and asylum for poor boys and girls. Hired men care for the boys and women for the girls. And these men and women are under supervision of certain men chosen by the government. But since these are all most hostile to our religion, it is easy to surmise the great harm facing the children who are almost all born of Catholic parents.

Indeed no opportunity is lost for completely uprooting the least trace of their faith. When the boys arrive at an age when they are capable of hard labor it is customary to place them with employers who are very often Protestant and very often in areas where there is no Catholic so that they cannot preserve even a trace of their parental religion. Sectarian ministers of all shape and color visit the island to fill the minds of the children with their errors. No priest comes there from the city. The Father from our college does what he can for the salvation of these poor little souls.

The Father entrusted with this work for this year toils hard to remove very many obstacles and put things on a firm basis. Since he could in no way celebrate Mass, he obtained permission from the Most Reverend Archbishop to bring them Holy Communion. He heard confessions as he could in some corner of a room. Enough was done, however, to provide hope that many souls have been snatched from Satan's snares and that yet others will be. The situation has been called to the attention of many Catholics. New supervisors there are not ill-disposed to our faith and, with God's help, it is expected that in a short time these children will enjoy all the benefits of their religion. Things have reached the point where the Father has been given a room for Confessions and the new supervisors have allowed an altar to be erected for celebration of Mass.

Worthy of note is a certain conversion to the true faith. There were two Protestant girls among the boarders in the convent of the Religious of the Sacred Heart. Though their father had been born of a Protestant family, in his twelfth year he was received into the Catholic Church and baptized by one of our Fathers at Georgetown College. Twenty years ago he married a Protestant and, as commonly occurs, he completely abandoned all practice of religion. But the divine mercy, which had earlier pursued the father, was directed toward his daughters. Hence, with the consent of her parents, the older girl of 16 years, when enlightened by the light of Catholic truth, was admitted to the baptismal font. Then her sister, six years younger, when gravely ill, was so insistent in asking to be counted among the daughters of the Church that this favor could in no way be denied her. When she was close to death, both parents came to the convent. Then her father was persuaded to seek genuine consolation where it can be found, in the sacrament of Penance. He agreed and made this noteworthy comment that he had never doubted the Catholic faith and had always held the deepest reverence for the Jesuit priest who had received him into the Church. At all these events, the mother, who had been against our holy faith, was shaken and her prejudices set aside. Thus, it was not hard to bring her to speak with our priest. And so, a few days later she was baptized in the presence of her daughter and husband. This daughter, to whose prayers we may owe the fact that both parents returned to the Church and to works of devotion, now desires only one thing, the happy day when she can give and consecrate herself totally to God in religious life. To this prayer her parents have already given their approval.

Another Protestant girl met with greater difficulties. Her tutor and parents were most hostile toward the Church and especially toward the Jesuits. They made it clear to her that she would meet many obstacles if, in obedience to her inner voice, she were to embrace the Catholic faith. Still she was moved by the strongest determination, and the case was brought to the Vicar General. He approved that she be privately received into the Church for, as he said, once these girls are received into the true fold, rarely or even very rarely do they succumb to any danger of losing their faith. So, happily baptized by one of our Fathers, the girl seems fervent and brave for now and for the future.

Let me make this final statement about Protestantism: many young Protestants are enrolled in our Jesuit high schools and inexplicably the Society of Jesus is useful even for such young people. For instance, even those students who do not ask to be received into the Church, due to lack of interest or to the force of their passions, nevertheless they often reject irrational opinions about Catholics. And they always remain well disposed toward our holy faith, even though not all of them know and believe in their hearts that it is the only Church of God.

### 5. *On Ministries in Convents.*

The Fathers visit nearby convents, where certain spiritual fruit can be obtained. In the United States the number of such residences is large. How much they help to advance the cause of God can be understood from the fact that several bishops believe and hope that they will be means for the salvation, enrichment, and expansion of the Catholic Church, especially in the future. This year one of our Fathers gave the Spiritual Exercises to the girls in four academies, as they are termed. Though he said not a word about the religious life, he found many girls inclined toward this manner of life. In the same residences he helped many who wanted to return to the Faith, and succeeded in that work, as we have written above.

### 6. *On Ministries among Priests.*

Among our ministries the most useful seems to be spiritual retreats to priests, even though, through nobody's fault, they are rather rarely undertaken. It seems that for the future they should be offered more often. Thus far, especially in neighboring dioceses, certain Fathers have been repeatedly asked by the Bishop to give the Spiritual Exercises to priests. This year, the Bishop of Albany asked the Rev. Father Superior to send a priest to give the Exercises in his diocese. A priest was sent who for years counted many priests of this region among his former students; nevertheless, he knew that many others had a poor opinion of the Society. God blessed his work and, even at the end of the first day, all of them admitted that never before had they been so moved. On the third day they exclaimed: "Would that for the past 15 years we had such a retreat!" As the retreat drew to a close, in the presence of all his clergy and in their name, the bishop, with very deep affection, thanked our Father and afterwards said to him that he would not want to change a word of all that he had said and that, as far as it lay in his power, he would arrange that in the following year the same Father would give the same Spiritual Exercises. Moreover, the priests showed their appreciation through kind letters and generous alms. During the solemn Mass celebrated by the bishop, in which all the priests communicated, the final address was delivered to a packed, devout crowd of the faithful, especially men.

Several times in the course of the year, either in Canada or in the United States, the priests of the college gave the Exercises with happy results. Our men derived the deepest happiness from the hope that, in the next year and the following years, lay people and especially priests will use the spiritual experience of our Blessed Father Ignatius more often, more easily, and with practical results. Great help for that goal will be the likely result of Fordham's recent purchase from the Archbishop of the ecclesiastical seminary which adjoins the college property. There for the first time in many years, a retreat will soon be offered in the former seminary to the priests of this large diocese.

### 7. *The Usefulness of Missions in This Region.*

We hope that in the near future some of our Fathers may be assigned exclusively to give Missions to the people. Judging by what happened in the diocese of Albany as mentioned above, one may surmise how much can be done in this field.

With a sad heart, the Bishop there saw how few men in his cathedral came to the sacraments, even in the Easter season. Therefore, he immediately thought that the priest who had already directed the retreat for the priests should be invited to give the Exercises exclusively for the men of the parish. The priest came to the parish, spoke as apostolic men do, and this was the fruit of his talks: in the cathedral 800 men, and in other churches very many others received Holy Communion, among whom there were quite a few former public sinners.

Delighted by this second success, the Bishop sent the priest to another place where there was deadly discord between the people and the pastor. Matters had gone so far that parishioners no longer wanted to receive the sacraments. But, with the help of God, in short order all discord was healed; about 300 men have received Holy Communion on Sunday; the Rosary Society, which had been nearly dead, has been revitalized and restored to its original fervor.

### X.  Oct. 1, 1860 to Oct. 1, 1861
### *College, Community, Retreat House, Parish Residence*

This year the total number in our Community was 50, of whom 15 were priests, 7 were Scholastics, 28 were Brothers.

The Fordham community lives in three separate dwellings. The first one, by far the most important and largest, houses the university with its college and community, where the Rev. Fr. Superior of our whole North American Mission lives. The second one is the Retreat House, with one priest and two Brothers. And the third one is the parish Residence with two priests and two Brothers who will finish their novitiate on next September 4. The latter were chosen from four candidates in the Canadian novitiate; they were judged suitable to begin the novitiate.

What regularly helped or enabled some members of the community who were certainly unequal to such a variety of works and burdens was the fraternal love by which each one readily supports others along with observation of rules and zeal for souls. It is appropriate to call to mind three Jesuit Brothers who for a long time have made considerable contributions to the students. Two of them have shared a watchful authority over the students as prefects. The third [Br. Julius Macé] has taught music, an art in which he so excels that it is said he has no equal in the whole wide region, and the boarders esteem him so highly that they would hardly accept other teacher in his place.

*About Our Students*

In the lamentable American civil war which has torn America apart, no loss was suffered at the college, as was to be feared, either in the number of the students or in any important studies. The use of the sacraments flourished among all at the college as well as a taste for devotional books, and that manly spirit of religion which, indeed, would be honored certainly among Catholic people, but in these times is more difficult even as it is more necessary. Obedience was such as to leave hardly anything to be desired. With their seniors outdoing them in every good example, younger members excelled in piety, both expressly for the propagation of the faith and in other ways as well. Happy results were produced both by way of spiritual exercises and festive celebrations occurring throughout the year. At midnight on Christmas Eve all shared Communion after kneeling before the crib and venerating the Divine Infant. A solemn procession in the campus garden, with customary splendor, marked the feast of Corpus Christi.

*Academics*

With regard to studies: as already has been done for two years, exams were given privately or with public honors. In a public exam, a humanities student dealt with literary and critical difficulties in the whole of Horace, and two from the first class of basic grammar with all the historical, mythological and grammatical questions of Lucian's dialogues. They showed themselves prepared in their responses and, though examined long and rigorously, did not stumble even once.

In the upper classes, philosophical or historical essays in writing were required nearly each week. They regularly went so well that they demonstrated equally their erudition and diligence. ... [In one Academy] historical, political, and literary issues were being debated oratorically, [since] young men should be introduced to the art of public speaking, which is so important in a country of this kind. A large number of outstanding clerics and laymen regularly attended these twice-yearly public disputations, adding special grace. Many newspapers then spread the news about these events.

The other Academy was inaugurated this year with favorable beginnings, and we hope it will be of great use for promoting studies and increasing the good reputation of the College. This Academy is solely concerned with more carefully investigating and widely spreading history as far as possible throughout the lifetime of our young men. An older individual is admitted into the Academy provided he has written previously with distinction about some historical problem. Learned men from the clergy and citizenry have politely, not to say gratefully, accepted honorary certificates of admission that had been offered them. A gold medal for the best biographical treatise furthers this project. The first medal was donated by the Archbishop, this year's, however, by the mayor of the city.

We recently inaugurated another kind of similar prize to be given to the second year philosopher who best deserved it. This has no other purpose except to inflame our youth ever more with a love of study and of every fine achievement. As a new honor, that prize was conferred solemnly in mid-July in the presence of two thousand citizens. Also heard with huge applause, as ever, were the sparkling rhetorical performances of selected young men. At that time, too, sixteen baccalaureate degrees and three masters degrees were conferred. As regularly happens in addressing these graduates, the extern guest-speaker launched into praises of the whole Society and, specifically, of Fordham University that modesty forbids one to repeat. Not only modesty, but their very abundance excludes from these pages the praises later loudly proclaimed by the press.

### Pastoral

Our external works will now be concluded in short shrift. Our two resident priests quite constantly care for the Fordham parish of about six hundred faithful, largely Irish. At certain times of the year they require help from several of the college priests. We have slightly but satisfactorily restored a narrow building for the parish and added to it an organ and other amenities. In addition to gifts from the faithful, we spent almost seven thousand francs on our own.

Spiritual exercises for priests are given in three different dioceses: New York, Albany, and Hamilton. In each one of these places, all priests were living by the same rules that at the time were customarily observed by religious; they were a kind of living theatre, very much suited to inspire parishioners' piety. After the retreats they expressed thanks to the retreat director; they did so publicly and in writing, with everyone's signature added.

Many groups of religious women were also given exercises for a triduum before taking vows or renewing them. For a solid eight days, however, the Spiritual Exercises were given to Sisters of the Immaculate Heart in Reading and at St. Joseph's, then to the Sisters of Charity at Mt. St. Vincent's and, separately, to their women students, then to the Visitation Sisters in Brooklyn, and then to the Sisters of Mercy in New York and in New Haven, etc.

At the thirteen Missions that our Fathers gave there were about three thousand communions, and there were other good results besides: validated marriages, many abjurations of heresy, instances of the restoration of family peace and harmony.

To give some examples: the people of Binghampton, a very religiously-committed group, expressed such joy from the mission from which they had benefited, that the pastor had to forbid by a specific command the whole populace from following our Fathers all the way to the train station. Oneida parish in New York State had a different experience. The flock consisted of eight hundred parishioners scattered in many little market-towns. No matter how much the pastor labored for their salvation, hardly any sign of religion was visible, and the Church mourned her own loneliness. Imagine the fright of our Fathers who heard of this! But then imagine the solace of the same people and the thanks and joy of the good pastor when he suddenly saw hardy men trudging on foot eight, ten, fourteen miles in the depth of winter to hear the preaching, and when he saw those who had been away from Mass or confession for fifteen, thirty, fifty years coming devotedly in the church daily, with humble hearts, bewailing their former lives!

In the cathedral of Hamilton, Canada, one of our Fathers, with the help of two Tertian fathers along with diocesan priests, spent thirteen days hearing confessions. Very many there, who had fallen away from the Catholic faith, rather well-known by name and by their teaching, were taken back by the Ordinary into the bosom of the Church. There was such a gathering of Protestants to hear the true word of God that, to stop their exodus, a nearby Protestant chapel that had been closed was reopened. But in vain! More Protestants even from their newly opened chapel came back to the Catholic building, at last spewing out from their hearts and mouths the errors they acknowledged.

> XI.  December, 1863 to Oct. 1, 1864
> *College, Community, Retreat House, Parish Residence, Jesuit Seminary*

[*In December, 1863, the Province of France was divided. The New York/Canada Mission became part of the Province of Champagne, in whose Annual Letters this account appears.*]

This year (1863) the total number in our Community was 75, of whom 20 were priests, 28 were Scholastics and 27 Brothers.

### 1. *Student numbers.*

At the start of this year the student census of Fordham College was more promising than the alarming crises of war allowed us to hope for. Indeed, we had serious reason to fear that with a sharp drop in enrollment, we would have to increase our crushing burden of debt to provide needed operating funds. In fact, that fear appeared groundless from the very beginning of classes, for such a crowd of young men showed up on opening day that the losses of last year's graduates were not a problem.

### 2. *Students' religious observance.*

Yet there would be little or no reason to celebrate the growth in numbers if it were not matched with solid moral standards and promotion of authentic devotion. The result has been progress in observance of house rules in the student hall, progress in esteem for the masters, a warm comraderie among the boys, and progress in the generous, attentive practice of their true religion.

Some boys in the student body are affiliated with one or other non-Catholic sect. Yet, not a year passes without at least one among them turning from errors of dissent and solemnly professing the Catholic faith. We Jesuits do nothing whereby we would seem to actively promote such conversions. It is the example of peers and the kindness of the masters and the very beauty and solemnity of Catholic ritual that move them powerfully to embrace the true faith.

### 3. *The devout death of a boarding student.*

The whole house was saddened by the death of one young lad. He was a boy of sharp intelligence and competitive drive, but it was his innate modesty that endeared him to all. Our grief was borne more easily as we witnessed his unshaken courage in his sufferings and the angelic piety that enabled him to see death itself as gain. When the illness finally confined him to bed, he continually and fervently conversed with God.

Fingering his Marian chaplet day and night, he often begged the Blessed Virgin to lead him swiftly to the heavenly Court. The infirmary Brothers who constantly took turns at his bedside and his comrades who vied to attend him experienced a deep devotion as they observed his ardent longing for death and his peaceful composure amid such suffering. Frequently, with eyes fixed on heaven, he kept repeating in a loud voice: "Come, let us go to the homeland of the blessed!" until, in fulfillment of his desire, he breathed forth his innocent soul.

4. *The Good Name of the College.*

Very many of our former students continue to maintain until an advanced age the same good will toward Jesuits and the college that they had when being trained by us. How much they value the training they received from the teaching of Jesuits can be shown by this fact, that they are unwilling to commit their sons to other than Jesuits for formation in both liberal arts and morals. The educational plan and methods (*"ratio institutionis"*) given by us also receives commendation from the fact that, after they complete their studies with a praiseworthy record of talent and piety, many enter diocesan seminaries or religious cloisters to embrace a more perfect mode of Christian life.

The ball games that are organized for the recreation of our students have attained some renown, both for the enthusiasm of the players themselves and for the significant crowds of people who come to watch them. In addition, they greatly promote closer bonds between our students and youths from neighboring colleges who previously were strangers.

Challenges to compete are publicly posted here and there by the Fordham youths and other nearby colleges. The challenges are accepted. The day of the contest is fixed. The contestants descend into the arena. The battle is engaged; the interest of the spectators sharpens the enthusiasm of the contestants. Referees are standing by, skilled at settling disagreements between the competing lines of battle. The victory is proclaimed, and those on whom fate has not smiled freely concede the palm of victory to their fellow contestants in good spirits. They go off together to wipe away the memory of their unlucky outcome with a feast prepared for the occasion. Some spectators inform newspaper reporters of the contest and its outcome, and they describe the whole event in the paper, as though it were a momentous happening worthy of being handed down to their descendants.

5. *Jesuit Ministries.*

The priests who are assigned to the ministry of teaching do not devote their time only to the affairs of the college. Instead, if there is time left over from their ordinary occupations, as on Saturdays and the vigils of some feast days, they leave home so that they may devote their spiritual ministry in the parishes around Fordham. And so, after their weekly labors at the college they spend their time until late at night in hearing confessions, in preparing for the divine liturgy the next day at ten or eleven o'clock and also delivering sermons to the people on the truths of Christianity. Moreover, it often happens that a priest says Mass and presents the nourishment of the Gospel in two parishes, four or five miles apart, on the same day. Beyond that, where there is need, he often visits the sick and administers the sacrament of baptism. And all this is in addition to his school work! But during the summer vacations even longer expeditions are undertaken, and they water with the dew of their heavenly eloquence the shores of New Brunswick, Nova Scotia, Prince Edward Island, or Newfoundland.

### 6. *Missions in Vermont.*

Since the previous letters have made no mention of the missions conducted during the last year by a parish priest from our house within the borders of Vermont, we consider it appropriate to follow up this matter with more details here.

Once a series of pious exercises was initiated in any parish of these regions, it is amazing with what enthusiasm and zeal all the Catholics tried their best to take part in them. And many of them had to travel fifteen or twenty miles to reach the church where the exercises were held. Even ladies of the night deserted their houses and foot patrols. Among these many were found who more than once spent the whole morning in church fasting up to noon, so that, having washed away the stains on their newly discovered conscience, they might be renewed by the Eucharist. Sometimes people would even participate in the Sacred Meal at night, at seven or even eight o'clock, sometimes even later. When asked why they were willing to abstain so long from food, since they could receive Communion the next day, they replied that they did this so that their wives and children might be able to go to the sacraments the next day.

Over the space of about thirty years, only two priests carried on apostolic ministry in these widely scattered areas; from this one can easily imagine how many people during this time were unable to profit from their ministry. Because of such a lack of priests the following unfortunate situation also developed. Some non-Catholics, especially those who enjoyed the greatest authority and wealth, often lured Catholics into moral practices incompatible with their Catholic belief. Among these quite a few had entered into marriages witnessed by Protestant ministers or magistrates of the regions where they lived.

In the course of time, as soon as the Bishop of Burlington took over the governance of his new diocese, he firmly decreed that it was forbidden to provide the sacraments to such Catholics unless they made public reparation for their public offense. But it was never necessary for any of our priests to impose such severe treatment on anyone. Whoever was asked whether he was willing to obey the orders of the Bishop, as long as he begged pardon from a merciful God, declared without delay that he was prepared to do everything required. Accordingly, shortly before the beginning of the solemn offering of the Divine Sacrifice some gathered each day at the entrance to the sanctuary and, renouncing verbally the evil they had done, humbly begged for the forgiveness of their brothers. Not even one person was found, in so many parishes of so large a diocese, who refused to return in such a way to graced communion with God and his Church.

Everyone who reflects upon the situation of these Catholic people will admire this proof of, I might almost say, daring piety. For very many of them are oppressed by poverty and most of them live bound to the domestic service to Protestants. At times some mistresses of households where they work absolutely forbid them from helping the mission. Very often, to get to the distant church, they must either borrow or rent horses. Thus, they put up with all these inconveniences both at the beginning of winter and in its full depth, the months of January and February, when everything there lies frozen under the most extreme cold. But if some among the Protestants mentioned above either totally forbade or grudgingly put up with the attendance of Catholic servants at the sacred services, a great percentage of them, on the contrary, indicated that they so highly approved of their religious practices that they themselves by their own example compelled some of the faithful to assist properly at the exercises of the mission. And especially on those days when a discussion was set up on some topic controverted between Catholics and Protestants, so large an audience assembled to hear it that Catholics and Protestants had to press tightly together within the church. Even the ministers of the sects themselves, also clothed in solemn garb, listened to the speaker with no less attention than if they proceeded from the mouth of some undefeated athlete of the sect in question. Our speaker had to exercise great circumspection lest, if he directly attacked the remarks of the heretics, this might unleash an aggressive attack against the Roman faith. Rather, by carrying on these discussions as though they were engaged together in completing and building up the fullness of truth, he had infused great power into them to dissolve the opposing errors and also draw men of good will gently toward conversion to the true religion.

And so every expedition of this kind that was carried out by Jesuits resulted in a joyful conversion of many Protestants to the Roman faith. It is amazing, moreover, how much such conversions, celebrated by a public and solemn ceremony, contributed to strengthen Catholics' perseverance more and more firmly in their holy commitments.

### 7. Some Pious Incidents.

It seems important to tell the story here of an outstanding example of divine predestination. A certain girl in the town of Swanton-Falls, a member of an Anabaptist congregation, had heard from a Protestant preacher about the necessity of baptism to obtain eternal beatitude. She was more than fourteen years of age, but had not yet been washed by the waters of regeneration. Upon returning home, she broke out in tears and begged of her parents a very great favor, that they allow her to be washed in the saving font of baptism as soon as possible. There was nearby a kind of pharmacist who learned that the young girl was in sharp pain from major toothaches, and that no matter what was done she would clearly not get well. He kept talking about and offered to sell her a kind of fluid material to be inhaled; he said it was the only way to be cured; he had discovered it only recently. The girl unfortunately believed him and wished to try the medication. She did and, upon imbibing one or two drafts of the horrible vapors, she was seized violently with very painful contractions of the nerves and shortly thereafter had a mental breakdown. A doctor was immediately summoned. But no matter how skilled his efforts, all was in vain. The girl spent the whole night in a semiconscious state, so that while they were conferring about her critical condition no one thought about her request for baptism. The next morning when our Father was taking a bit of breakfast he heard a kitchen worker talking about the unfortunate case of the girl and mentioning at the same time her strong desire to receive baptism, a desire she had explicitly mentioned the day before. Right away our Father requests that her parents be asked if they would allow him to come to her so that he could make her wish fulfilled. The weeping mother consulted with the doctor who agreed immediately, and our Father was called. Promptly she was washed in the holy waters of Baptism and enrolled in the Christian army. However, the ceremonies had hardly been completed when she breathed her last; her face was peaceful like an angel's. It seems clear that the girl was kept living on earth just long enough to be born in heaven.

8. *Piety towards the Blessed Virgin.*

Our Catholic people have been accustomed to showing themselves very eager for devotions to the Most Blessed Virgin. Almost everyone wishes to be enrolled in the Scapular of the holy Mother. In the entire state of Vermont you'll perhaps not find 100 men who do not wear those blessed garments. You would see crowds of mothers with young children or leading them by hand or carrying them in their arms; they show them to the priest from the grating of the sanctuary so that, after he had invoked blessings on the children he would put the cloth of the Blessed Virgin on them at the mothers' request. Therefore, what prevents us from hoping that she, who single-handedly has crushed all heresies, would keep the faith of Catholics flourishing with a vital spirit and make it better day by day, though they live among heretical seductions, and that she would bring to the church a stability which later produces the certain fruits of salvation?

9. *The Jesuit Theological Seminary.*

What remains is that we write a few words about the Jesuit theological seminary that has been started up a second time at Fordham. The Maryland province disbanded its seminary in Boston and our theologians there had to return home. So a School of Higher Studies for Jesuits, which did not function at all for four years, was started up again in early September, 1863, with fourteen scholastics of our province, and six from the Missouri province of whom two are philosophers. Their quarters were the buildings which the Right Reverend Archbishop had sold to us on the year before. Three professors divided up among themselves the whole of dogmatic theology. But one of them fell ill at the end of the year and since he continued to be sick, we were deprived of his talent, holy injunctions and example that we had received from him earlier.

Meanwhile, from among the theologians six had been commissioned as catechists by whom about 180 young people were instructed in Christian doctrine. And, we must not neglect to mention the outstanding diligence of one man in advancing devotion among the young people in the parish. Lest the benefits of First Communion too quickly disappear, he organized young people of both sexes into two sodalities and increased the good effort that was begun through the catechism in a wonderful way through his pious exhortations. And he also worked effectively among adults. Among them he propagated the devotion of the Living Rosary, and he gave a kind of new life to the work of the parish library which had languished.

## XII. Oct., 1865 – Oct., 1866

*[Though the following is found in the book of Annual Letters, as you can see it is not a letter particularly about Fordham — although some familiar names are revisited — but about the American Mission in general, complaining about the lack of cooperation with the Campagne Province's attempt to tell the story of its mission in America. Recall that we are only three or so years away from a total administrative break with the old world of France.]*

Again this year we didn't get the expected letters from America, though they were very much desired. It is not up to us to judge those who skipped the tasks that obedience and charity required. As for us, we're sorry that we can't narrate the many great works that our brethren did for the praise of God and of the Church. We especially regret that we don't have the means to offer the usual and well-deserved praise in these letters for those whom God called for the reward of their labors.

Fr. Remi Tellier should be specially praised as a man of outstanding virtue who deserved well of the Society and especially of our American Mission. [He was rector-president of Fordham during 1854-59; those were very difficult years because of frayed relationships with the Archbishop of New York. His final and most important assignment is mentioned next.] He led that Mission as Superior General for six years, from the day he took office to the last day of his life [Jan. 7, 1866]. He was worthy of the esteem and love of all, since he governed bravely and graciously. We were glad to learn the summary of a life so well and fruitfully spent was about to be written by a Jesuit. Fr. Tellier came from the diocese of Soissons [in north France]. He lived 69 years, a Jesuit for 47 years. "His memory is held in benediction," for he was "of the seed of those men through whom salvation was brought to Israel."

And we must mention the names of two whose death was specially precious in the sight of God, namely, those who in the course of 1864 and 1865, toiled daily for the sick in hospitals at the risk of their personal safety. One of these was Fr. George Laufhuber; the other was Fr. Joseph Pavarelli, who was from the Jesuit province of Venice. Of the latter some reports have come to us and they will be summarized here.

When Fr. Joseph Pavarelli first came to the New York Mission, he was attached to the residence at Guelph [Canada]. A man who had all kinds of virtues, charity above all, he was praised for his human and pleasing conversation, his whole being was dedicated to preaching the word of God, hearing confessions, teaching Christian doctrine to the young, visiting the sick day and night. Long distances or inclement weather did not deter him. Therefore, his life matched the high opinion of him held by all, as the account of the following fact will prove. On a certain day an old man came, asking that three Masses be celebrated by one of the holy Fathers (his expression). Asked whom he judged to be holier than the others, he named the Italian priest. And his confidence did not deceive him. For behold, in a few days, he happily reported that the grace he sought had been granted. Shortly thereafter, Fr. Pavarelli was sent to New York. There God gave him a "difficult struggle to win," he was perfected in a short time and received an everlasting crown of glory.

You can see Blackwell's Island from New York City. Those whose desperate need makes them do terrible things, those afflicted with contagious disease, those who are insane are assigned here. More than 30 thousand enter this place each year. There our Fathers purchase a great harvest gained through great labor. And there death always threatens. Two of our Fathers had already died when Fr. Joseph, like a brave soldier, received that post. He did everything to win for God the souls of both the Catholics and even the Protestants. Lest anyone without religion should perish, he applied himself as much as he could to learning German.

He had just completed the third month of this kind of work, when he was seized by a deadly contagious disease. Sensing that the end was near, he gave himself up fully and freely to the will of God, and he had nothing else in mind except to prepare himself for his last agony. In his final days he fell into a delirium and yet he did not stop saying religious words, at times mentioning the name of heaven or purgatory, at times recalling the passion of Christ and saying: "How short is the way of the Cross," or reciting the litanies of the Blessed Virgin or other prayers. He yielded up his soul to God the day before the vigil of Christmas.

During the time his body was displayed, the serenity of his countenance moved and attracted people to a religious sense. And indeed his obsequies were the occasion of events that had never happened before. Thus, although his body was brought out at 7:00 A.M. in the middle of winter, a violent wind raged and rain mixed with snow was falling, men and women patients processed in a long line all the way to the river bank, about a half mile away. There his body was to be placed in a boat to be brought to the Fordham College cemetery.

The civil magistrates who are in charge of the hospital testified of their own accord in a public statement to their sense of gratitude and justly deserved reverence at the deaths of the three priests and they decreed that testimony should be sent to the Most Reverend Archbishop.

The reports contained in this volume will perhaps seem to many to be too brief. This poverty comes from a shortage of documentation on the part of more than one of the Missions. To meet this problem in the future, all of our Brethren for their love for the Society, are asked to carefully write down and let us know whatever occurs to them worthy of note. It will be of some advantage if those, to whom the task of gathering information, do not put off that task to the end of the year. Instead, let them have as an almost permanent rule to prepare valuable reports by keeping their eyes and ears open wherever they are.

Part III

"A kind of early hope"

The College and Parish of St. Francis Xavier

CHAPTER 7

## REV. JOHN LARKIN, S.J.

### Priest, Philosopher, Theologian, Charismatic Orator

Fr. John Larkin was the founding president of the College of St. Francis Xavier. The account of his life that follows is from the *Annual Letters* of the Province of France[9] for 1858–1859. It sketches in broad strokes the struggles of an institution to be born in hostile and uncertain surroudings, struggles that will be described in greater detail in Chapters 8 and 9. It reminds us that, behind these struggles, there are always *people* of faith and hard work.

"Fr. John Larkin was born on February 2, 1801, of Irish, honorable and prosperous parents [Elizabeth Jones and John or Charles Larkin], at Newcastle-on-Tyne in the English province of Northumberland. He did his early education successfully in the

Catholic Ushaw College [in Durham]; there one of his teachers who deeply impressed him, was the distinguished [historian Rev. John] Lingard. A fellow classmate who became a lifelong very close friend was the future Archbishop and Cardinal [Nicholas Patrick] Wiseman. So he always regarded his stay at Ushaw College as fortunate.

After college, Larkin followed Bishop Slater [as his secretary] to the Island of Mauritius, but he soon returned to Europe and began a two-year theology program in the Sulpician seminary in Paris and joined the Sulpicians. Then he sailed for America, completed his studies and was ordained at Baltimore [on Aug. 26, 1827]. [In 1828] he began teaching philosophy and mathematics at [the Sulpician] College in Montreal. On Sundays he also preached to the people. In both teaching and preaching he rapidly revealed the wide range of his talents. Well versed in all kinds of literature, outstandingly knowledgeable in Latin and Greek, he not only published a Greek grammar that was used in the Sulpician College, but also in alternating order, he prelected his classes using either language. So well did his students master his lessons that they gave the public defense of theses in either language, Greek or Latin, according to the choice made by their adversaries.

His students benefited greatly from their educational experience; and his good example of solid doctrine and virtue impressed their youthful minds and hearts. In addition, his students found it very easy to imitate their brilliant professor's clarity and precision. The students specially accepted their beloved teacher's teaching about God.

Similarly, the people at his Masses were very pleased when he preached. The man who translated Latin words skillfully into Greek spoke beautifully in the pulpit in English and in French as the occasion required. In fact, he spoke English beautifully, such that each listener could take his words for music.

At a time when things were going very well for him, he constantly and earnestly prayed to God that He provide an opportunity for him to meet someone from the Society of Jesus. The answer to his prayers happened when in 1840 Fr. Peter Chazelle, S.J., formerly the Rector-President of St. Mary's College in Kentucky, accepted the invitation to come to the Montreal seminary to preach an eight day retreat. Larkin made a general confession during that retreat and soon entered the Jesuit novitiate [on Oct. 24, 1840, at age 38½] at St. Mary's. In a few months he was assigned to the [newly begun] college at Louisville first as dean and then as superior of the house until the college was abandoned to assure a successful initial move into New York. [At St. John's College, Fordham, he was vice-president and dean for a year, 1846-1847; the next year he devoted to founding what later became the College of St. Francis Xavier in New York City. That work was cut short when he was reported to be appointed bishop of Toronto. With superiors' permission, he fled to Europe to cancel that burden and succeeded in that goal.]

He ... was in France during 1850 and 1851, first for tertianship in the province of Lyons, then at Laval to prepare for an examination on all of theology. Thereupon he was rector for three years at Fordham College. Next, for two years he did pastoral assignments in London and elsewhere [e.g., Westminster, Liverpool and Newcastle]. He was appointed official Visitor to the Irish vice-province [a task he did not complete because his New York brethren urgently needed him home]. Upon his return to America, he spent the last three years of his life in the New York College in the sacred ministry of preaching, hearing confessions and exercising the priestly public ministry.

Though promotion to the episcopate had twice been offered to him, he twice preferred a humble service of God in the Society of Jesus. Everyone who lived with him for a long time agreed that he seemed always self-controlled and never showed a sign of impatience. Although he was rector of colleges in difficult times and was hard pressed due to the shortage of material things and of students, nevertheless he did not act precipitously or as though he were in a rush, and did not seem to contradict an opponent. He always seemed to be calm, and his modesty made him always silent about himself. He was strong in facing hardships, and ready to face major problems. Throughout those times, his wonderful prudence helped him solve cases of conscience, becoming all things to all people.

To advance the cause of goodness he would often accept for spiritual direction mostly persons of low status (and even be obsequious to them), although he might also accept some men of great knowledge and authority, for the same purpose. Everyone who knew him well admired this excellent Father's virtue much more than his learning though that was immense. And no one was known to have ever complained about him.

Father John shined as an orator; the skills and qualities that combine to make someone an excellent orator were found in him: a big and impressive body, manly elocution, graceful and, when necessary, emphatic gestures; a strong, resounding voice that was so pleasant that as long as he spoke his listeners were delighted with the sound of his voice and they did not tire of hearing him. But the main thing about his preaching was that his knowledge seemed to be inexhaustible and a divine love seemed almost to flow out from him, truly a bright and shining light; and finally, a feature that is very important for winning over the listener, he projected the peacefulness of a beautiful soul through the agreeable sound of his voice. Thus rambunctious youths, so impatient of protracted speech, were struck with amazement and remained in their place through hours as he orated learnedly and at length.

He was always prepared to preach, and it often happened that what he said *ex tempore* included a very accurate quote of Scripture. Besides, this marvelous man so excelled that, once when he had been ordered to honor secular solemn ceremonies [by his presence], he suddenly and beyond the usual practice and expectation changed the solemn ceremonies into opportunities for preaching the Gospel. And not only did no one, Protestant or non-religious, complain or disapprove, but also, if I may say so, his success there crowned his accomplishments as a speaker. His speaking successes equaled his courage in undertaking the challenge. At least three times people remember such triumphs.

The first of all these events which the *Annual Letters* carried at length took place in 1843 on the anniversary day of American independence from the English yoke near Louisville, where our Father, then prefect of studies in a college in that city, was almost forced to talk by outstanding citizens. He spoke for two hours on Christian liberty from the pure Gospel. He spoke in priestly vestments, including a stole, in the open air before twenty thousand citizens of all kinds.

The site of another triumph of uncertain date, was in a large Protestant church on the topic, Genius. Through a long definition, and in a roundabout way the orator at last sailed through the topic in such a manner as to brand Luther and Calvin with deserved disgrace, and his words were received with loud and long applause.

The scene of his third triumph was Philadelphia. Father spoke shortly after a certain Catholic church had been set on fire by seething sectarians. He spoke in the public auditorium of the Library. After recalling the burning of the Library of Alexandria, he brought up the topic of the recent fire in their own city. At the very mention of the fire his friends began to be anxious and confused for they felt that some of the people were disturbed, some were guilty or involved in the crime and they would not control their anger at the speaker. Father was not concerned. He continued the sermon he had begun and crafted his speech so well that all were satisfied, and finally his speech produced praise from all.

In such hostile situations and on such unfavorable topics, whom was he following? What sacred pulpits, what crowds of priests and faithful had to elicit such a result? Truly he excelled in conducting the Spiritual Exercises of our Holy Father, St. Ignatius. Almost every Jesuit who heard him expound the Exercises thought that he was indeed fortunate. He was so clear in proposing the "points" for meditation, so passionate in impressing those who heard him regarding practical results from the retreat, so versatile in his knowledge of the Jesuit *Institute* and in examples of major issues! He received no lesser results when he gave the Exercises to other clergy and laypeople and similar praise came from them. Especially brilliant were his treatment of The First Principle and Foundation [*De Fine Hominis*], The Two Standards, and The Last Judgment.

But he confirmed his public speech by the example of his private life. His piety was very tender, and he was accustomed to ask God most sincerely for the grace of perseverance. By the manner in which he preached on compunction of heart and fear of the Lord he proclaimed what he deeply felt: outstanding devotion to the Holy Spirit, and charity toward the souls of the deceased, and he bound himself by what is called 'the Heroic Act'.

Towards the end of his life, though not advanced in years, as though warned of his closeness to eternity, he gradually fled concourse with others, insofar as he could. He did not leave the house unless he was forced by some necessity; he abstained from reading newspapers. He stayed in the sacred tribunal [confessional] for hours; and, although he was hard pressed by crowds of penitents during the Jubilee, and was bothered for a long time with a throat ailment, outwardly he showed a more than usual cheerfulness.[10]

On December 11, 1858, he had spent five or six hours in the church hearing confessions. At 7:30 P.M. he went to the dining room and while he was eating, his arms became distended, and he said distinctly to the Father sitting beside him, "I'm finished" [*Actum est de me*]. He said nothing more but fell into the hands of the Father seated beside him, and then he fell to the floor in an attack of apoplexy. He was brought to his room, given absolution and extreme unction, as well as the help offered through ritual prayers. Meanwhile, three physicians had been called, and after they consulted about his case, they did blood letting from a vein. But he did not recover consciousness.

The next day, a Sunday, people heard the sad news with great sorrow. Soon parishioners of high and low estate, and Father's friends, crowded the residence. That whole day into late at night near his corpse there was a combination of tears and prayers.

Fr. Superior decided on a delay of the funeral because of the strong urging of outstanding people that his funeral should be as solemn as can be allowed. His body, clad in priestly vestments, was laid in state in the church. His face seemed like one who was still breathing, and gave off a bright hue of his pure soul, and reflected the wonderful kindness of his heart, and unique reverence.

Later a large number of clerics and outstanding laypeople accompanied the funeral when he was buried in the Fordham College cemetery. There on separate days a solemn funeral ceremony was held for him, first in the seminary, and then in the college. Everybody praised him [*Defuncti laus in omnium ore erat*]."

CHAPTER 8

## THE EARLY YEARS: ST. FRANCIS XAVIER COLLEGE AND PARISH

For these early years, no Fr.Minister's diary has been found, such as the one for St. John's College that we saw in Part I. But there does exist a document entitled *A History of the House* [*Historia Domus*].[11] The following selection from it gives us a useful framework for events to be described at greater length in Chapter 9.

### 1847-1848

After our Fathers had taken over St. John's College, which is situated in the village of Fordham near New York, in response to his invitation, the bishop made known his wish that they also take care of a parish in the city. That could not be done at the time they first came to the college. However, our Fathers were later allowed to buy a former Protestant church on Elizabeth Street. It could easily accommodate nearly 350 people [the *History* says 3,500, but probably the author meant 350] for divine services.

A contract to purchase the church was drawn up in the beginning of July but it included immediate payment of 3,000 scudi [$5,000]. Fr. Larkin had been sent with 5 cents to the City to get a church and a school. But with the help of Divine providence, a friend loaned the money in a way that was advantageous to him and to us. The church was solemnly dedicated by Bishop McCloskey within the year . . .

With the approval of the Mission Superior, Rev. Fr. Boulanger, and once the lower floor was made sufficiently suitable to conduct classes and serve students, the new college in New York was opened on September 8, 1847 with 60 students. That number kept increasing, so that we expected that we would have 130 students in the following year. The students were divided according to age into four classes. In the two higher classes the rudiments of Latin, in the lower classes elementary English were taught. The teachers were Fr. Lebreton, who was also Minister, Brothers Nash, Baxter, and a young layman named O'Reilly. Fathers Petit, DeLuynes and Verheyden worked in the various church ministries.

With the help of God, everything was going well and we were happy. But then on Saturday, Jan. 22, 1848, the feast of the Holy Name, it all came to an end. Consumed in a fierce fire, the church was leveled to the ground in barely an hour. This seemed to be the cause of the fire: under the church there was a furnace which had some defects that resulted in spreading flames on every side. A workman's carelessness perhaps caused a certain part to break and thereby the flue for the release of hot air did not function. The fire raged on and on. All the wood in the structure was ablaze and there was no chance of preventing the fire from ruining the whole building.

In the fire almost all the sacred vestments and things needed for the church went up in flames. However, there was time to get from the flames the chairs, boards and many other things that are needed in schools. Those items were brought to the church of St. James and placed in the undercroft of the church. And there, with the consent of the pastor, classes were continued without any interruption, but not without a loss of some students. In the meantime, our Fathers fulfilled their sacred functions regularly at the church of St. Vincent de Paul, a church for the French living in New York.

The Fathers desired to rebuild the church without delay. But Fr. Larkin thought that the place where we were was not suitable for building our church both because the place was not good for a school and because of the impossibility of obtaining a structure that would be adequate for both our church and our school. He judged it would be opportune to sell our property and build our college and church elsewhere in a suitable place. Fortunately indeed it happened that before the fire we were insured against it. So after the fire we received 10,000 scudi ($16,700). The Insurance Company offered a suggestion: that we sell the property for 9,500 scudi ($15,865). Besides, right after the fire, with the permission of the bishop, collections were taken up in numerous churches for the building of a new church. In addition, private citizens were asked for gifts that could be given over a fixed time schedule. Hence, after selling other goods and reducing expenses, to replace the church ornaments that were burned, about 1,600 scudi ($2,670) were left.

We rented a house in a better part of the city, at 77 Third Ave., for 700 scudi ($1,170) a year. We occupied it in the beginning of May and taught school there. But the small size of the place and its inconvenient location forced our Fathers who had been serving in the church to perform their various sacred ministries with pastors living in the city. Yet the teachers continued to teach, each one in his own room. One can image how hard this must have been for them.

1848-1849

Fr. Larkin was the Superior. The teachers were Fathers Ouellet and Lebreton, and Brothers Nash and Baxter, and a young layman named Warner. Brothers were Garvey and Coté. This year nothing memorable happened except the death of Fr. Lebreton who died peacefully [*patienti animo*] after many months of great pain. Fortified with the sacraments, he slept in the Lord on Oct. 10. Br. Bidwell, a scholastic novice, took his place in the classroom.

On Oct. 1 Fr. Jouin, fleeing from the Italian persecution, stayed in our house for help in learning the English language.

After Fr. Larkin had obtained permission, even enthusiastic approval, from the archbishop, he planned to lay the foundations of the [new] college this year. Property had almost been purchased when a papal bull was sent to Fr. Larkin announcing that he would be made bishop of Toronto. He replied to the Pope and asked that he be freed from facing such a great burden. While we awaited the outcome of the appointment, the work of building the college seemed to be put off to another time.

1849-1850

The Superior was Fr. Larkin; the teachers Fathers Bienvenu and Jouin, Brothers Nash, Gardiner and Baxter, and the same young layman mentioned above; and the Coadjutor Brothers Garvey and Coté.

This year the school began with 80 students. There were four classes in which the Latin language was taught. This year instruction in the rudiments of German was also provided.

After two months into the new year Fr. Larkin was sent to France where he made his third year of probation [Tertianship] which seemed to have been made with the special help of Divine Providence. For shortly after he set out a letter arrived from the Pope appointing him to the see of Toronto. Later it developed that Fr. Larkin, through Fr. General's intercession with the Holy Father, was freed from the episcopacy.

Fr. Ryan was appointed in place of Fr. Larkin on Oct. 25.

In the beginning of February, 1849 we bought eleven parcels (lots) of land in a better part of the city. In the shape of a parallelogram, each lot extends 25 feet on the street and 120 in depth. The result is that the surface on each side should be designated as part of the church.

The title of the vendor to ownership of the property was discovered to be unsettled because it was before the courts. So we withdrew from the contract. But then, through our agents, Terence Donnelly and D. Glover, a lawyer, under maximum secrecy, we bought for 36,000 scudi ($60,000), 10 other parcels, the land where the college and church now stand between 15th and 16th Streets going north, and between Fifth and Sixth Avenues going west.

Lest there be any block to the difficult transaction, on April 5th, Mr. T. Donnelly completed the business in his own name. He then transferred the entire property to us. When it became known that the property belonged to the Jesuits and that they were going to build a college and church on it, the neighbors did their utmost to prevent us from taking possession of the land and would gladly have paid us a higher price if we had been willing to sell to them. They made their offer, but in vain.

When the plans for the college had been drawn and a place reserved for a domestic chapel, which had to be rather large, since the Bishop made it clear that he did not wish us to have a church which was not a parish church, Father Ryan went to the Bishop to ask him to allow the public to attend the services in our chapel. The Bishop gave permission and added that he wanted us to have a church but only on this condition that the church be a parish church. Hence an agreement was made between the Bishop and Father Boulanger that we would build the church but turn over the deed of ownership to the Bishop. In the meantime, until the debt which we have contracted for both the church and the college has been paid off, we will receive the entire income from the church. Furthermore, by written agreement, the Superior of the Mission will name the parish clergy, always assigning two to care for the parish. They will receive a stipend of 1,000 scudi ($1,670) and the right to the additional income commonly referred to as the pastor's stole fees.

In order to hasten the construction of the church the Bishop gave permission for two of our Fathers to collect money in the city. With great effort they collected 7,000 scudi ($11,700). One of the two, namely Father Driscol, deserves special mention.

In addition, two Fathers, Father De Luynes and Father Maldonado, were sent to Central America to raise money, and, in the course of a year, collected 15,000 scudi ($25,000).

On July 12, excavation for the foundations of the new college were begun and toward the end of October the roof of the college was in place.

On the Saturday within the Octave of Easter Father Kohler arrived from Canada and took up residence with us.

### 1850-1851.

Father Ryan was Rector from February 3, Father Jouin, Minister and teacher. Other teachers were Fr. Bienvenu, Fr. Kohler, Brs. Baxter, Gardiner, Nash, and one young lay teacher, Mr. Warner. Fr Driscol worked in the parish. Coadjutor Brothers were Garvey, Chouvey, Raguet, Pilz, and Welsh (who taught in the elementary school).

This year we began our school in the same building as last year, since the college was not yet completed. The number of boys attending was 90. The highest class in grammar was added this year. In addition we began a course which is called the commercial course.

On the September 24th the Bishop laid the cornerstone of the church with great solemnity.

On November 25 we entered the new college. Not all the boys who began to attend our school this year followed us into the college since some of the parents thought that the college was too far away from their homes. For this reason the college began with about 80 boys but their number increased day by day until near the end of the year the number of our students reached almost 120.

One thing for which we should thank God is that, although the walls of the college, which had been just roofed over, had not yet dried out, and our furnace in its still unfinished state could give no heat, thus making it necessary for a number of Ours to live in cold and damp rooms, not one of the community fell ill.

Before the church was finished, the college auditorium was used as a public chapel and the Fathers even heard confessions there. However they had not yet been given the care of the parish. That was given only after the Friday within the third week of Lent when, upon the completion of the church crypt, all the parish ministries, could be carried on there.

On July 6, 1851 the Archbishop dedicated the church to divine worship under the invocation of St. Francis Xavier.

### 1851-1852

Fr. Ryan was Rector, Fr. Du Ranquet, Minister and Prefect of Students. Teachers were Fathers Kohler, Jouin, Regnier, Thiry, Brothers Doucet, Nash, Gardiner, Sherlock and a young layman named Moyt and Coadjutor Brother Welsh. Other Brothers were Joset, Chouvy, Vachon, Raguet, Pilz, and Garvey.

School began with 120 boys. In the past year the class of Humanities (*Humaniarum litterarum*) has been added to our classes.

A few days after he had made his annual Spiritual Exercises, Br. Joset suddenly became sick and slept in the Lord, well fortified with the Sacraments. His body was brought to the village of Fordham and buried there.

In February we bought another piece of property [a lot] adjacent to the college at a cost of 3,500 scudi ($5,850).

Fr. Ryan made arrangements for the Religious of the Sacred Heart of Jesus to teach the girls of our parish. They opened school in the crypt of the church on March 18 and plan to build a house in the parish limits where they can also house their school. Also they teach Christian doctrine on Sundays to the other girls who cannot go to school. Furthermore in the evening they also teach Christian doctrine to the girls who attend Protestant [public] schools so that Catholic girls may be brought back from the impieties of those institutions.

In addition, the Brothers of Christian Doctrine (*Frères de la Doctrine Chrètienne*) undertook a similar care for the boys in our parish. Fr. Ryan bought a piece of property for 3,500 scudi ($5,850) to build a parochial school there. Finally, a house was rented for 500 scudi ($835) where the brothers began to teach on May 17. Attendance at their school this year was 250 boys.

Fr. Tellier came from Canada at the end of February and on March 15th he was appointed to replace Fr. Du Ranquet as prefect of studies. On May 7 Fr. Du Ranquet set out for Montreal in Canada, and from the same city Fr. Férard was sent to our college, as Minister of the house in place of Fr. Du Ranquet.

On June 4 Fr. Ryan also went to Montreal to make his Tertianship. Fr. Tellier was acting rector in Fr. Ryan's place and Fr. Driscol was acting procurator.

Departures this year from our community and from the Society were Br. Welsh who died and Br. Shea, a scholastic who was sent from Fordham to our college to help us as a teacher.

An outstanding picture of St. Francis Xavier, patron of our church, was sent us from Rome; the saint is depicted being borne to heaven by angels. Very Rev. Fr. General offered us the picture, which was painted by Br. Augelligri.

During the vacation in August, Fr. Ryan returned to us after he had made his last vows in Montreal on July 31, the feast of St. Ignatius.

# CHAPTER 9

## ANNUAL LETTERS TO ROME OF THE XAVIER COLLEGE AND PARISH

The beginnings of the College and parish of St. Francis Xavier were not easy. It was tried by fire (the loss of the church which also housed the school's classrooms), by flight (charismatic Fr. Larkin rushing to Europe to avoid a higher appointment) and by death (39 year-old Fr. Lebreton, the Fr. Minister and teacher). Furthermore, public perceptions of the school for some time were unfavorable when it was compared to successful public schools. "Compared to those fine [public] schools," Letter V below summarizes its early public image: "the College of St. Francis Xavier is: first, a late-comer; second, it's very poor; and third, its building looks more like some rundown factory than a school. How could it ever be a fit venue for the academic fray and students' hoped for prosperity? Further, its teachers come and go; some of them don't speak good English. People generally think that Xavier takes in only mediocre students, not the elegant or urbane. Rough-spoken to boot. So they'd hesitate to send any high-quality Catholic student here and suspect that those who do have more virtue than money."

Virtue is indeed central to all these Letters. They are filled with edifying stories about last minute conversions, huge numbers of confessions and communions, reconciliation with the Church, special care for prisoners and down-and-outers, the practice of the faith in the face of persecution and the general disdain from others. Often this virtue has a pugnacious edge to it, to make "the power of the true Catholic religion" known and accepted by Masons, Protestants and anyone else. Apparently the latter were no slouches either — pressuring Irish Catholic maids and young Catholic workers in factories, blocking access to Catholic ministry among prisoners and public orphans and other hostile actions that expressed their hostility to the Catholic faith..

Toward the end of the Civil War, the Xavier Jesuits launched a ministry to 'Africans'. One letter notes, as Fr. John O'Malley pointed out in the Prologue, that, though liberated by the war, "the liberators avoid the liberated like they'd avoid the plague."

### I. 1847-1848

*[This first Letter is actually from the Fordham Jesuit Community, explaining why, in that first year of its existence, Xavier could not report on time.]*

We will now take over the responsibility that would have ordinarily been incumbent on our brothers in New York City, i.e., providing an account of the opening of their College, its progress, and the events of the past year. They themselves, it would seem, no longer have much left to write about, since their church has been destroyed by fire, the Jesuit community in the city has been dispersed, and their fellow workers and the youngsters in their schools have also been scattered. So there is nothing much of consequence left for them to write about. A few items of lesser importance nonetheless remain which we would like to include in our letter.

Last year's Annual Letter gave an account of the circumstances which led to our decision to open [a new] college. We should now let you know how that decision was implemented. After our very successful work in the city on the occasion of the diocesan Jubilee, we asked for a church and a place in which we could establish our community. Upon receiving our request, the Bishop Hughes promptly offered us the Church of St. Andrew which he had earlier desired to give us. That church however was heavily burdened with debt and, because of its location, it was not highly esteemed in the city. A church which had formerly belonged to the Presbyterians and, before that, had been owned by the Universalists, seemed to be preferable on the basis of both its cost and its location. Furthermore, the Reverend Coadjutor Bishop [John McCloskey, the first president of St. John's College and future first Cardinal Archbishop of New York] proposed that we buy it.

The structure *[at Elizabeth and Walker Streets]* was purchased in the month of May, 1847, and remodeled so that it could serve as a Catholic church. Four school-rooms were made ready underneath the church so as to accommodate 200 pupils. After the solemn blessing of what was now a Catholic church at the beginning of September, the college was opened.

There were five Priests, three Scholastics, and one Brother in the Jesuit community. *[The 1848 province Catalogue, the first time the Community was named, listed the members as follows. The priests were: Rev. John Larkin, the founding Rector, Rev. Peter Lebreton (who died on 10/10, 1848), Rev. Charles deLuynes, Rev. Nicholas Petit, Rev. Peter Verheyden, and Rev. Tiberius Soderini. Scholastics were Michael Nash and Richard Baxter. The Brother was John Roy. However, earlier, in 1847, there had been another scholastic and one other priest.]*

Three classes of the lower school were begun. After a little while, however, one of the Fathers was obliged to give up teaching for reasons of health and a novice was assigned to take his place. 115 pupils were registered in the school, 20 of them were under the age of nine, six under the age of 12, and the rest were under the age of 15. Although they were fairly unruly at the start, their behavior gradually improved. Ultimately, after they had been given a retreat, they began to show some signs of piety — a source of consolation to both their teachers and their parents.

The Sodality of Our Lady was established in the school on the Feast of the Purification, but, the loss of the church by fire has left the Sodality with neither a place in which to meet nor the means which are required for it to carry on its activity.

In the evening before the third Sunday after the Epiphany [Jan. 22, 1848], as our Fathers were hearing Confessions, an extraordinary degree of heat was felt in the church. Flames from the furnace, after first consuming the schoolroom desks, set fire to the classroom walls from floor to ceiling. Finally, when there was no hope left of putting out the fire, nothing remained for us to do beyond saving what we could from the burning building. It took the whole night to bring the fire under control and keep it from spreading beyond the church. This disaster aroused universal sympathy for us from the spectators, and, with one exception, the daily papers were unanimous in expressing their regret. Indeed, it did not pass without comment in the city that a neighborhood business establishment, whose workers were seen dancing with joy during the fire, was itself destroyed by fire before the week was over. Certainly, before it was destroyed, the church had begun to be visited frequently by the faithful.

The city's Catholics were drawn to our church by the dignity in which its liturgy was conducted,the attractive decoration of the church, the excellence of its liturgical music, and the high reputation enjoyed by its preachers. From the Sunday after the blessing of the church, professions of faith began to be made by new converts, hardly a week going by without one or more Protestant coming over to the Catholic Church.

## II. Oct. 1,1850 to Oct. 1,1851

In the new house our community consisted of 5 priests, 3 scholastics, and 4 Brothers.

At the end of November of 1850, we were fortunate to move from our old house [at 77 Third Avenue] to a much newer one [on 15th Street]. Yet, in the new residence, we first had to cope with a nasty, miserable batch of health problems. It was to be expected that filling our lungs with the very damp air in our new quarters would be a problem. Yet, with God's help, we came through it all safe and sound.

Now, one of the Fathers who are engaged in neighborhood pastoral ministry received a sick call, but happened to find out the man was a Mason. So he thought that the first thing to do was to help the man to part company with that evil society. Having finally achieved this, he did not hesitate to refresh the dying man with the Sacraments. A few days later our friend died. In a spirit of revenge, some Masons concocted a plot to press the involved Jesuit either to provide the deceased with solemn funeral services, which would certainly cause great scandal, or, if he refused, to face a multiple false charge of sinning against freedom and charity itself.

They were just about to spring the trap on our Father when a devout physician, a known friend of our cause, heard about the foul plot. He immediately approached the priest and said to him, "Let's go! I want you to come with me right away to bring our professional help to a woman who's desperately sick." The priest gets up and hurries to the street with the doctor. When they both had gone a considerable way, the doctor said, "No further need for hurrying or for going farther. I'm sure you are safely away from the schemers." He then opens up and tells the whole story. Both share a good laugh and felicitate each other, with the priest naturally protesting the doctor's friendly deception. But on the other hand, who was going to feel shame or disgust over the aborted plot? Was it our Masons, flattering themselves over an injustice that cries for redress? Not unless they have managed to bring shame and embarrassment down on their own heads.

Now what will I say about our tiny band of confessors, so few they can scarcely satisfy half of their penitents? Truly, this situation never before caused such a pious, yet painful demand for our men as it did during the recent Jubilee celebration. Honestly, you would have seen a mixed crowd, jammed tight and deep, practically besieging our Father confessors. Some of these people actually waited without food all day long. Some attempted to force their way to the confessionals. Some even were desperate enough to link arms or they would break through the tribunal itself! Some were heard to say, "I've been waiting from early morning to evening;" and another in reply, "And I through the whole night as well." But meanwhile what about our own men? Truly, from weariness, sleep privation and hunger, they were almost lifeless.

Then, too, despite their smaller number, we must mention the assorted activities of our "off-the-chart apostles" [*quasi supra modum apostoli*]. For example, they teach Christian doctrine to the boys, provide the widest possible circulation of good books, and guide adults who have not yet been renewed in Holy Eucharist, some toward confession and then to the Eucharistic table.

We are heavily involved in the care of prisoners. This is all the more edifying for the fact that this is an unattractive ministry, hardly of pastoral interest to minor Protestant clergy. For instance, our men won considerable esteem when their devoted help at long last bore good fruit with an unfortunate sailor. Condemned to death by hanging, he was racked with despair. Then we wrapped him in such fatherly care that we won him for God. Now people see him, spirit serene, features composed, not at all terrified of death itself. In fact, he congratulates himself that he is able to make the expected journey, safe and sure, toward repentance and supreme happiness.

In these particular prisons many are held for drunkenness. Wine-besotted, prostrate in the streets, completely out of their wits, they are locked up by order of the judge. Who would piously and mercifully work with and welcome these wretches, so disgusting to all, other than a Catholic priest? Their conversion is very difficult, but not entirely impossible.

Let's take for example a certain Irishman who inflicted every kind of cruelty on his wife. He was brought to one of our Fathers, and after he went to confession, he seemed to be changed into a new man. However, when he returned home, wine overpowered the sacrament and again the sacrament overcame the wine. But finally he prevailed and joined the Temperance Society, and so the man who had been a scandal to everyone, in the end became a source of edification to all.

There are a good many Catholic maids who work for Protestants who try in every possible way to corrupt them and turn against their faith. Very, very few of them are known to have allowed themselves to be thus overwhelmed. In fact, very many of them are so firm in the faith that they would rather be thrown out of the house than desert the sacraments. Likewise, some of these women eat nothing but bread on Friday and Saturday to avoid eating forbidden foods. Hence, at times their employers give them off on these days to let them be free for their pious practices.

You'll also find Protestants who contribute money to help build a Catholic church, on the ground that otherwise there won't be enough loyal Catholic maids for them. And it sometimes happens that maids win over their employers to God. I would call these women "Imitators of the Apostles." One of them was plagued by an unusual and very pious scruple because she baptized the six infants of a certain Protestant when they were close to death. She felt that she had assumed and, as it were, usurped a ministerial role that belonged to a priest.

Finally, I cannot fail to say a very few words about the college students. Skipping other issues since almost everything here is in line with the practice of the Society, I shall conclude this annual report with one incident. A poor man used to beg on the streets. He was afflicted with smallpox. Everyone who crossed his path would avoid him so they would not catch this terrible disease. One of our students had, like everyone else, walked rapidly past the poor man. But he soon had a change of heart and, moved by pity, returned to that man, chiding his own pitiless heart as follows: "What's this, why won't I give the poor man a coin? Why not offer him a word of consolation? Well, even if he does infect me, I shall approach him and wash and console him." After he had done this, on the same day he did indeed catch the same disease. But after a while he was healed and got better. Doesn't one who marches into virtue with such a stride lead us to expect that he will make great spiritual progress?

III. Oct. 1, 1852 to Oct. 1, 1853

1. The number of our men: At the start of the year, the total number in our community was 20, of whom 11 were priests, 3 were Scholastics, 6 were Brothers. Of these, during the past year one priest made final Jesuit vows, and another Scholastic unhappily returned to the world. [The Vice-Rector, from Nov. 1, 1849 to Sept. 1, 1855, was the Rev. John Ryan.]

2. Spiritual progress: Thanks to the kindness of the good God, and under the care of Superiors, this year there appears to have been better observance of the rules and progress in fervor and mutual charity.

3. Ministries: Besides the usual ministries, the principal growth is due to our founding or strengthening new classes and Sodalities.

First, we note a challenging object of our prayer, namely, to establish a class for small boys to be taught by the Brothers who claim the venerable De Laval as the founder of their Institute. But this effort met a powerful obstacle in the lack of available money. Yet the enormous charity of many has so met the huge expense that one can truly appropriate the brilliant phrase of the Apostle, "Having nothing, but possessing everything." To attain this goal, there was much buying and selling, many musical concerts and symphonies, financial drives everywhere, and donors' public listing except for those whose modesty and humility had them make gifts anonymously. Thus, for example, when a certain workman of slight means gave about thirty francs, one of our men asked him, "My friend, what is your name so that I may put it on our list?" The response, "It does not matter, God knows it and that's enough for me."

You may infer how much spiritual benefit these boys in the school are deriving from us. Formerly, they had been either left to themselves and thus became generally lazy and prone to evil habits, or their education has been entrusted to Protestant teachers. Almost as soon as they were put in the care of their new teachers, they were changed into new people. In the eyes of all, they demonstrated the power of the true Catholic religion to reform morals.

Whatever has been said of the boys should also be said of the girls whose education has been admirably undertaken by the Religious of the Sacred Heart, either gratuitously or through charges which are merely enough to meet expenses.

So that I may recount something edifying, I will narrate one or two conversions. A certain girl, educated by the nuns whom I have mentioned, had been born to Protestants but soon found the Truth and was moved to embrace Catholic values. She wanted to abjure her former creed immediately. Thus, in fulfillment of her vow, during the solemn Mass in the presence of many witnesses including her father, a man noteworthy among Protestants both for knowledge and honors, she manifested such peace of soul and she spoke so strongly in professing the Articles of Faith that, after the ceremonies, her father had to exclaim: "As I see it, only the Catholics make the administration of the sacraments both noble and worthy of veneration."

Hardly a year later, the same priest who had received the devout girl's abjuration of heresy, was called to her sickbed. Just as she had always maintained her Catholic faith, even though her parents were not Catholic, so too with bravery and steadfastness she bore the pains of her sickness, in spite of everyone's despair of her life. When she recognized her confessor at his approach, "Father," she said, "the Lord is kind enough to call me to heaven, through his great mercy and the accumulation of his many gifts, even though I am unworthy. Would this world still have delights for me? So, not unwillingly, but rather joyfully and happily I will say farewell to this world." Soon, strengthened by the sacraments, she peacefully fell asleep in the Lord. A Protestant woman present, marveling at the girl's peacefulness and ready departure from life, said, "If this is the way Catholics die, then I wish to become a Catholic so that I may die as a Catholic."

I will make almost the same statement about a young man, formerly of our college, who died prematurely when he was hardly seventeen. Since he knew in his heart that he was closer to death than to life, his first request was that the Catholic priest he brought to him whom he had known to be residing in our college. But when the lad's parents caused delays due to their anxiety lest the presence of a priest induce excessive fear, the young man insisted and finally succeeded. When our priest stood there, the lad was so far from fear that he derived deep consolation. But due to the lack of time, the young man immediately made his confession and was strengthened by the last sacraments. So great was the youth's devotion that, though his grandmother had always been a Protestant, she spontaneously knelt beside the deathbed, prayed according to the Catholic rite, and seemed to adore the Blessed Sacrament. God brought it about that the dead youth converted the living.

IV. Oct. 1, 1857 to Oct. 1, 1858

The total number of our community this year was 23, of whom 10 were priests, 4 scholastics, and 9 Brothers.

It is seven years since the New York Jesuits started a double apostolate, the College of St. Francis Xavier and the parish of the same name. Up to now they have written often about the school, but practically never about the parish. At last they have written fully and informatively about the parish.

The parish is one of twenty parishes in the city, centrally located, and boasts that there are more than 10,000 Catholics within its boundaries. The church and the college were built and opened at the beginning of 1850.[12] The church is 100 feet long and 80 feet wide, with a basement which is almost the same size but it is too small to meet our daily increasing needs.

That there is such impiety and immorality is no surprise in such a city with such a trading center and such an enormous port like this. Who wouldn't be surprised that in the same city there coexists a small space, which glows with fervor and genuine lively faith, in our neighborhood? The proof of our success is the steady increase in good works : in our first year, 1851, our church had 18,000 Communions. The number has constantly increased to more than 50,000 this year, 1858. One third of the penitents come to our confessionals from different and even remote parishes. They come because they receive more help for their needs here than they usually get elsewhere.

This year four members of the Xavier community are the principal workers in the parish. There are five Masses each Sunday, two include sermons. There are so many people for each of the Masses that often some have to be turned away. The same holds true in the basement of the church at the nine o'clock children's Mass which includes beautiful congregational singing. More than one thousand children return in the afternoon for religious instruction. They are divided into two groups, those preparing for first communion, and those who have already received. [13]

Later in the day there are Solemn Vespers with Benediction of the Most Blessed Sacrament. It's then we bemoan the lack of space in our church. If it were two or three times larger it would scarcely hold the eager crowd. Many non-Catholics are attracted by the music of our excellent choir, and the expert organist who leads them. The rest of Sunday is taken up with parish organizations.

There are five or six flourishing organizations. There is a "Living Rosary" of about a thousand members, divided into the customary groups. [14] There is a Marian Sodality now of about 200 single men, most of whom are young. There is another group starting up composed of young people learning their catechism. For assisting those in need, we have the Vincentian society, and a similar one for women called the *Benevolent Society*. Both groups are very helpful in assisting the continuous flow of poor immigrants who come here from all of Europe to these parts.

There is, besides, a special work here of reconciling Protestants. It is growing slowly, but definitely. Over the past three years the numbers who have given up their errors have increased from 29 to 36 to 49. Each month, on different Sundays the members of the Marian Sodalities and the Living Rosary receive communion as a group, a wonderful example to everyone. These groups gather together to recite the whole rosary after Vespers each Sunday, and once a month the Father moderator gives an appropriate talk.

The power of divine grace shone beyond measure during the Jubilee last year. It lasted for the month of December. At that time over eighty thousand confessions were heard in the church of St. Francis Xavier. For the first three weeks at least six priests were hearing confessions, and sometimes twelve. They usually stayed in the confessional until 11:00 PM. On occasion crowds of more than 100 had to be turned away until the next day. Many had to return three or four times in vain. They assemble here from all parts of the city. They come, moved by some inexplicable impulse, the prodigals and the suffering , with souls burdened with every type internal misery; they undergo joyfully the burden of difficult confessions. They saw clearly the finger of

God, in the single voice of His vicar opening to them and pouring forth the mercies of heaven.

In the midst of this work, the very much loved ("*desideratissimus*") Father John Larkin fell a victim of his zeal (see the profile of his life, from the *Annual Letters* in Chapter 7, above). His death deprived the city of a very strong and important worker, Everyone thinks that he will help all of us as powerful patron in heaven.

There are few cities like this under the sun, hence apostolic zeal is expressed in strange ways and circumstances. Since most of the Catholic inhabitants are people who were driven from Europe by need or ambition, they usually do not stay here very long before better opportunities drive them once more further into the rest of the States. Hence for many years we have bid farewell to people we have cared for or reconciled to God. Likewise, we receive and help many so that there is no respite from general confessions and preparing adults for their First Communion. This year, 1858, we have prepared more than 200, about half from either sex. We are helped in a wonderful way by the zeal of the faithful, especially by Catholic housemaids, particularly those from Ireland.

### The Irish Housemaids

A great number of these Irish heroines have crossed the ocean for no other reason than to gather some small income in service of American families, among Protestants, so that they can send it all back to their poor old parents. In a foreign land, hostile to their faith they will suffer and do anything rather than offend in any way their faith or neglect their spiritual life. You see worthy models of the early Christians, very often bereft of human help or companionship, in the midst of mockery and temptation, being lorded over, reproached and raged at by their masters, you see them after they have undergone these cruel experiences, but they remained utterly faithful to every religious duty.

During Easter, or other times of the year when it is time to go to confession, they don't hesitate to leave a wealthy family, putting in peril where and how they will live in the coming months. Thus when they can enjoy Sunday or even daily Mass they curtail the already brief time allotted them for sleep. They shine like lamps in this heretical world with the brightest piety, Christian modesty, and the rest of the virtues. Hence though some face insults, remarkably very many don't, and moreover they are sought out as servants. When many Protestant women move outside the city, they make the offer to cover the expenses of their Catholic employees and grant money and effort to build Catholic churches in their neighborhood. It is no surprise that some of these upper-class women who have seen the quality of their employees' lives have embraced the Truth. We have heard an American woman saying that her eyes had been opened by the moving spectacle of a maid, newly arrived from Ireland, throughout all of Lent refusing to break her fast until noon, not taking even a few drops of coffee although she was working very hard.

### A Medical Student

There are other noble examples of this strong faith from other walks of life. A young medical student, who had been educated in a Jesuit college, was attending one of the premier institutions of our city, where all of the professors and all the students, except himself, were Protestants. By chance he heard a professor speaking from his rostrum somewhat disrespectfully of the Most Holy Virgin. He kept his pain to himself at the time. Later when he was alone, he wrote a letter to the professor, reproving him because he had publicly with no justification mixed religion with an issue that was a medical issue only. He was in the audience and was personally attacked when he impuned the honor of the Immaculate Virgin. And finally, demanding by right (*pro jure expostulans*) that in the next public lecture he make up for the public affront by a public apology. Next day, to the stupefaction of his audience, the professor stopped suddenly in the middle of his lecture, read in a loud voice the letter which he had received from his Catholic student, and said that he deeply regretted that he had verbally attacked the religious faith of one of his students and promised in the future not to give a basis for anyone to make such a demand.

Piety moves all of the faithful of the parish, when it comes to works of mercy or religion. Eight times last year money was collected in our church for the sake of works other parishes; more than 20,000 francs were collected, this was above and beyond the ordinary Sunday offering. Two years ago there was an outstanding effort of Catholic women to expand the hospital [St. Vincent's]. They held a sale at the Crystal Palace. There were twenty tables, one from each parish in the city. The income after two weeks was 180,000 francs. One fifth of that was from our parish table.

### V. Oct. 1, 1858 to Oct. 1, 1859

The total number of our community this year was 27, of whom 13 were priests, 5 Scholastics, and 9 Brothers. The rector, from Sept. 1, 1855 to Aug. 15, 1860, was the Rev. Michael Driscol.

The Fathers and Scholastics taught the following subjects: philosophy, mathematics, rhetoric, humanities and grammar; English; French. Business arithmetic was made available for those who wished it outside the regular curriculum. Four priests did pastoral work in the parish; other priests preached and heard confessions when teaching duties allowed them the time; likewise the scholastics taught catechism, gave homilies to youths, and moderated Sodalities. Our men were moderators of seven different Sodality groups in the school and parish.

As a general statement, most would say that the fruit of our good works was more manifest than usual, thanks especially to the seven Sodalities.

Our responsibilities are basically three: a college, a parish, and a variety of other ministries in the neighborhood.

The sudden death of Fr. John Larkin in December of 1858, taken from us in the midst of his work on the Jubilee, was a big blow not only to this community but to the whole Mission. It was mentioned in the recent letter describing the Jubilee. His praise will be sung in the proper place.

*Challenges the College Faces*

There are many reasons why our college, the only one like it for Catholics in a city this large, has made less progress than we had hoped both in winning the citizenry over and in getting students. Now that some of those basic reasons have gone away, we are can finally set our hopes higher.

In this country, every state [*civitas*] looks on the education of children as its responsibility. Teachers chosen by public officials and honored with rich rewards accept the responsibility of imparting, free of charge, every kind of learning to any boy [*puero*]. Universities, academies, colleges and high schools are well endowed with public money. They make available not only instruction but provide each student with classical texts, maps and whatever other supplies are needed, all at public expense. To head off fights and protests, the law does not allow any religious instruction. It boasts (believe it if you like) that it doesn't favor any sect. As things now stand, since a real liberal arts kind of education is not allowed there, and since over the years they have attained a certain good reputation, even well-off and well-esteemed citizens don't hesitate to send their children to them. Some Catholics surely in good faith also don't hesitate to do the same; they are taken in by the example of others or are confused and trying to save a little money. But the unfortunate youths pay a high price for such training in the liberal arts. Their childrens' young minds soon forget or grow to disdain and almost always neglect Catholic teachings.

Compared to those fine schools, the College of St. Francis Xavier is: first, a late-comer; second, it's very poor; and third, its building looks more like some rundown factory than a school. How could it ever be a fit venue for the academic fray and students' hoped for prosperity? Further, its teachers come and go; some of them don't speak good English. People generally think that Xavier takes in only mediocre students, not the elegant or urbane. Rough-spoken to boot. So they'd hesitate to send any high-quality Catholic student here and suspect that those who do have more virtue than money.

Yet despite all our difficulties, we have the sweetest of rewards: our faculty, each and every one, recognizes that the students we've had are worthy of their 'virtuous' parents. The students are pious and have the luster of true morality; they take direction easily; they're classy competitors; they are marvelously teachable for literature and other subjects; they're as ready to study as to play. There are 250 of them, and in their course of studies you'd never catch one of them using improper language or reading dirty books.

*The Parish*

Now let's move on to pastoral care. Given all the Catholics in our city, there are neither enough churches nor priests to go around. So our goal is to provide opportunities for as many people as possible to fulfill their Sunday obligation. Masses go on in the upper and lower church one after the other from 5:00-10:00 A.M., Mass after Mass, crowd after crowd. The children's Mass has its own time and place; often 90 of them attend. But even more than the numbers, what strikes you, if you look at them seriously, is their modest bearing — something you never see these days — a frank spirit of openness on their faces, all the more attractive because so rare. You could not but be impressed by their piety, whether they're saying the rosary or singing the litanies and hymns. After a brief sermon geared to the little ones, they're sent home. For catechism, however — which we really work on —the rest of the children go to the lower Church. Six hundred of them in two groups: one, pre-First Communion, the other, post-First Communion. Boys and girls in both. Their instruction is basically a little history in story form about the faith, a few prizes handed out, songs, etc.

In the upper Church, another seventy young people, slightly older, receive more substantial instruction. Who these lads are and how they got here is what is really interesting. Most are found on the highways and the byways by the St. Vincent de Paul Societies. Or they work in factories where they're constantly worn down by aggressive proselytizing by all sorts of ministers. In a city like this, imagine what a cesspool it's like when young poverty-stricken people are corrupted by bad books and bad advice and then sucked into the churning tide of apostasy. It's young people like this whom we welcome with kind understanding, urging them to return to the faith or hold onto it as the case may be. Then, when they're strong again, we tell them to do the same favor to their co-workers or their relatives.

The young workers' Sodality has been an enormous help to us. Almost every month the Father Moderator of the Sodality invited ten or twelve neighborhood youths to return to a good life and either be introduced to the Lord's Table or return to it after long neglect. And once they're on the right path, they're so grateful they ask to join the Sodality themselves and then go out and invite others to do the same. One big responsibility toward young workers, many of whom are quite ignorant of their faith, is to prepare them for First Communion. When they were asked to help out on this, the young worker Sodalists jumped right in. With one of our Fathers as moderator, one or two evenings a week and even though they're already exhausted from a hard day's labor, they do the tedious work of teaching the catechism and prayers, with a lot of word-for-word repetition, for an hour and a half. For girls, everything is in the successful hands of one woman volunteer.

One of our priests who visits local prisons was greatly consoled recently. An 18-year old — devoted to his poor parents, helping them with his income, a straight arrow, kept the commandments, trusted by his Protestant boss, but not afraid of making his boss angry by saying Catholic children shouldn't go to Protestant schools. He suddenly gets unlucky. He takes a week's vacation with a group of friends whose lives were much less upstanding than his. It never happened before, but he gets drunk. So the group is walking around town with him drunk. Someone in the group carelessly bumps shoulders with a passerby. An argument starts and then the fists fly; someone is stabbed to death. His pals say Roger, the 18-year old, did it. He's arrested and put in prison whence he is to be taken off and executed a year later. He couldn't remember who stabbed who in the fight because he was in such a fog.

At first he took his fate very badly and was all churned up inside. But slowly he was lifted up to a sense of God. He became a different person. He began a spiritual workout. He worked at accepting this execution. So much so that our Father thought he might be being too brutal toward himself. With all his spiritual reflection and sighings, he didn't get more than three hours sleep a night and that on a bare table. He ate only once a day, content with the bread the prison served in the evening. He'd see his relatives only three or four times a week for a very brief visit, so they wouldn't distract him from God. Instead, he welcomed anyone who could bring a little of God's light into his life. He spent whole days and much of the night at his prayers. He was so into it that no profane considerations interested him any more.

Some friends held out hope that his sentence would be reduced if he'd only appeal to people in high places. He would have none of it. He resigned himself cheerfully to God's hands, even to death. And in the meantime, if his piety was simple, so was his zeal. It moved his fellow prisoners, old cronies of Satan that they were, to confess their wickedness from the heart and become their better selves. He even won over the prison chaplains who, though most were Protestants, couldn't be more amazed at his long prayers and fasting. His truly saintly preparation for death certainly stirred up a lot of people. Our Father who was with him at the end brought a lot away from the experience. He found the young man the same in his last moments as he was in prison, disdaining all bodily considerations, all the pain. His heart was fixed solely on God's will for him and on the Passion of Christ. All the witnesses marveled how calm his face was and how peacefully he concentrated on his prayers on his way to die, and the serenity and constancy on his young face in the place of execution. Without a doubt, he found life also in death and, in the severity of human justice, he found the grace and mercy of the Supreme Judge of all of us.

## VI. Oct. 1, 1861 to Oct. 1, 1862

The total number of our Community this year was 30, of whom 16 were Priests, 4 Scholastics, and 10 Brothers.

Eleven members of the community did their duty for the students by teaching or keeping discipline or both, three by hearing confessions. The following subjects were taught by the Fathers and Brothers of the community: Latin, poetry and rhetoric, logic, metaphysics, and ethics; history, chemistry, trigonometry, analytic geometry and algebra; astronomy, physics, chemistry and natural history; geometry. A Brother taught graphic arts and calligraphy. There are four young graduate lay auxiliaries: one taught chemistry, three taught in the elementary school.

Two academies and two Sodalities of the Blessed Virgin Mary flourished.

One priest was the pastor of our parish; four assisted in this work as part of their proper assignment and almost all priests also assist; likewise, four did catechetical work, four directed Sodalities as well as the Rosary Group, Daughters of Mary, the Workers group and the Boys' group. Work with the Negroes has begun.

Two Fathers stayed permanently in nearby Blackwells Island for all kinds of parish work. Besides, specific assignments were given us in many prisons of the city and the vicinity, hospitals, parishes, schools, religious houses and conservatories.

*Good News for the College*
The college's status was improved with the additional title and rights of a univer-

sity. Many Jesuits together worked in both the college and the parish. They worked hard, heart and soul, at both projects. And it's no wonder that a great a harvest of works had been gathered through the combined efforts of so many companion-workers. For, "A brother who is helped by a brother, is like a strong city (Prov. 18, 19)." Certainly there was a union of hearts and minds. And there were times of poverty and occasions when patience needed to be exercised; these often foster fraternal charity. For while the new section of our building was being constructed, old shortages of space created a problem, finding places needed for both the Jesuits and the students. It helped in all ways, above and beyond the charity "which suffers all things," that we saw the new structure rising before us day by day; that gave us a kind of early hope and a sense of having it already.

Finally, at the end of the scholastic year, we began to enjoy the benefit of true possession [of the new building at 39 West 15th Street, later known as the Lynch Building]. Indeed, the new building is adjacent to the old one but is superior in every dimension: 120 feet long, 60 feet wide, 83 feet high from ground to roof, [all] surmounted by a 20 foot tower with a gilded cross dominating everything.

There is nothing taller in the whole city, and so from it one can have a clear view both of the whole countryside north of the city and of lands across the river. There are four floors. The community refectory and the elementary-school classrooms are on the ground floor which is two feet below ground, as is customary here. The grammar-school classrooms and the office of the prefect of discipline are on the second floor. A reception hall, high-school classrooms, a chemistry lab, and a room for teaching physics and natural history are all on the third floor. Lastly, the top floor, which has a height twice that of the others combined and a breadth coextensive with the house, contains only an auditorium which is very beautiful by reason of its size and decorations. The ceiling is remarkable for its frescoes. The huge frame of a musical instrument, decorated with large representations of David and St. Cecilia, dominates the scene.

There is surely reason why we should give great thanks to God that so necessary a building was completed in such terrible times, and that our total building cost less than expected. And we owe no less thanks that these difficult times should bring an increased rather than decreased enrollment, with day students numbering more than 300. And we owe the greatest thanks that so many ordinary people with devotion, toil, and complete obedience abounded such that we never had a more prosperous year.

And we owe no small thanks that we have gained the title and privileges of a university [granted in 1861]. A university here is more general and more adaptable than is usual elsewhere. Although it is of less honor than elsewhere, it is no less important, since it has the associated right to confer any degree, not only to our own college students but also to anyone who comes from anywhere and passes suitable examinations. And so this year we undertook to exercise this right, with the institution of a doctor of laws degree for one of our laymen studying law, two masters of arts degrees for previous graduates, and 15 baccalaureate degrees for our philosophy students.

No small help to promote solid devotion has been the junior sodality of the Queen of Angels. Many of our former philosophy students left here with a fixed determination, confirmed during three days of recollection, to join the ranks of the clergy.

Many public literary exercises were held throughout the year. But the crowning one was held at year's end in the presence of parents and priests. Students seemed to be received with sincere applause; they pleased the audience with their twin display of modesty and learning. The higher Academy ran two disputations with musical interludes. An awards ceremony, which completed the academic year, surpassed all of the above. For then for the first time we utilized the now nearly finished auditorium. Since the Archbishop was out of the country, the Vicar General presided. The older students delivered worthy speeches. Singers from the rest of the youth, finding a suitable place to use their voices and assisted by the best group of choristers, left a lasting impression of their songs and of the day with the audience. So much for the college.

### The Parish: Confessors, Prison, Aspirations

Let us look at the more weighty and so certainly more enduring things about the parish and its associate sodalities and catechism classes. We have only summarily dealt with these things before. Only a few things are reported about the stable ministries that we take care of locally. But to offer at least an overview of so many and so fruitful works, our activities beyond the college seem to be divisible in three ways according to the different types of persons ministered to. One will be of pious groups of whatever kind, the second of prisons and hospitals, the third those with Negroes.

Using the above categories, therefore, the following groups are assiduously cared for by hearing confessions and giving exhortations. First, Christian Brothers, brothers special to this region. Second, the girls' school in the parish. Third, the Sisters of the Good Shepherd and, we assume, their penitent girls. Fourth, Sisters of Charity of Mt. St. Vincent, also called Fort Hill, on the route between New York and Fordham. (These sisters are nuns in the full canonical sense and distinct from the French Sisters of Charity of St. Vincent.) Fifth, two residences of the Religious of the Sacred Heart, one in the City and the other of seventy nuns in Manhattanville; we care for both the nuns and their resident and extern students.

All our priestly ministry for prisoners or other unfortunate persons is focused specially in four places:

1. The city prison called the *Tombs* [15]

2. The *Central House Of Correction,* a place called *Sing-Sing,* where a priest works four times a year, covering the whole place by staying five or six days in succession in the several individual sections there;

3. One of the nearby islands, Randalls Island, where an orphanage has very many children; the Catholic and Protestant children are mixed together. There the zeal of one of our Fathers finally overcame hundreds of difficulties set up by a Protestant magistrate; the Father was able to make his way through them and continued his practice of going there twice each week, Thursday and Sunday. Now the institution is completely open for us and that's very advantageous to the unfortunates living there.

4. The final institution is *Blackwells Island,* like the other three places but much more desolate; two of our Fathers lived there this year and gave it their continuous care; each week in turn they come back to live for a week at the Xavier residence. Wretchedness there is seen in five places: a hospital, a morgue, a poorhouse [*ptochotrophio*], a

prison, and a house of correction. The residents number six thousand, most of whom are Catholics. This field rendered fruit a hundred-fold that first year. Almost every day six died well fortified with the sacraments. Countless individuals changed their lives for the better. More than two hundred and twenty returned to mother Church.

Our final topic concerns the many thousands of Negroes in this city, almost all of whom are members of Protestant sects; they have their own churches and clergy; the church is the social center of those sects. Of course, any Negroes who are Catholic or are becoming Catholic are admitted to our churches. But in this most free society, customs and traditions reign supreme and when they feel despised and often rejected by some, very few come to our churches. For that reason, it occurred to our men that at least their youths could be brought together separately, that as many of them as possible could be convinced to go to their very own school, and thereby be renewed in religious knowledge and sacramental practices. A scholastic assists in this work on Sundays and teaches about Christ to a crowd of those who come to the school; there is hope for commendable progress but not for penitents. However, the project still is in the growth stage [in herba].

Indeed, a volume would not be large enough to explain adequately so many great projects that are taking place every hour for the praise of the divine mercy. If they are forgotten, pious edification will be lost. These few words are written to pass on their achievements.

### A Prison Chaplain's Experiences

The Father who works in the prison or the workhouse [triremibus] was accustomed to talk individually as he went from cell to cell; after a few words of greeting, he would say the following to help open their hearts to him: "I am a Catholic priest. Are you also a Catholic?" Sometimes he heard this response: "Father, indeed I am not, but I feel that I ought to be; my mother is (or was) Catholic." During the month of July that was the way a youth about 24 years of age replied; he said he had not been baptized. The Father pursued that point: "Are you sure?" "Very sure," he replied, "My mother often said so, especially because my Protestant father, now dead, prevented my being baptized by a Catholic priest." A short time later, now very well disposed and sufficiently well instructed, the young man was just washed with the illuminating water of baptism when in tears of joy he burst out : "I beg you, Father, go to my mother (he used her true name). She doesn't care at all about religion. But with very little work you'll call her back to a better feeling for her religion if you tell her about God's mercy towards me. Furthermore, my two younger brothers and a younger sister have not yet been baptized; and my two adult sisters have been baptized by a Protestant minister. With God's help, you'll convince all of them without difficulty, to be baptized and at the same time persuade my mother to follow her religion.

And when the family got together the Father found them very well disposed, and learned that they said morning and night prayers which their mother led. In a short time, since the truth of the faith was accepted, the pious desires of the brother and the children were accomplished.

One day when our Father was at the prison an unfortunate old man is brought there; he was believed to be drunk but actually was paralyzed. Since he really didn't know English, our Father spoke to him in French. Straightway he was overcome with joy and his eyes overflowed with tears. He was from an excellent family in Normandy but was fraudulently deprived of his wealth by a stranger, and immigrated to America to avoid scandal at home. He looked on prison as a safe harbor. After 40 years absence, he returned to the sacraments.

A Protestant guard pursued a prisoner, a recent Catholic, to rejoin his sect. His very quiet response was: "I thought that I was free to follow my conscience and that here at least my soul would not be enslaved along with my body." At that response, the guard got angry and threatened to punish him. The prisoner replied again quietly: "Lucky me, if it should happen that I suffer for such a cause as this."

## VII. Oct.1,1862 to Oct.1,1863

The total number of our community this year was 32, of whom 14 were priests, 5 scholastics, and 13 Brothers.[16]

Twelve Priests and Scholastics taught subjects ranging from elementary Latin to the biennium of philosophy; a Brother taught calligraphy and writing; four were prefects of discipline; one catechized students; three taught the sacraments; four lay externs taught in the lower school.

Four did pastoral work in the parish, two in prisons, four in nearby islands. Four heard confessions or taught catechism in convents or conservatories, one took care of Negroes, two traveled on missions.

### The College

We finally achieved the long-standing desire to have a building suitable for the ever-growing number of students and to have the institution raised to the level of a university. In response to an invitation, at the beginning of September, 1862, crowds of students, their parents and relatives, participated, not only in the Mass of the Holy Spirit with its appropriate sermon, but also in the dedication of the new building [the Lynch Building]. Then, during the chanting of the Litany of Loretto, under the display of fifteen beautiful banners depicting the mysteries of the rosary, in a long procession we left the parish house and, from top to bottom, we blessed each part of the building, its halls and courts, consecrated them to the infinite God, and dedicated them under the double title of the Blessed Virgin Mary and St. Francis Xavier. Since a full description of the entire building is contained in another report, only this needs to be said, that we have obtained so much that more could hardly be desired.

As was to be expected, the number of students in the college rose to some 375. This increase was largely due to the favor the clergy of the city, many of whom graduated from either of our schools, Xavier or Fordham. At their own expense, several priests have supported our students, some two at a time, some three, some even six; some of those assisted students offer hope of augmenting the sacred militia.

Only extern students are accepted at the college, with the exception of day-scholars or semi-boarders, mostly Irish; they are not kept there more than about six hours daily, from nine in the morning till slightly past three in the afternoon. For each level there are two sessions: the first from 9 A.M. till 11:30, the second from about 1:00 P.M. till 3:15. The time between the sessions is given to a half-hour of private study, games, and breakfast, because the homes of many are too distant for them to go home for a meal and return back again. Since there is a lack of study halls [*communibus museis*], the boys study privately in their classrooms under the supervision of teachers.

Games are played between teams, and classes are pitted against each other, either because games are played better against equals or because boys usually get to know few others besides their classmates, since levels are separated from each other over most of the remaining hours. Hence, if anything untoward should happen, it usually is contained within one class and there is less danger that the whole body be infected by an evil spirit. Since they are day students, if a boy suffers an offense in the College and returns home he quickly forgets everything and the next day he comes to school with no memory of the fault. Furthermore, since most are of Irish blood, they are used to having father, mother, and sister say nothing about priests except with the deepest reverence. This parent-teacher collaboration is a double support for good training because this custom is in our favor, even though it often does not promote fairness [*consuetudo illa, saepe inimica justae observantiae*]. But the frequent parent-teacher meetings contribute to the authority of each. For these reasons, we receive remarkably malleable youths and mold them in a very supportive manner.

It must be admitted that Latin and Greek literature is held in low repute in a place where the clergy is the only state of life which requires such knowledge. And that the study of literature does not contribute a thing to men totally dedicated to making money. So we cannot exaggerate our amazement or the heights to which our spirits and hopes are raised when we see year by year not only increasing numbers of applicants to our school, but their enthusiasm and proficiency in their studies. For, if you except those few whom you can find anywhere, the rest manifested such determination to complete their tasks that they needed bridle more than goad. In nearly every class, even the youngest, several kept studying late into the night lest their classmates surpass them. Hence parents often complained to teachers: "Alas! I'm afraid that such damnable toil may damage the eyes, head, and body of my dear boy. Isn't it your responsibility to set some limit to such enthusiasm?" Perhaps under obedience, though assignments were unfinished, two boys were forced to go to bed and, unable to sleep, for a solid hour were heard to repeat: "I didn't finish my work. What will the teacher say? Victory will elude me. My rival will win." Finally, it became necessary for the prefect to forbid anyone to extend homework beyond two and one-half hours.

Though one may obtain a sure indication from what has already been said, still, private examinations and public defenses also demonstrated the progress made. In the customary examinations given in the middle and end of each year, most fared satisfactorily. But in every class there were some, and in three classes most, who did so well that there would hardly be any studies in which more could be expected. With outstanding results, each class presented a public competition before the parents. In this effort, the enthusiasm of the youngest was so brilliant that victor and vanquished shared honors. Even more than in the past, the public argumentations of the philosophers, an exhibition so dear to every American, received great applause, especially from the many priests who attended. When the defense was over, the Most Reverend Archbishop himself rose and, according his custom, kindly addressed the speakers. Moreover, with unusual praise he extolled the surrounding group of classmates so that sincerity and joy in speaking may exhibit a kind of brilliance shining forth from purity and innocence, a brilliance far more valuable than any type of applause.

Who could not detect this brilliance of the angels as the source for these blessed youths? Most of them are nourished by the bread of heaven each month, and some more often. Some show their first zeal for the souls of their parents or classmates. Many teach catechism to uneducated young people, either in their parishes or to a group gathered in our parishes. When some of these lamented that their ears were often assaulted by blasphemies against the name of God, they enrolled as many Catholics and others in the Holy Name Society which met twice a month. If anyone of their number had fallen into blasphemy since the preceding meeting, he would openly confess it and undertake whatever penance the others should prescribe.

As a joke, a teacher had said to a certain misbehaver who was perhaps too saucy of manner: "You will have made reparation after you have made the Way of the Cross." Later, after he had dismissed all the pupils, the teacher visited the chapel, completely forgetting his statement, only to behold the same undisciplined lad devoutly engaged in making the Stations of the Cross.

More than any other time, the month of Mary called forth the devotion of all classes: class by class, altars were erected and beautified with all kinds of flowers and lighting; from their small funds, the boys were moved to prepare solemn festivities never known before.

All who witnessed the public ceremony honoring the Virgin Mary confessed that they had never seen the like. Prepared during the previous year, the fifteen banners, drawing from the mysteries of the rosary, proclaimed the union between the lives of the Redeemer and Redemptrix. Emblems broadcast the devotions special to each Sodality; . . . many attracted attention. One could hardly count the flowers and candles carried in the crowded procession. Among other offerings, a golden heart was borne along, carrying the names of teachers and pupils.

### The Parish Mission

This was the sixth year in which our church had been renewed by the solemn spiritual exercises of a mission. Moreover, since the sacred triduum of the Japanese martyrs took place at the same time, there seemed to be a double reason for undertaking the mission. The date chosen for beginning the exercises was the first Sunday of Easter. To lead the mission, by the favor of God, we successfully invited two Fathers of the Missouri Province who were already known for their many activities and their conversions of Protestants.

The following schedule was observed: at 9 A.M. and 3 P.M. the service was offered to those with leisure or less demanding obligations. But for all those who had to work from 7 A.M. to 6 P.M., at a bit before 5 A.M. one the missionaries celebrated Mass and gave a sermon more suited their needs. But after 7 P.M., the hour by which most classes of society have stopped working and when the subsequent silence of the night gives hope for more abundant results, three sermons were given at the same time in separate locations for different audiences: in the College for men only, in the lower church for the other gender, in the upper church for anyone. As soon as the mission was advertised, more people than one could imagine came from all parts of the city. Long before the evening starting hour, the College and both churches were so full that no room remained even for standees and many had to go home in sorrow. In the three locations at the same time there were easily six or seven thousand people. Often two hundred Protestants attended to hear words favorable to them; they were attracted either by Catholic friends or by the subject matter; effective books were distributed, especially one by our own Father [Francis X.] Weniger [1803-1888], *Protestantism and Infidelity*, a work that has given light to many readers.

With the blessing of God, both for Catholics and for Protestants, the benefit of the mission has exceeded all expectations, so much so that it has no precedent and resembles a miracle. It would be a far happier blessing if more time and a greater number of priests had been available. Confessions numbered about 25,000, and Communions in our church alone, 20,000. Starting on the third day of the mission, for entire days the confessionals were staffed by fifteen priests and often, especially in the evening, by more than twenty. It is hard to believe the joy of the faithful when 63 Protestants of different backgrounds and ages were led to embrace the true faith. Some abjured their heresy before a few witnesses, but most did so with full solemnity in the presence of a huge crowd, and this was done twice. On one occasion, 24 abjured, on the other, 13. Many were shouting: "Never have we witnessed so grand a triumph." The first to enter the sacred font was a popular Protestant minister. When he chanced to come by the doors of the church in the midst of the sermon and wondered at the huge crowd standing in the street, he asked what was happening. An Irish girl replied: "Look, in that church a priest is now proving that outside the Catholic Church there is no salvation." Touched by the novelty of the idea and by his longing to listen, he made his way through the throng as well as he could. As often in other situations, the preacher was exhorting the non-Catholics in words such as these: "My friends who are forever pounding your Bible, I beg you to read and reread it; I think that, if you read it properly, it will not be long before you recognize the true Church, for the Bible is completely Catholic. If what I say gains little credence from you, I ask you to come to me and I promise to show you the truth about every point about which you have doubts." So the heretical minister came and, after discussing at length the contested doctrines, he said: "Indeed, till now I have been blind about the Bible. These teachings remarkably coincide with Catholic doctrine. I will study the rest." And soon a bright light shone on what had been his simple thinking.

As the crown of the mission came the foundation of the devotional group called the Consolers of the Sacred Heart of Jesus, which our missionaries in the American West, by indult of His Holiness, usually establish after any mission. On the spot, 1,400 of the faithful enrolled; and this association gained its greatest increase particularly from this devotion which our Savior has entrusted to our least Society; to foster this devotion the members are asked to participate in the most Sacred Sacrifice and the Benediction of the Blessed Sacrament on the First Friday of each month.

Celebrated in this manner, the solemnity of the martyrs of Japan dawned upon us. No one would claim that those martyrs had no part in the graces received. During the rest of the year, the parish had no blessing greater than that mission. Yet no one is to make lesser account of the other blessings which, like rivers in their quiet but continual flow, lengthen and strengthen their richness.

This year, great effort was expended to maintain religious silence in the church.

*Other Parish Activities*

Omitting others for now, let us mention some of our principal ministries: devotion to administering the sacrament of Penance, catechizing, and care of the several sodalities. One may conjecture that our parish includes 16,000 souls. One cannot count how many from other parishes in the city celebrate the sacrament of Penance in Jesuit churches. By continuous service, four Fathers try constantly to keep up with this work.

The work of catechesis is somewhat relieved by the two parish schools in which the children are duly prepared for first Communion, the boys by the good Brothers, the girls by the Religious of the Sacred Heart, and at times the pastor presides over the Sunday gatherings. But far more numerous are the children who attend either no schools or public, and therefore Protestant, schools. Besides, we meet many adults of different ages who have received no sacrament beyond baptism and even that may be doubtful. Awaiting confirmation or advancement in sacred doctrine are those who have recently received First Communion.

There are also the unfortunate blacks, adults and children, for whose freedom so much free blood has been shed. But, now the liberators avoid the liberated like they'd avoid the plague. What has thus far been done for each of these groups? Since a suitable gathering place is still lacking, service to the Africans proceeds slowly. Still, something has been provided for adults and children of color: several adults have been received into the Church, and about 40 children assembled, 20 of whom have been properly instructed, examined, and admitted to First Communion.

Much more easy and pleasant is the situation with white adults, who are gathered in our house and publicly or privately instructed. This year about 200 of them have been received, a third of them married men. We have been successful and rejoice in that part of our ministry to adults, children, and adolescents.

About 800 children who are not in parochial schools gather each Sunday in the lower church to be instructed as a group either by devoted laity or by our students, both of whom of their own accord have offered their services. If rumor is believed, throughout the entire city there is no other catechesis comparable to ours.

At the same time the Religious of the Sacred Heart offer a similar program of catechesis for girls. Each year about 500 are admitted to First Communion and, around the same time, they are confirmed. Once these candidates have been thus instructed, on each of the following Sundays, in the same or greater numbers they gather in the upper church for a homily on persevering in their catechesis. There was a solemn conferral of prizes during which about 20 girls, with energetic, simple hearts, presented proof of their studious habits, and brought home a holy picture or sacred medal.

To give a specific example, a boy preparing for First Communion was often thinking of the wretched state of his Protestant father. Finally, afire with extraordinary zeal, the boy approached one of the priests and said: "I beg you, Reverend Father, go to my father. As you know, he lives entangled in heresy, and I would not want to be eternally separated from him." Our Father willingly went with the boy and, after a few weeks, the father abjured his heresy and, with his exultant son received the Eucharist and Confirmation. When a 12 year old girl had answered poorly in catechism class and was asked whether she attended school, she replied: "I can't. Two years ago my father died. My mother serves sick soldiers in Washington; at home I alone take care of my younger sister and two little brothers. Indeed I send them to school, but I cannot go with them because the whole house depends on me." All of this was seriously and simply related.

But there are even greater marvels. One of our Fathers was concerned about the reading of any heretical book and had singled out by name the Bible used daily to begin all the athletic competition of the Protestants in this city. He said that ecclesiastical authority had expressly forbidden such reading, and stated that "You can abstain from such reading without difficulty because the public law gave freedom in this matter." After a short interval, a teacher noticed that an 11-year-old Catholic boy usually did not take part in the daily game till the reading of the Bible had been finished. Suspecting the reason, he threatened to give the laggard a beating unless he took part in the game from the beginning. Next, the words were followed by threats. Yet for two solid years the generous boy preferred daily lashing, which was severe, to placing his faith in danger. Another boy was steadily rejecting the same reading. With his eloquence fruitlessly exhausted and finally stricken by rage, the teacher whipped the naked boy so badly that he drew blood from all of his little body; then, after a pause, he eagerly asked: "Will you read it finally?" When the boy again refused, he beat him more severely. In short order, the matter became known outside the school; it seemed so serious that it came to court; but the case seemed a little hostile to Protestantism [*causae hereticae*] and was thrown out of court. But Catholic citizens decided that a gold medal be given to the young confessor of the faith. There was one who would risk his life because or his fidelity.

We will mention only two of the Sodalities (which had been noted as the third heading among parish works): one for adult workers, the other for youths made wretched because of dangers to their health. Some years earlier, the very work of catechesis gave birth to such heroic service. In 1857, after the usual celebration of a general First Communion, many of those who either participated in the Protestant sports or worked for Protestants realized the danger to their faith and morals. Of their own accord they began insistent requests that we form them into a Sodality. Nothing could have pleased us more than such requests. It seemed best to join together in one Sodality, not only the petitioners but others of similar age, for among them there was hope that as many apostles would be formed as members were admitted. Nonetheless, lest perhaps that first little flame feed only on straw, a Father tested spirits more surely, at the same time sharpened their desire, and at first imposed delay upon delay. Then, when he thought the time ripened by pondering, he chose to admit only a carefully chosen few out of the many applicants. These were deemed worthy of being the strong foundation for raising the building. Upon them no easy rules were imposed, two of which were: 1) that each make monthly confession and Communion; 2) that, if any member did anything unworthy, his name would be given to the director. This was done in late 1857. Then, early in 1858, when the members were not more than 33, that small but enthusiastic band of warriors pushed for another wish, to be associated with the Prima Primaria in Rome under the title of the Immaculate Conception of the Blessed Virgin Mary, with St. Joseph as patron. When the Father Director had written to Rev. Father Provincial and to Rome, the prayers were properly answered before the end of the same year. Then, when the project was progressing in every way, around October, 1863, there were 139 admitted, about 200 candidates, of whom 46 were on probation, 61 were postulants, and 83 aspirants.

As a sign of the holy fires burning in the group, there is a kind of treasury of spiritual offerings written on lists like: so many Masses attended in honor of the Blessed Virgin Mary, so many rosaries offered to gain a definite grace, so many brief hymns recited in honor of St. Joseph, etc. That treasury was created in early November, 1862. Nine months after its inception, such offerings numbered 8,569. Moreover, the group had its own library which the members, though poor, expanded by more than 700 volumes, and not one volume has been lost, so carefully have the librarians guarded them! If readers harm any book, one of the members repairs the damage gratis. The good young people have not disappointed the hopes entertained for their apostolate; due to their zeal several of their contemporaries have been called back from heresy and many of their parents have been converted to a better life.

Examples abound of remarkable constancy in the faith. One member wrote to a friend: "I have a father who is involved in the unholy sect of Freemasons and thus hates the Catholic Church; my mother is Catholic to the bone, and I gladly follow her. So when my father had heard that I belonged to the Marian Sodalists and that my little brother was under instruction for his first Communion, he exploded in anger: 'I would rather see you damned in eternal fire than raised in the Catholic Church.' With these words he banished us from his sight. So I am not allowed to go the 25 paces to the nearest church, but with my whole heart I cling to the Church and the Sodality." When another had fallen from a height and should certainly have died, he escaped safely and said about our wonderment: "What's so remarkable? My scapular was protecting me." Another gave equal credit to the same scapular when he was not completely burnt in a fire.

Another sodality is also flourishing, composed of older workers, and in seniority and numbers it surpasses the first. For, born about ten years ago under an unknown title, it soon took the patronage of the Blessed Virgin Mary and was likewise joined to the Prima Primaria in Rome; it now has about 250 members. Most of them are employed in mechanical skills and offer an effective example by joining wondrous integrity of life with fervent piety. Every month they receive the Body of the Lord as a group, and several receive more often. During the mission in question, their zeal was demonstrated first by their leading many Protestants to the sermons, then by helping them consult the missionaries. When one man by chance had heard that there were many difficult obstacles in the way of young men who wanted to become priests, first he asked whether he might be allowed to offer anything to help the needy among such candidates, and the next day sent 300 francs with the message: "How pained I am that to this sacred work I cannot offer 10,000 more and myself as well."

*Visits to the Official Houses of Detention.*

We undertake whatever priestly ministry is needed in public prisons nearby or at a distance. In the city itself the only prison is the one commonly called the Tombs, where vagrants, drunkards, criminals as well as youths guilty of lesser crimes are kept for a short period awaiting their sentences. Some will be freed after a few days, others are assigned to prisons. A position was opened there for two Jesuits, one to appear twice a week, but the other to come less often.

The main work there is to prepare each prisoner to confess his sins properly. When he leaves this place [he will go to] other prisons, where he might be able to meet one of the Jesuits there, or [he may visit] one of us at the college later. That happens frequently.

Young men are pleased to be called by name when the priest is present. A large number of them, previously poorly instructed in religion, are glad to come back after they are invited to take instructions, as they are free to do. Recently after one returned home, he told a parent that he had made a promise to remain a penitent of a certain Jesuit. He was faithful to the promise for a time but then later forgot. The parent said: "I will take you with me," and therefore both came to seek forgiveness. It is not unusual that one success will bring two or three others like him. Each week about thirty alcoholics will pledge themselves to abstain. Of these at least a half will keep their word, but the rest, you might readily believe, after a few days or weeks, will return to their former habit.

In the same place there are many young Catholics, about twenty years old or more, not yet admitted to the Sacred Banquet. These are also being instructed either in prison or at a college later. A certain one of these by chance assisted a soldier close to death from the wounds he had received, for there was not any priest at hand to fill the need. Concerned about the faith of some one close to death, he decided to offer as much help as he could. So he interrupted and asked : "Are you at peace in your conscience?" The soldier replied : "I will indeed reveal everything to you. I was born in New York and at first I was the worst among the evil-doers and was sent to prison. There I revealed my sins to a certain visiting priest; from that time on I led a sufficiently good life and now I die peacefully" and he gave the name of the priest.[17] The other replied: "I also know that priest and will report everything about you to him." And he did so.

There is another prison far more notorious, in which the full penalties are exacted. It is situated at twenty leagues from the city in a place named Sing-Sing. Jesuits seldom go there but stay for a long period when they do. This year two Jesuits went there, one for three or four visits, the other for six. On each visit, each of them stays three or four days. Since they visit those in solitary confinement, it is easy to understand how much solace there is for those who are condemned to hard labor and constant silence. Catholics were freed from sins and non-Catholics were taught the true doctrine; of the latter thirty-one returned to the Church while they were in prison.

Furthermore, there are other houses of detention on one of the nearby islands, which over the years have almost completely been left to Jesuits' care. This situation developed in years past but things have gone too far; so now it would be proper to review the situation there from the beginning.

### Pastoral Care for Three Nearby Islands

Plenty of small islands surround the city of New York, which itself is entirely on Manhattan Island, at the mouth of the Hudson River. Three of these islands on its east side, almost a kilometer away from the city, are fairly close to each other, and ignored by a great many books and maps. *Blackwells Island*, the largest, or rather, the longest of the three, is two kilometers in length, followed by *Wards Island* to its north, and lastly by with a small bay on its west. Each has become a dumping-ground for the city's ills, overseen by Charity Commissioners [*Decemvirorum*], appointed by the City Council [*a senatu publico*], and who are, by the way, Protestant, as most, if not all, of these officials usually are. And each island has its own share of misery. Wards Island harbors indigent Irish and German immigrants, while *Randalls Island* shelters orphans of both sexes from two years of age to fourteen, and a multitude of the blind, deaf, and variously maimed; Blackwells, the largest island, has five times as many of the sick, poor, and deranged, plus petty criminals serving time or simply being held there to keep from mischief.

You'd be amazed to know that, with barely a third of the city's Catholics figuring in the census, more than four-fifths of them turn up in these wards and shelters. Still, you can't be too astonished when you consider that each of these places is brimming with poor people and that, in this part of the world, Catholics, and especially the Irish, are conspicuous for their poverty. As for the jails, the accused can post bail and remain free until the trial ends. Few Catholics, however, can even imagine making bail. One of our Fathers, in his comments, intimates why that's the case. Once, by chance, both he and an official were looking from a prison window on a crowd of nearly 500 inmates on a field below, all of whom, whatever they were doing, did it quietly at an official's direction. Such docility and compliance of so many people struck the priest; he mentioned it to the official, who replied: "If, indeed, I had any say in the matter, I'd at once easily release 400 of that crowd you're looking at, and replace them, quickly, with 400 of those who put them here." The majority of accused Catholics, who haven't bail money, even lack the means, by letter or otherwise, to inform their kin. You'd be right to surmise that, in other respects, the Catholics shut up in such places aren't of the better sort but, the fact that most are Irish makes them easier to reform.

These islands, then, are just ready for harvesting, but, for the longest time, workers were too few for the task. Before 1859, in fact, no Catholic priest had as yet set foot on *Randall's Island* where, besides a hospital for the maimed, there were more than one thousand children orphaned or else abandoned by their destitute parents. These children, mostly born Catholic, but living and breathing naught but Protestantism on the island, were to be indentured, whenever possible, to Protestant families. The vast majority, however, was to be sent out west and, likewise, dispersed among Protestants.

The orphanage itself is a complex of twelve buildings, each 50 x 150 feet, three-storied, and all inter-connected. It's impressive, indeed, but doesn't have an inch reserved for Catholic worship. There is, to be sure, a Protestant chapel, with a minister who legally provides sermons and ceremonies. A matron is in charge of each building, and all but one of these women are Protestants. A Methodist minister, a diehard sectarian, and likewise very devious, runs the entire compound. The minor officials, on the contrary, are almost all Catholic.

The Reverend Archbishop resolved to end the slaughter of so many innocent lambs, and in whatever way he might, finally turned to us in 1859. And so, Rev. Father Superior ordered a priest from Fordham [Rev. Louis Schneider, *Mission. excurr. in Randall's Island*, was at Fordham until 1860, and was now on the staff of the College of St. Francis Xavier] to undertake the task. The Rev. Father Superior made it clear to him that there seemed to be scant hope for this mission, considering the difficulty involved, but, nevertheless, the Archbishop wanted him to do whatever he could, no matter how little. The priest, who also served as a teacher in the Second Division, part-time chaplain and catechist with the employees, obediently shouldered the burden laid on him. Yet, he could work there only on his days off, Thursdays and the summer vacation. He began, therefore, to go to  once a week, starting in the fall of 1859. It can scarcely be told how much it cost him, in terms of toil and persistence, to plow a furrow in that thicket. So full of thorns were his early attempts that, terrified, he almost gave up.

The first one he had to win over, or else overcome, was that Methodist director who, together with a like-minded minister, had sworn that nothing Catholic would get through to his orphans. To be ovecome, also, was the head warden, a veritable Cerberus, who was the director's minion. But, opportunely, a new director took charge of the children. Granted he wasn't Catholic, and knowing full well that whatever he could do to hinder the priest would earn him praise, much less blame, from his superiors, this basically good man, nonetheless, was always ready to help our man. The matrons, in turn, were easily enough won over by kindness and, (what exceeded all credulity, most of all the priest's), by gifts of Catholic piety such as statues, medals, crucifixes and prayer books. All of the women took these things (bought for the considerable sum of 500 francs collected in alms) not only without a second thought but also with many thanks. In the meantime, the priest had to gain the trust of everyone else and so, eager to check things out, as it were, he toured the whole facility, with praise for much of what he saw and kind words for every official. He even convinced two of the city's tabloids to send free copies to the orphanage daily. Ingratiating himself like this, which in itself was quite a feat, he was able to talk each week about religious matters with 100 girls between seven and fourteen, grouped into sewing circles and to 350 boys; he was able to visit the sick as often as he wished.

One thing more remained to request, space for saying Mass and suitable for hearing confessions. Such issues depended on the director. Whatever our Father might do for this purpose, either using persuasion, gifts, or other approaches with the director, or working directly with the house supervisors or indirectly with powerful friends, all was in vain. The one argument that was used to oppose everything that the Father did was: "We've never done that before; it's not our custom." But it was altogether necessary that the confessions of the unfortunate people there should be heard, and those who were soon about to be transferred elsewhere especially desired it. Our Father was able to hear confessions wherever he could, in the kitchen, in the barn, outdoors, even beyond the walls, behind bars, or in the freezing playground. Nearly all the sick went to confession, and two of them died shortly thereafter. The man of God responded fearlessly to the Protestant minister who wanted to prevent these spiritual ministrations. The priest stated that the service must be provided, even against the will of the minister or even of the Commissioners.

But then the appearance of the situation began to change. After living through five months with these troubles, our Father goes to the Commissioners. Kindly received, he so begged and orated that their president was persuaded and gave him letters to be presented to the minister in charge in which he indicated that it seemed right and certainly most acceptable to him if a suitable place for hearing confessions would be provided for the Catholic priest on each of his weekly visits. When he received these letters, our Father enjoyed a double triumph, because his right was acknowledged and sealed both to make his weekly visits and to hear confessions. However, he celebrated his triumph a little too soon. For when the minister had read the letters in the presence of our Father, he was at first dumbfounded. Soon, filled with bitterness, the man promised a room if there would be any necessity for it. Two weeks later, in his customary benign manner he upset our Father as he instructed him that permission granting him a room had been amended. The Commission had decided that the Catholic priest had the right only once a month to speak with the boys. He proceeded to insist that the law was clear and poclaimed that unless he willingly complied with it he might have to be removed from office. Our Father's calm response was: "Your are right. But I am going to have that law changed." Others eventually took care of the matter.

The rumor of these disputes spread throughout the city. In case after case, the Commissioners, all of them Protestant, got the message of the reports. So Catholic leaders decided to remedy the situation by means of a petition to the city officials; they managed to have the current Commissioners supplanted by others, one a Catholic, the rest men of good repute and generous disposition, who really seemed concerned about honesty and justice. In place of the bosses' henchman, a new director took over the orphanage. He himself was a Protestant but he enjoyed the favor of the Catholic commissioner, was friendly to our Father, and tended to favor him over all the other chaplains. So from then on there was a change in the state of Catholic affairs. A proper place was finally provided for confessions, and a just arrangement was made for the priest to meet both boys and girls. Three or four youths from the Vincent de Paul Society were admitted to catechize the boys; later some Sisters of Charity came for the girls.

Meanwhile, plans were being made for a real building, one with a large school hall devoted to religious affairs, a suitable Catholic altar and other facilities for the ordinary faithful; the plans were to be presented to the mayor. In the school hall there would be a large partition and behind it a huge closet in which objects for Mass would be kept; they would be hidden on ordinary days. But on holydays a tabernacle would appear in the recess with candelabra and vases for flowers. The folding doors themselves and the objects that would be seen would be harmonized with the style of the entire altar, it ssteps and other appurtenances. Need is truly the mother of invention.

All preparations completed, on the first Sunday of September, 1860, a year after our entrance into the institution, we introduced the Sacred Mysteries there, and that had never happened before on that island. At that time our Father who created the mission there was transferred from Fordham College to Xavier and, now relieved somewhat from some of his duties at home, was able to visit his island twice a week, on Thursday and Sunday. There's barely an hour for Mass with a homily; after Mass the children separate to get their religious instruction apart, the boys with catechists from the Vincent de Paul Society and the girls with the good Sisters. Meanwhile, the good Sister (*Sunamite*) has breakfast for the priest in the same place. From the start almost 400 people would attend, namely 40 men, 70 women, 200 boys, and 80 girls. The children came willingly and gladly, and, considering that children everywhere are noisy and restless, these were remarkably well-behaved in such a common space. They are all, however, still required to attend Protestant services; yet, the more they get of Catholic worship, the more their horror of the Protestant, and their faith increases day by day as they compare one with the other. As to the sacraments, a good many began to receive Communion on Sundays, and those who reached the proper age for it, made their First Holy Communion. Thus did our happy priest *reap his harvest sowed in patience.*

June 22, 1861 dawned differently and quite brightly for the island and the orphanage with the arrival, for the first time, of the Archbishop, who confirmed 319 people. To be added to this number, actually, were those who hadn't as yet made First Communion, that is, those children who were about to be shipped out west. The idea was to help them, as much as one could, to keep the Faith amidst dangers so many and great. The sight, however, of the lame, the blind, the mute, and so many other unfortunates, prostrate at the bishop's feet was truly Gospel-like. As Christ once did with similar crowds, his Grace gently consoled and encouraged them. Astonishing, too, was the resolve shown by the 80 girls in the group. They, like their Protestant teachers, had it in mind that Confirmation had to be received fasting. So, thinking that the solemnity would not begin before 9 a.m., they started to fast at 8 p.m. the previous night, so simply and quietly that no one at the ceremony even suspected what they had done. The next day, which was Sunday, renewed the joy when 100 children shared in the Divine Banquet for the first time. All who witnessed it, Catholic and Protestant alike, were deeply moved. Later that year, on the Feast of the Immaculate Conception, all were moved again when nearly 200 approached the Sacred Table with utmost fervor and spiritual delight.

The good work did not cease to go on after that, with help (which was mentioned above in anticipation) from the Sisters of Charity who were of double service, both teaching the children, and embellishing the altar and the music. Who would hesitate to refer all this to Divine Providence and, along with us, to thank God for them?

*Blackwells Island*

Further, it appears that this work led to something eminently good, because it opened the way, and energetically so, to Blackwells Island, of the three islands the biggest and most crowded with human misery. For up to 6,000 souls usually live in its five institutions, three of which, a hospital, an asylum, and a poorhouse maintain the sick, the mad, and the indigent, while the other two serve as jails, one for minor offenses, the other for hard time. However, for every hundred petty criminals released daily, another hundred enter, rounded up from the city's streets and squares. Blackwells Island is, truly, a huge field for the harvesting, but it also demands much and constant attention. Indeed, up to 1861, a single priest, already overburdened with parish duties, took care of the whole island, making the rounds of its shelters two or three times a week, and doing a task by no means easy but far from matching the need. Therefore, after we began the mission, on the archbishop's insistence, we took on Blackwells Island also.

Fr. John Jaffré, as his necrology reports in the latest *Annual Letters,* was the first Jesuit to go to Blackwells Island, happily taking up the post on Easter Monday, 1861. But this tireless old man worked so hard that, after a few months, he fell ill and died. His death was a reminder that even two stronger men, working night and day, could barely cover the whole place. And so, following the late Fr. John, two priests from Xavier came to the island and, once in place, lived at public expense, eating at the common table with other administrators. Shortly thereafter, many Jews, Chinese, and Protestants in the hospital began to convert. Christmas Mass was celebrated with unusual splendor, for our Father, having found among the indigents some who knew how to read music and play various instruments, arranged a solemn high Mass on the order of a concert, complete with chorus and orchestra. It was an unbelievable delight for all present, among whom were most of the island's authorities, although all of them were Protestant.

The record for the last half of that first year show 5,000 Confessions, 4,400 Communions, 750 Extreme Unctions, 330 conversions and just as many adult First Communions, 270 child Baptisms, and 2,000 pledges of sobriety.

From the start of this ministry on Blackwells Island to the beginning of 1862, 450 converted to the True Faith, and 253 in this one year alone. Many of these, after being baptized, went on to claim their heavenly reward. In general, these conversions require very little persuasion. Most people, after a brief colloquy, and, especially, through the intercession of the Holy Virgin, are induced to embrace the Faith. Why, there were even Protestant women who, in a wonderful way, helped our Fathers in making converts; they suggested to other Protestants that they see a priest to help them solve their problems of conscience. They were the occasion many prisoners died in the True Faith.

Some of these women, though, were bitterly anti-Catholic and did all they could to hinder the priests. The ministers, too, seeing their chapel with barely 30 or 40 devotees on Sundays and the Catholic chapel (which holds 1,200) brimming with so many of their own converted flock, began a vigorous push to get rid of our Fathers. In the meantime, they would gladly preach in public spaces to whatever listeners had gathered there, remained there and listened with attention. But what can those unfortunate people do when even top city officials favor our mission with public praise and funds, and when the time is near for us, by joint wish of the bishop and the city, to take charge of the third island as well?

VIII. December, 1863, to Oct. 1, 1864[18]

Our community members this year totaled 28, of whom 16 were priests, 3 Scholastics, and 9 Brothers.

*Associations Founded for the Alumni*
As a means to foster Christian piety more vigorously among the young people who took their studies under our direction we created two organizations, one religious, and the other literary. The group's name in English is The Xaverian Association.[19] Their members meet regularly once a month, and the literary branch of the association meets a second time to have serious discussions on important issues, and they do so using scientific methods. The same purpose is proposed for the religious group that popularly distinguishes Marian Sodalities; our group's practices do not differ from those that Sodality members practice; that is, they meet regularly on certain days to profit from some solemn prayerful activities that they do together, attend Mass together, and hear a religious exhortation that befits their own condition of life.

*The New Large Building* [later called the Lynch Building]
Great expectations had been raised for our recently-completed large building. Those expectations were wonderfully fulfilled when the structure finally opened its doors. Three public presentations were scheduled to take place in the building at different times. In the first, a member of the Jesuit Maryland province gave an excellent talk on the beneficent effects of Catholic doctrine regarding political liberty.
Shortly thereafter you should know that Dr. Ives analyzed the history of philosophy; he was formerly an Episcopalian bishop but now is totally involved in promoting Catholic issues and projects among New Yorkers. Third, Mr. O'Gorman, an important orator in our city, spoke about the beauty and background of the works of Oliver Goldsmith.
We owe an outstanding debt of gratitude to the organist; he is easily the leading figure among the New York musicians. In the same hall a formal concert was presented during which the famous oratorio, "Moses in Egypt" was performed to the applause of a full house. The income from such performances has been assigned to the student library which at the beginning of July has already boasted of about 2500 volumes on its shelves.

*The Storm Against Us from Some Student's Insolence*
One event disturbed the generally favorable routines of the college and so the view of the Fathers has been that they should deal rather severely against some students for some misbehaviors. A few of the more audacious philosophy and rhetoric students considered sending information to a newspaper and having it printed in the popular

press. When faculty members were informed of this plan, they showed its ringleaders why it would be inappropriate for students to take on such a project and they enumerated the special embarrassments that would follow from such a destructive attack. It would harm the good name of the college and would weaken college discipline.

But the young men were not influenced by these warnings, were obstinate in their plan, whispered against their teachers and began to learn ways of bringing about its publication. Thereupon, a newspaper, called *The Vindicator* was printed. What we had anticipated was what actually did happen. At a critical point, the name of the college was stated, and an unjust charge of thoughtlessness and rashness (*inconsiderantiae ac temeritatis*) was made against the Fathers. But they could not let such a great obstinacy go unpunished. And so the names of three of the principal leaders of the faction were dropped from the list of students and the others were easily brought around to attend to their duties. In that way peace and the observance of the rules was promptly restored to the young men at the college. However, it did not require a long delay to make clear that the three plotters had been motivated more by thoughtlessness and juvenile levity than by any morally perverse state of mind. An indication of this was the fact that two of them soon took on the clerical life in a diocesan seminary, and our Fathers learned that the third truly did such penance that that they did not hesitate to take him back into the college.

### The Life and Death of a Student

George was a student of the humanities when his final illness took him away. The boy's eager enthusiasm, Christian piety and exactness in keeping rules and laws made people marvel at him. His father, a Protestant, showed how strongly he felt whenever he thought about his beloved son's purity and naturally-good habits. The adolescent's uprightness was projected in the appearance of his angelic countenance and also from every aspect of his body. He served Mass daily. Very loving toward all who lived in his house and in the school, he was diligently on guard lest he might cause them anything that was less than pleasant. When he was slipping into his final illness and afflicted with continuous pain, he turned his eyes and his mind to the crucifix. That was how he could always bravely bear his pains. Accepting the divine will, he yilded up his life very peacefully, at age fourteen. He left not only for those in his home a great longing for him but also, for all, an example of an innocent life that will not be easily forgotten.

### The Conversion of a Former Student

A life completely different from George's was that of a youth who left this world after spending a few years of study in the College. Caught up in the vortex of public affairs, he was not concerned about eternal salvation and long neglected his duties as a Christian. Even when he was felled with a deadly disease no one at home could persuade him to respond to their prayers that at last he look to his soul; rather all his friends had the experience of hearing his groans of horror of religious talk or even at the sight of a priest. One of our Fathers hears about his crisis of body and soul, hastens to his house, and orders that it be announced that he wishes to see his former student. There's a wonderful force in that word! The sick man immediately consents, he receives

Father in a friendly way, shows himself convinced. He voluntarily begs to be fortified with the sacraments of the Church and receives them with great piety. His family is consoled about his premature death by the fact that he died in the embrace of the Lord.

## The Marian Devotions during May

This diary will close with an account of our students' pious exercises during the month of Mary to show that in cold parts of our America no less spontaneous movements of lively piety are demonstrated than they do in more fortunate parts of Catholic Europe. Throughout that month you'd believe that each one of the schools was changed into something like a sacristy. Images of the Blessed Virgin adorned with tapestry, candelabras and flowers capture students' attention and create a certain heavenly atmosphere for scholastic activities. You see two boxes placed in an appropriate place for the young people. One box is for money to keep the ornaments in good shape, in the other they place papers containing the written intentions of the students or express their daily devotion to the most pure Virgin.

The month opens and also ends with solemn prayers of supplication about which it is worth saying that many Protestants who happened to be brought along to the devotions were moved by the experience. In the procession the students march in using two routes: one is to proceed directly from their home room to a nearby place in the church; the other is to find their way from the public street and enter through the church's main door. They create a impressive procession and each class competes with others in pious rivalry competition regarding their signs, standards, banners and other ways of distinguishing themselves for the altar decorations. Led by altar servers carrying the sign of the cross, the standards of Christ the Lord and the Blessed Virgin are brought in, and the students read their signs which have no set function in the solemn ceremony. In order come the standards in which the mysteries of the holy Rosary are listed to make each of them known to every class in the school. The standards and a certain number of students went together both to better keep the laws of symmetry and to create some competition among the boys; for the permission to stand out is not given to all students, but given in view of their diligence in studies and the uprightness of their behavior. At the end of the procession under their own banner come the Sodalities of the Guardian Angels and of the Mother of God along with the advancing column of singers. After them a carrier of grains, then a chosen group of girls of whom some, garbed in celebratory clothes, carry floral wreaths, others bear before them garlands of flowers enclosed in silver cases Those decorations the boys entwine around the head of Mary's statue; they do that task out of a sense of devotion, beginning in early May. You see an image of the Heart of Mary, constructed with great difficulty of solid silver, all gilded with gold; the names of all the students are inside the case. There is a custom here that every year, money is collected to take care of making a new image which they dedicate to the Immaculate Virgin at the end of the year. A boys' choir and the clergy are the final ones in the procession.

When they come to the altar the priest who is about to say Mass first blesses the pages in the little chests and then the silver heart. When the Mass is over, inside the church the prayers of supplication begin and end with the formula of consecration and the offering. Then Benediction of the Most Blessed Sacrament follows. Finally, after again kneeling as is the custom of suppliants, they all return in an orderly way to the college where they came from.

PART IV

*"Among us"*

The Fordham Cemetery: New York and Beyond

CHAPTER 10

THE FORDHAM CEMETERY HISTORY

OVERVIEW

1847-1889

Near the Fordham University church and adjoining Faber Hall, there is a small graveyard that has often been referred to locally as the "Jesuit cemetery." Like the Jesuits who journeyed from afar to reach New York, this cemetery involved a journey as well — less distant or arduous for those involved, to be sure, but real and interesting nonetheless.

The first Jesuit burial at Fordham took place on July 11, 1847, a day after Br. Joseph Creeden's death. An Irish-born novice Brother, he died at age 26, two months and a week after entering the Jesuit novitiate at Fordham. After his burial, another 60 Jesuits were interred near him, as well as nine students, three seminarians, and three workmen. One of the Jesuits was Irish-born Fr. Eugene Maguire who died at St. Mary's College, KY, on June 11, 1833, at age 33, and whose remains were brought from Kentucky and re-interred at Fordham in November, 1850. In addition, that first cemetery included a vault for three members of the Rodrigue family.[21]

The site of the first or "old" cemetery was a hillside of the property that later became a part of the New York Botanical Garden. It was described as about a quarter of a mile from the present administration building. It was however, in an area of 26.85 acres that were condemned in 1885 by New York City through the right of Eminent Domain. The transfer of ownership was completed by payment in 1889.

The loss of the property created a crisis among the Jesuits regarding the past burials and future ones. One group favored purchase of a separate section in St. Raymond's cemetery which was several miles distant from Fordham. But when a report was circulated about that likely purchase, some of the senior Fathers were saddened. Fr. Isidore Daubresse, a 1846 pioneer Faculty member, long associated with Fordham, and one of the most venerated members of the province, expressed their concerns in writing. They appealed to the consultors and asked that the graves be retained on the college property both to respect the dead by having them *"apud nos"* (among us) and to honor their own religious poverty.

Their appeal was successful: the decision was to keep the graves. Permission to open a new cemetery had to be obtained from the New York City Board of Health (Fordham was in that part of Westchester "annexed" by New York City in 1874). That board sent an inspector who was shown two recommended sites, the orchard and the vineyard. He chose the vineyard. Numerous other approvals had to be obtained and Fr. Patrick Dealy, the former college president who had helpful contacts in the city, was instrumental in obtaining them.

On January 7, 1890, the college obtained permission from the Department of Health to remove the bodies from the "Bronx Park" provided the work "be done in freezing weather and under the supervision of the district medical sanitary inspector." The requirements of the Health Department were fulfilled by the end of the month in which the permission was granted.

Thus from January 21 to 28, 1890, remains were transferred from the old to the new cemetery, the present site. The remains of 60 Jesuits, in addition to three diocesan seminarians, nine students, and two workmen were transferred. The remains of two individuals who were buried there were not found; more will be said about them in Ch. 11. At the time of the transfers, three recently deceased Jesuits, temporarily kept in a vault in St. Raymond's cemetery, were interred in the new site. The new cemetery was blessed on January 30, 1890, thereby surely making it a separate and special "sacred site." The details of the transfers and of the blessing were carefully recounted in the Fr. Minister's diary.

The Fr. Minister at that time was Rev. Joseph Zwinge, S.J. (assigned at Fordham from 1879 to 1883; 1889 to 1891; 1894 to 1897); he provided many details of the cemetery transfer both in English in his diary, and in Latin in the *Liber Defunctorum, Sommaria Vitae et Elogia* (The Book of Our Deceased, Life Summaries and Eulogies). We will refer to it throughout as the *Liber Defunctorum*, and we cite it generously in Appendix I in connection with the cemetery move. Here is an example of an entry for Jan. 23, 1890, translated from the Latin: "We transported [the remains of] Fathers Tissot, Legoüais, Schemmel, and DeLuynes ... and Brothers Joset, Fauris, Proulx, Séné...."

In the same *Liber Defunctorum* the total expenses of the transfer and the head-stones were calculated at $1,203.83. The expenses were mostly for materials —lumber for boxes; carbolic acid; marble for posts and headstones (the marble work was finally completed by June 23, 1891); labor (nine outside workers, five college workmen, a contractor and his assistant).

Since the deceased came not only from Fordham but also from the College of St. Francis Xavier, St. Peter's College, Jersey City, and from Jesuit parishes in Manhattan, they all shared in the costs of the transfer.

From January, 1890, to January, 1909, sixty-four additional Jesuits were buried at the new site. A list of the honored dead and a current map of their graves can be found in Appendix II. After 1909 there were no other burials in the Fordham cemetery because a cemetery was opened at that time for locally deceased Jesuits at the novitiate of St. Andrew-on-Hudson, Poughkeepsie, NY.

### 1910 to 1959

Like many a country cemetery, little attention seems to have been paid directly to the Fordham cemetery from the time of the last burial until plans were being made to build Faber Hall. It was not completely neglected: the grass was cut and repairs were made when necessary. During the later part of these years some individuals tried unsuccessfully to decipher inscriptions on many of the tombstones. Perhaps the general lack of attention was due in part to the original placement of the cemetery entrance. In 1890 when the new cemetery site was being planned it seemed logical to put the cemetery entrance on the south side of the plot, facing what was then the main roadway, just as was done for the entrance to the nearby church. The inscriptions on the tombstones would naturally face that entrance. In the course of time, the former main roadway got much less use, being replaced by a road on the north side of the plot. Obviously, from there passersby saw only the uninscribed back of the stones.

The original placement of the cemetery entrance, marked by its two white marble posts, can be verified in a 1931 blueprint of the campus. The blueprint was made by Charles F. Giraud, Civil Engineer and City Surveyor, 645 E. Tremont Ave., Bronx, and was on display in the office of the campus engineering architect.

Two changes were made in the cemetery probably during 1951-1953. The entrance (marble posts and gate) was moved to the north side. The cemetery was thereby made much more accessible than formerly. And a stone and brick wall-like structure, surmounted by a kind of monstrance, a symbol of blessing, was erected on the south side where the original entrance had been. The decorations in the new structure were an occasion for a letter retained in the University Archives.

Maurice Ahern, then the University Archivist, wrote to Fr. Ignatius Cox, S.J., to defend the religious orthodoxy of the artistic symbols used in the cemetery. Mr. Ahern associated several artistic details with Christian concepts or teachings (e.g., the Circle stands for eternity; the trefoil for the Trinity; the 6 pointed star, used by early Christians as well as by the Jewish people, for God's power extending everywhere). Ahern's letter of November 18, 1953, is the only document found about the modifications to the cemetery made between 1951 and 1953.

The reason for regarding those years as the likely dates for these changes are the following. Before 1951 two documents do not depict the present north entrance or the stone and brick structure at the former south entrance. The documents are the above mentioned 1931 blueprint and a less-sophisticated 1950 chart of the cemetery. At the other time-frame, the letter of M. Ahern in 1953 clearly refers to items that were then in place. Hence we conclude that the changes at the south and north side of the cemetery occurred in the 1951-1953 interval.

A final major cemetery-related event in the 1910-1959 period took place during March 20-23, 1959. The remains of 38 Jesuits were moved from the west side to the south side of the cemetery to facilitate the building of Faber Hall. That transfer enabled builders to erect scaffolding and move materials readily according to their needs. Unfortunately, records of the details of this final transfer could not be obtained because of the later bankruptcy of the builder of Faber Hall and the death of the then-funeral director. However, there is a professionally drawn blueprint of the cemetery which recorded the details of the result of the transfer.

1960 to 1998

During the period from 1960 to 1998 two developments in Jesuit Community and University relations affected the cemetery in contrary ways (ownership and non-ownership). On July 1, 1969 the University and the Jesuit Community signed an agreement that legally separated the Jesuit Community from the university, and created the Jesuits of Fordham, Incorporated. Loyola Hall and Faber Hall together with some adjoining land were deeded to the Jesuits. Thereby the cemetery was included in the holdings of the Jesuits of Fordham, Inc.

But by the 1990's the numbers and needs of the Jesuits on campus changed considerably. A new agreement was made with the University in January 25, 1995. In effect, in exchange for Spellman Hall and its surrounding gardens, the ownership of Faber Hall and its adjoining garden area was transferred to the university. The adjoining garden area included the cemetery and so from that time the Jesuits no longer owned the cemetery.

A change that followed the transfer of ownership was the removal of hedges around the garden area and around the cemetery. This development raised the concern that the cemetery might become an easy target of vandals. Over the years some tombstones had been damaged, either by vandals or by natural deterioration. Physical plant employees had repaired them on numerous occasions.

1998 to 2000

Jesuit concerns about the cemetery, especially its appearance and the respect due to the memory of those interred there, was brought to the attention of the University President, the Rev. Joseph A. O'Hare, S.J., who promptly appointed a university committee to study what should be done. Jesuit and lay representatives of the university were members of the committee, which was chaired by the Rev. Gerald R. Blaszczak, S.J., then Rector of the Jesuit Community and University Chaplain.

At the committee's recommendations the following changes were made:

• A metal fence partially covered by hedge was erected to protect the area. Besides the hedge, bright flowers were planted to beautify the area.

• New granite low slant markers were put in place of the almost illegible old Vermont marble tombstones which were gradually disintegrating in the face of modern acid air pollution. The granite replacement markers are more resistant to that problem. The markers were all placed to face towards the present entrance on the north side of the cemetery. For historical reasons, a row that contained the earliest tombstones was retained, but slant markers were also provided for that row.

• The markers state the individual's name, dates of birth, entrance into the Society, and death. Each stone also names his place of birth, if known, and place of death, as well as IHS (with a cross rising above the H — a characteristic Jesuit emblem for Jesus) at the top of each stone, and R.I.P. (*Requiescat In Pace*) at the bottom. The older tombstones provided much of the same information but were written in Latin. They gave the nationality — born (*natus*) in France/Ireland/Austria/, etc. — but not the local birthplace of the deceased. Typically, the markers for those who were not Jesuits contain only the vital statistics that are known about them.

 • A plaque was erected by the walk beside the northeast side of the cemetery. It reads as follows:

IN THEIR HOPE OF THE RESURRECTION HERE LIE THE REMAINS OF
124 SONS OF ST. IGNATIUS LOYOLA: 68 JESUIT PRIESTS;
44 JESUIT BROTHERS; 12 JESUIT SCHOLASTICS;
77 OF THEM HAD ASSIGNMENTS TO FORDHAM.
OTHERS BURIED IN THE SAME CEMETERY FOR WHOM AND WITH WHOM
THE JESUITS LABORED ARE: 3 DIOCESAN SEMINARIANS,
9 STUDENTS AND 2 COLLEGE WORKMEN.
MAY THEY REST IN THE PEACE OF CHRIST.

On October 19, 1999, a blessing of the new slant markers and a rededication of the cemetery marked the completion of a journey begun long ago by Jesuits who first set out from Kentucky. Many members of the Community were present at the blessing in the cemetery and at a Mass in the Loyola Hall chapel that followed it.

\* \* \* \* \*

CHRONOLOGY

The following chronology, therefore, can be set forth for events described in this chapter:

1847
*July 11* - First burial in the old Fordbam cemetery on a hillside, east part of campus: of Joseph Creeden, aged 26, Irish-born Jesuit novice Brother.

1850
*November 1* - The remains of Irish-born Rev. Eugene Maguire were re-interred in the Fordham cemetery. He was the only Jesuit who died in St. Mary's College, KY; at age 33, he expired on June 11, 1833. The Jesuits came to Fordham from St. Mary's College in 1846.

1889
*April* - After payment of $93,966.25 New York City took title to over 26.85 acres of the east campus, which included the college cemetery; the property was taken by the authority of the state 1884 New Parks Law. Those acres later became part of the New York Botanical Garden. Thereafter the cemetery could no longer be used and so for a short time three Jesuits' bodies were kept in a vault in the St. Raymond cemetery.

1890
*January 21-28* - The remains of 61 Jesuits (including the three who had been in St. Raymond's), three seminarians, nine college students, and two workmen were transferred to the new cemetery near the university church. The remains of a Brother and one workman were not found. The transfers were meticulously documented in Latin and English by Fr. Joseph Zwinge, S.J., the Fr. Minister (administrator).

1890

*January 26 -* First burial in the "new" cemetery: Fr. James Perron, aged 72, French-born former French army officer and administrator in the province who was regarded as a model Jesuit.

1909

*January 24 -* Last burial in the Fordham cemetery: New York-born Fr. William O'B. Pardow, aged 62, formerly Jesuit provincial superior and famous preacher.

1931

Campus engineering blueprint showed entrance to the cemetery was on its south side (Fordbam Rd. side). A cemetery chart dated 1950 confirmed that entrance.

1950-53

Sometime during these years the entrance gate and its white marble posts were moved to the north side of the cemetery, and a brick wall, surmounted by a monstrance-like blessing symbol, was erected on the south side.

1959

*March 20-23 -* To facilitate the building of Faber Hall the remains of 39 Jesuits were moved to the west and south-west sides of the cemetery.

1998

*September 22 -* Rev. Joseph A. O'Hare, S.J., appointed a committee to study the most appropriate way to insure the sacred character of the campus cemetery.

1999

*October 19 -* At the committee's suggestion, the deteriorating tombstones were replaced by low granite markers. The cemetery and the markers were blessed by the Rev. Gerald Blaszczak, S.J., Rector of the Jesuit Community, in a well-attended ceremony.

2000

*April 5 -* A permanent plaque was placed beside the cemetery to bear witness to those interred in "God's Holy Acre."

## CHAPTER 11

## WHAT DOCUMENTS CAN TELL US

Documentation provides the building blocks of any history. This is true in the case of the Fordham cemetery. The Fordham University Archives contain numerous documents which provide information about the cemetery and the people buried in it. Among them are the following:

1. the hand-written *LiberDefunctorum* we saw in Chapter 10.

2. several Fr. Minister's Diaries which detailed daily happenings in separate hand-written books (covering 1846-59, 1860-87, 1899-1900);

3. a list of the deceased (*Liber Continens Nomina Defunctorum*) and charts of the cemetery sites. The most important charts were dated 1887, 1890, 1931, 1950, and 1959;

4. an unsigned *Workman's Diary*.

5. Jesuits' assignments are published in their province Catalogues. In earlier days the whole province Catalogue was written in Latin and each one's tasks were stated in abbreviations that were readily understood by those who knew Latin. Province Catalogues were an important source for information about individuals in this study.

6. A manuscript entitled *St. John's College, Fordham, N.Y.*

7. The *Annual Letters* we referred to in Parts II and III.

8. The *Woodstock Letters*.

Despite the documentary record, myths perdure. Two such are still circulated about the Fordham cemetery. The first myth runs: "There are no human remains here." The second myth attempts to prop up the first: "Only the head-stones were moved from the Botanical Garden, the part that used to belong to Fordham. Perhaps a few token bones were brought over. The rest of the remains were left."

These myths became so widespread that student campus tour guides were instructed to repeat that story. Those who questioned their account were informed that it was "common knowledge."

Yet the documentary evidence is clear:

First, the careful reporting by Fr. Zwinge in Latin and in English of the transfer of the graves, naming those whose remains were transferred on each of the days when work, was done in January, 1890.

Second, several charts of the graves in the cemetery: one drawn up in 1887 with comments later inserted after the 1890 removals; the others dated 1890, 1950, and 1959. They suggest the conviction of the knowledgeable and truthful chart-makers that they were dealing with a genuine cemetery, not a "phantom" one.

Third, another confirmatory source concerning the transfer of the graves is the unsigned hand-written book, entitled *Workman's Diary*. The diary was very likely written by Br. William Donovan, S.J., who was also buried at Fordham. (At one point in the diary he noted that "tomorrow is my birthday" and he was the only one in the community who had a birthday on that day.) Being a farmer, he reported on weather and events that pertaining to weather, such as out-of-doors activities on campus like construction. Thus for Jan. 13, 1890, he noted "We had too very wet days this week but weather is now fine and clear. They commenced to dig the graves for removing the corps [sic] from the grave yard." And on Jan. 28, he wrote "They finished in removing all the bodies of the dead from the old grave yard to the new one in the garden." Apparently he wasn't aware of the two missing corpses but he confirmed the main issue that we have been investigating.

Fourth, the "no human remains' myth totally ignores the sixty-four additional Jesuits buried — *not* reinterred — between 1890 and 1909.

As for the second myth — that only the headstones were transferred from the `old cemetery' to the new one — we have to distinguish between two different groups in the cemetery, Jesuits and non-Jesuits.

The claim that the Jesuits' tombstones were transferred from the old to the new site is clearly inaccurate. *No* headstones were used on the Jesuits' graves in the first cemetery. Instead, a black-painted wooden cross was erected over each Jesuit's grave and his name and some vital facts about him were written in white paint. The vital facts were the following: name and grouping in the Order (priest, brother, scholastic); national origin and date of birth; place and date of death. In addition, on the top of each cross there was this inscription: "*In spem Resurrectionis hic Jacet* (In hope of Resurrection, here lies [name inserted])." On the bottom of each cross 'R.I.P' (*Requiescat In Pace*) was printed,

Many of these crosses and texts were sketched and can be seen in the *St. John's College, Fordham, N.Y.* manuscript referred to above.

Though there were no headstones for the Jesuits in the old cemetery, the graves of most of those who were not Jesuits *did* have headstones of various sizes and models. Their variety in size and design argues that they were probably provided by their friends or relatives. Those headstones *were* moved to the new site, although in an area separate from the graves of the Jesuits. But, according to the *Liber Defunctorum*, so were the bodies.

We ask, then, why did the myth persist that there were "no remains" in the cemetery? It seems somehow to have sprung out of one or other of the following anomolies:

The remains of one Jesuit, Br. Joseph Creeden, and one college employee, Joseph Kessel, are not in the new cemetery because they wre not found in the old one. Br. Joseph Creeden, a novice brother, died on July 10, 1847 before taking his first vows. He was the first Jesuit who died at Fordham and undoubtedly for that reason his brethren felt a special need to memorialize him. In *St. John's College, Fordham, N.Y.*, we read, "This Brother's body was not found in removal of 1890, although we dug for it for 3 days. His place was left vacant in new cemetery and a head stone (*sic*) erected over an empty grave. J. Zwinge."

Joseph Kessel at the time of his death in 1855 was a lay employee of the college. He had an unusual background because he had been a Jesuit brother in Rome; he left the Order there, at a time of great political unrest. While he was at Fordham he applied to be restored into the Society but by the time of his death no response had been received regarding his request. Since his remains were not found, there is no marker or memorial for him in the new cemetery.

And there is the case of Fr Achilles Sarria's remains.[22] Fr. Sarria was born in Naples, Italy, May 11, 1824, entered the Jesuits August 1, 1844, and died June 28, 1873. He was a member of the Mexican province. After he vigorously denounced the Freemasons during a sermon, "... he learned that the police were waiting for him outside the church. He therefore left by a back door and escaped to Vera Cruz, from which place he hastened ... to New York. On the way he contracted yellow fever, from which he died in a few days after finding a refuge with his brethren of the Society in New York"[23] The main mystery about him is that Fr. Zwinge reported that his remains were transferred from the old to the new cemetery and placed between Fathers Monroe and Tissot. But later charts, admittedly drawn up when most of the tombstones were becoming undecipherable, omit his name. A possible explanation is that his remains had been claimed by relatives or Jesuits of his home province and no record was kept of this event.

And there is the argument about Fr. Eugene Maguire (his name was often also misspelled as McGuire). He was the only Jesuit who died at St. Mary's, KY whose remains, some 17 years after his death, were transferred to the Fordham cemetery. Yet a distinguished Jesuit recalls kneeling in prayer many years ago at Fr. Maguire's tombstone in Kentucky. His remains *had* been moved but the tombstone was retained, possibly to keep a memorial of his having been buried there or perhaps as a memorial to human indecision or laziness.

But all this proves is that, in one case, a memorial was placed over Bro. Creeden's empty grave, that no memorial stone was provided for Joseph Kessel, that Sarria's grave seems missing, and that people were still praying over a stone in Kentucky even when Fr. Maguire's remains were no longer there. Hardly evidence, from the predominant documentary evidence presented above, to substantiate the myth that *all* the graves are empty.

# CHAPTER 12

## BIOGRAPHICAL PROFILES

*A WIDENING WORLD*

The real contribution of the cemetery documents is to enable us to garner a picture of how Jesuit ministry developed in the New York/Canada Mission from those first years at Fordham and Xavier. Yes, many of the Jesuits in the cemetery call our attention to the day in, day out issues faced by those two specific institutions. But the roll of the cemetery dead also lets us catch sight of new configurations and shifts based on apostolic demands beyond Fordham and Xavier. The pioneer Jesuit companions might have wanted their dead to remain "among us," but the *lives* of these dead Jesuits took them far and wide — and to serve not "us" but anyone in need. While not earthshattering, these new configurations and shifts enlarge our view of Jesuit history in the latter half of the 19th and early 20th centuries.

For example, two of those interred in the Fordham cemetery illustrate the regional shifts in the Society of Jesus's work in North America. Fr. James Perron had been Superior of the New York/Canada Mission from 1866 to 1869, a role going back, as we have seen, to Fr. Clement Boulanger. By the time Fr. Perron died in 1890, that Mission would no longer exist, since the New York region was joined to the Maryland Province in 1879. This meant that New York Jesuits could now expect to work in earlier ministries established by Maryland such as the College of the Holy Cross and Boston College, both founded out of the Maryland Province in 1843 and 1863 respectively. Fr. Perron's colleague in the cemetery, Fr. William O'B. Pardow, was in fact Provincial of the Maryland-New York Jesuit Province from 1893 to 1897 and had the job of deciding which Jesuit went to Fordham or Xavier or Georgetown or anywhere else for that matter.

This perhaps explains why, of the fourteen former college presidents buried in the Fordham cemetery, six were presidents of Fordham and three of Xavier, but two were president of Boston College, one of Woodstock College and Seminary, another of St. Peter's College and another of Georgetown.[22]

Another aspect of those early *Annual Letters* — the largely polemical relationships between Catholics and Protestants — is belied in part by three cemetery Jesuits: Fr. Louis Jouin, born in Germany of Huguenot parents, was for over 30 years a renowned teacher, linguist, philosopher and writer at Fordham. Fr. Francis Monroe, nephew of U.S. President James Monroe, had been an officer in the U.S. Navy during Commodore Matthew Perry's 1853-54 visit to Japan and converted shortly after. He taught mathematics, sciences, and history at Fordham and the College of St. Francis Xavier. Fr. Henry Van Rennselaer, descendant of early Dutch (Calvinist) settlers in New York, was a widely admired pastor and personality at the St. Francis Xavier parish, NYC.

The birthplaces of the Jesuits in the cemetery are also revealing, especially in the differences between the pioneers and the those who followed. The changing pattern of national origin among these Jesuits can be clearly observed from the chart below.

## PIONEER JESUITS COMPARED TO THE TOTAL GROUP

| 1846 PIONEERS Place of Birth | | | ALL WHO DIED, 1847-1909 Place of Birth | | |
|---|---|---|---|---|---|
| | No. (47) | Pct. | No. (124) | Pct. | |
| France | 19 | 40.5 | 27 | 21 | France |
| Ireland | 11 | 23.5 | 46 | 37 | Ireland |
| Canada | 6 | 13 | 6 | 5 | Canada |
| Germany | 3 | 6 | 8 | 6 | Germany |
| USA | 3 | 6 | 27 | 21 | USA |
| Italy | 0 | | 6 | 5 | Italy |
| Other | 5 | 11 | 4 | 5 | Other |

The 'big three' contributors to the 1846 pioneer group were France, Ireland and Canada. Native French speakers were in a clear majority. By 1909 the total pattern had changed. The "big three" contributors were Ireland, France and the USA. Native English speakers were now in the majority. The language change was clearly a function of developing educational and pastoral needs of the changing population patterns Jesuits were starting to deal with.

Insertion into this new and rapidly changing culture could have its adventurous side as well. Despite rare references made to the Civil War in the *Annual Letters* of St. John's College and Xavier, Jesuits were actually serving as military chaplains in that conflict: for the Union, Frs. Michael Nash, Thomas Ouellet and Peter Tissot, and for the Confederacy, Fr. Joseph Prachensky.

The other thing the lives of the dead teach us is that Jesuits in the educational ministry always seemed to be doing a lot of pastoral work as well — missions, prisons, hospitals, helping out in parishes and convents, relief work, etc. Recall the story (Appendix III) of the two Fordham Jesuits, Frs. Henri du Merle and Charles Schianski, who never quite made it to the Fordham cemetery but died in Montreal as a result of their labors among the typhus-stricken Irish immigrants there. In any case, this traffic between the educational and the pastoral seems quite fluid by modern standards. Indeed, some Jesuits back then thought the pastoral sphere was upstaging the educational, but this would change with the growing number and size of educational institutions needing to be served.

The average age of the Jesuits who were buried during 1847-1909 was 52. Today it would be 73.5. The youngest Jesuit in the cemetery is Br. Joseph Proulx who died at 17 years and 8 months; the youngest scholastic is Edward O'Connor who died at 20 years and 4 months; the youngest priest is Fr. Eugene Maguire, age 33, reinterred at Fordham in 1850 from Kentucky.

The oldest Jesuit in the cemetery is Br. William Hennen who died at age 89. Several other Brothers lived into their 80's: Br. Charles Alsberg, 86, Br. Émile Risler, 83; Br. Jeremiah Garvey, 82; Br. Philip Ledoré, 81; Br. Frederick De Pooter, 80. Only two priests reached the the four-score mark: Fr. Thomas Legoúais, 83, and Fr. Louis Jouin, 81.

Causes of death are mentioned for only 32 of the 124 deceased Jesuits, with a dozen different diseases or causes of death being named. Pneumonia was identified most frequently as the cause of death (7 times), followed by typhoid fever (6), consumption (4), heart trouble (3) and apoplexy (1). Two had unusual causes of death: one in a railroad car accident, and one from asphyxiation during a fire at Xavier.

This final section offers information about each of these individuals. For some — nine young students, three seminarians, two former college employees — little has been learned. The situation is understandably different for the Jesuits. Some were in the public eye and we have a wealth of information at hand about them. At least a modest amount of information is available for most other Jesuits, gleaned from the documentary sources described ealier.[24]

It is also important to recall the *genre* of most of the documents we cite here. They are encomia — laudatory and at times unrelentingly flattering. History's warts are graciously omitted, on the principle no doubt, *nil nisi bonum de mortuis* (say nothing but good things about the dead).

Still, the collective picture is quite amazing. A pattern emerges of a lot of hardworking Jesuits. These were men who could be sent anywhere in the service of Christ. They were ready to do any job. A symbol of their solidity and steadfastness are the 37 Jesuit Brothers buried in the cemetery. Coadjutor Brothers, as they were called then, supported the priests' efforts in any way they could. For many, that meant cooking meals, doing marketing and buying, managing a farm, directing an infirmary, housekeeping, and similar works. Now as then, Jesuit Brothers also used their special talents to serve God as artists, musicians, artisans and teachers. And their presence back then made it possible for the colleges, if not to exist, then at least to run economically enough to enable them to take in the number of poor students that they did.

All of these — priests, scholastics and brothers along with their lay helpers —set a new stamp on the tentative, embattled life of the nascent Catholic Church in America. The deep spiritual motivation of the men interred in the Fordham cemetery is evident at every point. That is praise enough. A young student, David Arelland, perhaps expressed it even better in the October 1890 *Fordham Monthly*:

## In the College Cemetery

Nigh to a little vineyard of the earth,
Long laborers in the vineyard of the Lord
Here in God's acre share their meet reward –
The sleep He giveth His beloved. Their birth
And death, the date and place (alas the dearth!)
Are all the marble monuments record.
Yet was each life e'en as an angel's sword
Wielded unseen but making felt its worth.

Yonder at eventide the dresser reaps
The gems from off the crown of Vintagetime,
Easing the vine of all its purple heaps;
The while these dead are garnerers in a clime
Where plenty, aye gratuitously leaps
Without the fear of blight from drought or time!

*Individual Profiles*

For individual graves, the identification code is: B (born), E (entered the Society), + (died). The bracketed part of the code, e.g., [I-R-7], gives the location of the grave in the present cemetary as is illustrated on page 268.

BR. CHARLES ALSBERGE, S.J.
B. Dec. 31, 1789 in Ooteghem, Belgium (other dates found)
E. Oct. 8, 1827 [I-R-7]
+ March 16, 1876 at FC: Lived 86 years

Charles Alsberge (earlier catalogues had Alsberg) was admitted into the Society in Belgium after a long probation. He completed his noviceship at Montrouge (near Paris) and served faithfully as tailor and sacristan in various houses of the Society in Belgium until 1836, when he was sent to the New Orleans Mission. There he labored for ten years. In 1847 he received his final appointment: to Fordham College where he spent his remaining thirty years (1847-1876) as tailor.

His whole life in the Society was a model of the life of a faithful, pious Jesuit Brother. The delight with which, even when almost blind, he labored for the Lord touched all who witnessed it. Finally, all his physical vigor having faded away, rather than broken by any disease, he quietly fell asleep in the Lord.

BR. PATRICK BACON, S.J.
B. Dec. 31, 1813 in Abbeyleix, Co. Laois, Ireland
E. Aug. 26, 1851 [J-R-3]
+ Sept. 27, 1870 at FC: Lived 56 years

Little could be learned about Br. Patrick Bacon except his Jesuit assignments. He made his novitiate at Fordham. Then he was assigned for a few years to do household tasks at St. Joseph's parish in Troy, NY. His next assignment was the same one he had to the end of his life, doing household tasks at Fordham from 1858-70. Fr. Minister's diary noted only this about his death: "Brother Bacon died this morning at 1½. The burial will take place tomorrow morning at 5½."

BONAVENTURE BEAVEN, Fordham student
B. July 16, 1843 in Mexico [A-6]
+ March 15, 1857: Lived 12 years

All that has been learned about Bonaventure Beaven, besides the vital statistics recorded above, is that he "had scarlet fever for about three weeks, and, having recovered, died of congestion of the lungs."

REV. HERMANN BLUMENSAAT, S.J.
B. Feb. 23, 1845 in Arnsberg, Westfallen, Germany
E. Apr. 11, 1874 [F-R-6]
+ May 5, 1901 in NYC: Lived 57 years

Hermann Blumensaat left Germany at age twenty-one to avoid the army and support his mother. His companion in his early years here was Henry Heide. They became successful partners in a candy manufacturing company, but Hermann gave up his business interests when his mother died. At age 30 he decided to become a Jesuit priest.

His novitiate was at Sault-au-Récollect, Montreal; philosophy, theology and ordination were at Woodstock, MD. He then spent four years ministering to a German congregation in 87th St., NYC. However, Blackwells Island (later Welfare Island) became the site of his ministry for the last fourteen years of his life. On that island five city institutions (Women's Lunatic Asylum; the Workhouse; the Almhouse; the Penitentiary; the City Hospital) were devoted to the sick in body and mind; they usually totaled about 8,000 souls, three-quarters of whom were Catholics. Chaplains like Fr. Blumensaat were kept busy all day ministering to their population's spiritual needs and was likely to be called any hour of the night to attend the dying. He never took a vacation. His knowledge of Latin, German and French (he was less skilled in Spanish and Polish) enabled him to assist many needy and helpless immigrants by communicating with them in their native tongue.

A short article on him in the *Woodstock Letters* noted that "Fr. Blumensaat is delighted with the opportunities for doing good which he possesses on Blackwells

Island." He indicated that "at least 15,000 different people, punished for [less serious offenses at this place], are susceptible to the influence of a priest; many of [them] would otherwise never call upon that influence"[25] He was able to continue his devoted apostolic work until 1901 when "owing to overwork and exposure, he was attacked by pneumonia" and died at St. Vincent's Hospital.

Words used to describe Fr. Blumensaat were: bright student, happy disposition, obedient to superiors, devoted to friends and beloved by them; a Catholic priest [who labored] "devotedly, zealously, untiringly" for his flock — a description of a truly holy man.

Appreciations and biographical data about him were written by his friends, Henry Heide and Fr. Samuel Frisbie, on the occasion of the unveiling of a tablet memorializing Fr. Blumensaat in the then-new Catholic chapel (1910) on Blackwell/Welfare Island, NYC.[26]

BR. CHARLES BRENDLE, S.J.
B. Sept. 12, 1826 in "Berg," Würtemberg, Germany
E. Mar. 1, 1855 [I-R-4]
+ Jan. 9, 1887 at FC: Lived 61 years

Little has been learned about Br. Charles Brendle besides his vital statistics and an early notation about him that his special talent was that of *faber lignarius* — carpenter. After making his novitiate at Fordham he remained there for ten years (1858-1867), following his special talent as cabinetmaker. Later he was transferred with the same assignment to two other places: the College of St. Francis Xavier, NYC, and the parish of (later St. Ignatius), NYC.

REV. JAMES BRODERICK, S.J.
B. June 8, 1851 in Athlone, Co. Westmeath, Ireland
E. Oct. 26, 1875 [G-R-6]
+ Oct. 21, 1905 in NYC: Lived 54 years

After studying philosophy in Belgium, James Broderick seems to have had serious health problems. In 1882, for instance, he was assigned to St. Thomas, MD, as "*cur. val.* (caring for his health," and doing private study; then, after a year of teaching at Georgetown, he continued his regency during 1885 and 1886 at Las Vegas, N.M.(an unusual assignment at that time because it was far away from his province). After theology and ordination at Woodstock, MD, he did parish ministry at Alexandria, VA and in 1891 and 1892 he taught at Gonzaga High School, Washington, DC, before making his tertianship in Frederick, MD.

In his few years of active ministry after tertianship he was assigned to numerous places: Whitemarsh, MD, for a year; and Chapel Point, MD, where he was also superior, for three years; the missions in Jamaica, B.W.I., for four years; Holy Cross, Worcester, MA, where he was also Minister for a year; and his last assignment was to hospital work in Randalls Island, New York City.

BR. JOHN BUCKLEY, S.J.
B. June 23,1842 in Curraghturk,Co. Limerick, Ireland
E. Oct. 29, 1871 [I-R-6]
+ July 21, 1876, in NYC: Lived 34 years

Not long after John Buckley had immigrated to this country the Civil War broke out, and he enlisted in the Union army, which he served for four years.

After his noviceship, he was sent to Fordham where he worked on the farm with fidelity (1873-1876). However, for several years a disease had been developing inside him, and he was finally forced to desist from hard labor. He was sent to the College of St. Francis Xavier, NYC, to be closer to his medical treatment. However, soon after his transfer, he died, fortified by the last sacraments and edifying those about him by his patience.

BR. MALACHY BYRNE, S. J.
B.   Feb. 2, 1813/15 in Tynanstown, Co. Meath, Ireland
E.   May 28, 1857 [C-L-2]
+ Feb. 12, 1873 at FC: Lived 58 years

Malachy Byrne was admitted to the Society for the New York-Canada Mission in 1857. After his noviceship he was engaged first at Guelph, Canada, in various domestic occupations and afterwards at Fordham (1860-1873) as a stone mason.

He suffered from several infirmities, which he bore with patience and humility and died a pious death at Fordham.

REV. MICHAEL J. BYRNES, S.J.
B. May 29, 1843 in Elphin, Co. Roscommon, Ireland
E. Sept. 8, 1858 [G-L-2]
+ Feb.10, 1907 in Jersey City, NJ: Lived 63 years

Michael J. Byrnes made his novitiate and his classical studies in Frederick, MD, from 1858 to 1862. During 1862-65 he taught math and French at Holy Cross College, Worcester, MA, and did the same in the next three years at Boston College. In 1868-74 he studied philosophy and theology, all but the first year at Woodstock; he took his first year of philosophy at Georgetown. His first assignment as a priest was to Boston College where he taught the humanities, math, and rhetoric. In fact, for some time he specialized in teaching rhetoric since he later taught it at Holy Cross during 1877-81, at Fordham for a year, and at Boston College from 1883-88.

Beginning with 1889, leaving aside the college teaching arena, he was able to function at times as parish priest and at other times as high school teacher. Thus he did parish work at Xavier parish, NYC; Washington, DC; St. Joseph's, Philadelphia; and St. Mary's, Boston. He also taught for brief periods at Gonzaga, Washington, DC; St. Joseph's, Philadelphia; and Loyola, Baltimore.

Fr. Byrnes was clearly a multi-talented person who devoted his talents to the development of the minds and souls of his students and his parishioners.

### REV. PHILIP CARDELLA, S.J.
B. Apr. 3, 1831 in Fano, Pesaro, Italy
E. Oct. 22, 1846 [H-R-3]
+ July 17, 1901 in NYC: Lived 71 years

Fr. Philip Cardella had transferred from the Roman province to the Maryland-New York province in 1882, after a fruitful apostolate in Nicaragua. When he was in New York for some years, he was quoted as saying, surely with some satisfaction: "He who, as President of Nicaragua, banished me from the Country is now in New York, an exile."

Fr. Cardella, an Italian, became an apostle of the Hispanic community in New York City. He was also honored by being named the Tertian Instructor at Frederick, MD, in 1898; he had previously held the same position elsewhere.

Fr. Cardella "had all the appearance of an aristocratic son of Italy, military in his step, plump of body with a large head amply furnished with mixed black and gray curly hair." He was "unable to talk without free hands and arms. He always carried an umbrella, rain or shine, and if he wished to insist upon a particular point he would hand his umbrella to his companion to hold, until he had put the decided finishing word [and hand flourish] to his thought, and then, with the same precision, would take it right back to await his companion's answer."

"For some years he was director of the quarterly conferences of the New York Archdiocesan clergy." This appointment was symbolic of the special respect accorded him by the Society and the Archdiocese.

### REV. PETER CASSIDY, S.J.
B. May 13, 1845 in Westport, Co. Mayo, Ireland
E. Aug. 11, 1865 [F-R-9]
+ Jan. 19, 1902 in NYC: Lived 57 years

When Peter Cassidy was four years old, his family emigrated from Ireland to Brooklyn, NY. Peter attended the College of St. Francis Xavier and after graduation taught there for a year. But during a retreat under Fr. Daubresse, he decided to become a Jesuit.

Having made his novitiate and early studies in Canada, he returned to Xavier to teach there for three years during his regency. He completed his theological studies at Laval, France. After ordination he served for 27 years in many Jesuit colleges, such as Boston College, Fordham, and Georgetown. His favorite college work, in which he experienced great success, was teaching poetry and rhetoric.

He was rector-president for three years (July 1, 1888 to October, 1891) at St. Peter's College, Jersey City; the college program there was begun in 1877.

Fr. Cassidy was also very successful in giving retreats and missions as well as in offering spiritual direction. A sketch about him in the *Woodstock Letters*[27] contains several pages of descriptions and praise and of his efforts in this kind of work in which he was engaged exclusively in the last few years of his life. Highly lauded were his "admirable use of Holy Scripture which he quoted with great unction; 'the word of God alone' he would say, [I must] put forward and I but the mouthpiece.' With him it was the living word. ... To some who owe their spiritual growth to his guidance, he is their hope of heaven."

Fr. Cassidy was described as a man of perfect order about his person, his room, even his style of writing; perfectly honest, even blunt in his candor; the manliest of men, an unselfish gentleman, capable of deep feeling withal ... of tender affection, which, however, he not easily or often manifested. ... Altogether a lovable character, a sincere and out-spoken friend." When he praised a person or a performance, he did it so heartily that there was no suspicion of his sincerity.

His obituary recounts his sufferings from malaria and his attack of pneumonia during a two weeks' mission at St. Ignatius Church. When physicians realized they could do no more for him, he was fortified with the Last Sacraments and the prayers for the dying. The account ends with this statement repeated by many: "May God give us all as peaceful and as happy a death, as in His mercy he gave to good Fr. Cassidy."

Fr. Cassidy's funeral Mass was held at St. Ignatius church, NYC, said by Fr. James Fagan, the Socius to the Provincial, and attended by Bishop McDonnell, about sixty priests and a filled church.

REV. JOHN CHESTER, S.J.
B. May 6, 1854 in Caledonia, NY
E. Aug. 14, 1871 [I-L-1]
+ Dec. 20, 1906 in NYC: Lived 52 years

John Chester received his early education at Gonzaga College, Washington, DC, and entered the Jesuit novitiate at Frederick, MD. He studied philosophy at Woodstock, taught during regency at Holy Cross and Georgetown, but became ill and went to New Mexico for a year. He returned to Woodstock for theology and ordination. During his priesthood he taught at Fordham and Holy Cross. Then a series of financial posts followed: procurator at Georgetown for a short time, followed by ten years as province treasurer. His last assignment was treasurer at St. Andrew-on-Hudson, Poughkeepsie, NY.

His associates regarded Fr. Chester as an untiring worker for the sick and the poor; he was specially kind and helpful to those who did not enjoy good health. Because his assignments brought him into the financial world, he became a personal friend with many prominent business people.

REV. PHILIP CHOPIN, S. J.
B. Oct. 28, 1823 in Montandon, France
E. Aug. 3, 1848 [B-R-11]
+ Jan. 16, 1864 in NYC: Lived 40 years

After Fr. John Jaffré, the pioneer full-time chaplain at Blackwells Island lasted only one month there (most likely because of working beyond his strength), it became obvious that an additional chaplain was necessary. Fr. Philip Chopin was appointed to be one of the two new chaplains. He had been teaching philosophy and higher mathematics at the College of St. Francis Xavier, NYC. One of his students, Dr. Charles Herbermann, wrote of his professor years later: "He was a French gentleman not remarkable for ... his skill in teaching, but a pious and self-sacrificing religious" (p. 130).

Fr. Francis Maréchal was also appointed with Fr. Chopin in replacement of Fr. Jaffré. Apparently their personalities were quite different: Chopin "had the knack of smoothing over difficulties at the hospital," while Maréchal did not hesitate to face problems head on.

In the early years at Blackwells Island, there was a lot of opposition to the work of the priests. For example, some young physicians did not like their presence and penalized poor defenseless patients for attending Mass. They would ask patients if they had been at Mass that morning. If the answer was yes, their response would be: "If you were well enough to go to Mass, you are well enough to go home." And they were cruel enough to send home a number of these poor people.

But due in part to Fr. Maréchal's strength and Fr. Chopin's suavity, the situation gradually changed on Blackwells Island, and for years Catholics were well treated there.

During Fr. Chopin's two years of ministry at Blackwells Island, "he received hundreds of Protestants into the Church. Finally, he himself was laid low, by the scourge" of typhoid, "a martyr of . . . zeal and charity" like his fellow Jesuit chaplains on those islands, Fathers Jaffré, Laufhuber and Pavarelli.

MR. THOMAS M. CONNELL, S. J., Schol.
B. July 20, 1868, in Baltimore, MD
E. Aug. 4, 1884 [E-R-9]
+ Jan. 13, 1892, in NYC: Lived 23 years

Thomas Connell left Loyola College, Baltimore, to enter the Jesuit novitiate at Frederick, MD. After studying philosophy at Woodstock College, he was assigned to teach at Xavier, NYC. Before the end of his first term there, he was hospitalized for a month before his death. In the hospital his mother and his brother were in constant attendance; his brother, Francis M. (1866-1935), was later an outstanding Jesuit educator. During Thomas' illness he impressed others by his patience and his resignation to God's will. "He died without a struggle ... and was buried in our peaceful little cemetery at Fordham, whilst the pure snow kept ... falling gently."

REV. JAMES CONWAY, S. J.
B. Mar.15, 1849 in Cranagh, Co Tyrone, Ireland
E. Aug. 25, 1869 [F-L-2]
+ Aug. 12, 1905 in NYC: Lived 57 years

"Father James Conway had a meteoric flight through Woodstock where he was appointed to teach in 1892-93. He was a thorough student and scholar trained in the German Province and assigned to the Buffalo Mission. Thence he came to New York and taught and wrote in various houses. He added his quota to the school controversy by his pamphlet *The State Last*."[28]

During the short period of his teaching at Woodstock he was recognized for his religious observance, hard work, and thoroughness.

For many years he presided over the New York Archdiocesan theological conferences. In 1902-1903 he was honored by being appointed the first Instructor of Tertians at the new Noviceship of St. Andrew-on-Hudson at Poughkeepsie, NY. His last assignment was at Fordham (1903-1905), teaching metaphysics, ethics, and evidences of religion. He died at Fordham.

MR. MICHAEL S. CORBETT, S. J., Schol.
B. Mar. 6, 1875 at Nenagh, Co. Tipperary, Ireland
E. Aug. 14, 1892 [F-R-5]
+ Oct. 31, 1899 in NYC: Lived 24 years

He made his noviceship and study of the humanities at Frederick, MD. Probably he had health problems because he was assigned only one year to the College of St. Francis Xavier, NYC, doing student prefecting and teaching. After that year he was assigned to study theology in Woodstock. Again this was a departure from the usual course of studies, which prescribed several years of philosophy preceding the study of theology. This special arrangement again was possibly done in view of his health problems.

He died in his parents' home which was in the vicinity of Van Corlandt Park near Fordham College.

BR. PATRICK CORRIGAN, S. J.
B. May 2, 1821 in Drumkeeron, Co. Fermanagh, Ireland
E. Dec. 14, 1873 [H-R-10]
+ Oct. 11, 1894 at FC: Lived 73 years

Patrick Corrigan immigrated to Quebec and then moved around Canada before coming to Marquette, WI. At a mission there he met a priest who urged him to make a Jesuit retreat of election to help him decide his vocation. He did so and entered the novitiate of the New York-Canada Mission in Montreal. After his novitiate he was assigned to Fordham. For many years he cared for the Fordham cemetery. He remained there to the end of his life (1876-1894), except for two years spent at Xavier and Jersey City.

He was a mason and stone cutter and worked hard at his trade till two years before his death. At that time he assisted Fr. Jouin in his book-bindery. When he died he was well fortified with the last rites of the Church.

MR. JOHN T. CRANE, S. J., Schol.
B. Feb. 23, 1878 in Miners' Mills, PA
E. Aug. 13, 1897 [F-L-3]
+ Dec. 8, 1905 at FC: Lived 27 years

John Crane made his novitiate at Frederick, MD, and studied philosophy at Woodstock, MD. Then he was assigned to regency at Holy Cross, but he did not finish even the first term there.

Mr. Crane was sent to the Fordham infirmary on November 8, 1905, and died there a month later. During that month he received frequent visits from relatives and Jesuits. He was called by a Jesuit classmate a "lovable saint." The same man wrote of his life as "faultless" and praised his tender devotion to the Blessed Virgin. Asked about prayer in his serious illness, he said it was "very hard to pray in this condition" but added that "it was easier if someone suggested little ejaculations" which he could repeat after them.

He was praised for his Jesuit obedience and for his heroic patience during his sufferings. His contemporaries thought that he should be regarded as a model Jesuit.

BR. JOSEPH CREEDEN, N.S.J.
B.  Apr. 26, 1821 in Ireland
E.  May 2, 1847 [B-L-1]
+ July 10, 1847: Lived 26 years

Joseph Creeden, like many of his countrymen, sought the refuge of the New World during the time of "The Great Hunger" in Ireland. Many of the refugees booked passage on unsanitary, disease-ridden ships, often called "coffin ships" for the number who died on board. Apparently Joseph was on one of those ships. About two months after he entered the novitiate at Fordham, he became gravely sick from "an illness contracted on shipboard," as noted in the Fordham *Liber Defunctorum*. During his illness he gave an excellent example of great patience and self-abnegation.

Though he was the first Jesuit who died at Fordham, his death and burial were noted with extraordinary succinctness in the Fr. Minister's diary. Thus we read there on July 10: "*Moritur Frater Creeden, nov. coadj.* [Novice Brother Creeden died];" and on July 11: "*De more sepelitur idem frater* [The brother was buried following our usual funeral customs]."

When the remains of other Jesuits were removed from the old to the new cemetery site at Fordham, his remains could not be found, in spite of workers spending three days searching for them. Nevertheless a tombstone was placed over the space that was assigned for his remains. A special memorial was later erected for the first Jesuit who died at Fordham.

JOHN CREMIN, Diocesan Seminarian
B. 1824 [A-1]
+ April 12, 1849: Lived 25 years

The *Liber Defunctorum* records a hard-to-read Latin inscription on his tombstone: "Here in peace rests John Cremin, a mature exemplary young Irishman 25 years of age. Cruel death on April 12, 1849, snatched away a hope for the church and one loved by his friends. The seminary students with tears collected funds for this monument to commemorate their very holy and popular classmate."

BR. PATRICK CROWE, S.J.
B. Feb.18/28,1817/8 in Carlow, Ireland
E. Jan. 10, 1845 [J-R-5]
+ Dec. 23, 1869 at FC: Lived 51/52 years

Patrick Crowe was one of the last to enter the novitiate in St. Mary's, KY; of course, he continued his novitiate and took his first vows at Fordham. From those days until shortly before his death, Br. Crowe's assignment was to be manager of the Fordham College farm (1847-1869). As such, he must have been knowledgeable about all aspects of farming, orderly in his habits, and skilled in dealing with many farm workers. His skills in farming and in directing other farm workers must have been specially approved by his Superiors.

In the early days of the college the farm was an important factor that kept costs of the residential students to a minimum. The large, productive farm extended from the rear of the present Administration Building to the Bronx River. A section it is now a part of the New York Botanical Garden. Over the years many Jesuit Brothers tended the farm until it was discontinued years after Br. Crowe's time.

BR. BERNARD CUNNINGHAM, S.J.
B. July 1,1817 in Knockbegg, Co.Roscommon, Ireland
E.  Sept. 9, 1853 [C-L-3]
+ Mar. 11, 1874 at NYC: Lived 57 years

Bernard Cunninghan entered the Society for the New York-Canada Mission in 1853 at the Fordham novitiate. Shortly thereafter he was assigned to the College of St. Francis Xavier in New York City. There his functions were to supervise the dining room from 1856 to 1874; from 1861 to 1874 he also dispensed supplies.

His rector testified that he was a most faithful brother, always most desirous of advancing in the way of perfection.

BERNARD FRANCIS CURRAY, Diocesan Seminarian
B. March 24,1834 in Albany, NY
+ Oct. 17, 1856: Lived 22 years [A-3]

His original tombstone read in part as follows: "Here Lie the Mortal Remains of Bernard Francis Curry / Student of Theology in St. Joseph's Seminary / Born in Albany, March 24, 1834 / Died in New York, Oct. 17, 1856."

The spelling of his surname on his tombstone (Curray vs Curry) differs from that found in other sources about him. In the first Fordham cemetery (now a part of the New York Botanical Garden), only his tombstone or memorial and one other was written in English. All the other tombstones and the Jesuit wooden crosses in the cemetery were written in Latin.

MAURICE DALY, former Fordham student
+ 1849 [A-4]

Maurice Daly was said to have worked at a New York newspaper after his student days, according to Fr. Louis Jouin. When  dying he expressed the wish to be buried at Fordham, and the burial here took place on Aug. 14, 1855, six years after his death.

We do not know where his body was temporarily interred or other details about him, except for a reference to him in Fr. Thébaud's memoirs.[29] He wrote: "Poor Maurice! he was a boy of talent, feeling a strong inclination for politics and journalism. No sooner had he obtained his degree than he associated himself with Denman, the editor of the *Truth Teller*. ... It appeared probable that he would succeed in giving to that old paper a new lease of life. But death struck him ... "

REV. ANATOLY DANDURAND, S. J.
B. July 29, 1826 in Quebec
E. Sept. 9, 1846 [B-R-10]
+ Sept. 20, 1862, in NYC: Lived 36 years

Anatoly Dandurand entered the Jesuit novitiate in Montreal, Canada. After that he studied philosophy for two years at Fordham. Then he was assigned to teach Latin and mathematics at St. Mary's College in Montreal. Next, he taught for three years at the College of St. Francis Xavier, NYC.

While at Xavier one of his students was Dr. Charles Herbermann who wrote of his professor: "I have never come across a better professor of mathematics and science, nor a more upright, honest gentleman" (p. 130).

From 1858 to 1862 he studied theology, four years in four different places: the first year in Laval, France; the second year at Vals, France; the third year at Boston College; and the fourth year at Fordham where he also taught chemistry, natural history, trigonometry and calculus. His final year must have been very busy.

## REV. PATRICK FRANCIS DEALY, S. J.
B. Apr. 7,1827 in Rathkeale, Co. Limerick, Ireland
E. Oct. 31, 1846 [E-R-7]
+ Dec. 23, 1891 in NY: Lived 64 years

Patrick Dealy was the first Fordham student who became a Jesuit, though he had had no Jesuit teachers and he had not received a Fordham degree. His education in the Jesuits required him to study not only at Fordham but also at Montreal, France, Austria, Belgium, and finally Rome.

His usual teaching assignment was English literature. He taught in Fordham (1853-1855; 1864-1866; 1881-1886; 1889-1891), Montreal, and the College of St. Francis Xavier in NYC. While at Xavier he founded the Xavier Union (later named the Catholic Club) which, with a thousand members, became a stimulating influence on many leading members of the Catholic laity. For many years he was the spiritual director of this group.

Fr. Dealy was President of Fordham during 1882-1885. One of his successors in the Fordham presidency, Fr. Robert Gannon, believed that under him "a new era began at Fordham," since older, conservative views yielded to more modern ideas. During his administration the old seminary building was refitted, the Science Building (later called Thébaud Hall) was begun, military drill (R.O.T.C.) was introduced, sports (baseball and football) developed, the *Fordham Monthly* was started and the grounds beautified. During his presidency New York City by eminent domain began the process of annexing 26.85 acres of the campus, the part between Southern Boulevard and the Bronx River, for later use by the New York Botanical Gardens. By 1889 the city paid $93,966.25 for those acres, a sum regarded even then as "absurdly low."

After Fr. Dealy retired from the presidency, he spent his remaining years in parish ministry in New York City, Boston, and Philadelphia. A characteristic or pattern of his ministry was his sponsorship of the local Sodality of Our Lady.

Fr. Dealy was distinguished as a professor, pastor and administrator. He was one of the best known priests in New York, due in part to his charming personality and the interest he took in others. Cardinal McCloskey esteemed him highly, asked him to be his confessor, and regarded him as his best contact among New York Jesuits. The Cardinal also appointed him to lead the first American group pilgrimage to Rome.

Fr. Dealy died of pneumonia on Dec. 23, 1891, at the residence of St. Lawrence O'Toole (later St. Ignatius Loyola), NYC; he contracted the pneumonia after he had visited a dying person. He was buried at Fordham on Christmas Eve.

His name is well known to generations of Fordham students and alumni because an important multi-functioning stone structure in the center of the Bronx campus, Dealy Hall, honors his memory.

## REV. CHARLES HIPPOLYTE DeLUYNES, S. J.
B. July 29, 1805, in Paris
E. Sept. 5, 1841 [C-R-13]
+ Jan. 20, 1878, in NYC: Lived 72 years.

Though Fr. Charles de Luynes was at Fordham only for 1846-1847, doing parish and campus ministry work, he was an important personality in Jesuit communities whose influence was probably based upon the unique combination of learning and attitudes they perceived in him. Dr. Herbermann encapsulated his reflections on his friend when he described him as: "a superior theologian, an omnivorous scholar, familiar with both the old and the New World and a warm-hearted friend." Herbermann also wrote of him as an enthusiastic American who took the greatest interest in the Republic" (p.134) and who was "notwithstanding his French name, a patriotic Irishman" p.152).

Though he was educated and ordained in Paris, he often described himself as "Born in Paris of Irish nationality." He was Paris-born because his Irish father, Edward Joseph Lewins, a lawyer, had been sent there in 1797 to negotiate a loan for the United Irishmen who planned to separate Ireland from England. After a long stay in Paris his father did not succeed in obtaining the loan. But he could not return home because of his part in the rebellion. The family remained in Paris, changed their name, and prospered in business and in higher education.

While young Charles de Luynes was studying theology at the seminary of St. Sulpice he was inspired by Bishop Flaget to join him as a missionary priest in Kentucky. In 1833 he did that and was assigned to several important posts in the diocese of Bardstown (the seat of the diocese and the name of the diocese; both were later changed to Louisville). De Luynes met the Jesuits in Kentucky, was strongly attracted to them and joined them as a novice in 1841.

From his first days in the novitiate his superiors recognized his gifts in languages (English, French, Spanish, and classical languages), in pastoral counseling and in preaching. They encouraged him to develop those talents since they would help make his later work very fruitful. The Jesuit novitiate adjoined St. Mary's College and by 1842 he was a member of the college faculty teaching the Latin classics.

He arrived at Rose Hill from Kentucky with others on Aug. 9, 1846, and did priestly ministry on and off campus. Then in 1847 he was assigned to what became the College of St. Francis Xavier and church in New York City. Except for two years in Troy, NY, and his trips to Mexico (1851-1853 with Fr. Charles Maldonado) and Chile (1855-1856) to gather money and donations for both Xavier and Fordham, his headquarters and the focus of his priestly service remained the Xavier church and College.

His pastoral actions particularly edified many people. For instance, Dr. Herbermann described the dignity and recollection that characterized him at Mass: "He rarely took less than a full hour to offer the Holy Sacrifice.... The Canon of the Mass especially was said with a solemnity that impressed all those who assisted ..." (p. 144). His preaching was said to be like that of his Xavier brethren who were "impressive preachers [not aiming] at high-flying oratory, earnest speakers, practical and clear and ... as far as Father de Luynes was concerned, rather inclined to be lengthy" (p.148). His sermons on texts from St. Paul were specially appreciated.

The high regard in which he was held can be judged from the fact that the Provincial Council of Baltimore in 1855 proposed that he become the Bishop of Charleston. There was a report that he was in fact appointed to that see. However, before the official document arrived, de Luynes arranged to leave New York on a begging trip to Chile until another was appointed to that office. While in Chile, he sought benefactions from wealthy friends for the struggling colleges in North America. Thus Fr. de Luynes served both Fordham and Xavier at the same time when he sought sanctuary from the unwelcome appointment. His purpose in traveling abroad was to prevent his being officially notified of the episcopal appointment. Many individual Jesuits have done that to avoid receiving such special honors, even honors in the Church.

It was indeed honor enough to be seriously considered to be bishop in one diocese. However, Fr. de Luynes was also strongly suggested by New Orleans Archbishop Blanc as a candidate to become his coadjutor bishop.

Contemporaries described Fr. de Luynes as a courtly man, of comely and impressive appearance (six feet tall and proportionally broad, with piercing eyes that a biographer claimed brought discomfort to the wicked), a deep and original thinker, an impressive, earnest and gifted preacher whose powerful bass voice was easily heard in large churches. Testimonials include statements like the following. He was praised as "admirable as a pastor, ... known and honored for his benevolence, ... Loving all in God, he left nothing undone whereby he could possibly render his ministry profitable to the people." Church historian John Gilmary Shea described him as "learned, [with] a clear and penetrating mind" and, as a result ... "he enjoyed universal esteem."

De Luynes had friends among the rich, especially among the local Hispanic wealthy class (at one time he was the only Spanish-speaking priest in New York). Those wealthy friends enabled him to show generosity to his numerous friends who were poor; among that group were many famine-forced exiles from Ireland.

He died at the College of St. Francis Xavier of gastritis; he had chronic dyspepsia for many years.

A lengthy profile of Fr. de Luynes by his friend, Dr. Charles G. Herbermann was published in *Historical Records and Studies.*[30]

BR. FREDERICK De POOTER, S. J.
B.  Mar. 3, 1811 at Broechem, Anvers, Belgium
E. Apr. 18, 1842 [D-L-3]
+ Apr. 19, 1891 at FC: Lived 80 years

Frederick De Pooter served in the army of his country before he served his Lord in the Society of Jesus. Though most of his Jesuit life was spent in the New World, he remained a member of the Belgian Province.He first came to Fordham on June 18, 1847. In the following year he was sent to Fort William, Canada, where he remained as cook and gardener till 1853 when he was transferred to Sault Ste. Marie, Michigan. Then he was transferred to Fordham, where he remained till his happy death, on the day when he had just completed his forty-ninth year in the Society. Thus he served at Fordham during 1847-1848 and 1854-1891. He was a gardener who took care of the vineyard and the bees. Fordham students knew him from that work.

Stories were told about him to illustrate his robust constitution and spirit. For instance, on his way from the missions he lost his money and in order to make his way home he worked for a time in the coal mines. Later, in the year before his death, he had gone to pick apples in Scarsdale, and on his return, being thoroughly wet from the rain, he slept in the barn.

Known to be generous [*magni animi*] towards others, he was hard on himself. Some illustrations of his physical penances have been reported. Thus, he was said to sleep on a bed of corn stalks and use a broom as his pillow. At times he made a crust of bread his supper and breakfast.

REV. JOSEPH DESRIBES, S. J.
B. July 29/30, 1830 in Issoire, Auvergne, France
E. Oct. 5, 1849 [F-R-10]
+ Jan. 19, 1903 at FC: Lived 73 years

Joseph Desribes was a member of a devout Catholic family that numbered four Jesuit priests among its members. When young Joseph reported at home that the teacher in the local school informed his class that Jesus was not God, only a great man, his parents decided to send him to a Jesuit school in Belgium.

He entered the Jesuits at Avignon for the province of Lyons and taught in several colleges of that province. When he came to America in 1857, he taught and was a prefect in the Jesuit College in Alabama, Spring Hill College. He was also ordained there during the Civil War. But in 1866 he went to France for additional study and returned to Spring Hill two years later. The climax of his fourteen years at Spring Hill occurred in his dispute with the local Episcopal bishop concerning custody of two French children. Fr. Desribes was directed in the will made by the father of the children to return them to relatives in France. The Episcopal bishop fought the case through several courts, but Fr. Desribes finally won his case.

After he left the college, he did priestly ministry in Alabama for three years. But at a time when province changes were made, he asked to be transferred to a northern province and his request was approved. So he did priestly ministry in Cincinnati, southern Maryland, Blackwell's Island, NY (1882-89), and other places until finally in 1895 he was assigned to do parish work at St. Lawrence O'Toole's parish (now St. Ignatius Loyola), NY. There he was specially remembered for his generosity, self-sacrifice and devotion to the sick. When his health failed he was moved to the infirmary at Fordham three months before his death.

Though Fr. Desribes' speech always preserved a certain foreign accent, he was everywhere liked as a preacher for the clarity of his language and the originality of his ideas. He was described as pious and courageous, especially in defense of the faith.

REV. JOHN B. DeWOLF, S. J.
B. July 21, 1821 in Michelbeke, Belgium
E. Sept. 24, 1844 [E-L-3]
+ Apr. 9, 1895 in NYC: Lived 73 years

Fr. John DeWolf devoted many years of his life to parish pastoral ministry, for instance, at Leonardtown, MD (1862-74), Frederick, MD, at Alexandria, VA (1882-88), and other places. In addition he taught French, theology, and philosophy at Georgetown, Holy Cross, MA, and St. Joseph's College, Philadelphia. In 1889 he came north and, functioning out of the Xavier parish, served at Hart's Island for four years, and at Randall's Island shortly before his death.

The *Woodstock Letters* reported Fr. DeWolf's saying Mass for the first time on Feb. 15, 1889, in a new Chapel in Hart's Island. There he served "from 200 to 300 prisoners, some 1,400 insane and 150 orderlies."[31] A few years later the same source reported the activities that accompanied his golden jubilee. He celebrated a solemn high Mass in the Xavier church that was filled with friends and admirers, among whom were many of his penitents. Later that day "the modest, humble father listened meekly to his praises ... in an English address, an English poem, and a Latin ode." At the end of the ceremony "Fr. Cardella made appropriate remarks in his original way."

He died in Randall's Island of pneumonia, and was buried at Fordham after funeral rites at the College of St. Francis Xavier.

BR. WILLIAM DONOVAN, S. J.
B. Jan.10, 1822 in Goulstown, Co. Kilkenny, Ireland
E. Aug. 17, 1850 [H-R-6]
+ Dec. 16, 1896 at FC: Lived 75 years

At age 28, William Donovan entered the Jesuits as a novice Brother at Fordham, and after completing his noviceship stayed at the same house among the "Old Brothers" for a year as cook.

As was common in those days, he was transferred to numerous residences and returned to several of them. Thus he was more than once at Fordham (1861-1864;

1888-1897) and at Ft. William, Ontario (1856-60; 1864-72). Other assignments were to The College of St. Francis Xavier, NYC, West Park, NY, and Conewago, PA.

A document about him compiled in the year of his death reported that his occupations at the different places included: cook for ten years; care of the wine cellar for ten years; treasurer for six years; in several places he was gardener; his last assignment at Fordham was *ad domum* (varied work in the community residence).

He was the author of the anonymous manuscript *Workman's Diary* now in the Fordham University Archives. The diary shows his love of outdoor agricultural and gardening work. It also confirms the Fr. Minister's report about the dates of removal of bodies from the "old" cemetery to the new one.

REV. EDWARD DOUCET, S. J.
B. May 12,1825 in Three Rivers, Quebec
E. Sept.7, 1844 [D-R-11]
+ Dec. 9, 1890 at FC: Lived 65 years

Edward Doucet entered the Jesuits in Canada and made most of his novitiate there, but he came to Rose Hill in time to pronounce his first vows at Fordham on Sept. 8,1846, and thereby became the first of many others to make his Jesuit vows at Fordham. He served Fordham during most of his adult years (1846-1852; 1859-870; 1874-1880; 1883-1890).

After his first vows at Fordham he spent the next four years there teaching the youngest students and did the same for two more years at the College of St. Francis Xavier. He then returned to Fordham to complete his philosophical and theological studies and be ordained. In 1859 he was assigned to Rose Hill as prefect of discipline; in the next year he wore many hats: vice-president, prefect of studies, of health, and of discipline.

In 1863 he was appointed President of Fordham, at age 38. He was among the youngest in that position. During his presidency, he helped draw up the plans for the First Division building. But after a one-year presidency he had to resign because of poor health. He traveled to France in November, 1864, to recuperate there. But he also did pastoral work in France and later became professor of English at the Jesuit college at Amiens. In 1868 he returned to Canada and became dean at St. Mary's College, Montreal.

In 1871 Fr. Doucet was again assigned to Fordham where he spent the remaining years of his life except for short assignments at parishes in the New York area and at West Park, the Jesuit novitiate. He taught many courses in philosophy: metaphysics, ethics, logic. the history of philosophy, and the philosophy of religion.

He was an excellent musician and an outstanding preacher in both English and French. He was also a close friend and defender of Edgar Allen Poe, the poet and storywriter, who lived nearby for some time and loved to wander about the college grounds and mingle with the Fathers. The author of Fr. Doucet's obituary lamented the fact that his ill health and weak eyesight prevented him from putting finishing touches on his numerous essays on historical subjects. He believed that his written reminiscences of Poe would have been specially appreciated.

People sought out Fr. Doucet as a confessor because he was specially discreet, understanding, kind, and straight-forward. Above all, priests found in him a wise counselor. He was friend alike of the poor and of the wealthy.

Through 30 years he suffered from various illnesses. In his last years he faced the hardship of blindness and various other infirmities, with truly heroic patience. Finally, full of merits, he flew off to heaven on Dec. 9, 1890, supported by the sacraments and the consolations of religion. Venerated by Jesuits and those close to Fordham for his knowledge and prudence, his piety toward God and his love for the Society, he was buried in the new Fordham cemetery before a large crowd.

## BR. JAMES DOYLE, S. J.
B. July 25, 1851 in Kilkenny, Ireland
E. Aug. 11, 1877 [H-R-9]
+ Aug. 31, 1898 in NYC: Lived 47 years

James Doyle at age 26 entered the novitiate at Frederick, MD. We do not know how he spent his earlier years. His multiple skills must have been appreciated in the novitiate since he was kept there for more than a decade as he fulfilled various functions in different years: assistant tailor, manager of the dining room, cook, treasurer, and beadle of the Brothers. Between two stints at Holy Cross, MA, he was assigned to Troy, NY, and Holy Cross in Worcester, MA. In those places he performed the same variety of functions as he did in Frederick except for tailoring.

Br. James Doyle died, as the *Liber Defunctorum* says at "the Italian Church on Elizabeth St." [Nativity] in New York City. Unfortunately, we have not found an obituary for him or any account of his personality.

## BR. WILLIAM DOYLE, S. J.
B. Dec. 31,1811 in Liberty, Co. Kilkenny, Ireland
E. Nov. 17, 1851 [C-L-4]
+ Apr. 5, 1874 in NYC: Lived 62 years

At age 40, William Doyle entered the novitiate for Brothers at Fordham and was retained there as carpenter for three additional years. Next he was assigned for four years to the College of St. Francis Xavier, New York, as carpenter and receptionist. He spent a year at Troy doing varied tasks and a year back at Fordham as carpenter. His final assignment in 1865 to the day of his death was at the College of St. Francis Xavier as carpenter, assistant infirmarian and cook.

At Xavier he was regarded as a pious and faithful observer of the rules and an example of all the virtues of a good Jesuit Brother.

REV. MICHAEL DRISCOL, S. J.
B. May 7, 1805 at Ennis, Co. Clare, Ireland
E. Sept. 7, 1839[ D-R-1]
+ Mar. 4, 1880 at FC: Lived 75 years.


    began his adult life as a skilled laborer and soon became a priest, a college professor and college president. Born in Ireland, he immigrated to the U.S.A. and found employment as a stone mason near Bardstown, KY. In 1834 he visited a priest who convinced him to enter the nearby St. Mary's College.

A few months after he was graduated with a B.A. degree, at age 34, he entered the Jesuit novitiate and thereby became one of the first novices in the Kentucky mission. Due to the dire needs of those times he and other pioneer seminarians had to teach during their seminary training. He was ordained a priest on September 10, 1844, and later that month, was made dean of St. Mary's College and remained in that post until the Jesuits left Kentucky for Rose Hill.

He arrived at Fordham with a group of other Jesuits on July 29, 1846. There he taught mathematics and Latin, and was also appointed director of the diocesan seminary by Bishop Hughes. But in 1847 Driscol, with several other Fordham priests, responded to a request for help from Jesuits in Montreal to assist them in their priestly ministry to Irish immigrants stricken with cholera. Fr. Thébaud, his rector, recalled Driscol's response to his invitation to minister to the plague-stricken: "I found him delighted with the prospect of beginning his labors among his countrymen, at the cost of his life if necessary." He served the immigrants in their emergency sheds, caught the fever, recovered, and then was pastor of the immigrants in St. Patrick's church in Montreal for several years.

On his return to New York, he taught at the College of St. Francis Xavier, NYC. On September 8, 1855, he became Xavier's third President and pastor of the parish until Aug. 15, 1860. His regime was marked by a 30% increase in the student body, a broadening of the curriculum and an improvement in scholarship.

After completing his term as President, he devoted his life to giving retreats and doing parish work mostly in Troy, NY, in Montreal and in Yonkers. Accounts about him mention the fact that he heard confessions in the Irish language; as is the case with many immigrants whose first language may be Italian, French or Spanish, many Irish immigrants felt more comfortable using their native Irish language when confessing their sins.

Fr. Driscol was "a tall, stately man, with a serious, yet gentle expression of countenance," and an impressive, dignified bearing. He was manly and determined and did not hesitate to urge others to act "calmly and quietly." He was praised for his executive ability in organizing the work of both the St. Francis Xavier parish and the college. "A born orator," his warm, sympathetic heart never failed to reach the hearts of his hearers in important pulpits and in private contacts. With qualities such as these it is no wonder that he was considered a likely candidate to be raised to the episcopacy. In summary, he was regarded as one of nature's true noblemen.

HENRY LEMERCIER DUQUESNAY, Fordham student
B. Feb.1853 in Kingston, Jamaica [A-8]
+ Jan. 29, 1865: Lived 11 years

The above vital statistics are all the facts we know about this young man. Nevertheless, through the kindness of Rev. Gerard L. McLaughlin, S.J., regional archivist of Campion College, Kingston, Jamaica, W.I., we have learned about his family. In the New World the Le Mercier DuQuesnay family first settled in Haiti. Then, after a revolution, they moved as refugees to the island of Jamaica "where they were the mainstay of the Catholic Church from 1800 to about 1840." Many members of the family then migrated to French New Orleans but others remained in Jamaica where they are still prominent today.

BR. JAMES DWYER, S. J.
B. June 6, 1862 in Wappingers Falls, NY
E. Aug. 14, 1879 [ I-L-2]
+ May 5, 1906 in FC: Lived 44 years

At age 17 James Dwyer entered the Jesuit novitiate at West Park, NY, which was not far from his home, and he was assigned to do varied tasks there for an additional two years. His later assignments included Boston College, 1883-93: at first, assistant manager of the dining room; later, assistant procurator, buyer; Gonzaga College (Washington, DC), 1895-96: sacristan, varied domestic tasks; Woodstock (MD), 1896-97: bookkeeper, and varied tasks; Holy Cross (MA), 1898-99: assistant cook, receptionist; St. Ignatius Loyola (NY), 1900-04: manager of the dining room and receptionist; then, care of the physical plant; Fordham,1905-06: assistant infirmarian. We have no further information about him.

BR. MARTIN EALY, S. J.
B.Nov.11, 1830 in Ballinrooaun, Co.Wexford, Ireland
E. Mar. 24, 1855 [H-R-8]
+ July 9, 1897 at FC: Lived 66 years

Before he entered the Jesuits Martin Ealy spent two years of his life as a sailor out of New London, CT. He entered the Jesuits at Fordham under Fr. Thomas Legoüais, then the Master of Novices. After his noviceship he remained at Fordham for two years at various posts and then went to the College of St. Francis Xavier as cook for a year. Next he was assigned to Quebec for two years as cook, buyer and general houseworker.

In 1865 he came south to Troy, NY, for three years as cook, buyer, and treasurer. And then he was at Fordham again as cook for a year. In 1869 to 1876 the parish of St.

Laurence O'Toole had the benefit of his services doing housework, cook, buyer, etc. Then he came back at Troy for fifteen years doing his usual varied activities.

In 1893 when he was over 60, he returned to Fordham for limited posts as receptionist and general housework. We have learned little else about him.

MR. ROMUALD M. ECHEVERRIA, S. J. Schol.
B. Nov. 6, 1868 in NYC
E. Aug. 13, 1888 [H-R-4]
+ May 26, 1898 at FC: Lived 30 years

Romuald Echeverria made his noviceship at Frederick, MD, and upon its completion was sent to Holy Cross to prefect students and teach French, math and Latin for three years. He did the same at Fordham for a year.

He studied philosophy at Woodstock, MD, during 1895-96. Then he was assigned to teach Latin at Boston College. However, a dark cloud of ill health always hovered over him: "*Fuit aegrotis fere semper* (he was almost always ill)." He had been sent to Denver, Colorado, in an unsuccessful quest for good health. Finally, he was sent to Fordham where he died.

HENRY MALORY EDDRINGTON, Fordham student
B. in Tampa, Florida
+ Jan. 31, 1872 [A-10]

In an attempt to learn at least his date of birth, a written inquiry was sent to the Sacred Heart church, the "mother church" of Tampa. A telephone response was received on June 9, 1999: "Checked records from 1816 on and no person of that name was baptized here. No surname like that is in the local telephone book." Thus, we know nothing but the place of his birth and the date of his death.

BR. JAMES EGAN, S. J.
B. May 10, 1814 at Birr, Offaly, Ireland
E. Sept. 13, 1855 [I-R-2]
+ Jan. 19, 1892 at FC: Lived 78 years

James Egan made his novitiate at Fordham and remained there for seventeen years as cook. After four years in Canada he returned to Fordham where he spent the remaining years of his life as cook for one year, and as assistant cook for thirteen years.

For the last three years of his life he was unable to work because he suffered from cancer in his right hand and leg. His pain was excruciating. Yet Br. Egan bore it all patiently and died peacefully.

REV. JAMES FAGAN, S.J.
B. Feb. 20, 1856, in NYC
E. July 29, 1873 [G-R-8]
+ Apr. 28, 1906, in NYC: Lived 50 years

James Fagan began his education in the New York City public schools and at the age of thirteen entered Fordham. A few years later he became a novice at the Jesuit novitiate near Montreal. He was sent abroad for further study: to Roehampton, England, for classics, and Louvain, Belgium, for philosophy. At Woodstock College, MD, he completed his theology program and was ordained there.

He taught at St. Peter's in Jersey City as a scholastic, and as a priest he taught both at Fordham and at the scholasticate in Frederick, MD. Later he was socius to the Jesuit provincial, and college dean at Fordham, Georgetown, and Xavier. During the last three years of his life he was director of studies and vice-principal at Loyola School, NY. There he impressed many by his keen sense of justice, love of knowledge, and high moral/intellectual ideals. He furthered his ideas on education through many public lectures and conferences, praising especially the *Ratio Studiorum*. But he was also well acquainted with current popular educational movements and frequently spoke at Catholic and public-nonsectarian educational meetings.

Fr. Fagan "had a mind of such intense, ceaseless activity that it burnt out the delicate fuse, and the vibrating high-strung nervous machinery suddenly stopped." He died in what is considered the prime of life, and was interred in the Fordham cemetery.

Hard on himself, he was sensitive and helpful to the sinner. People came all over for his counseling services. Tributes to his memory referred to him as "distinguished for his unfailing kindness, his unflinching courage in the performance of ... his duty even in the face of much opposition, and his spirit of prayer." He was specially devoted to the Blessed Sacrament. Though well acquainted with the main issues of the day he talked by preference of spiritual topics. "Truly has he left to those who knew him well an inspiration and an example."

BR. PATRICK FARRELL, S. J.
Oct. 16,1838 at Dunmanaway, Co.Cork, Ireland
E. Dec. 7, 1867 [D-L-2]
+ Apr. 7, 1891 in NYC: Lived 53 years

Patrick Farrell entered the Society in Canada. His life in the Society was characterized by the virtues of humility and obedience. He was employed as cook and in other various offices about the house. During the last year of his life he was porter at the College of St. Francis Xavier, NYC. In this office he displayed patience and tact.

One who knew him well from his novitiate to his death declared that he never knew him to offend against charity or hear him criticize superiors. He was ill during his last four months of life; during that time he edified others by his recollection and patience. He died of consumption in a New York hospital.

BR. FRANCIS FAURIS, S. J.
B. June 11, 1798 in Vachères, France
E. Feb. 2, 1825 [B-L-4]
+ June 23, 1859: Lived 62 years

In 1825 Francis Fauris entered the Jesuits in the Lyons Province. Later he served in many French houses as purchasing agent but was caught up in the 1848 revolution, escaped a violent mob intent on mayhem and managed to get to Fordham where the 1848-49 catalogue stated that he was in charge of supplies. Then he was transferred to the Jesuit parish in Troy, NY, where he remained until just before his death. In Troy he wore many hats: cook, buyer, doorkeeper, etc., and did that work while giving edification as an excellent religious. His obituary noted that, though he underwent a great deal of suffering, he never complained.

He was sent from Troy to the infirmary at Fordham for the sake of his health but died there within the month of his arrival.

JAMES CHRYSOSTOM FENNEL, Diocesan Seminarian
B. July 19, 1827 in NYC [A-2]
+ April 17, 1850: Lived 22 years

In our day, only some of the words on James C. Fennel's original tombstone can be read. But a manuscript booklet in the Fordham University Archives provides the full inscription: "*In spem resurrectionis hic jacet Jacobus Chrysostomus Fennel, Neo-Ebraci natus, anno salutis 1827 jul. 19, susceptus anno 1845 in Ecclesiam Catholicam atque Seminarium ingressus anno 1848 Jan. 29. In pace CHRISTI anno 1850 april 17 quievit consummatus.* (In the hope of resurrection here lies James Chrysostom Fennel, born in New York on July 19, 1827, received into the Catholic Church in 1845, entered the Seminary in 1848, [and] on April 17, 1850, was snatched away and brought to rest in the peace of Christ)."

JOHN FERNANDEZ, Fordham student
B. 1854 in Costa Rica [A-9]
+ March 5, 1870: Lived 16 years

The Father Minister's diary contains the following entries:
March 5, 1870: "*Pie obdormivit in Domino, hora 11½ A.M Joannes Fernandez, annos 16 natus, qui inter optimos numerabatur alumnos.* (John Fernandez, one of our best students, slept piously in the Lord [died] at 11:30 A.M.)."
March 6, 1870: "*Exsequia defuncti alumni Joannis Fernandez. Solemnis cantata*

*Missa. Adsunt praeter alumnos ... Praefecti ac Magistri ... P. Rector.* (Funeral for the deceased student, John Fernandez. Solemn sung Mass. Present at the funeral Mass, besides the students, [were] Prefects and Teachers [and] Fr. Rector.)"

Nothing else has been learned about him.

BR. JAMES FITZGERALD, S. J.
B. Mar.31, 1848 in Hohnstown, Co.Kilkenny, Ireland
E. Feb. 20, 1880 [G-R-7]
+ Mar. 22, 1906 in NYC: Lived 58 years

James Fitzgerald came to America when he was quite young. We do not know about his earlier life, but at age 32 he entered the Jesuit novitiate at West Park, NY, and remained there until the novitiate was moved to Frederick, MD. A series of transfers brought him to St. Inigoes, MD, St. Joseph's, Troy, St. Mary's, Boston, and in 1901 to St. Ignatius, NYC, until the end of his life.

Though he was in pain and realized he was terminal, he kept working until the end. Having cooked the dinner for the community at 6:30 P.M., he was anointed at 9:00 P.M. and died at 2:30 that morning. That night he received the Last Sacraments calmly and with devotion. Then he shook hands with those present in his cheery way and took leave of them happily. About a half hour before breathing his last, he gathered all his strength and cried out his last words, "My Jesus, I give you my whole heart and soul." He was praised for his humility, strong sense of obedience, and devotion to work.

REV. JOHN FITZPATRICK, S. J.
B. July 13,1832 at Blackditches,Co.Wicklow, Ireland
E. Aug. 21, 1857 [D-R-2]
+ Oct. 31, 1880 in NYC: Lived 48 years

John Fitzpatrick made his novitiate at Sault au Récollet near Montreal. After that during 1860-63 he was assigned to prefect and teach many subjects (geometry, trigonometry, religion, philosophy and Latin). During 1864 to 1867 he studied theology at Fordham and was ordained. In 1869 he did parochial work at St. Joseph's in Troy, NY. In 1871-73 he was back at Fordham where he taught geometry and was prefect of discipline. In the following year he made his tertianship in Montreal. The rest of his life, except for two years of parochial work at Troy, he spent at Fordham as prefect of both discipline and students' health. In his final year he was in charge of the parish church at Fordham.

REV. MICHAEL FLYNN, S. J.
B. July 16, 1837 in NYC
E. Aug. 18, 1856 ]F-R-1]
+ Dec. 8, 1897 in NYC: Lived 60 years

Michael Flynn was born in New York City but was sent by his parents at any early age to Ireland and spent several years of his boyhood there. On his return he was enrolled in Xavier but did not complete the program there. Instead, he entered the Jesuit novitiate in Canada and taught at St. Mary's College, Montreal. After studying philosophy in Boston he made regency at Fordham, "having charge of the three grammar classes." His theological studies and ordination (1872) were at Woodstock, MD, followed by a return to Fordham.

In the twenty-five years of his priestly life he had numerous changes in assignments. Besides Fordham, he was assigned to Troy, Jersey City, Georgetown, Holy Cross, West Park and Woodstock. While he was at Woodstock as librarian his health began to fail and he was sent to Fordham as likely more congenial for his health; there he remained until the end, teaching history and Latin, as well as looking after the house library. He died in St. Vincent's Hospital, NYC.

When he was at St. Michael's parish in Troy, he was reported to have specially "endeared himself much to his" parishioners. His contemporaries praised him for his kindness, being painstaking in fulfilling his duties, and for patiently and cheerfully bearing his sufferings. "He was a devout religious and charity was his most striking virtue. He never seemed to detect the faults in [others] but saw only the good qualities, and looked at everything in a charitable light."

REV. GEORGE FOERTSCH, S. J.
B. Aug. 8, 1810 in Sesslach, Bayern, France
E. May 2, 1847 [C-R-4]
+ Dec. 22, 1869 at FC: Lived 58 years

At age 37, he began his novitiate at Fordham under Fr. Thomas Legoüais and after the novitiate immediately began the four-year study of theology and ordination at Fordham.

For the next four years he was engaged in teaching and other academic work at Fordham; in the different years he was assistant to the prefect of studies, teacher of German and Latin. In 1857, however, with the exception of a year (1959) in Paris, his work was changed to more parochial activities in Buffalo, at St. Michael's (1961-64) and later (1865-69) at St. Ann's.

The *Liber Defunctorum* reports that Fr. Foertsch was born in Bavaria but the more authoritative *Catalogus Defunctorum, S.I.* adds the place named above, Sesslach.

REV. SIMON FOUCHÉ, S. J.
B. May 9, 1789 in Paris
E. Sept. 11, 1832 [C-R-5]
+ June 29, 1870 at FC: Lived 81 years

Born during the French Revolution, young Simon Fouché was brought up by his priest-uncle, while his mother posed as his uncle's wife for the priest's safety. We have learned little of his childhood and later years in what must have been very "interesting times" until he was ordained a diocesan priest for Paris in 1816. But, after serving there as spiritual director for five years, in 1821, he decided to go to the New World. Shortly he was in the diocese of Bardstown, KY, where he taught in its seminary. However, in 1831 he made a retreat directed by a Jesuit and after it, he decided to become a Jesuit.

After his noviceship at St. Mary's College, KY, Fouché taught at that college. In addition, from 1840 to 1846 he was also spiritual director of the nearby motherhouse of the Sisters of Loretto, and was helpful in the modernization of the Sisters' constitutions.

Fr. Fouché came to Rose Hill on Aug. 22, 1846 and became the first Jesuit treasurer of the college, and in addition, he taught literature and mathematics. He must have been regarded as a successful treasurer since he was assigned to that office from 1846 to 1855 and from 1861 to 1863.

In 1855 he was assigned to the College of St. Francis Xavier, NYC, where for four years he was spiritual director and librarian. Thereupon he was back at Fordham as assistant procurator for a few years. He returned to Xavier for the last six years of his life.

Fr. Fouché was remembered as vivacious in both action and speech and specially companionable, a man who was very religious, and "the most amiable and gentle of teachers and scholars."

REV. THOMAS FREEMAN, S. J.
B. Apr. 5, 1841 in Fort Ellis, Nova Scotia
E. Sept.7, 1866 [J-L-2]
+ Oct. 14, 1907 in FC: Lived 66 years

In his early life, Thomas Freeman faced a constant struggle with hardship and in his later boyhood he worked on an Atlantic coastal schooner. The family finally moved from Nova Scotia and settled in Rhode Island where he received his primary education. At first he studied with the Sulpicians in Montreal with the intention of joining their congregation. After teaching for a time at their Grand Seminary, he concluded he was better suited to enter a religious order. He entered the Montreal Jesuit novitiate  He studied philosophy at Fordham and Woodstock, and theology at Louvain, Belgium.

His inclination toward sciences became obvious early on. He was granted a year of study at the Columbia University School of Mines for what was to be his life's work; by modern standards that preparation was inadequate but in those days it was special and helpful.

While he pursued the study of theology at Louvain, Belgium, he also assisted a famous Jesuit scientist Fr. Renard, who later left the Jesuits and became curator of the Royal Museum in Brussels.

Fr. Freeman spent eight years teaching physics and chemistry in Woodstock from 1890 to 1898. He was reported to have been remarkably lucid in his scientific explanations. Furthermore, he had a dexterity and practical turn which proved very valuable in preparing for and doing experiments. He was keen in observation and quick in detecting flaws and difficulties in practical problems, as well as in providing remedies. He was able to impart his knowledge in graphic ways to others, thereby making the transfer of knowledge a pleasant operation for the learner.

In addition to teaching at Woodstock, he taught physics and chemistry, sometimes one, sometimes both, at the College of St. Francis Xavier, Boston College, and of course Fordham. For some years he furnished the Scientific Chronicle for the *Catholic Quarterly* and his articles there were said to have doubled its circulation. His outside priestly activity focused on the needs of the deaf, especially at St. Joseph's Institute in the Bronx. In the last few years of his life he was an invalid due to stomach cancer.

"He was a man of absolute sincerity and simplicity of purpose, a patient and constant toiler at his task until the end, concerning himself very little with the outside world and seeing few but the most intimate friends." One such friend was Bishop Michael Tierney of Hartford who gave the last absolution after his Requiem Mass.

Fordham showed its special respect and admiration for him by naming its physics building Freeman Hall.

REV. JOHN GALLIGAN, S.J.
B. Dec. 28, 1858 in Canton, MA
E. Aug. 5, 1876 [F-R-4]
+ July 2, 1899 in NYC: Lived 41 years

John Galligan made his novitiate and his classical studies in Frederick, MD. He studied philosophy in Woodstock, MD. Regency from 1884 to 1887 was in an unusual place, Las Vegas, New Mexico, where he taught English, arithmetic and Logic. It was likely that his health was a factor in his assignment to New Mexico's dry climate.

In 1888 he returned to Woodstock for four years of theological studies and ordination. His first assignment as a priest was at St. Joseph's College, Philadelphia, where he taught Latin and mathematics for several years.

He returned to Frederick in 1895 for tertianship, and remained there for an additional year to teach the classics to young Jesuits.

St. Joseph's College reclaimed his services in 1897, this time as both Minister and prefect of studies. His final assignment on July 2, 1898, was Rector of Gonzaga College in Washington, DC. He planned extensive re-decorations in the church; his successor carried out those plans.

In 1899 he came to New York to attend the Jesuit provincial congregation but became ill and died in St. Vincent's Hospital.

BR. JEREMIAH GARVEY, S. J.
B. Jan. 1, 1794 in Shandrum, Co. Cork, Ireland
E. July 1, 1845 [I-R-9]
+ July 28, 1875 in NYC: Lived 82 years

Already 51 years of age when he entered the Society, Br. Garvey was for many years impeded from most activities by partial paralysis. The greater part of the day he spent in prayer, especially saying his beads. He was assigned to Fordham during 1847-1848 and 1851-1852.

BR. THOMAS GORMLEY, S. J.
B. Apr. 8, 1832 in NYC
E. Oct. 29, 1871 [E-R-10]
+ Jan. 1, 1893 in NYC: Lived 60 years

As a youth Thomas Gormley was remarkable for his piety and devotion to his religious duties. He often expressed the wish to dedicate his life wholly to God's service but was urged to defer his hope and to care for his aged mother. When she died, he entered the Jesuit novitiate at Montreal at age 39.

He had learned the trade of plumber, and he owned property on 5th Avenue and 16th Street, which he later disposed of in favor of the College of St. Francis Xavier. After the novitiate he spent most of his Jesuit life at Xavier doing the plumber's work. He was familiar with every part of the many buildings, and when there was trouble with water pipes he could solve the problem promptly.

During the last ten years of his life, he was a constant sufferer from a complication of diseases, and yet he never uttered a complaint. He accepted his sufferings as a gift from the hand of God. On the morning of his death he received Holy Communion at Mass, returned to his room, and, feeling unwell, went to sleep. When he awakened at the sound of the fire alarm, he lost his way in the smoke-filled corridor and instead of finding the stairway entered a room and was overcome there by the smoke. His death was caused by suffocation.

Br. Gormley "was one of those quiet, unobtrusive men who by the unconscious loveliness of their lives seem to be born for the purpose of edifying those with whom they come in contact." His self-sacrifice, kindness, generosity, attentiveness to the wants of others, obedience, humility were qualities that others noted about him. One described him as "a kind friend, an edifying brother, a man of God."

REV. CHARLES GRESSELIN, S.J.
B. Nov. 26, 1818 in Hiesville, France
E. July 6, 1841 [B-R-12]
+ Aug. 15, 1864 in NYC: Lived 45 years

Before Charles Gresselin entered the Jesuit novitiate in Laval, France, he had studied the humanities for seven years, philosophy for one year and theology for two years. After he took his first vows he was assigned to Brugelette in Belgium for the study of the classics and philosophy. Then he was sent to Laval for theology. Until the 1980s Jesuits were ordained after the third year of the four-year course in theology. However, Gresselin was not ordained until after he completed his fourth year of that study; we do not know why.

His first assignment as a priest in 1848 was to teach various philosophical disciplines to Jesuits at Brugelette and other subjects such as the history of philosophy for other students. During 1850-53 at the seminary at Bruges, he taught logic, ethics, metaphysics, dogmatic theology and church history.

After making his tertianship in 1854-55, he was assigned to the New World and to New York. During 1855-60 he was at Fordham teaching seminarians. For two years he was also the Minister of Jesuit Scholastics and Prefect of their health. The courses he taught were the following: Dogmatic theology, Sacred Scripture, the Sacraments, natural theology, canon law, logic, and metaphysics.

In 1861 the Jesuit theologate was moved to Boston College until the new Scholasticate at Woodstock would open in 1869. Fr. Gresselin's last assignment was to teach at Boston College. But gradually because of his excessive work he developed heart trouble. One winter he spent in Jamaica and in Cuba, but his health did not improve. Yet in 1864 he was appointed acting Prefect of Students and taught Sacred Scripture; in addition he was prefect of the Community library.

The Somervogel-deBacker bibliography of Jesuit writings (vol. 3) reported the fact that Fr. Gresselin composed materials for a tract *On the Faith* but burned the manuscript before his death. Somehow that act symbolizes the glowing talents he displayed in his short life and the disappointment many must have felt at his early death.

REV. NICHOLAS HANRAHAN, S.J.
B. Oct. 31, 1831 in Templeshambo, Co. Wexford, Ireland
E. Sept. 12, 1856 [E-R-4]
+ Apr. 9, 1891 at FC: Lived 60 years

Nicholas Hanrahan joined the novitiate at Saint Acheul in France and was for a time a Jesuit Brother. He came to Fordham in 1857 and was appointed to take charge of the boys in the capacity of prefect. But soon he became a scholastic studying rhetoric, philosophy and theology.

After his ordination Fr. Hanrahan began to teach at Fordham and to do the detailed work that fell to him as assistant prefect. In 1871 he was made assistant procurator, and in that position he had the opportunity to do a great deal to improve the grounds at Fordham.

From 1874 till 1888, he was a Fordham professor, prefect, and treasurer. As financial manager he made a legion of friends for himself and his Order as indicated by the large number of letters of condolence that poured into the college for several weeks after his demise. Every living alumnus of Fordham seemed to have lost in him a dear friend and a well-known landmark of Fordham memories. He served at Fordham during 1857-1859; 1864-1888; 1890-1891.

He spent two years (1888-90) at the Jesuit parish in Troy, and in his priestly ministry there he was distinguished by his devotion to the poor and suffering. He returned to Fordham in the summer of 1890 and died peacefully there with a religious resignation to the supreme will of God. The cause of his death was said to have been bronchitis.

### REV. HUBERT HEINDENREICH, S.J
B. Mar. 13, 1848 in Rheinberg, Rheinland, Germany
E. Aug. 24, 1874 [E-R-5]
+ June 29, 1891 in Jersey City: Lived 43 years

Hubert Heindenreich went to the Gymnasium in his native Germany and took up the machinist trade. But at age 22 he came to Washington, DC, and was tutored in Latin by a priest to whom he confided his hopes for the future. At age 26 he entered the novitiate at Frederick, MD, and five years later he was ordained at Woodstock. After several other assignments he came to St. Peter's College, Jersey City, three years before his death.

On the college commencement day he had exerted himself to an extraordinary degree and had not eaten anything till late at night with left-overs. The result was a severe attack of indigestion and then cholera from which he did not recover.

Fr. Heindenreich won great admiration and friends based largely on his intense activity and earnestness. It was expected that he would be long remembered for his manly character and other virtues.

### BR. WILLIAM HENNEN, S.J.
B. Nov. 25, 1800, Crombach, Westfallen, Germany [now Belgium]
E. Nov. 9, 1839 [D-L-1]
+ July 4, 1890 at FC: Lived 89 years.

A great way to become popular with young boys is to be a good baker at a school. That's what Br. Hennen was for very many years.

He had been drafted into the Bavarian army and stayed in that service for ten years. After leaving the army, he began to seek out how to spend the rest of his life. Attracted to the religious life, he found no satisfaction in the options available to him at home. But he had a strange dream or a revelation in which he saw his "place in creation" embodied in a beautiful house with a church nearby. This experience and similar ones have been regarded by some as "mystical."

He began to search for the house. He wandered through various countries and cities, such as Belgium, Germany, and France; he came to America and continued his search in New York, Philadelphia and other places, including Bardstown. As he was about to despair of what began to seem a foolhardy adventure, an old man approached him, touched him and said, "I will show you your place in creation." The old man led him to St. Mary's College, explained his mission and then disappeared. Though St. Mary's was not the house William Hennen sought, he stayed and, at age 39, entered the novitiate on November 9, 1839. He was first a Scholastic novice (preparing for priestrhood) because he had earlier studied in a Belgian *petit seminaire* for the priesthood. But later superiors decided it would be better for him to become a Brother and he accepted that change. He remained in Kentucky until 1846 when he and most of the other Kentucky Jesuits were transferred to Fordham.

When he first saw Rose Hill with its mansion and its new and lovely church, he recognized it immediately as the "place" of his vision. Brother Hennen could hardly contain himself. He felt happy enough to die. Instead of dying at that time, however, he lived to serve the "place" with joy for forty-four years (1846-1890). His service included being baker (he was called the "tutelary genius of the bakeshop"), carpenter, refectorian, mechanic, repairer of clocks and watches, etc. The old chronicle which told this tale concluded by saying that he died in his "place in creation" with beauty and peace, showing the wonder of God in his Saints.

For several of his later years, he was a kind of hermit because of his failed hearing. Yet he fulfilled all his spiritual duties and spent almost the whole day reading and praying. He was buried with his rosaries in his hand. The details of his life are in themselves an extraordinary eulogy.[32]

REMIGIUS HILLENMEYER, college employee
B. 1784 in Alsatia.
+ Aug. 3, 1860: Lived 76 years [A-13]

Mr. Remigius Hillenmeyer knew the Jesuits in Kentucky and came with them to Rose Hill where he was employed in the college. His work was described thus: *"ipse plantavit pomarium nostrum* (he planted our orchard by himself)." He was buried in the same grave as George Thompson (see below).

Besides his dying far from his Kentucky home, there was another consideration that persuaded superiors to bury Mr. Hillenmeyer at the college: his son, Peter, was a Jesuit priest at the time the father died; Peter was born on June 29, 1824, entered the

Jesuits on Oct 30, 1844, studied theology and was ordained at Fordham; he taught at Fordham in 1855-7. He made tertianship in France during 1859-60. Then he is said to have gone to England where he died in a Jesuit house, though he had left the Order.

## BR. FRIDOLIN HOEFELE, S. J.
B. Feb. 19, 1820 in Gräfenhausen, Baden, Germany
E. July 24, 1857 [H-L-1]
+ Aug. 9, 1894 at FC: Lived 74 years

Fridolin Hoefele (sometimes spelled Haefele) made his novitiate in Canada. After he took his vows he was assigned for a short time to Montreal and to the College of St. Francis Xavier, and then for almost thirty years to Fordham (1862-1894). At those places he plied his carpentry skills. For instance, at Fordham, besides many smaller jobs, he built structures which served their purpose for a long time but no longer exist, such as a separate carpentry shop, a refectory and a chapel, in the former Jesuit provincial residence on West 181$^{st}$ St. Br. Hoefele was noted for his great patience, demonstrated in bearing with a chronic complaint from which he suffered for forty years.

## REV. JOHN JAFFRÉ, S.J.
B. Sept. 25, 1800, in Auray, Brittany, France
E. Sept. 28, 1819 [B-R-9]
+ May 10, 1861 in NYC: Lived 59 years

John Jaffré completed his Jesuit formation in 1835 and spent the first seven years of his priestly work in Vannes, Brittany. After 1842 the Jesuits returned to Canada, and Fr. Jaffré offered himself for work there. To prepare for it he studied English for two years at Stonyhurst College, England. In many ways his work in Canada was successful: he was a very impressive preacher and parish organizer, particularly in the Chatham area. However, some opposed him because "his headstrong attitude and tendency to ignore the recommendations of others" which undermined his ardent zeal and remarkable energy. At any rate, in 1860 he was appointed the first Catholic chaplain for New York City's public institutions on Blackwell's Island.

A tribute to Fr. Jaffré's work and devotion in New York is given in "A Historical Sketch of the Missions of New York and Canada" by A. Weiss in the *Woodstock Letters*, vol. 3. There he was identified as "a former missionary of Upper Canada, [who] started daily from the College [Xavier], visited in turn each of the [five] institutions [on Blackwell's Island, NY], and after displaying a zeal which in presence of so much misery, nothing could moderate, returned home at night completely exhausted, only to begin his work again the day following. In one month's time he was in his grave, a victim of the typhoid fever. The pioneer in that good work had fallen."

In the three years after his death, Jesuit chaplains Fathers Philip Chopin, George Laufhuber and Joseph Pavarelli also succumbed to the same disease and all buried in the Fordham cemetery. Surely, they should be accounted martyrs of charity.

BR. MICHAEL JARRY, S. J.
B. Mar. 4, 1793 in Pontivy, France
E.   Sept. 10, 1825 [B-L-2]
+ May 1, 1848, at FC: Lived 55 years

Michael Jarry's early education was provided by his parish priest who hoped he would take Sacred Orders. But circumstances required a change of plans, and he joined the Jesuits as a Brother. He made his novitiate partly in France, and partly in Italy (province of Turin). After his novitiate he was assigned as tailor to several residences of the French province in Italy. Then he was sent to America via New Orleans; he joined the Jesuit Community at St. Mary's College, KY, in 1835 and was tailor and did household work.

He continued to do that work faithfully until May 10, 1843. A note in the manuscript *Catalogus Primus* in the Fordham Archives reveals that he became paralyzed on that day; his infirmity was apoplexy that stayed with him until he died. However, he went with the others in 1846 to St. John's College, Rose Hill, NY, Fordham. In view of his illness his final assignment was to look to his health and pray. He was the first vowed Jesuit to die at Rose Hill; Br. Creeden died before him, but he was a novice at the time of his death and had not taken public vows.

Br. Jarry was regarded as a model in many ways, a talented, industrious, pious and devout, very charitable, a well-beloved Jesuit.

BR. FIDELIS JOSET, S. J.
B. Feb. 12, 1802 in Courfaivre, Switzerland
E. Oct. 26, 1822 [B-L-3]
+ Jan. 12, 1852 in NYC: Lived 50 years

Fidelis Joset was the third child in a family of five boys, four of whom became priests or religious. A long *Woodstock Letters* obituary on his Jesuit brother, Fr. Joseph Joset, contains some details about other members of the family. There Fidelis is identified as "the wild one of the family" who later became a Jesuit Brother.

He entered the Jesuits in the Upper German province and served there for 25 years, assigned to cooking and maintaining residences. However, in 1847 he and other Jesuits fled Germany because of the political turmoil there. When he arrived in New York, Fr. C. Boulanger, Superior of the New York-Canada Mission, sent him to help two priests who were serving newly settled German Catholics in Wilmot (now St. Agatha), Canada. Br. Joset cooked and cared for the priests for two years until ill health forced him to seek a transfer. For a year he was stationed at St. Mary's College, Montreal, as cook. His final assignment in 1850 was to Fordham where he died two years later.

REV. LOUIS JOUIN, S. J.
B. June 14, 1818 in Berlin, Germany
E. Aug. 20, 1841 [F-R-3]
+ June 10, 1899 at FC: Lived 81 years

Louis Jouin, was born in Berlin into a French Huguenot family. After an early education in a French school in Berlin, he worked in Prussian Poland and there converted to Catholicism. He decided to leave his country and become a missionary. But before getting legal permission to leave he had to promise never to return to his native Prussia. Then he made a six-week journey to Rome mostly by foot, and there after several interviews with Fr. General Jan Roothaan he was received by him into the Jesuit order. He made his novitiate in Rome and studied philosophy in the Roman College. That was a time of terrible political turmoil in Italy and Jouin's life was affected by it. He had a shortened experience of regency teaching, and early ordination (April 30, 1848).

After being expelled as a "foreign Jesuit," he traveled to Geneva, Marseilles, Paris, and then London where the provincial counseled him to go to America.

In early October, 1848, Jouin arrived in New York at age 30. He was a priest, though he had not yet completed his theological studies; he took the study of English as his first task. This he did, along with other work, at the College of St. Francis Xavier, NYC. In 1852 he began his long association with Fordham, and typically combined study (the completion of four years of theology under the seminary professors) with numerous other activities. With the exception of a brief periods of rest and work in Canada (1872-78) and at The College of St. Francis Xavier (1878-80), he was at Rose Hill from 1852-1859; 1861-1872; and 1879 until his death. He was regarded as the link between the pioneers and those who began the college's new century.

The range of the courses he taught is remarkable and gives an idea of his talents. Some courses he offered practically every year: ethics, natural theology, metaphysics; other subjects these days would be considered unusual for a philosophy professor: math at various levels, physics, chemistry, Spanish, Italian, German, and French. Besides the languages that he taught, he could speak fluently in English, Latin and Polish and "was well versed in Hebrew, Greek and Gaelic," as his former rector, Fr. Campbell, asserted. Among his other activities were those that might be called "service to the community:" Minister, sub-minister, spiritual father, parish priest, Sodality director, and librarian. Like Fr. I. Daubresse before him, the archdiocese honored him in appointing him for many years to preside over conferences of the priests' Cases of Conscience.

Fr. Jouin wrote five books on philosophy and theology, and each of his books passed through four editions and were textbooks in many colleges. His writings reflected characteristics of his teaching since he was said to be specially clear and concise, factors that gave him the reputation as a remarkable teacher.

In his later years his hobby was bookbinding for the college library. He was skilful in lithography and by that means produced many of his writings for his own students.

With his death an era that began at Fordham with a largely European-trained Jesuit community definitely came to an end. At the time of his golden jubilee as a Jesuit in 1891 and after his death in 1899 numerous tributes were published about him particularly in the *Fordham Monthly*. One read, "For over thirty years ... Fr. Jouin has been connected with ... Fordham, and during that time his labors as director of the diocesan *Casus Conscientiae*, professor of philosophy and author, have endeared the genial gentleman to thousands ...."

Fr. Campbell wrote that Fr. Jouin "was not in any way puffed up or proud of [his talents]. He was ever a humble religious and simple as a child. It was this quality which made him the life of the community recreations, for he was ever genial, always ready to enjoy a little joke even at his own expense."

In a booklet published probably in the early 1930's by the College Book Store and containing many photos of Fordham, the building known today as Hughes Hall was identified as Jouin Hall. Fr. Thomas Campbell's profile of Fr. Jouin, with a portrait, was published in *Historical Records and Studies*.[33]

BR. JOSEPH KAIN, S. J.
B. Dec. 22, 1822 in Magherafelt, Co. Derry, Ireland
E. Mar. 14, 1853 [H-R-7]
+ May 6, 1897 in NYC: Lived 74 years

At age 31, Joseph Kain entered the Jesuits in the novitiate near Montreal, and during 1856-60 functioned at St. Mary's College, Montreal.

During the 44 years of his Jesuit life, Br. Kain was assigned to many different Jesuit houses; the ones at which he spent a number of years were the College of St. Francis Xavier (8 years), Fordham (7 years; 1861-1865; 1871-1873), Montreal novitiate and St. Mary's College (6 years), and St. Lawrence O'Toole (4 years).

While in most of his assignments he did many tasks, his services most in demand were as infirmarian and custodian of the clothesroom. An assignment that Br. Kain received for three years (1884-87) was an unusual one in his time and an honor to his abilities. He was the Brother Socius to the Provincial, Robert Fulton. At the same time the Father Socius was Fr. William O'B. Pardow, a future provincial.

REV. ANDREW P. KEATING, S. J.
B. Mar. 25, 1843 in Enniscorty, Co. Wexford, Ireland
E. July 28, 1860 [E-L-2]
+ Mar. 29, 1895 in Jersey City; Lived 52 years

Three-year-old Andrew Keating and his mother immigrated first to St. John's, New Brunswick. They later moved to Boston where Andrew was introduced to Latin and to the Jesuits. He joined them, and after his novitiate he taught as a regent in succession at three Jesuit colleges: Loyola (Baltimore), Gonzaga (Washington, DC), and Georgetown (Washington, DC).

After ordination he exercised his priestly ministry in six different Jesuit parishes. His final assignment was to teach and conduct sodalities at St. Peter's College, Jersey City. But he was a sick man and did not last out that one year.

He was praised as "humble and kind, good-hearted, jovial, and charitable, always ready to oblige others, though somewhat timid and nervous when he had to appear in public and preach. As a religious he lived an exemplary life and was beloved by all."

PATRICK KEON, Fordham student
B. Nov. 14, 1856 in Ireland
+ March 19,1873: Lived 16 years [A-12]

In the Minister's diry for March 19, 1873, there is the notation that Patrick Keon, *"unus ex alumnis nostris, obdormivit in Domino hora 11½ P.M.*(one of our students, slept in the Lord [died] at 11:30 P.M."

Nothing else is known about him.

BR. MICHAEL KEYS, S. J.
B. July 8, 1826 in Athy, Co. Kildare, Ireland
E. Sept. 18, 1858 [F-R-7]
+ June 6, 1901 at FC: Lived 75 years

We don't know when Michael Keys came to this country, why he came, where he settled down or friends or relatives who preceded him here. At any rate, he entered what was then the Jesuits' New York-Canada Mission at its novitiate for Brothers in Montreal, Canada in 1858. The year after he completed his noviceship he served at St. Mary's College, Montreal, as assistant cook.

Br. Keys was assigned several times to Fordham: 1862-1863; 1871-1873; 1878-1879; and 1901, his final assignment. The other places at which he served were several Jesuit residences in Canada: Chatham, Guelph, and Manitoulin Island. In the U.S.A., besides Fordham he worked at St. Peter's, Jersey City, , NYC, and Troy, NY.

In the residences his work varied from place to place; some of them were: cook, sacristan, general domestic work; receptionist; custodian of the supply room; book-keeper; keeper of the wine cellar.

Before 1892 his name was spelled Kays in catalogues; after, it was spelled Keys.

BR. NEAL LAFFERTY, S. J.
B. Mar. 22, 1828 in Glasgow, Scotland
E. July 20, 1854 [J-R-6]
+ July 25, 1866 in NYC: Lived 38 years

In his dozen Jesuit years Br. Neal Lafferty was assigned after vows to only one place, Fordham College. After his noviceship there, he was the assistant dean of discipline for two years. Then for another two years he was assistant to the college academic dean. There were two more years again as assistant to the dean of discipline and to the procurator. In his last two years he functioned in many tasks: sacristan, assistant to the college dean, custodian of the clothesroom, and assistant procurator. His Fordham service extended from 1857 to 1866.

### REV. JOHN A. LARKIN, S. J.
B. Feb. 2, 1801 in Newcastle-upon-Tyne, England
E. Oct. 23, 1840 [B-R-8]
+ Dec. 13, 1858 in NYC: Lived 57 years

Fr. John Larkin was the first Jesuit dean and vice president (1846-1847) of Fordham, and the second Jesuit president of Fordham (1851-1854). He was also renowned an inspiring orator and personality.

The reader is referred to Chapter 7 of this book for further details about him.

### REV. GEORGE LAUFHUBER, S.J.
B. Mar. 5, 1820 in Lerchenfeld, Neunkirchen, Austria
E. Sept. 7, 1854 [C-R-1]
+ Feb. 22, 1865 at NYC: Lived 45 years

George Laufhuber studied at a seminary in Austria and was ordained a diocesan priest. The *Liber Defunctorum* tells how he consulted a famous Jesuit missionary about becoming a Jesuit. The Jesuit recommended instead that he become a Redemporist, which he did. But his heart was not at rest, and so after he obtained a dispensation from Rome, he entered the Jesuit novitiate of the Champagne Province. He completed his novitiate at Sault-au-Récollet, near Montreal, and spent a year reviewing his theology at Fordham. He was then sent to Canada to serve in the Guelph parish from

September, 1857, to December, 1859, and to look after German immigrants who were dispersed throughout the countryside. He evangelized those he found and initiated the building of churches and schools in Catholic settlements.

After working a yer at St. Michael's in Buffalo, he was transferred to New York City in 1864 and ministered to typhoid patients quarantined at Blackwell's Island. At breakfast on his first day there a woman asked him if he had a wife and children. Father replied that a Catholic priest does not have a wife because not having a wife [enables] the priest to be [devoted] totally to God, whereas the man who has a wife has a divided heart, etc. The woman was the wife of a Protestant minister.

At forty-five years of age, he died of typhoid while serving in this ministry" like his fellow Jesuit chaplains on those islands, Fr. Jaffré, Fr. Chopin and Fr. Pavarelli.

REV. PETER LEBRETON, S. J.
B. Jan. 27, 1809 at Josselin, France
E. Nov. 10, 1830 [B-R-2]
+ Oct. 10, 1848: Lived 39 years

Peter Lebreton completed the Jesuit course of studies in France and Switzerland. In 1839 he came to St. Mary's, KY, and made his tertianship year there. After that he was procurator at the college for several years, taught Latin, and did parish work in the vicinity of the college.

He came to Rose Hill on June 29, 1846, in one of the early groups to leave Kentucky to get ready for the arrival of others. He had to arrive early because he was assigned to fulfill the office of Minister for a year. Thus he became the first Fr. Minister (Administrator) of the Jesuit community at Fordham (1846-1847).

The next year his assignment was to Fr. Larkin's "New York College" which later became St. Francis Xavier. However, after a year and a few months there and many months in pain which he suffered patiently, he died with the strength that flows from the sacraments.

In 1847 the "Catalogus Primus," which reported vital statistical data about individuals, gave some facts about Fr. Peter Lebreton. In that source we read of his place of origin and his dates, as above; his physical strength and health, mediocre; his education, Greek and Latin literature, two years of philosophy, three years of theology; his ministry to date, two years prefecting, two years teaching, 4 years as procurator, five years of parochial ministry and one year (1846-47) as Minister.

The DeBacker-Sommervogel Jesuit bibliography reported that Fr. LeBreton wrote a book, *The Devout Manual,* published by Dunigan, NY, in 1840.

BR. PHILIP LEDORÉ, S. J.
B. Feb. 13, 1800 in Quiberon, Morbihan, France
E. Oct. 11, 1822 [I-R-5]
+ Apr. 14,1881 at FC: Lived 81 years

Philip Ledoré had spent eight years as a seaman before becoming a Jesuit Brother in France. After ten years devoted service at St. Mary's, KY, he traveled to Rose Hill as a pioneer member of the community there.

An anecdote about Br. Ledoré, "a Breton like myself," was recounted by Fr. Thébaud, his rector. He wrote that the brother deferred planting vegetables and flowers until late spring because of the vagaries of Kentucky weather; but finally he was convinced to use glass-covered beds to control conditions that favored growing vegetables.

At Fordham for 34 years (1846-1881) Br. Ledoré faithfully fulfilled various offices, such as baker, gardener, manager of the clothes room, etc. In many ways his long life at Fordham symbolized the religious self-sacrifice, dedication, hidden service, and generosity of the over 170 Jesuit Brothers who served God at Fordham from 1846 to 1998.

REV. THOMAS LEGOÜAIS, S. J.
B. April 26, 1793 in Nantes, France
E. Oct. 31, 1821 [C-R-11]
+ May 15, 1876 in New York: Lived 83 years

Survivor of the French Reign of Terror, Paris-educated doctor of laws, theology professor in France and Spain, Master of Jesuit Novices, first Jesuit chair of the Fordham theology department, first Jesuit Fordham librarian — these are some of the associa-

tions linked with Fr. Legoüais' name. He served at Fordham from 1846 to 1871.

But equally striking about Fr. Legoüais was his size. Everyone who wrote about him mentioned his size: diminutive, "a pigmy in stature." His height was a trifle under five feet; he was said to have been denied entrance into the Jesuits because of his size, "until he obtained the special consent of the [Jesuit] General." He had trouble mounting a horse or re-mounting after falling from it. But he was also portrayed as a giant in the vineyard of the Lord.

In his years at Fordham Fr. Legoüais offered spiritual leadership and personal counseling to a wide range of clients, from the college President to the youngest student. In addition, he served for many years as special counselor to the mission Superior, and was regarded as "One of the most influential ... [local] Jesuit[s]" of his day.

Years after his death an admirer wrote that Fr. Legoüais' "boy-like proportions [provided a sense] of magnetism for the American boy." Another wrote that he was "an immense favorite both with pupils and with the laity." A biographer summarized his life as one of quiet, unassuming "self-sacrifice and earnest Christian work." Archbishop Corrigan testified that "for many years he was the favorite spiritual director and confessor of the students at St. Francis Xavier [College] and Fordham."

BR. JULIUS MACÉ, S. J.
B. Nov. 8, 1822 in Nantes, Brittany, France;
E. May 27, 1847 [D-R-6]
+ Aug. 11, 1889 at FC: Lived 66 years

Julius Macé had studied music at the Conservatory in Paris under the famous Bertini and was one of his favorite students. When he applied to enter the Jesuits he was given the opportunity to study for the priesthood but instead he preferred to be a Brother. At the end of his first year of novitiate at St. Acheul in France, he and seven other Jesuits (3 priests and 4 brothers) were sent to New York. He completed his novitiate at Fordham and was assigned there for the rest of his life (1849-1889).

He served God largely through music: he was professor of music for nearly forty years and played the organ in the parish church (the present University Church was also the local parish church for many years) and in the students' chapel on formal occasions, as well as the piano on less formal occasions. "No festival of the Church, no college holiday ... ever came and went... without being [made...] brighter and more festive by [his] musical genius. ... He was gladdest and most contented when he was given, and when he felt, the assurance that his musical performances had made [the students'] lives at college more bearable and more homelike."

An anecdote about Br. Macé and his musical talent concerns a performance given by Louis Gottschalk, the composer, who had learned that, as he said, "There is someone here tonight whose musical talent I consider superior to my own." He insisted that Br. Macé join him on the stage, and according to the story, they played a duet.

He suffered much from infirmities that caused him to be bent almost double, but no one heard him complaining. His special joy was being with the students, and they reciprocated.

Qualities mentioned about him were: cheerful, pious, ardent, devout religious, humble, patient, specially devoted to the Blessed Virgin, stable, unassuming, self-sacrificing.

BR. HENRY W. MACKEY, S. J
B.  June 15, 1873 in Summerhill, Co. Tipperary, Ireland
E. Jan. 17, 1897 [F-R-8]
+ Oct. 5, 1901 at FC: Lived 28 years

Henry Mackey made his novitiate at Frederick, MD, and upon its completion was assigned to St. Ignatius Loyola, NYC. His responsibilities changed in each of his three years there. In the first year he took care of the heating plant. In the second year he had charge of the dining room and the wine cellar, and he did general household work. In his third year and final year, he was assigned to do cleaning work in the parochial school and was sacristan.

When he caught consumption, he was sent to the Jamaica mission. After he spent a short period there, he returned to New York and died in Fordham.

REV. EUGENE MAGUIRE, S. J.
B. May 22, 1800 at Slane, Co. Meath, Ireland
E. Jan. 8,1825 [B-R-1]
+ June 11, 1833, at St. Mary's, College, KY: Lived 33 years

Eugene Maguire was admitted to the Society at Montrouge, France, after he had completed studies in humanities, philosophy, and theology. Some of those studies were done in Ireland, and some in France. After taking additional studies in physics and mathematics, he taught the latter in two Jesuit colleges in France.

In October, 1832, he was sent to teach at St. Mary's College, KY. He must have been specially welcomed there, not only for his many gifts but for the fact that at that time he was the only Jesuit whose primary language was English. But he would not be there long. In the course of 1833 he suddenly caught the cholera and died in the following June. Receiving the Last Sacraments with great faith and piety, he said: "How much I love the Society! How sweet (*dulce*) it is to die in the Society." With such sentiments, he died in the Lord.

His remains were brought from St. Mary's, KY, to Fordham by Charles Gilbert on the evening (*vespere*) of November 1, 1850. That night they were placed in state in the chapel of the Blessed Virgin Mary; the next morning a Mass for the dead was said for him in the presence of all the community; after that they went in procession after the bier to the burial ground. Psalms were sung and the remains of their "very beloved Father" (*carissimi Patris*) were interred for a second time on November 2. His remains were later interred for a third time when the "new" Fordham cemetery was opened in January, 1890.

REV. JOHN McDONNELL, S.J.
B. July 12, 1814 in Killarney, Co. Kerry, Ireland
E. July 1, 1846, at Rome [B-R-4]
+ Jan. 14, 1852, at FC; Lived 37 years

According to the *Annual Letters* of the Province of France for 1852-53, "John McDonnell was born in Ireland on July 12, 1814. After he had successfully completed his studies and graduated *magna cum laude,* he was sent as a missionary to North America. We can't give account of the details of his achievements there because his modesty prevented it. But this much we can say, that from that time forward his health was always bad. And he was highly esteemed there and was sent to Rome to reconcile souls and end a controversy between the bishop on the one hand and both priests and lay people on the other hand. But when he brought the issue to the hoped-for conclusion, John said farewell to the world and having been admitted into the Society, he entered it at Rome on July 1, 1846.

He went to Acheul [France] to make his novitiate. When that was finished he was sent again to North America [to Fordham] and there worked at his own studies and at prefecting students. He always demonstrated his talent as an excellent conciliator not only among Jesuits, but also among the students. At his final life crisis, like a tried and true soldier of Christ, he persevered in his assigned task until Jan. 13. After he had finished his morning duties at school, he had an attack of apoplexy, and within the space of an hour, he breathed forth his spirit. He lived 37 years, 6 months, 1 day; he was in the Society 5 years, 6 months, and 13 days."

Fr. McDonnell's official assignments in his last year at Fordham (1852-53) were the following: Sub-minister, Catechize workmen, Teach English, history and arithmetic, hear confessions of nuns, House consultor.

## REV. FRANCIS X. MARÉCHAL, S. J.
B. March 4, 1826 at St. Cassin, France
E. Oct. 14, 1852 [B-R-6]
+ Jan. 13, 1882 at NYC: Lived 55 years

Francis Maréchal was also known as Joseph Ansault; we do not know why he used the two names. After completing his novitiate in France, he was sent to Fordham to complete his theological studies and was ordained in 1856. He was ordained so shortly after his novitiate because of his earlier studies as a diocesan seminarian.

After ordination, during 1857-60, he ministered to the Catholics settled in the region between Guelph and Georgian Bay. He was then recalled to New York and began ministry at Blackwells Island, where he remained from 1862 to his death, except for 1870-73 when he was assigned to Chatham in Canada.

After Fr. Jaffré, the pioneer full-time chaplain at Blackwells Island, had lasted only one month there, it became obvious that two chaplains were necessary there. So Fr. Francis Maréchal and Fr. Philip Chopin were appointed to that task. For how they fared as a successful team, see above under Fr. Chopin.

Fr. Maréchal himself died the victim of a railway car fire. He was returning from Troy in a train that was destroyed in a rear-end collision at Spuyten Duyvil on Jan. 13, 1882. He was burned to a crisp and was identified only through his breviary. Needless to say, his brethren and the general public were shocked to hear of his sad death.

## REV. FRANCIS X. McGOVERN, S.J.
B. July 9, 1841 in NYC
E. Oct. 9, 1875 [H-R-5]
+ Nov. 11, 1897 in NYC: Lived 56 years

Francis McGovern made his Jesuit novitiate at Sault-au-Récollet, near Montreal. After completing his novitiate, he began his regency teaching Latin at the College of St. Francis Xavier, NYC, and during the next two years he perfected the students, taught calligraphy, and did private study at Fordham.

From 1882 to 1888 he studied philosophy and theology, and was ordained in Woodstock, MD. During the next two years he did parochial work at Troy and at Wards Island. He was procurator at Woodstock for a year, and, after two years of parochial ministry at Xavier parish, NYC, he made Tertianship at Frederick, MD. His final assignment for two years was again to parochial ministry at the Xavier parish, NYC. He died of apoplexy at St. Vincent's Hospital, NYC.

REV. NEIL N. McKINNON, S.J.
B. May 7, 1842 at Grand River, Prince Edward Island
E. Oct. 6, 1868 [J-L-3]
+ Oct. 9, 1907 in NYC: Lived 65 years

Neil McKinnon had studied for the priesthood in the seminary in Montreal and had been ordained a deacon when he decided to become a Jesuit. He made his studies in philosophy and theology at Woodstock and was ordained there in 1873. His priestly activities included work at the College of St. Francis Xavier, NYC, Fordham (1877-1880), St. Peter's College and parish, Jersey City, and finally St. Ignatius parish, NY, where he had his longest stay, fourteen years.

He was depicted by many as the ideal pastor, displaying virtues such as patience, gentleness kindness of heart, prudence as an advisor, zeal, charity, and forbearance; his life was a true supernatural one; he was loved by the rich and by the poor, by Catholics and by non-Catholics. His success as an organizer was proved by his planning and building the handsome new church and the Loyola School, as well as initiating work on the new parochial elementary school. The dedication of the new church took place on Dec. 11, 1898, with Archbishop Michael Corrigan presiding. The Apostolic Delegate to the U.S.A. was the celebrant of the Mass, and numerous outstanding diocesan and Jesuit leaders were in attendance. By special privilege of the Holy see, St. Ignatius Loyola was named as titular patron of the church with St. Laswrencfe O'Toole as co-titular, the feasts of both saints were be celebrated with an octave, of equal rite of the first class.[34]

Fr. McKinnon's "tall, gaunt figure and striking appearance" was "well-known throughout the city and marked him apart in any gathering." He seems also to have been regarded as among the most respected Jesuits among his peers.

He must have kept up his contacts with Prince Edward Island where he was born. At one time the late bishop there concluded that his best replacement would be Fr. McKinnon. So he went to Rome, visited Propaganda which apparently approved, then visited Fr. General and explained the situation, and his need for Fr. McKinnon as coadjutor bishop with the right of succession. However, Fr. General was not convinced.

"His funeral was a magnificent tribute of affection and respect from his numerous friends. His Grace, Archbishop Farley, said the Low Mass and gave the last absolution; priests from many parishes crowded the sanctuary to its utmost, while the church was filled to overflowing long before the Mass of Requiem began."

BR. PATRICK MacNULTY, S.J.
B. July 2,1809 in Drumgooland, Co. Derry, Ireland
E. Nov. 12, 1847 [J-R-4]
+ Sept. 11, 1869 at FC: Lived 60 years

Patrick MacNulty entered the Jesuit novitiate at age 38; we do not know what he did before 1847 or even when he came to the U.S.A. During his novitiate at Fordham among several tasks, he was assigned to supervise the dining room.

After completing his noviceship, he was assigned to Fordham for the remaining years of his life. His first functions were to do general household tasks. Then for about eleven years his duties included "*cur. lac. et lamp.*" which seems to have meant "cares for water basins in rooms and for the kerosene lamps in the residence." Br. MacNulty's last assignment was the same as his first one, to do general household tasks. The first time his surname appeared in the province catalogue, it was spelled McNulti.

BR. WILLIAM McSHEA, Novice Schol. S.J.
B. Feb. 15,1828 at Ballyshannon, Co. Donegal, Ireland
E. July 19, 1851 [B-R-5]
+ May 18, 1853 at FC: Lived 25 years

William McShea came to the Fordham infirmary in early May, 1853, as a second year novice from Sault-au-Récollet near Montreal. He had an advanced case of consumption. Shortly he was overcome also by typhoid fever. Fortified with the Last Sacraments of the church, he breathed his last at about 7:45 P.M., two months before he would have taken public Jesuit vows.

The Jesuit diary for May 19 noted that, because of the heat and the nature of his fever "that took away this beloved brother," he was buried early the next morning. At 5:15 A.M. the Office of the Dead was said in the church, followed by the funeral rites and a procession with the chanting of hymns and psalms on the way to the burial ground.

The diary also stated that all the college students of their own accord (*suo proprio motu*) attended the funeral ceremonies. In his very short time in the infirmary, he must have deeply impressed many individuals.

REV. DAVID A. MERRICK, S. J.
B. Feb. 19, 1833 in NYC
E.  July 21, 1853 [I-L-3]
 + Apr. 21, 1906 in NYC: Lived 73 years

Born into a prosperous and artistic family, David Merrick's early education brought him to several schools in the New York area until he finally entered Fordham in 1847 and was graduated there in 1850. Three years later he entered the Jesuits in France. Upon returning to America, he taught classics at Fordham and then at Montreal. For several years after ordination, he taught philosophy in Montreal and was English preacher at the Gesú there.

Much of his priestly life was spent in New York, first at Xavier where he did parish work such that his superior regarded him as providing invaluable assistance. He was praised for his zeal, singleness of purpose and untiring activity. Fr. Merrick was next made pastor of St. Lawrence O'Toole's 's church. There he completed the handsome basement of the new church, a work that required detailed financial and technical efforts; in addition he secured a state charter for the parish, which legally separated it from dependence upon The College of St. Francis Xavier.

In September, 1888, he was appointed president of the College of St. Francis Xavier, NYC. He remained in that very busy office for three years until his health began to fail, and he was then assigned to less pressure-laden tasks.

In administrative positions Fr. Merrick was distinguished by his conviction that his duty was chiefly to guide and direct others; he allowed those under him to develop their own skills and accept responsibility for their actions. He himself was a man characterized by intense personal energy. Dooley praised him as: "a zealous, hard-working priest [who] did not spare himself . . . as long as there was a soul in need. He was a father to the poor, and a father and savior to the sick, the dying and all in need of spiritual aid."

He is profiled in the *National Cyclopedia of American Biography*.

BR. CONRAD MEYER, S. J.
B. Sept. 14, 1820 in Hoevelhof, Westfalen, Germany
E. Dec. 16, 1861 [I-R-3]
+ Mar. 3, 1888 in NYC: Lived 67 years

Some years after coming from Germany, Conrad Meyer entered the Jesuit novitiate and took his first vows at Sault-au-Récollet. A sequence of assignments brought him to Buffalo, New York City, Algoma County (Michigan), Fordham, Jersey City, and finally, Xavier, NYC. There he was for twelve years the infirmarian and wardrobe-keeper. And there "he died a most edifying death, surrounded by the Fathers, who had learned to revere the hidden virtues of his life." In him his fellow Jesuits recognized and praised these qualities: humility, gentleness, modesty, willingness to oblige, fidelity, and charity.

REV. FRANCIS MONROE, S. J.
E.   Mar. 5, 1824 in Charlottesville, VA;
E. Aug. 11, 1855 [C-R-8]
+ Aug. 2, 1871 in NYC: Lived 47 years

Francis Monroe was a convert, a veteran officer of the U.S. Navy, and a nephew of the fifth President of the United States, James Monroe. Scion of a distinguished Virginia family, at age 17 through a friendly Congressman he obtained an appointment as a naval midshipman which required extensive study and practical work on shipboard. Thus he made voyages to the Mediterranean, England, Brazil, as well as in local waters during the Mexican-American war. The Naval academy at Annapolis was opened in 1845, and Monroe took his examinations there during 1846-47 for promotion. He was promoted to the rank of lieutenant and then was attached to the North Pacific Surveying Expedition with Commodore Perry, which brought him on shipboard to Japan and China. During that expedition he became a Catholic.

Besides the grace of God, two factors have been cited as influencing his conversion: the first factor was inspiration from reading the life of St. Francis Xavier; he had borrowed a life of the saint from Fr. Edward Doucet when he taught at the College of St. Francis Xavier, NYC. The second factor was the example of his elder brother, Col. James Monroe, who had converted earlier; his brother, incidentally, in spite of his Virginia origin, lead his militia regiment, the New York Twenty-Second, to the front in the Civil War. He was President of the NYC Board of Aldermen, a member of the New York State Assembly and Senate. The Monroe brothers were especially close when Francis was at Xavier, and James lived on 14th Street.

Shortly after Francis returned from the Perry naval expedition, he resigned his commission in the Navy after 13 years of naval service, seven of them as an officer, and applied to enter the Jesuits. He was accepted by the Jesuit Fr. General. Entering in 1855, he made his novitiate and studied philosophy and theology in France, and was ordained at Montreal in 1860. Only 11 years of priestly ministry lay before him.

He first taught physics, mathematics and astronomy for several years at the College of St. Francis Xavier, NYC, at St. Mary's College, Montreal, and at Fordham (1862-1865). Then he was appointed professor of rhetoric for two years at the College of St. Francis Xavier, NYC. In 1867-68 he taught higher sciences again at Montreal. Thereafter he did parish and mission-band work with headquarters first at Montreal and then at Fordham.

His classroom lectures impressed his students by his clear and interesting delivery. He was familiarly known by some friends as "The Captain," because nautical terms and reference to the sea naturally became a part of his vocabulary; it did not reflect his assuming special authority. Two other naval skills remained with him during later years: whittling and chess. On one occasion a knight on a chessboard was lost, but by the next day Fr. Monroe had whittled out a figurine that was superior to the lost one. Games of chess became the occasion for both relaxation and friendship-making; his habit of making humorous remarks during play "added spice" to the games.

In 1865 he was appointed moderator of the newly-created Xavier Alumni Sodality which later, under Fr. Dealy, became the prestigious Catholic Club. As moderator his principal duty was to provide the monthly sermon to the members. In the Xavier church he shared in the responsibility of preaching, and by invitation he preached in the Cathedral. Herbermann characterized his preaching as "original," "not eloquent" but "interesting and practical and in general popular" and "unquestionably homespun and quite familiar." Yet both his modesty and military background were revealed in his own description of his preaching: "I am no double-barreled gun, nor much less a revolver which you can shoot off as often as you please. I am nothing but an old-fashioned single-barreled blunderbuss and therefore I must ask you to listen patiently."

He returned to St. Francis Xavier, NYC, in September, 1870, to the warm welcome of friends. But he probably was suffering from "organic trouble" which required a surgical operation from which he failed to rally and died.

During his few years of teaching, he was appreciated by students on account of the justice and fairness which always characterized his actions. In his other priestly activity he was praised for his cheerful manners, tact, and urbanity. Physically, he was described as "a tall, straight, spare, square-shouldered man, of easy gait, calm and deliberate in everything, ... noted for [his] laconic wit and humor."

A profile of Fr. Monroe, written by his friend, Charles G. Herbermann, was published in *Historical Records and Studies*.[35]

## REV. WILLIAM MOYLAN, S. J.
B. June 24/28, 1822 in Armagh, Ireland
E. Nov. 14, 1851 [E-R-2]
+ Jan. 14, 1891 at FC: Lived 68 years

Irish-born William Moylan came to this country as a youth and, after his ordination as a secular priest, labored for some years among the Indians and fishermen at Cape Gaspé on the Gulf of St. Lawrence. His life in this cold region was blessed with much fruit for souls.

Fr. Moylan determined to consecrate himself still more perfectly by becoming a Jesuit. He did that in 1851 and after his novitiate was sent to teach the beginning classes at Xavier and then the classics at Fordham College (1855-1856).

His two years of teaching were followed by several years of work in the priestly ministry at St. Francis Xavier parish, NYC, and in California, teaching Rhetoric for a year at the Jesuit College in Santa Clara.

On his return from the west, he was made rector-president of Fordham beginning July 31, 1864. The appointment of Fr. Moylan to this post was said to have been an event which would have given much satisfaction to Archbishop Hughes, for he very highly esteemed his devoted friend and zealous priest; the Archbishop died several months before Fr. Moylan's appointment. His hopes for him were justified as Fr. Moylan proved to be a capable, decisive administrator. During his presidency the athletic facilities were enlarged, and the First Division building was commenced and completed.

After his presidency at Fordham, Fr. Moylan became the first Jesuit pastor at the church of St. Lawrence O'Toole (St. Ignatius). During his two years as pastor, he notably decreased the parish debt and secured remission of municipal assessments on the parish. Next he spent some years in Canada, where he attracted much attention by his eloquent, logical, and incisive discourses. From Canada he came back again to the States where he was engaged for many years in parish work at Jesuit parishes. For months before his death he was sent back to Fordham. There he died very peacefully.

He was praised for his uprightness and firmness of character, thoughtfulness of others, and sagacity in applying the right remedy at the proper time.

REV. SAMUEL MULLEDY, S.J.
B. Mar. 27, 1811 in Romney, West Virginia
E. Aug. 29, 1831 & Jan. 5, 1866 [C-R-2]
+ Jan. 8, 1866 in NYC: Lived 54 years

Samuel Mulledy entered the Jesuits at age twenty after studying at Georgetown College. Upon completing the noviceship at Whitemarsh, MD, he was sent to Rome for his theological studies in which he excelled, and was ordained there in 1840. Upon his return to the New World, he was appointed to some specially responsible positions: Master of Novices, Rector, Minister, and then Rector-President at Georgetown College; his brother Thomas (1794-1860), older than Samuel by 18 years, also held that post twice at that same college where Mulledy Hall still honors his memory. Samuel held the position of Rector-President of Georgetown College from only January 10 to September 6, 1845; it is said that his tenure was shortened because his addiction to alcohol became known; his successor in the office was his older brother, Thomas.

Leaving Georgetown temporarily, he did priestly ministry in Philadelphia. Later he returned to Georgetown where he taught dogmatic theology for two years and rhetoric for one year. Then in 1850 he left the Society; we do not have any details about his departure.

For the next ten years he was attached to churches in many different American cities: Boston, Albany, and Brooklyn. Finally, he was incardinated into the New York archdiocese by his good friend, Archbishop John Hughes. After a few years at St. Mary's, Yonkers, he was assigned as assistant to the pastor at St. :awrence O'Toole's parish. There in a relatively short time he favorably impressed the people and the pastor. The pastor, Fr. Walter Quarter, (whose brother, William, was bishop of Chicago) made a dying request to the Vicar General that Fr. Mulledy succeed him as pastor, and the request was honored. Two years later Fr. Mulledy himself was suffering from asthma and an aneurysm of the aorta. Reports of his serious condition reached his former brethren in Maryland and in New York. He had made known his strong wish to be re-admitted into the Society, "in order that he might have the happiness of dying therein," as Fr. Paresce, the provincial, noted in his letter to the Maryland province.

In 1890 a later Jesuit provincial, Fr. T. J. Gannon, S.J., quoted the following words of Fr. Joseph Loyzance, S.J., rector of the College of St. Francis Xavier in 1866, regarding the sequence of events: "On Friday morning, Jan. 5th, 1866, I sent a telegram and received the answer of Fr. Paresche: 'I authorize you to receive the vows of Samuel Mulledy.' At once I went to Yorkville. At noon on Friday, the 5th of Jan. 1866, [Fr. Mulledy] used the formula of vows in the small refectory of St. Lawrence's old residence, kneeling down. Towards the middle of the formula, overpowered by the feeling, he added the words of the Maccabees: '*Corde magno et animo volenti* (Heart generous and mind willing).' Stopped a little while and continued. After the vows we gave him the kiss of peace. He was delighted.

"On the same day he wrote a letter to Archbishop McCloskey letting him know the news and asking his Lordship to give St. Lawrence to the Jesuits."

Fuller documentation of these events can be found in Appendix IV.

The archbishop concurred with this request. Three days later Samuel died "a most saintly and edifying death." Since March 8, 1866 his church has been served by the Jesuits, and since 1899 it has been called the church of St.Ignatius Loyola in Jesuit Catalogues.

Fr. Mulledy personally was reserved in manner, kindly to all, zealous for his growing flock, hard-working to his "fingers' ends," a man of strong character, superior mental gifts and learning. A parishioner who knew him well described his sermons as clearly arranged, spoken with quiet dignity, always providing something for further thought. Thus it is not surprising that their "Fr. Sam," was loved and admired by the people.

MR. GEORGE A. MULRY, S. J. Schol.
B. Sept. 26, 1862 in NYC
E. July 10, 1880 [D-R-7]
+ Oct. 1, 1889 at FC: Lived 27 years

George Mulry was born into a distinguished family. His mother was Parthenia Crolius, a scion of an old New York ancestry, and his father, Thomas Mulry, was a leading figure in Catholic Charities and a successful banker (a ten-year president of the Emigrant Industrial Savings Bank; Mulry Square in downtown Manhattan was named in his honor). George was one of fourteen children, four of whom became Jesuits (the other three became priests; they were Michael, 1853-1884, Patrick, 1860-1895, and Joseph, 1874-1921, who was president of Fordham University during 1915-1919).

George entered the Jesuits at the novitiate at West Park, NY, completed two years of juniorate at Frederick, MD, and had two and a half years of the three-year philosophy program. But then he was diagnosed as seriously ill with consumption and was assigned to Fordham for the better care of his health.

What he achieved between his arrival at Fordham during the spring of 1887 and his death, was what distinguished him. His physicians claimed he would be dead by the following spring. But before the end of spring he prefected students, did secretarial record-keeping regarding students, worked with the senior (Parthenian) Sodality, and introduced the League of the Sacred Heart and other religious organizations blessed by the Church. In addition, he founded an association for the college workmen. He devoted his time with the workmen out of concern for  their physical and spiritual welfare; they agreed to follow regular religious practices, and their residence was renovated and a reading room upgraded.

Admirers of the statue of Our Lady in Queens Court, near the University Church, may be pleased to learn that Mr. Mulry is given major credit for the existence of the statue. "It is to his untiring efforts we mostly owe the beautiful statue of the Blessed Virgin on the campus" (obituary in the Fordham Monthly, Oct., 1889, p. 10). And he started a custom among the college students of having the May devotions on Saturday evenings outdoors before that statue of Our Lady. The same obituary quoted several sources that recalled that others found him extraordinarily attractive and that he used that gift to foster others' religious development, not his own benefit.

But besides his activities of infusing religious enthusiasm among college students and others, he used the time of his illness to grow spiritually. His personal pain he used as a way of understanding and assisting others in their troubles. Contemporaries recalled his patience, resignation to God's will, ingenuity, perseverance, prayerfulness, and in general, his "saintliness."

He died after New York City had taken title to the east section of the college property, and the city officials refused to allow further burials there. His remains, and those of two others, were kept in a vault in St. Raymond's Cemetery until the new Fordham cemetery was opened some 3½ months after his death.

REV. HENRY MURPHY, S. J.
B. Nov. 24, 1831 in Enniskillen, Ireland
E. May 19, 1855 [C-R-6]
+ Oct. 5, 1870 in Brooklyn: Lived 38 years

After the Murphy family emigrated and settled in the U.S.A., Henry, one of eleven children another two of whom were priests, did his first collegiate studies with the Sulpicians in Montreal. Then he entered the Society and made his noviceship at Sault-au-Récollet, near Montreal. When he was a novice he wrote his sister that he would prefer being the novice that he was over having the dignity of the U.S. presidency. After the noviceship he taught elementary French and English at St. Mary's College, Montreal. In the following three years he taught various subjects in the College of St. Francis Xavier, NYC.

In 1861 he reviewed philosophy as a student at Fordham, and during the following year he taught Latin to youths at Fordham. From 1864 to 1866 he studied theology at Fordham and for one year at Georgetown. Then he was ordained.

After ordination he returned to Xavier College and completed one year of teaching the classics till 1869, when he was sent to France. Upon his return the following year he died at the beginning of what would have been his second year of teaching as a priest. The Fordham Minister's diary has this notations for Oct. 7, 1870: "Burial of Fr. Henry Murphy who died on the 5th at his sister's place in Brooklyn" where he had gone for his health with superiors' approval.

This story was told about his effect on people: The class in 1868 was generally regarded by others who dealt with them as particularly unruly, a class that studied the humanities but "showed few signs of humanity." But through his patience and humility he tamed their wildness. When he suspected someone was about to make noises or play some trick he used to look at the class with a kind of deceptive kindness and, in a voice which was clear, gentle, and clever, he would say, "It seems to me that someone has become a bit crazy." Then he would wait in silence until all became orderly. And that always happened.

An indication of his effect on them was demonstrated when Fr. Murphy was sent to France for his health near the end of the Spring term. The boys showed their reverence for him in ways that were consistent with their immaturity. Without seeking permission, they absented themselves from class, surrounded him on the ship, all with hats off, while the most eloquent one among them read a speech. The speech lauded their professor with highest praises and thereby favorably impressed the other passengers and guests who witnessed it. Then as if they were saying their last farewell to him, they departed, but not for school. They spent the rest of the day playing games, prepared with joyful hearts to be punished the following day.

About a year before his death, in view of his precarious physical health, he wrote that if he died young "perhaps God foresees the dangers to which I would have succumbed and He will call me to himself lest my weakness destroy me. "

REV. MICHAEL NASH, S. J.
B. Sept. 24, 1824 in Whitechurch, Co. Kilkenny, Ireland
E. Apr.13,1844 [H-L-2]
+ Sept. 6, 1895, in Troy, NY: Lived 71 years

Michael Nash was specially known for his service as a Civil War chaplain and for his writings. He often spoke and wrote about that war and about the early Jesuits in Kentucky and Rose Hill.

After graduating from St. Mary's College, KY, he entered the Jesuit novitiate at that same place. He studied at Fordham, Laval (France), and Paderborn (Germany) where he was also ordained in 1859.

Upon returning to New York, he volunteered to be a chaplain in the Civil War in response to Archbishop Hughes' request for army chaplains, and was assigned to the Wilson Zouaves, "the roughest element in New York." He wrote eleven long letters about his experiences in the war which were published in the *Woodstock Letters*. Jesuit Fr. General Beckx received this report: "Fathers Tissot and Nash … are praised in the papers for their zeal and disregard of all risks, even death itself, in the thick of battle…"

Fr. Nash enjoyed relating the exploits of his Zouaves. But one of his brethren learned that in the face of overwhelming odds in the battle at Pensacola, they turned around and ran "to battle another day." That Father would seemingly confirm the stories by reminding the group in mock praise of the Zouaves' fleetness of foot at Pensacola.

At the end of his enlistment, Fr. Nash was appointed Fordham's Vice-president for an academic year (1864-1865). After that, he had various teaching and parish assignments in six different places until 1874. He was then appointed pastor at St. Joseph's, Troy, NY, where he remained for fourteen consecutive years until 1888. At Troy he taught an evening school for boys, seven of whom afterwards entered the Jesuits. After that he exercised his priestly ministries at two other places until he finally returned to Troy, where he died of apoplexy.

He was described as a master storyteller who could interest his listeners for hours; thus he was called "an eloquent, witty Irishman with a sense of the dramatic." He acknowledged his fiery temper and fought against it all his life. Another characteristic was his courage; in the army he was said to have been always ready to join a daring expedition. These qualities endeared him to soldiers and many who liked his military style. Some men reported that they liked his use of military knowledge when he encouraged them in their fight against temptations. Archbishop Corrigan wrote of him that he "was an exact religious, was much loved by the poor wherever he went, and did not spare himself in laboring for them."

FR. MICHAEL H. O'BRIEN, S. J.
B. Nov. 17, 1851, in Brooklyn, NY
E. Aug. 28, 1872 [G-R-9]
+ July 3, 1907 in NYC: Lived 55 years

Michael O'Brien entered the novitiate at Montreal, did a year of Juniorate in England, and studied philosophy at Louvain. He made regency in three colleges, Xavier, Fordham (1881-1882), and Georgetown. He completed his theology and was ordained at Woodstock.

His first assignment as a priest was to teach philosophy at Boston College, but in the next year, 1889, he was sent to Woodstock to teach in the seminary for two years. After two more years at Georgetown, he went to Xavier, NYC, where he taught philosophy for the rest of his years.

Fr. Michael O'Brien was studious and industrious; sedentary and averse to exercise, probably due to "corns" on the soles of his feet; above all, he was gracious and "a man of extraordinary charity."

REV. CHARLES J. O'CONNOR, S. J.
B. Dec. 1, 1843, in Dublin, Ireland
E. Mar. 19, 1861 [E-L-1]
+ May 5, 1894 in Jersey City: Lived 50 years

Charles O'Connor and his younger brother Edward (a Jesuit novice scholastic who was also buried in the Fordham cemetery) came to this country when they were very young. He was at one time a student at the old St. Joseph's College in Philadelphia and later at Xavier, NY. When he entered the novitiate at Montreal, he became one of the first novices of Fr. Perron (who is also buried in the Fordham cemetery); Fr. O'Connor felt a life-long affection and gratitude towards his Master of Novices.

His health was a cause of ongoing concern, and frequent changes marked his cycle of studies: Frederick, Fordham, Woodstock, Xavier, Montreal, West Park, and Fordham. Concern about his health was also the reason for his early ordination during the 1876 summer vacation by the Most Rev. John Loughlin, the bishop of Brooklyn. After ordination he was assigned to Xavier as prefect of studies and discipline. Then he was called upon to solve a problem that had arisen about the teaching staff at the boys' parochial school attached to the Xavier parish. Fr. Provincial assigned him to that task, and it became the great work of his life. In his twelve years in that assignment, he did more than solve the problem; he exercised a great influence on the moral training of the boys and young men in the parish. He strengthened the school in many ways and won the special gratitude of the parents.

Shortly before he died he told his provincial that his intense love for the Society motivated his zealous work for its interests.

He died of hepatitis in Jersey City, and his Requiem Mass was said there. The archbishop of New York attended his funeral services and gave the last blessing "to show, as he said himself, his appreciation of the labors of Fr. O'Connor for the children of his diocese." He was specially admired for his hard work and dedication for Catholic education in spite of his own health problems, for his zeal, [and] devotedness, especially for the young."

MR. EDWARD O'CONNOR, S. J. Schol.
B. Aug.19, 1846 in Dublin, Ireland
E. Aug. 27, 1864 [C-R-3]
+ Dec. 27, 1866 in NYC: Lived 20 years

As mentioned in the above paragraphs about his brother, they came to this country when they were very young. And Mr. Edward O'Connor died young, just a few months after taking his vows. Little more has been learned about him except that he "was a youth of great promise, as those who were with him as well as the words of his novice master attest."

REV. JEREMIAH O'CONNOR, S. J.
B. April 10, 1841 in Dublin, Ireland
E. July 30, 1860 [E-R-3]
+ Feb. 27, 1891 in NYC: Lived 49 years

Jeremiah O'Connor's father died about a month before the boy was born. That fact lay behind the special mother-only-son relationship that existed in his case. Mother and son immigrated to America and settled down in Philadelphia, where Jeremiah attended "old St. Joseph's." He decided to become a Jesuit and in 1860 began the usual cycle of preparation: novitiate at Frederick, a very fruitful regency at Loyola College, Baltimore, seven years at Woodstock. By special permission he was ordained a year early to accommodate his sick mother who hoped to see her son a priest before she died.

After tertianship he was sent to Boston College and on Dec. 18, 1879, became the Rector-President. His administration, regarded as successful in all essentials, ended in 1884.

The next phase of his life was pastoral ministry, first at St. Francis Xavier parish, NYC, for four years. Then in 1888 his next assignment was pastor of the church of St. Lawrence O'Toole (now St. Ignatius). After two and a half years of service at that church, he was involved indirectly in a tunnel disaster that led to his death. In Feb., 1891, a train tunnel accident involved many passenger deaths. Fr. O'Connor and other priests went to the scene to lend spiritual comfort. But he rushed there poorly protected from the cold and returned to his residence chilled through. Pneumonia set in, and his heart, lungs and kidneys were effected. He lingered from Feb. 23 to 4:40 A.M. on Feb. 27. Fr. Provincial said his low requiem Mass. "There was no speaking, but the obsequies were honored by the presence of the Archbishop, Msgr. Farley, two other Monsignori and about fifty priests"[36]

He was noted as a pulpit orator; "a rich … imagination, sparkling thoughts, … and musical voice" together with painstaking preparation were all elements in his success. His associates remembered him especially for his "kindly nature, warm heart, and love of the Society and of the priestly dignity."

BR. WILLIAM O'CONNOR, S. J.
B. July 1, 1825 in Gurtnaho, Co. Tipperary, Ireland
E. June 23, 1855 [J-R-2]
+ Dec. 25, 1870, at FC: Lived 45 years

At about age 30 William O'Connor entered the Brothers' Novitiate at Fordham. We have no record of what he did earlier.

His fifteen years of Jesuit service were all spent at Fordham (1855-1870), where he was infirmarian from the end of his noviceship to the day of his death.

We have no other information about him.

MR. CHARLES H. O'LALOR, S. J., Schol.
B. Jan. 15, 1870 at Boston
E. Aug. 14, 1888 [I-R-1]
+ Jan. 17, 1897, at FC: Lived 27 years

After Charles O'Lalor finished his studies at Boston College, he made his novitiate in Frederick, MD. In the following years he studied rhetoric for one year at Frederick. Then he studied philosophy at Woodstock, MD.

In 1895 for regency he was assigned to teach Latin grammar at the College of St. Francis Xavier, NY, where he caught consumption. In the following year (1896) he was transferred to Fordham where he was the assistant dean of students. His last listed assignment was "*cur. val.*," "caring for his health." A list of vital statistics about him less than a year before his death spoke of his *vires debiles* (weak health)."

MR. ARTHUR O'LEARY, S.J., Schol.
B. Feb. 2, 1869, in Newark, NJ
E. Aug. 14, 1885 [D-R-8]
+ Jan. 11, 1890, in NYC: Lived 21 years

Arthur O'Leary at age 11 attended St. Peter's College and continued there until he entered the Jesuit novitiate at age 16. In the Juniorate he showed signs of the consumption that would end his life. So he was transferred to Fordham for the better care of his health. He was regarded as "naturally gifted for literary studies."

MR. JEREMIAH O'NEILL, S. J., Schol.
B. Sept. 14, 1871, in Milford, MA
E. Aug. 14, 1891 [H-L-3]
+ Nov. 20, 1895, at FC: Lived 24 years

Having studied at Boston College, Jeremiah O'Neill entered the Jesuits as a novice scholastic in Frederick, MD, and spent the two years after the novitiate at the same institution studying the classics.

When his health deteriorated after a vacation, he was assigned to Fordham as "*cur. val.*" But the care was not successful; he died of consumption but spiritually fortified by the sacred rites. He had been in the Society for only a little more than four years.

REV. BASIL PACCIARINI, S. J.
B. Feb. 10, 1816 at Montone, Perugia, Italy
E. April 23, 1834 [D-R-3]
+ Oct. 1, 1884 at FC: Lived 68 years

At eighteen years of age Basil Pacciarini entered the Jesuit novitiate of San Andrea in Rome. He began his studies in that same city but completed his theology program in Georgetown. He was ordained in 1848.

After he finished his Jesuit course of preparation, he did priestly ministry in Charles County, MD, and then was assigned for two years working among the Indians of Maine. Shorter periods of parish work followed in Boston and Philadelphia. Then came an important period in his life: twenty years at St. Inigoes in St. Mary's County, MD. Soon after he arrived there, thousands of prisoners, Confederate soldiers, were housed nearby, and many profited by his spiritual services.

When his health began to fail at St. Inigoes, he was assigned to Fordham as Spiritual Father and chaplain to several convents. He died shortly after celebrating his golden jubilee as a Jesuit.

His obituary emphasized his great zeal for souls that helped him bring many adults back to the church, his simplicity combined with tact and a spiritual cunning for souls; in brief, his was "a holy and useful life crowned with a death precious in the sight of God."

LOUIS PALACIOS, Fordham student
B. 1833 in Venezula
+ May 22, 1851: Lived 18 years [A-5]

Little of Louis Palacios' original headstone can be read today. But fortunately a handwritten manuscript in the Fordham University Archives records the script for some of the headstones, including the one erected for Louis Palacios. It begins with the Jesuit emblem (IHS) and reads as follows in English: "Of your charity pray for the soul of Louis Palacios, born in Venezuela, died in St. John's College, May 22nd 1851 at the age of 18." The inscription then continues in Latin: "*Consummatus est in brevi Explevit tempora multa. Placita enim erat Deo anima illius. Propter hoc properavit educere illum de medio iniquitatis. R.I.P.* (Snatched away in a short while, he reached the fullness of a long life. For he was pleasing to God. Therefore He snatched him out of the midst of wickedness. May he rest in Peace)."

This was one of only two monuments that were written, if only partially, in English. The inscriptions on the other original headstones were entirely in Latin.

The page about this monument in the Fordham University Archives ends with this notation: "Monument of white marble." This tombstone must have been particularly notable in the old cemetery site, since all the Jesuit markers were black wooden crosses. This one was the largest tombstone in the cemetery, and because it was so different from the others, some individuals thought that a bishop was buried there. When the other decaying tombstones were replaced in 1999, this one and other marble stones from the first cemetery were retained.

Besides the content of the headstone we have no other information about Louis Palacios.

REV. WILLIAM O'BRIEN PARDOW, S. J.
B. June 13, 1847 in NYC
E. Aug. 31, 1864 [J-L-1]
+ Jan. 22, 1909, in NYC: Lived 61 years

William O'B. Pardow's father was descended from an old English Catholic family that kept the faith through all the trials of the Reformation period. When the family moved to New York, they got into the hardware business. Their business address also became a center for lay Catholic activities.

Young William received his primary education locally, first from the Sisters of Charity at old St. Peter's Church, Barclay Street. Then he went to the College of St. Francis Xavier and in 1864 received his bachelor's degree with highest honors in philosophy and religion.

Thereupon, following the example of many other family members, he applied for the religious life and was accepted by the Jesuits. He made his novitiate in Canada, studied philosophy at Fordham for one year and continued it at the newly-opened seminary in Woodstock, MD. Four years of teaching at Xavier was followed by theology and ordination in Laval, France. Tertianship was at Paray-la-Monial under the ascetical writer, well-known for preaching and practicing personal austerity, Fr. Paul Ginhac.

On his return to New York, he was assigned to teach at Xavier for five years. Next he was made first assistant [*socius*] to the Jesuit provincial for four years and later Instructor of Tertians at Frederick, MD. He impressed the priests with whom he was dealing with a sense of his personal love of Our Lord and with his practical use of Scripture. In 1891 he was rector of the College of St. Francis Xavier; he made several improvements in the college the next two years and was regarded as a strict, though fair, disciplinarian.

He was Superior of the Maryland-New York province during 1893-1897, and during that time he established the first foreign mission of U.S. Jesuits in Jamaica, B.W.I. After his term as provincial, he devoted himself as much as possible to giving lectures, sermons, and retreats for priests, nuns, and lay people. He was in constant demand as a famed speaker and as a retreat master, mostly throughout the eastern United States, but also at times on the west coast.        He was not the usual type of orator; his physical size was not impressive since he was small in stature and thin; he moved his listeners by the sheer force of a spiritual personality; he had a message to convey from Christ when he entered the pulpit; he delivered it with force, clarity and simplicity.

After two more years as tertian instructor and a short stay in Rome at a congregation of procurators, he was appointed pastor of St. Ignatius Loyola parish. There for the last two years of his life, he was besieged by requests for lectures, sermons, and retreats. Saying "rest is for eternity," he accepted too many of these invitations, and his earnest efforts in this work probably undermined by health and made him a victim of pneumonia and early death.

Archbishop Farley said the low Mass of requiem for him in St. Ignatius Church. Four other bishops and four hundred priests were also there, and the church was crowded with those who held tickets to attend. And several thousand others gathered outside the church, unable to enter but concerned to testify to their respect for their pastor by their presence. Some were impressed by the simplicity of the ceremonies: the low Mass and the fact that no eulogy was pronounced over him. But there were many who gave their own personal eulogies of him, a man who eloquently inveighed against sin in the pulpit, was recalled to be all kindness and sympathy in the confessional. He was praised for his readiness to preach and his success in reaching his hearers, his extraordinary zeal, kindness towards all, strong sense of justice, prayerfulness, love for the Society, and devotion to the Sacred Heart.

His biography, *William Pardow,* was written by Justine Ward who also edited some of his papers, using the title, *Searchlights of Eternity.*

REV. JOSEPH PAVARELLI, S. J.
B.  Nov. 6, 1822, in Casteldaldo, Italy
E.  July 28, 1842 [B-R-13]
+ Dec. 23, 1864, in NYC: Lived 42 years

Father Joseph Pavarelli came to the New World as a priest on loan from the province of Venice. He labored first in Guelph, Canada. There he impressed everyone by his virtuous life and zealous administration of the Sacraments. He was transferred to Blackwells Island where thousands of New York City's prisoners and dangerously ill patients were housed. Two of his Jesuit-chaplain predecessors had caught the contagion and died there (Frs. Jaffré and Chopin). Nevertheless, as an obituary says, "he took up his post like an intrepid soldier," and even undertook to learn German to be of better service. However, within three months he too caught the typhoid fever and died.

A huge crowd of men and women patients at Blackwells Island lined the shore to pay tribute to Fr. Pavarelli when his body was transported by boat for funeral at Fordham.

REV. ALPHONSE PELLETIER, S.J.
B. June 12, 1836, in Quebec
E. Sept. 7, 1857 [C-R-9]
+ Jan. 29, 1879, in NYC: Lived 42 years

Alphonse Pelletier entered the Jesuit novitiate at Sault au Récollet, Montreal, and at the end of his noviceship he was transferred to the nearby St. Mary's College in Montreal to teach French and Latin, as well as to prefect students. After that he was a Latin instructor at the College of St. Francis Xavier, NYC, for a year but was transferred back to St. Mary's, to complete his regency experience.

Prior to the opening of Woodstock, he studied both philosophy and theology at Montreal, where he also continued to prefect college students. He completed the course of formation in 1871 by making his Tertianship at Frederick, MD.

In the few years of his active ministry, he was the Fr. Minister (administrator) at Fordham (1872-1873), Montreal, and at Xavier, NYC. In addition, in 1873-74 he served as the assistant dean of studies at Montreal as well as Sub-minister.

CHARLES PENA, Fordham student
B. 1872
+ March 18, 1884: Lived 12 years [A-12]

We have only the above information about this youth.

REV. JAMES PERRON, S.J.
B.Sept. 1, 1818 at Authon, Loire-et-Cher, France
E.  April 16, 1846 [D-R-9]
+ Jan. 24, 1890 at FC: Lived 71 years

James Perron was educated at home until the age of eight and then studied at the Royal College of St. Louis in Paris until the end of his sixteenth year. Then he studied mathematics and physics for five years, and military science for two more years. After graduation from the Polytechnique College, he traveled through Europe and decided to enter military service in Algeria.

In his youth James' religious education had been defective. But a series of contacts with certain students in the Polytechnique College who were followers of St. Vincent de Paul, gradually produced a turn for the better in his religious practices. And his elder sister, in many ways *in loco parentis*, had given him a copy of St. Augustine's *Confessions* and that made him reflect on his own life. He wrote her: "They touched my heart and caused me to enter into myself." As a result he resigned his commission (he had reached the rank of captain) and planned to lead a life of retirement.

On his return home he spent a lot of time in prayer, in church, and in helping the poor. When he sought counsel regarding his life, the abbot of the Trappist monastery at Melleray, Brittany, advised him to enter the Society. James had inherited immense wealth and an estate from his father, a general, who had returned a millionaire from India. The general's son decided to sell the estate and other assets to be able to make gifts to the poor and to follow Jesus ("sell …, give to the poor, and come, follow Me") in the Society of Jesus.

At age 28 he was accepted into the Society and sent to San Andrea in Rome to make his first year of novitiate there because of the local strong opposition to his vocation. But after a year he was transferred to Issenheim in France for his second year of novitiate. Yet even before completing that part of his training he was sent to Brugelette in Belgium to study philosophy for one year. He was next assigned to go immediately to Laval to study theology; he was ordained in 1852.

He made his tertianship in 1853-54, and during that time he volunteered to serve on the missions. Apparently superiors hesitated to accept his offer because of doubts about his health. However, by 1860 when he was 42 years of age, he was assigned to go to New York. At the College of St. Francis Xavier, NYC, he spent his first year in the New World as Spiritual Father to the Jesuit community, and, of course, at that time he focused on the intricacies of the English language.

In his next thirty years be was twice Master of Novices, Superior General of the New York-Canada Mission (1866-69), second Rector of the seminary at Woodstock

College (1875-81), and twice Instructor of Tertians, all posts that are regarded as most important for the religious formation of young Jesuits. Appointment to those posts symbolized the esteem in which he was held.

In the summer of 1889 he was assigned to be spiritual father and conduct retreats at the new house on Keyser Island, CT. When he was there he wrote about his own retreat: "I have now to prepare myself for death which cannot be far distant." At the end of the year he went to Xavier, NYC, for medical treatment, and then about January 10th was moved to the infirmary at Fordham. Unexpectedly, he died in two weeks.

The Jesuit provincial, Fr. Thomas Campbell, celebrated Fr. Perron's Requiem Mass, at which there was no eulogy. But when he gave an exhortation to the community at the end of the annual visitation, he praised Fr. Perron's poverty and humility as the font of the other virtues. After the remains of those who were buried in the old cemetery were placed in the new one, he was the first to be buried in the new Fordham cemetery.

Traits and factors that were reported about Fr. Perron were: his charity, humility, meekness, proverbial kindness, and extraordinary devotion to the Blessed Virgin. In summary, contemporaries regarded him as "a saintly man, a living example of the virtues he urged on others, a religious animated with the purest charity." Because of his reputation for sanctity a lengthy sketch of his life in seven parts appeared during the 1890s volumes of the *Woodstock Letters*.

REV. CHARLES PETITDEMANGE, S. J.
B. May 15, 1826 in La Poutroye, Upper Rhine, France
E. Sept. 10, 1864 [G-R-3]
+ Nov. 2, 1903 in Jersey City, NJ: Lived 77 years

Charles Petitdemange made his novitate at Issenheim, France. Then "he studied classics in 1849 at St.Acheul … and philosophy in 1850 at … Namur, Belgium. Following this he began theological studies at ... Laval, France, but in 1856 moved to St. John's College, Fordham, N.Y., to complete his final years of these studies." He was ordained in 1857 and made his tertianship in Frederick, MD. For eight years he held varied posts in Montreal, Chatham, and Guelph.

In 1866 Fr. Petitdemange was assigned to the St. Laurence O'Toole parish (now St. Ignatius) in NYC. There he signed himself and was called Fr. Petit. His main work was "with the inmates on Randalls Island." He was said to have won the affection of the parishioners "as tender as was ever extended to any of his predecessors," perhaps as a result of his work with the children and his success in the confessional. He was praised as specially patient, kind and unassuming.

A year later he was moved to the parish at St. John's College where he remained until 1875. The following year he spent in a parish in Quebec City but was re-assigned to St. Ignatius parish that same year. He remained at St. Ignatius and later at St. Peter's parish, Jersey City, for the rest of his life, except for two years (1889-90) in Holy Cross College, Worcester, MA, as spiritual father.

REV. JOSEPH PRACHENSKY, S.J.
B. June 22, 1822, in Cheb, Czechoslovakia
E.  Sept. 3, 1839 [E-R-1]
+ July 8, 1890, at FC: Lived 68 years.

Born of Polish parents in what would now be called the Czech Republic, young Joseph Prachensky entered the Jesuit Austrian province. There his novice-master was Fr. Asum, who had been a fellow-novice at Polosk, in Russia, of Fr. Jan Roothaan, later the Jesuit General. However, during Fr. Prachensky's study of theology, at Innsbruck the Kossuth revolution at home influenced his superiors to arrange for his early ordination and for his transfer to the New Orleans Mission. He demonstrated the success of his theological study in his book, *The Church of the Parables* (New York, 1880; 1885).

He labored in that mission for 24 years. First he taught Classics at Spring Hill College, then did priestly ministry at New Orleans, and later became chaplain for 3rd Alabama Regiment during the first two years of the Civil War. He accompanied them in all their campaigns as far north as Norfolk.

After his wartime chaplaincy he made his tertianship in Fordham. Next he did priestly work for a year in each of these places: Troy, Canada, and the parish church at Fordham. His next regular assignment, which lasted 21 years (1868-1889), was the chaplaincy at the hospital on Wards Island, New York. Since 1847 that island mainly housed the Emigrant Hospital and Refuge which was supported by a state tax of $1.50 for each immigrant. The tax was collected from captains of ships containing immigrants. In later years Wards Island was used for other purposes.

Fr. Prachensky's vigorous lobbying and letter-writing on the religious needs of the immigrants persuaded the Board of Emigrant Commissioners to build a Catholic chapel and later a rectory on the island. He argued eloquently against the idea of sharing the same church for the several religions represented among the immigrants. His reported mastery of nine languages must have helped many people.

The golden anniversary of his entrance into the Jesuits was celebrated with considerable ceremony at Fordham on Sept. 5, 1889. The celebration demonstrated his power of attracting all those with whom he came in contact, and his use of his personal magnetism to bring them to the service of the Lord. His final assignment was to be "spiritual father" of the Fordham Jesuit community. He died there on Jan. 8, 1890, overcome with fever. In the morning he said Mass and died that afternoon. A solemn high requiem Mass was celebrated for him by Fr. John Scully, the Rector-president, in the church of Our Lady of Mercy on campus and it was well attended.

Fr. Prachensky was filled with the spirit of the Society. He knew well the first post-Restoration Fathers in Austria and used to tell many anecdotes about them for the edification of his brethren. He was a man of signal obedience.

REV. JOHN B. PRENDERGAST, S.J.
B. Mar. 14,1846, in Savannah, GA
E. Aug. 18, 1864 [F-R-2]
+ Sept. 13, 1898 in NYC: Lived 52 years

John Prendergast at age 13 was sent by his widowed mother to St. Hyacinth College near Montreal, probably at the suggestion of a visiting clergyman. He was a very good student, but toward the end of his poetry year in college, he became quite sick with an illness that was thought to be fatal. It wasn't fatal but in a sense it was fateful as it was the occasion of an increase in his piety and in his religious thinking. Later a friend convinced him to make a retreat at the local Jesuit novitiate. That turned out to be the turning point of his life. After a meeting with Fr. James Perron, he became convinced that he was meant to be a son of St. Ignatius Loyola.

His novice master at the novitiate was the same Fr. Perron who would soon become Mission Superior. He made his first year of philosophy at Fordham and then completed that study at the new seminary at Woodstock, MD.

He was next assigned to teach at the College of St. Francis Xavier, NYC, but during his third year of teaching his health broke down, and he had to give up teaching. In fact, his health was so bad that it was feared that he would not live to the time when he would be ordained if he followed the usual seminary course. So arrangements were made for him to be tutored in moral theology; his examination on that subject he passed brilliantly. He was ordained by Bishop John Loughlin in the Brooklyn pro-cathedral in the summer of 1875.

Fortunately, his health recovered, and he was appointed prefect of studies at Xavier; he retained that post from 1875 to 1878, and at the same time he became known as a very understanding confessor and excellent preacher with a highly intellectual, strongly Scripture-based approach.

After completing his tour at Xavier, he spent several years in Europe reviewing and deepening his theological background in Spain, France, and England; he made his tertianship in England. On his return in 1882, he began a six-year assignment back at Xavier. This time he was as professor of philosophy, and of course continued preaching in the church there.

His next appointment for 1888-90 was to be professor of Scripture at Woodstock College. This was a surprising assignment because his formal training for that post was minimal. However, his vast erudition after years of private study and research provided what formal training had not, and he was regarded as an outstanding seminary professor. After Woodstock, he was at Montreal and Baltimore for short periods, and then in 1893 was sent to the parish of St. Lawrence O'Toole (St. Ignatius) for the last years of his life. There he did priestly ministry with his usual vigor. His deep devotion to St. John the Baptist and his enthusiastic preaching about him inspired a benefactor to underwrite building a special Baptistery Chapel of St. John the Baptist in the church that was about to be erected. Fr. Prendergast planned the details of the baptistery, and in a way it is a lasting memorial to his work.

In 1897 his health gave way again, and he had to limit his activities. Finally, he was sent to St. Vincent's Hospital where he was "alone with God as he preferred, for he refused to see visitors." He went to his reward with "sentiments of the greatest piety and resignation."

Physically, he was tall in stature, thin, dark in complexion, and had dark hair. He was praised for numerous characteristics such as his independence of mind, vast learning, excellent preaching, vivid imagination, absolute dedication to truth and genuineness, vivid denunciation of sham and hypocrisy, and witty, interesting conversation. But some unnamed eccentricities against which he fought caused some to dislike him. Yet his admirers were legion. He was a man of solid spirituality who loved the old devotions, as well as the Mass, the liturgy, and the breviary. The Holy Eucharist was the center of his life.

BR. JOSEPH PROULX, S. J.
B. July 15, 1846 in St-Isidore, La Praire, Quebec
E. Oct. 29, 1861 [J-R-9]
+ Mar. 2, 1864 at FC: Lived 17 years

If our vital statistics records are correct, Joseph Proulx's entering the Jesuit novitiate at Sault au Récollet near Montreal, at age 15 years plus three months, was unusual. Surely, he must have convinced Jesuit superiors that he was exceptionally mature.

His only assignment at the end of his noviceship in 1863 was to Fordham as supervisor of the dining room but he died before the end of his first year there. Curiously, in the same province another Jesuit Brother with the same surname, and of similar age. Louis Proulx, S.J., b. 12/24/45, age 20, died on May 12, 1864, a few months after Joseph, at St. Mary's College, Montreal. Were they brothers or cousins? We do not know; the fact that they were born in different places (Quebec vs. Albany, NY) may or may not be pertinent.

MR. CHARLES QUINN, S. J.
B. May 6, 1848, in NYC
E. Aug. 11, 1865 [C-R-7]
+ Feb. 2, 1871, at FC: Lived 22 years

Charles Quinn attended the College of St. Francis Xavier before entering the Jesuits. After taking his vows, he was sent to Quebec to study the humanities. Then he was assigned to Fordham as a teacher and prefect. His efforts were blessed with marked success. However, consumption forced him to give up that work, and for several months he bore his suffering with patience. Characteristics of his life were kindness, zeal for souls, and a tender love of the Blessed Virgin.

BR. ÉMILE RISLER, S. J.
B. Oct. 30, 1821, in Cernay, Upper Rhine, France
E. Nov. 21, 1847 [G-R-4]
+ Mar. 17, 1904, in NYC: Lived 82 years

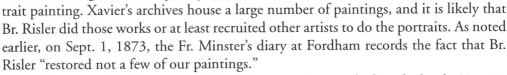

Émile Risler converted from Lutheranism and at age 26 began his novitiate at Issenheim in France. In view of his later activities as a Jesuit, he most likely had some training in the visual arts in his younger years.

He probably volunteered for the New World because shortly after his noviceship he was in New York and stayed there for the rest of his life. First he was at Fordham from 1850 to 1853; though he did some work there in 1873, he would not be assigned to Fordham again until 1902. The other years he spent at the College of St. Francis Xavier, NYC.

His main activity was devoted to art-related functions: doing and teaching calligraphy and portrait painting. Xavier's archives house a large number of paintings, and it is likely that Br. Risler did those works or at least recruited other artists to do the portraits. As noted earlier, on Sept. 1, 1873, the Fr. Minster's diary at Fordham records the fact that Br. Risler "restored not a few of our paintings."

As he grew older his non-artistic assignments increased, though the duties were probably light: sacristan in the chapel, custodian of the clothes room, and general housework.

When he was assigned back to Fordham in 1902, his task was general housework, but surely since he was in his 80s he could decide the particulars of that work. A summary statement about him in his Xavier obituary noted that while he worked he was always cheerful and that made him specially loved by Jesuits and students alike.

REV. JOHN ROBERTSON, S.J.
B. Mar. 22, 1847 in Charleston, NH
E. Sept. 7, 1875 [E-R-9]
+ Aug. 18, 1892 in FC: Lived 45 years

John Robertson was an Episcopalian and had probably been ordained in the Episcopalian church. When he went to England he became a Catholic and after a relatively short interval sought to join the Society in the English province and was accepted. He entered the novitiate at Roehampton and in due course was ordained. He worked at various priestly tasks in Bermingham and Glasgow.

He was then sent to the mission in British Honduras. After two years there, fevers and pleurisy made him very ill. He was directed to go back to his province by way of New York. When he arrived at New York he was exhausted and couldn't continue the trip. He was sent to Fordham, and two months later he died.

He was a man of great good will, equal to every task, joyful of spirit, a great lover of poverty who took only the worst for himself. Through all his illness he caused no trouble to others either in word, or countenance, or in any other way.

REV. VALENTINE H. ROCHFORT, S.J.
B. Feb. 29, 1871 in NYC
E. Aug. 14, 1889 [G-L-1]
+ July 7, 1906 at FC: Lived 35 years

Valentine Rochfort made his novitiate and later studied the classics at Frederick, MD. In 1893 he also did catechetical work with the deaf. He was then sent to Woodstock College for the study of philosophy until 1897. At that time he was transferred to make his regency at the College of the Holy Cross, Worcester, MA. There he taught general chemistry and college mathematics for four years.

After his regency he studied theology at Woodstock for four years. His first and only assignment as a priest was to teach chemistry and mathematics to the seminary students of philosophy at Woodstock College.

He came to Fordham from Woodstock for rest and medical treatment. Within a few days he improved very much. But the reports on July 7 that "Fr. Valentine Rochfort died suddenly this morning at 4:45 ... The Doctor's certificate gives cause of death as heart failure." For July 9 the diary continues: "Office of the Dead at 8:30 in college Chapel. Mass said by Fr. [William] Brett, Rector of Woodstock. ... 25 relatives and friends ... present in addition to the Community and about ten SJs from other houses."

BR. MICHAEL ROGERS, S.J.
B. Feb. 1, 1835, in Ogonnellae, Co. Clare, Ireland
E. Dec. 2, 1865 [G-R-5]
+ July 20, 1905, at FC: Lived 70 years

A reference to Br. Michael Rogers in an account of the new St. Andrew-on-Hudson novitiate in the *Woodstock Letters* (Vol. 31) provides this perspective on him: "Brother Rogers, who had complete charge of the carpenter work in St. Francis Xavier's and in the new Loyola School, 84th St., New York, came to St. Andrew in August 1902 to assist Father Walsh. The finer phases of finishing and rounding off the building developed under Brother Rogers' watchful care; scarcely a nook or corner but owes something to his intelligent skill, and patient, persevering effort."

"The first Holy Mass was celebrated in the new building by Father Walsh at midnight, on Christmas, 1902. ... Brother Rogers, Brother O'Sullivan and several workmen were present."

His carpentry skills and cabinet-making were much in demand. So he spent many years at the College of St. Francis Xavier, e.g., 1878-1883, 1887-1890; at Fordham, 1868-1871, 1883-1886, 1893-1895, 1904-1906; and at , 84th St., 1886-1887, 1902-1904. He was judged very competent in many skills, as indicated by his regularly being designated for "*omnia* (all kinds of work)."

### REV. MAURICE RONAYNE, S.J.
B. Apr. 2, 1828, in Dower, Co. Wicklow, Ireland
E. Sept. 12, 1853 [F-L-1]
+ Mar. 4, 1903, at FC: Lived 75 years

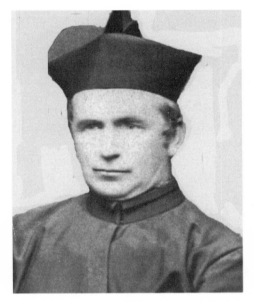

Maurice Ronayne made his pre-Jesuit studies at Maynooth in Ireland and Laval in France. He entered the Jesuit novitiate at St. Acheul, France. At any rate, his earlier studies must have been regarded as adequate enough for him to be assigned to study theology right after the noviceship, since he had taken the first years of theology at Laval. When he came to the U.S.A. in 1855 he completed the last year of theology at Fordham; Jesuits had traditionally been ordained after three years of theology, but in his case ordination was deferred until he had completed four years of theology in 1856.

The sites for his apostolate varied only between Fordham College and the College of St. Francis Xavier. The teaching of Rhetoric seems to have been his specialty. Thus, for a short period there was a pattern to his assignments: he would teach Rhetoric at Xavier for one or two years, then do the same at Fordham for the same time. But in 1865 The pattern changed. He was at Fordham 14 continuous years, teaching rhetoric, the history of rhetoric, and the history of philosophy; he also moderated the History Society and community Spiritual Father.

In 1880 he returned to Xavier for ten years, this time doing less teaching; he was the Spiritual Father and librarian. Then to Fordham, back to Xavier, and finally to Fordham as Spiritual Father and librarian. On Feb. 22, 1903, he was ailing and moved to the infirmary. Two days later, the Rector anointed him.

The Fr. Minister's diary for March 4, 1903, reports: "Fr. Ronayne died in the infirmary this evening at 7:45. He was conscious almost to the last. His patience and obedience were admirable. On March 5 it continues: "Fr. Provincial came this evening and will say the Mass tomorrow for Fr. Ronayne." On March 6: "Office of the Dead and Mass at 9 o'clock in church."

Fr. Ronayne wrote three books: *Religion and Science* (Collier: NY, 1879); *Religion and Science Historically Considered* (Kennedy: NY, 1890); *God Knowable and Known* (Benziger: NY, 1902).

BR. PATRICK ROONEY, S. J.
B.  Mar. 16, 1844, in Aghagower, Co. Mayo, Ireland
E.  Dec. 24, 1867 [C-L-1]
+ Mar. 9, 1871, at FC: Lived 26 years

In a short span of adult years before entering the Society, Patrick Rooney was said to have been a teacher in Ireland, then a member of the Irish Constabulary, and finally a merchant in New Haven, CT. After completing all this activity by age 23, he entered the Jesuit novitiate. At the end of his noviceship he was assigned to varied tasks at Fordham. But soon his health failed, and he died. For several months he bore patiently his cross of suffering.

ANTONIAS RUIZ, Fordham student
B. June 14, 1849 in Santiago de Cuba, Cuba
+ Jan. 30, 1864: Lived 14 years [A-7]

He entered St. John's College, Fordham, on June 29, 1863, and died seven months later. Besides the vital statistics above, we know nothing more about him.

REV. NICOLAS RUSSO, S.J.
B. Apr. 24, 1845 in Ascoli, Satriano, Foggia, Italy
E. Sept. 7, 1862 [H-R-2]
+ Apr. 1, 1902 in NYC: Lived 56 years

Nicolas Russo's father, a physician, wanted his son to follow in his career footsteps. But the son secretly wished to become a Jesuit, and when he was seventeen years of age he and two companions walked and begged their way to France. There Nicolas entered the novitiate at Pau, since the Jesuits were banned in Italy at that time. His first studies were in France, but he was sent to Woodstock, MD, for theology and ordination. Later, he taught at Boston College for ten years and was vice-rector and seventh president there for an academic year (September 1, 1887-July 4, 1888). He was assigned for a short time to The College of St. Francis Xavier and Georgetown.

Fr. Russo was the author of three textbooks, written in Latin (two on philosophy, one on religion). Up to 1891 his life was clearly in academia, but in that year the provincial asked him to accept a new challenge: a special apostolate to the New York Italian immigrants.

Fr. Russo threw himself with all his heart into the task. He began with a rented old bar room. Soon he was building a new church and separate schools for girls and boys. He created numerous clubs and religious associations to respond to the perceived needs of his Italian-Americans.

The *Woodstock Letters* index regarding him gives an idea of his many activities: Our [Jesuits'] Church for the Italians in NYC; founding of Our Lady of Loretto, NYC; his work at Boston; work in Bowery, NYC; an article he wrote, A Flying Trip Through Italy; his obituary; book review of his *De Philosophia Morali Praelectiones.*

His obituary recalled his tremendous physical, intellectual, and spiritual gifts and energy, as well as his patience, charity, and self-sacrifice.

MR. JOHN SAUZEAU, S.J. Schol.
B. Nov. 28, 1825, at Guerand, France
E. Jan. 13, 1849 [B-R-7]
+ Mar. 21, 1857, at FC: Lived 31 years

John Sauzeau completed his collegiate studies and for one year studied theology in the major seminary at Nantes. Then he felt called to the Society.

He made his novitiate and also reviewed Rhetoric for a year at St. Acheul, and then spent three years in prefecting college students at Brugelette in Belgium and in Paris. Finally, he was sent to America in 1855. His first task was to complete the study of theology at Fordham. For two and a half years he applied himself to this study. But several months before ordination on March 24, 1857, he died after a sixteen-day illness. Up to the end he had complete use of reason, and he received in good time all the sacraments that the Church provides for the terminally ill.

In the course of his illness he edified others by his patience, religious fervor and joy. Yet he had a serious mind and a brave spirit. He achieved well in his studies and hoped that he would some day be an indefatigable worker in the vineyard of the Lord. It was God's pleasure that his life be taken early, and he willingly accepted that fact.

REV. SERAPHIM SCHEMMEL, S. J.
B. Jan. 24, 1817, in Rouffah, Upper Rhine, France
E. Aug. 21, 1850 [C-R-12]
+ July 9, 1878, at NYC: Lived 61 years

A Latin obituary of Seraphim Schemmel began this way: "His nationality was French; his language was German; his body was small but his head was large." He studied for the diocesan priesthood and was ordained a priest in 1841 and served fpr 9½ years in a rural parish in his native diocese, Strasburg. But then he decided that he needed a different kind of life. He applied to become a Jesuit, was accepted, and after taking his first vows in Paris in 1852, he spent a year reviewing his Theology at Laval.

In the following year he was assigned to Fordham to teach dogmatic theology, Hebrew, philosophy and Holy Scripture in the diocesan seminary. He did that for five years (1854-1859). Next he taught philosophy in Montreal for another five years. He was back at Fordham for a few years and then a year at the College of St. Francis Xavier, NYC, and finally at the newly-opened Woodstock seminary teaching both dogmatic and moral theology until 1876. His teaching was said to be "remarkably clear in his expositions and explanations."

After he left Woodstock, he was assigned to Xavier to replace the recently-deceased Fr. Legoüais, a well-known confessor. Physically similar (both slightly built, stature small, one slightly above and the other slightly below five feet; but they differed in girth; it was said that what Fr. Schemmel lacked in height was abundantly supplied in girth). Their counseling was also said to be similar: clear, pointed, patient, gentle, always available and easy of access.

He was said to be personally timid, diffident (in teaching "he did not dare to look at his pupils"), and very humble. An obituary ends thus: "Quietly and unobtrusively he died as he had lived, a man of solid and well digested learning, but above all an interior man who seems never to have swerved, in any important detail, from the path of duty."

BR. JAMES SÉNÉ, S. J.
B. Apr. 4, 1793 at Lihon (Somme), France
 E. Sept. 27, 1815 [J-R-8]
+ Jan. 17, 1865 at FC: Lived 71 years

Before entering the Jesuits, James Séné had been a soldier for three years under Napoleon and was very devoted to him. Because he joined the newly restored Society when he did, he was later venerated as a pioneer member of his province.

After finishing his noviceship, and before he came to the New World, he served as custodian of the clothes room and as the infirmarian at several Jesuit residences in France and at the Jesuit seminary at Brugelette in Belgium. He was transferred to St. Mary's, KY, in 1838 where he fulfilled those same functions until he made the move to Rose Hill.

During his 19 years at Fordham, Br. Séné's duties shifted from work in the infirmary to gardening (care of the green house), caring for student housing, and prefecting students. He was one of the pioneers who came from Kentucky to Rose Hill in 1846 and continued to serve there until his death.

No formal obituary of Br. Séné has been found. Nevertheless, a letter in the Oct., 1891, *Fordham Monthly* recalled fond memories of him when the author and he were both at St. Mary's, KY. A. H. Garland wrote that Brother was "a dear soul to me, and one of the best friends I ever had. He was a soldier under Napoleon, and ... we used to talk of Napoleon in his hearing as a fraud, no soldier, coward, and so on, but oh! we had to get away quick. ... I believe I was then the youngest boy there, and was not very strong or of good health. For the first few months he would come ... and take me to the infirmary, give me a warm egg-nog, and put me to bed as carefully as a mother could. ... Precious old soul!" Surely this moving remembrance of Br. Séné serves well as an obituary.

BR. EDMUND SHANAHAN, S. J.
B. Apr. 3, 1836 in Moyne, Co. Tipperary, Ireland
E. Sept. 7, 1857 [G-R-1]
+ May 25, 1902 in NYC: Lived 66 years

Edmund Shanahan at age 31 entered the Jesuit novitiate at Montrouge in Paris. We do not know what his occupation was before he entered. And there is some confusion about the place of his years of novitiate. Possibly he did one year at Paris and one at Frederick, MD. His longest assignment in one place, for 16 years from 1872 to 1888, was at Loyola College, Baltimore. In other years he was at Holy Cross, Frederick (MD), Gonzaga (Washington, DC), St. Joseph's (Phila.), Connewango (PA), Woodstock (MD), Troy (NY), The College of St. Francis Xavier (NY), and finally, Fordham. He most of his assignments were as cook; at times he supervised service in the dining room. Nothing else has been learned about him.

BR. DAVID SHANNON, S. J.
B. Mar. 12, 1831, at Dromore, Co. Down, Ireland
E. May 16, 1856 [I-R-10]
+ July 16, 1874, at NYC: Lived 43 years

David Shannon came to America in 1852 and six years later entered the Jesuit novitiate after laboring as a mechanic for many years. From 1860 to his death he carried out various assignments at Fordham as dispenser, assistant manager of the farm, and director of the employees. He was for several years a patient sufferer, edifying all by his humility and charity.

BR. HILARY SPALDING, S. J.
B. May 15, 1823/4 in Nashville, TE
E. Nov. 26, 1848 [J-R-7]
+ Sept. 29, 1865 at FC: Lived 41/42 years

Two years after the departure of the Jesuits from Kentucky, Hilary Spalding, at age 24 or 25, a member of a well-known Catholic family, left neighboring Tennessee and came to Fordham as a novice Brother.

In 1853 he was included in the Fordham *Catalogus Primus* (vital statistical data) and in the *Catalogus Secundus* (evaluation of each one's prudence, talents, etc., probably completed by the rector). Br. Spalding's vital statistics in the *Catalogus* are those that are stated above, except that his year of birth, is given as 1824, rather than the year 1823 which is found elsewhere. Other factors about him were: his education, that he reads, writes, and can count; his judgment, sufficiently good; his health, mediocre; his experience/talents, good, as buyer and infirmarian.

After completing his novitiate, he was assigned for nine years (1850-1859) to several tasks at Fordham, mostly as infirmarian and buyer. In his last year there he was also assistant procurator.

From 1859 to 1865 he taught at the Jesuit Spring Hill College, Mobile, Alabama. Perhaps on the basis of his education or experience prior to entering the Jesuits or on the basis of his experience as procurator and buyer, he taught in the college Commercial Program.

During this period he was transferred from the province of France to the province of Lyons. We do not know how or why he came back to Fordham in 1865. At any rate, the Fr. Minister's diary, when recording his death, noted that he was "sick for a long time." Perhaps his sickness and early death was due to privations endured during the Civil War.

BR. MARTIN STOECHLIN, S. J.
B. June 24, 1826 in Hausgaum, Upper Rhine, France
E. June 7, 1854 [H-R-1]
+ Apr. 9, 1975 in FC: Lived 48 years

When Martin Stoechlin was a novice and before he had taken his first vows, he was sent to the Jesuit mission on Manitoulin Island, Canada. He remained there, worked among the Indian population, and engaged in domestic occupations until 1866. Then he was transferred to Buffalo where he spent four years as sacristan, buyer, and carpenter. When his health deteriorated in 1870, he was sent to Fordham, where he died a holy death after a long and painful illness.

REV. AUGUST J. THÉBAUD, S.J.
B. Nov. 20, 1807 in Nantes, France
E. Nov. 27, 1835 [D-R-4]
First Jesuit FC President, beginning July 15, 1846
+ Dec. 17, 1885 at FC: Lived 78 years

When at age 39, Fr. Thébaud was appointed the president of the college, he became not only the first Jesuit president of Fordham but also one of the youngest in that position and one of the few who left that post and later held it a second time. Readers may turn to Chapter 4 of this book for a full biographical profile of Fr. Thébaud.

REV. THEODORE THIRY, S.J.
B. Dec. 14, 1823 in Metz, France;
E. Sept. 11, 1843 [D-R-5]
+ Mar. 13, 1889 in NYC: Lived 65 years.

Theodore Thiry attended the Jesuit college, St. Clement's, in his native Metz. There he received his vocation and was accepted by the Society. He completed his noviceship and philosophical studies in France and Belgium, and when he applied for the American mission, he was accepted. He came to Fordham for theological studies and was ordained there by Archbishop Hughes in 1850. Then for eleven years he taught Latin and religion at the College of St. Francis Xavier, NYC.

The rest of his life was devoted to a stimulating apostolate at the Xavier parish where he was specially successful teaching religion to the young, hearing confessions, and inspiring parishioners to help the poor and spread the faith. He was for years in charge of the parish elementary schools, directed the boy's and young men's sodalities, moderated a literary society, the men's sodality, the St. Vincent de Paul Society, and the Holy Childhood society which at that time was dedicated especially to assisting the Church in China.

The cause of his fatal illness was Bright's Disease. His funeral Mass was celebrated by the Jesuit provincial, absolution was given by Archbishop Corrigan, and was attended by at least 3,000 grateful recipients of his religious ministries. The Xavier magazine summarized the many praises heard about him: "Among Catholics there were few men in this city better known and better loved than Father Thiry. The young men have lost a helper, the old men a tried and true friend, and the church of St. Francis Xavier one of its most earnest and zealous workers, a man of Apostolic Spirit."

GEORGE THOMPSON, college employee
B. in England:
+ May 15, 1869 [A-13]

[Buried in same grave as Remigius Hillenmeyer; information about R. Hillenmeyer can be found above.]

In the Fr. Minister's diary for May 15, 1869, a reference, translated from Latin, reported: "George Thompson, one of the employees, slept in the Lord [died] after an illness of some weeks. [He was] fortified by the Sacraments of the Church."

On May 17, 1869, the diary continued: "George Thompson [was] buried, Fr. Minister celebrated [the Mass], very many of the Jesuit Brothers and employees accompanied the bier. His body was brought first to the parish church and then to our cemetery."

REV. PETER TISSOT, S.J.
B. Oct. 15, 1823 at Mégève, Savoy, France
E.  Oct. 11, 1842 [C-R-10]
+ June 19, 1875 at NYC: Lived 51 years

Ripley's——Believe It or Not!®

Aug. 1969

FATHER TISSOT
HERO OF THE CIVIL WAR,
WHILE PRESIDENT OF FORDHAM
COLLEGE IN NEW YORK CITY
*WROTE A LETTER OF RESIGNATION
EVERY DAY FOR 5 MONTHS
–MORE THAN 150 LETTERS–*
HIS RESIGNATION WAS FINALLY
ACCEPTED IN JUNE, 1865

Peter had been a student at a Jesuit college in France, and had entered the Society at Avignon. While studying philosophy, he asked to be sent to America. Assigned to Fordham, he completed his studies there and was ordained in 1853.

For several years after ordination (1855-1860), he was the community Minister and procurator at Fordham. In his early years he also taught modern languages. However, his personal hope was to be engaged entirely in pastoral and missionary rather than in collegiate work. Thus he volunteered to be an army chaplain during the U.S. Civil War, and his offer was accepted.

Fr. Tissot was chaplain for three years of the New York 37TH Regiment, Irish Volunteers, known as the "Irish Rifles." General Philip Kearny said of Fr. Tissot that he was the model army chaplain: when his regiment was in action he always performed his priestly duties at the front of the line of battle. In fact, three horses were killed under him during battles. Yet Fr. Tissot himself wrote later that the best place for a chaplain in battle was at the hospital station just behind the front lines where he could serve the largest number of individuals.

He was captured on June 30, 1862, and imprisoned, During his brief imprisonment, he labored for the salvation of his charges as if he were in church. On July 19, 1862, he was pleasantly surprised when he was released with no conditions during a mid-war exchange of prisoners. A profile of Fr. Tissot and one year of his wartime diary was the basis for "A Year with the Army of the Potomac" in *Historical Records and Studies*, III (1904), 38-87. The diary revealed his concerns for the soldiers' religious needs, his ministry of the Eucharist (he prepared a surprising number of soldiers for First Communion), and his quest for Fordham alumni and for fellow chaplain-priests.

Shortly after his release from the army, Fr. Tissot was made acting President of Fordham. He stayed in that role only from January 23 to July 31, 1865, since he protested his unfitness for that honor in daily letters for six months to his superiors, and they finally yielded to him. Ripley highlighted his daily resignation letters in his "Believe It or Not" column. After his acting presidency, he returned to his position of college procurator until 1873.

Only in the last few years of his life was he allowed to devote all his time to the activity that he desired most: giving missions and retreats. He did that all over the country with indefatigable zeal and wonderful success. So it is not surprising that his one major publication was a religious book entitled *The Real Presence*.

General O'Beirne described him this way: his "darkened olive complexion framed
... eyes that sparkled with merry twinkles of humor ... scholarly [appearance] ... pol-
ished elegance. [His outstanding traits were:] unswerving, unalterable ... moral courage. ... [His was] a great soul [with] lofty principles."

Fr. Campbell wrote that Fr. Tissot gladly accepted his appointment as military
chaplain, though his quiet, retiring nature was averse to such activity. Campbell added
that his later missionary work, done mostly alone, ended his life prematurely because
of the excessive work it required of him. Most observers recalled him as a shy, refined
gentleman whose memory was held in benediction among the clergy and laity.

## REV. MICHAEL X. TOMEI, S. J.

B. Sept. 17, 1792, at Tivoli, Italy
E. Nov. 12, 1814 [B-R-3]
+ Dec. 10, 1850, NYC: Lived 58 years

Michael Xavier Tomei entered the Jesuit novitiate in Rome the year the Society was
restored. After his studies and ordination, he had a distinguished academic history:
professor of philosophy at the Roman College, rector at Spoleto, Forli, and Fermo, then
professor of moral theology and prefect of studies at the Roman College. He wrote
books in Latin on logic and on ontology.

In 1848 Fr. Tomei was among a group of scholars who sought refuge in the United
States from turbulent political conditions in Italy. He had been at Georgetown and in
July, 1850 hoped to return to his own Roman province. However, the political situation there was still very unsettled. In view of that fact, before he was able to set sail for
Rome, Fr. Clement Boulanger, the Jesuit Superior of the Mission, offered Fr. Tomei a
teaching position in St. Joseph's Seminary at Rose Hill, which was gladly accepted. He
was able to vindicate administrators' evaluations of his abilities by students' favorable
responses when he taught in the seminary, though he was there for only a few months.
In the annual edition of the *Catholic Almanac* that recorded names of the faculty of St.
Joseph's Seminary at Fordham, he was listed as Professor of Moral Theology (1850).
But a massive heart attack shattered his plans and the plans of others for him. He died
a very pious death, recognized as a learned scholar and an expert teacher.

## REV. HENRY VAN RENNSELAER, S. J.

B. Oct. 21, 1851, in Ogdensburg, NY
E. Oct. 31, 1878 [I-R-8]
+ Oct. 3, 1907, in NYC: Lived 55 years

Descended on his father's side from the early Dutch settlers and on his mother's
side from Rufus King, an American ambassador to England, Van Rennselaer was an
Episcopalian seminarian and was close to ordination in that church. However, in 1876
he, his sister, and a clerical friend were received into the Catholic Church in Paris
during a trip to Europe. On shipboard during the return trip to America, he met
several Jesuit missionaries and was deeply impressed by them. Later, after a retreat at

Manresa he entered the Jesuits and made his noviceship in England. He returned to New York for further study and taught at Loyola College, MD, and at Fordham (1883-1884).

He was ordained in 1887. The St. Francis Xavier parish, NYC, became the focus of his apostolic ministry. Yet his zeal for souls was universal, not limited to any special group. The widespread admiration felt for him and his personal effectiveness was indicated by the fact that more than 3,000 people attended his funeral.

His biography, *The Life and Letters of Henry Van Rensselaer*, written by Edward R. Spillane, S.J., was published by the Fordham University Press in 1908.

BR. GEORGE VAUGHEN, Novice Br. S.J.
B. Jan. 14, 1847, in NYC
E. Nov. 12, 1868 [J-R-1]
+ Oct. 22, 1870, at FC: Lived 23 years

George Vaughen entered the noviceship for Jesuit Brothers at Fordham and died a few weeks before he was able to make his public vows. Very little has been learned about him. Reference to him in a cemetery book gives only his vital statistics, as listed above. The Fr. Minister's diary noted in his regard: "Brother George Vaughen died this morning at 10¾. Buried next day at 1½ P.M."

BR. DÉSIRÉ VAURENTERGHAN, S. J.
B. Jan. 5/7, 1824 in Ghent, Belgium
E. July 20, 1860 [I-R-8]
+ Sept. 7, 1875 in NYC: Lived 51 years

Désiré Vaurenterghan at age 36 entered the novitiate in Sault au Récollet, near Montreal. After that he was assigned to numerous places in the province: Fordham, Buffalo (St. Michael's), Troy, and Xavier.

During his fifteen years as a Jesuit he was assigned to many different tasks in the above four houses: painting, gardening, baking, and "*ad domum*" (various unspecified household functions). We have no further details about him beyond what is contained in an obituary.

In his brief obituary he was praised thus: "He was a model lay-brother, as remarkable for his piety and regularity as for his skill as a workman. He fell a victim to a malignant form of black typhus which took him away in a few days" (*WL*, vol. 19, 408).

REV. THOMAS WARD, S. J.
B. Dec. 8, 1864 in Jersey City, NJ
E. Sept. 27, 1888 [G-R-2]
+ Nov. 18, 1902 in Jersey City, NJ: Lived 37 years

He was the oldest of seven children and decided that after finishing grammar school he should go to work to help family finances. He worked as a cooper to age twenty. Then he decided to act on his hope to become a priest and went to night school to learn Latin and Greek. When he realized his night school results were unsatisfactory, he enrolled among the day students at St. Peter's College, Jersey City, and worked at barrels on holidays, afternoons and evenings. After two years of college, he applied to the Society but was told he wasn't yet adequately prepared.

Yet he would not give up on his goal, and when he heard that he might be welcomed in the Jesuit Rocky Mountain Mission, he applied and was accepted. He made his noviceship in Wisconsin, philosophy and theology, and was ordained in 1899 at St. Ignatius, Montana.

Having achieved his heart's desire, he wore himself out in a few years of labor in the Northwest. Seeing the state of his health, superiors decided to send him east to Frederick, MD, for tertianship in 1903. But there his health deteriorated, and he was sent to St. Francis Hospital in his native Jersey City. He got worse and worse, but suffered very patiently, with perfect resignation to his death, and edified others by his prayer and devotions.

He was recalled as unsparing of himself in ministry, jovial, open-hearted, empathic towards others, and a model religious and model priest.

REV. JAMES WELLWORTH, S. J.
B. April 22, 1850 at Roscrea, Co. Tipperary, Ireland
E. July 30, 1873 [D-R-7]
+ Mar. 22, 1890 in Troy, NY: Lived 39 years

James Wellworth's family came to this country when he was about nine years old and settled in Troy, NY. In 1871 he came to Fordham for two years, and then entered the Jesuit novitiate. He studied philosophy and theology at Woodstock College, MD and after ordination did parochial work for a year at St. Thomas, MD.

After completing his tertianship, he was sent to take charge of the hospital work on Blackwells Island, NYC. He would spend only seven months on the laborious mission when God called him to his reward. But in that short time he gave to all on the island, officials and patients, an example of Christian and priestly virtues, which, they said many years ago, would not soon be forgotten. The *Liber Defunctorum* says of him, "He was a vigorous man not only in body but also in virtue: ... patient, long-suffering without complaints or quarrels."

He was absorbed in his work, and wholly forgetful of self, the last one to dream that he was doing anything that should attract attention. One incident is told of him which gave great edification. A patient in his last illness refused to see him or talk with him. This patient, finally, became unconscious, and for a whole night Fr. Wellworth sat by his bedside, waiting and praying for a moment's consciousness to be granted the man, in which to make his peace with God.

Fr. Wellworth was called to Troy a few days before his death to be present at the profession of one of his sisters, a Sister of St. Joseph. On arriving at Troy he became ill and died of pneumonia after only a a few days' illness.

In his last moments he was delirious, but the wanderings of his mind were in harmony with his life; he imagined himself assisting at the death-beds of fever patients.

REV. RICHARD J. WHYTE, S. J.
B. Nov. 17, 1824, in Dunbell, Co. Kilkenny, Ireland
E. Jan. 25, 1855 [E-R-6]
+ July 14, 1891, in NYC: Lived 66 years

Richard Whyte was born of a family that figured quite prominently in Irish affairs in the days of Daniel O'Connell. He studied medicine at Trinity College, Dublin. In the 1840's he came to this country, and in 1846, when hundreds went west in the search for gold, Dr. Whyte was among that number. In California, where his sister was superior of a convent, he practiced medicine for a number of years.

In 1855, when he was 31 years of age, he felt that he had a religious vocation. He entered the Society of Jesus in the Maryland Province.

He assisted in parochial work at Boston College for three years. Then he was transferred to Fordham where he taught the history of philosophy, rhetoric, and evidence of religion, which he did with much success. In 1874 he was transferred to the College of St. Francis Xavier, NYC, where he taught the same courses as he had in Fordham and did parish work for the remaining years of his life. His Jesuit assignments seem to indicate his change of interest from his former specialty, doctoring, and allied areas like natural sciences, for religious and literary endeavors.

In Fr. Whyte's last attack of disease (asthma and pneumonia), in spite of the torture of his sufferings, he displayed great patience.

*We offer here two reflections from a modern perspective on the materials presented in this book. As we saw, those materials consisted in the main of documentation of one sort or another. They traced a course from Boulanger's blow-by-blow account of the decision to come to New York, to the dramatic origins of Fordham and Xavier, to the spread of early New York Jesuits into ministries far and wide — ministries whose humble record is found on tombstones in the Fordham Jesuit cemetery. We have asked two scholars to reflect on these developments, one from the perspective of the long Jesuit educational tradition, the other exploring the significance of those early Jesuit lives for the Church's encounter with the 'new world' we find ourselves in today.*

## JESUIT EDUCATION: A CONTINUOUS TRADITION

It is an honor to be asked to make some reflections on *How the Jesuits Settled in New York.* Puzzled at first about the reason for this request, I recognized several possibilities, the first of which might be my life-long association with one of the institutions treated in the book, Fordham. It is seventy-two years since I first set foot on the Fordham Campus as a freshman in Fordham Prep and sixty-two since I received my diploma from Fordham College, In a long career as a Jesuit teacher I have never held a permanent appointment in any institution which was not affiliated with Fordham University. The history of my own life and the history of Fordham have coincided to a large extent.

Another reason for the request might be my lasting interest in the history of the Church and of the Society of Jesus. By profession, I am supposed to be a philosopher, not a historian. Nevertheless there are many ways of doing philosophy. My way has been to study the relation between systematic philosophy and Catholic theology, keeping in mind that the latter cannot determine its own nature and limits correctly without reflecting on its relation to philosophy, nor, on the other hand, can philosophy — *pace Descartes* — escape a certain narrowness of perspective if it systematically excludes from consideration the revealed data studied by theology.

But — and this is the relevant point of my reflections — I'm equally interested in how history has in the past shaped the way in which that relation between philosophy and Catholic theology is construed. As Church historians know, the Church's major religious orders have drawn on upon their distinctive style of Catholic theology in forming their spiritual world-views. This is particularly true of the Society of Jesus. Furthermore, the spirituality and humanism characteristic of the Society, which, from the early years of its existence, have given Jesuit education its unique identity, were the result of *a specifically Jesuit integration of natural knowledge and divine revelation,* an integration that could not be made without the use of a sound philosophy. For that reason, Jesuits, advised by Superiors who knew their history, have been guided by their own integrated theology and philosophy of education in the direction of their schools.

Historians of the Jesuit tradition in education who overlook that fact can easily go astray.

### Bearers of a Tradition

Brought back to life after the Napoleonic Wars, the nineteenth century Society of Jesus, to which early New York Jesuits belonged, placed great weight on its recovery of an authentically Jesuit spirituality and on renewed dedication to the specific type of apostolic and educational work for which the Society had been known before its suppression in the eighteenth century.

Modifications might be demanded in these works if they were to be carried on in the changed intellectual and cultural climate of nineteenth century Europe and America. But no such alterations, if they were of any significance, were to be be made on the responsibility of individual Jesuits. Any adaptation of the traditional Jesuit *Ratio Studiorum* made in the light of American educational demands had to be approved by European superiors, who usually had no personal experience of America. Justification for them could not be made in terms of mere expediency. Major Superiors had to know precisely what was being proposed. And so, by the rules of their Order, missionary Jesuits were obliged to submit regular reports on their apostolic and educational projects. As conscientious Religious, they did so carefully, honestly, and intelligently. Nineteenth century American Jesuits knew very well that their European superiors would not approve of what they were doing or planned to do in America unless these enterprises were judged to be compatible with the apostolic and educational tradition to which the whole Society was dedicated. Therefore, in order to compose the reports of their activity translated for us in *How the Jesuits Settled in New York*, the early New York Jesuits had to have already reflected very carefully on what they were about and convince themselves that what they were doing could be justified as an authentic form of their Jesuit apostolate. For that reason their reports to France and Rome, private internal Jesuit documents as they are, give the reader a precious insight into what the men who founded Fordham and Xavier honestly thought about their colleges as Jesuit institutions.

### Fidelity to Tradition in a New Land

Life was not always easy for the New York Jesuits. In Fr. Hennessy's book we read about the struggle of well-educated Europeans to design a traditional Jesuit education for young Americans unfamiliar with it. We read as well about the energy and diplomatic skill needed to carry on their pastoral ministry to the sick poor in public hospitals in which anti-Catholic staff and administrators consistently tried to impede their work. Another recurrent theme in the reports is the constant risk to the health, and even to the lives, of Jesuits assigned to the hospital apostolate. The early reports from the college and parish of Saint Francis Xavier reveal the energy and ingenuity with which Jesuit parish priests, many of whom had been born and educated in continental Europe, carried on their pastoral work for the immigrant Irish and the neglected Negroes living in the city.

The prescribed form for official Jesuit reports and the added obligation that these reports be written in Latin did not encourage originality and novelty in their composition. But these reports, after all, were not written for the entertainment of Superiors. They were intended to be trustworthy factual reports, accurate and fundamentally honest in their content, written for the information of Superiors living in another country. In their pages therefore we find out what sort of men these early Jesuits really were, how they went about their work, and what they honestly thought of the new land to which they had come. Though fully aware of the difficulties often placed in the way of their work, these early Jesuits, almost to a man, wrote enthusiastically about the unique advantages which the New World held out for their Jesuit apostolate. They obviously liked their American students and their immigrant parishioners.

Those who wrote the reports contrasted the basic fairness of their treatment in America with the systematic discrimination from which they had suffered under the anti-clerical liberal governments of Europe. Whatever individual Americans might think about them, the American republic and its institutions had not proved more hostile in principle either to Jesuits or to their faith. Jesuits in fact were much better off in America than they had been at home. Royalists though they might have been in France, the Fordham Jesuits made a point of celebrating the national holidays of the American Republic in their school, and they wrote to their Superiors in praise of the speeches given by their students at those celebrations.

A Diverse and Talented Community

The community that came from Kentucky to Fordham, although it belonged to Province of France, was multi-national in its composition. France, Ireland, Italy, and central Europe were represented in its membership. A number of its members could converse easily in several languages. The highly educated William Stack Murphy, an Irishman who had been educated in France, was equally fluent in French and English and, while studying theology in Rome and working as a Jesuit teacher in Spain, had also gained a good speaking knowledge of Spanish and Italian. Two other members of the Fordham community were facile enough in Spanish to be sent on an extended fund raising tour of Mexico.

Murphy, who had been dean of St. Mary's College in Kentucky, may well have been the best educational theorist among them. He had shown himself to be a very effective teacher at Billom, a well-known Jesuit college in France. Archbishop Lamy of Santa Fe, who had been his student there, remained in touch with him and came to visit him on at least two occasions. Murphy was thoroughly acquainted with the updated scheme of Jesuit liberal education, designed in France by Father Jean-Nicolas Loriquet and then implemented in the celebrated College of Saint Acheul. One group of French Jesuits brought the Loriquet plan of education with them to America and implemented it in their college at Grand Coteau, Louisiana. After some modifications in it, made after consultation with the Maryland Jesuits at Georgetown, the Loriquet plan became the basis of early Jesuit education at Fordham.

Because of recognized skill as a Jesuit educator, Murphy was later appointed by the Jesuit General as Provincial of Missouri. The Flemish Jesuit pioneers of that Province had not enjoyed the educational advantages of their French confreres on the East Coast, and, in what in many ways was still a frontier society, the Missouri form of Jesuit education had not been able to measure up to the General's expectations. Murphy was sent west to help his Missouri colleagues in their effort to design and implement the traditional form of Jesuit education, an effort which ultimately succeeded. After five years as a fine Provincial, he left Missouri and joined the French Jesuits in New Orleans.

Other talented Jesuits assigned Fordham were physically more robust. As Fr. Hennessy tells us, John Larkin, the founder of Xavier and a successful Rector-President of Fordham, was an impressive public figure and a popular preacher. At first a Sulpician priest, assigned to teach theology in Montreal, Larkin had joined the Jesuits in Kentucky and came with them to Fordham. His great success in New York almost proved to be his undoing, and he was forced to go to Europe and argue strenuously to fight off an episcopal appointment. Isidore Daubresse was not the popular figure that Larkin was but he was a highly respected moral theologian, and, like Larkin, had to argue strenuously to prevent his designation as a bishop. Auguste Thébaud was an excellent administrator and a popular author. Although a Breton, as Rector-President of Fordham, he knew how to cultivate a largely Irish-Catholic public. Despite the tension between the Fordham Jesuits and John Hughes, Thébaud remained on good terms with the imperious Archbishop and, as far as we can discern, they remained good friends.

Not all the early Jesuits wanted to spend their lives as educators. The pastoral needs of New York, Quebec and the Indian Missions further west in Canada could not be ignored, and so some of the Jesuits who came to Fordham or Xavier did not stay there for long. One such was Michael Nash, an Irishman who entered the Society in Kentucky and came to Fordham as a Scholastic. Although an intelligent and zealous man, Nash made no claim to be an intellectual. He felt at home as a military chaplain in the Civil War and as a long-term pastor in Troy. Like many other Jesuits at the time, his interest lay more in the active than in the academic way of life. Yet Nash became a distinguished Jesuit.

The Uniqueness of the New York and Canada Mission

For a number of reasons, the New York and Canada Mission was different in its outlook from the neighbor Jesuit provinces of Maryland and the Missouri. While both of them were independent, self-governing American entities, the New York and Canada Mission, on the other hand, remained dependent on its mother Provinces of France and Champagne until 1870. Until that time, to meet its apostolic responsibilities, the Mission had to carry on its work in two different countries speaking two different languages. Of necessity, this gave the New York Jesuits an international outlook that other American Jesuits did not share. Its ties with Europe linked their Mission closely to that continent, and, in the troubled years before and after 1848, a number of Jesuit refugees made their way to America through New York. Many of these exiles lived with Fordham Jesuits for a time and some with Xavier Jesuits, often under difficult conditions, either to complete their Jesuit theological formation or to perfect their English before taking up apostolic work in other parts of the United States. New York had become one of the nation's major ports of entry and, for that reason, Jesuits working in other parts of the country often stayed for a time at Fordham or Xavier either while going over to Europe or returning from it to America. Thus, contact with fellow Jesuits from all over the country became a fairly common occurrence at these two Jesuit houses. The early New York Jesuits were unlikely therefore to suffer from the narrow provincialism of which the native-born American Jesuits of Maryland have been accused. But, close as their ties to Europe remained for many years, it is interesting to note how few of the New York Jesuits showed any interest in returning there. Clement Boulanger, the brilliant founder and long-term superior of the Mission, did return to France, but the bulk of his subjects did not follow his example. They had come to stay.

The Jesuit Way

I notice that I have been focussing on the passing down of a Jesuit tradition from Europe to America and all that entailed. It dawned on me that I have lived through a similar transition in my years at Fordham, and I suspect Jesuits at Xavier and the other Jesuit institutions mentioned in this book could say the same.

The Fordham to which I came in 1932 bore little physical resemblance to the Fordham where the early Jesuits had worked. The University Church and the Administration Building had been remodeled. Hughes and Dealy Hall had been built in the nineteenth century and Collins Hall had gone up at the start of the twentieth. Fordham's major expansion between World War I and II had added the Gymnasium, Freeman, Larkin and Keating Halls, together with the Duane Library, to an impressive array of buildings on the Rose Hill Campus. Bishops and St. Robert's Halls had been joined to St. John's Hall to create the present Queen's Court. Fordham's Manhattan Division, first occupying several floors of the Woolworth Building and then in its own building at 302 Broadway, was home to its Schools of Education, Business Administration, Social Service and Law. Fordham had now become an urban university, even more so, since, with the exception of a small group of boarders, the students of Fordham College still commuted to the campus from their homes.

Despite these changes, however, the Fordham of that time remained much closer to the early Fordham than the Fordham of today. The University was still controlled by the Society of Jesus, and Jesuits were more numerous and visible on the Fordham Campus than they are today. The Jesuit General still appointed Fordham's Rector-President and still had a word to say about the content of its liberal arts curriculum. Fordham College was organized along American lines but its program of studies would still have been familiar to the faculty and students of Jesuit schools through out the world. Latin remained a requirment for its A.B. The first two years of the Fordham College curriculum emphasised the study of literature, Poetry in the first year and Rhetoric in the second. Although a variety of electives was offered, a designated series of courses in systematic philosophy was prescribed for every student in Junior and Senior year. That program of studies can be traced back to the Jesuit colleges of St. Ignatius' time, and it was the program prescribed for Jesuit schools by Father General Claudio Aquaviva in the first edition of the Jesuit *Ratio Studiorum*.

The Fordham Jesuits of the 1930s were not content just to carry on their educational tradition. They advertised that fact. The main lecture hall in Keating Hall, opened in 1936, and intended for the philosophical instruction of the whole senior class, took as its model the lecture hall of the Gregorian University in Rome. As he did in Rome, a single professor gave his lecture from an elevated podium, and some of those professors, like Joseph Murphy and Ignatius Cox in their heyday, did that quite effectively. The formal lectures were attended by a small group of the professor's assistants. They helped him in the correction of the students' papers and also worked more closely with them in small groups to help and guide them in their understanding of the professor's course.

On the stained glass windows of the former senior lecture hall in Keating Hall we still can see the portraits of Jesuit saints who also had been scholars. The legend inscribed over Keating Hall's main entrance reminded its student readers of the historical connection between Fordham and the Jesuit institutions in Maryland and Kentucky from which their university claimed descent. On the top of Keating Hall's outer walls the seals of every Jesuit high school and college in the Maryland-New York Province were carved in stone. The message meant to be conveyed by the architecture of Keating Hall could hardly have been clearer: Fordham represented an educational tradition older and more universal than itself.

A second great period of expansion after World War II changed both the physical appearance and the organizational structure of the University. To accommodate a large influx of boarders, Martyrs' Court, Alumni Court, Tierney and Millenium Halls were built on the Rose Hill Campus, and Hughes Hall, the former home of Fordham Prep, and Finlay Hall, the former Chemistry Building, were transformed into dormitories. Finally, after years of waiting, a university library adequate to meet its needs of a major university was built on the Rose Hill Campus. A new down-town campus at Lincoln Center became the home of a liberal arts college linked closely to the college on the Rose Hill Campus. The law school and the graduate faculties of business and social service were also located there.

The autonomy required for schools and their departments in the conduct of a modern university, the size and the diversity of its faculty, and the transfer of the University's control to its lay board of trustees have made it impossible for Fordham to remain the type of Jesuit school it was at the time Keating Hall was built. That does not mean, however, that the Jesuit tradition of education is no longer viable. Fordham is still proud of that tradition and has shown no desire to abandon it.

From the early days of Jesuit education, one of its defining charactistics was an explicitly integrated view of God, the world and man. The Jesuits' Christian God was a personal being, and human beings, made in God's image, were free, responsible persons. Created by a personal God, the world in which the Jesuit student lived made sense, and, properly educated, the student's intelligence would be able to show him how to find the meaning of that world, enable him to work well in it, improve it, and, by doing so. enrich its society, and thus return to God. A Jesuit school understood itself to be a community of teachers and learners working together toward a common end, and that end was the harmonious cultural, moral and religious development of the individual student whom God had entrusted to its teachers' care. That Jesuit view of man and of the world in which he lived accounted for the content of the Jesuits' curriculum and the *cura personalis* which characterized their way of teaching. Fordham has not given up that Jesuit vision of education.

From their beginning, social concern was another characteristic of Jesuit schools. The Jesuit college was usually the base of Jesuit pastoral activity. Through their Sodalities, its students were urged-to work for the sick and poor of the neighborhod about them. Faithful to that heritage, the early Jesuits based at Fordham, were also pastors showing great concern for the sick poor. One Fordham Jesuit, as we know, lost his life caring for immigrants, dying of cholera in Canada during the Irish famine. In their Xavier parish, Jesuits worked very hard to protect and educate the poor and neglected Irish and Negroes living in New York.

That type of concern did not die out with the early New York Jesuits. In the opening years of the last century, it inspired the work of Father Terence Sheely, whose many-tiered social activities resulted in the establishment of Fordham's School of Social Service. In the 1930s, Jesuits set up their celebrated labor schools in the metropolitan area to train responsible leaders for the labor unions of that time. One of those Jesuits was John Corridan, whose work out of Xavier on the waterfront later became famous. Another was the young Joseph Fitzpatrick, who labored at Xavier and at Fordham and was among the first to recognize the social, educational, and pastoral needs of New York's growing Hispanic population. Over the years, Father Fitzpatrick enabled Fordham to organize its resources to improve the lot of New York's minority population. Humanistic education and social concern were never formally linked together in the Jesuit educational tradition. They came together in a natural and coherent way, coming, as they did, from the Jesuit vision of God, the world, and man.

*How the Jesuits Settled in New York* has made available for us documents that were buried in Jesuit archives here and abroad. They had to be located, assembled, and then translated from nineteenth century Latin into modern English. The book has made an invaluable contribution to our knowledge of Jesuit education and its link to Jesuit pastoral and social activity in New York. To help him in his translation of the text, Fr. Hennessy assembled a team of fellow Jesuits well versed in Latin, familiar with the customs followed in the whole Society before Vatican II, and conversant with the style in which official Jesuit correspondence was written at that time. If the work of assembling and translating these documents had not been done at the present time, in all likelihood it could never have been done, and the historical data made available through this book would soon have become, for all practical purposes, inaccessible to most historians and educators and that would have been a serious loss to scholarship.

Gerald A. McCool, S.J.

## Ministry and the Lessons of the Fordham Jesuit Cemetery

In 1998 the Jesuit cemetery was an eyesore on the otherwise well-tended, Rose Hill campus of Fordham University. Many of the tombstones were disintegrating, some illegible, others vandalized. It was apparent the cemetery had seen no recent burials, and it was widely believed that the cemetery contained no human remains. Even though Fr. Hennessy demonstrated such a belief was incorrect, the cemetery had become something of a curiosity — some even said, an anachronism.

Once it was decided something ought to be done about the cemetery, the question was "what?" Some recommended that we take down the dilapidated stones and in their place erect a plaque honoring the memory of all those who had been buried there. Still others argued that there was no place for a cemetery on a modern university campus. Not a few objected that a renovation of the cemetery could not be justified at all, given the cost.

We decided, nonetheless, to keep the cemetery, to renovate it, to beautify it. Further, the new markers were to be made of granite for permanence sake, and designed for easy reading. Each marker was to provide dates of birth, entrance to the Society, death, and local birthplace. There is, of course, something of folly about what we did. But it is the folly of faith and of love. It is the folly of recognizing that however long ago they died, these men belong to us, and we to them. And that includes the dozen lay people who grace the cemetery as well. These lay people were diocesan seminarians, young college students or employees, all of whom shared in fulfilling the college goals through their own development or by assisting others to do so through effective services. They and we make up a family, the Jesuit family. 'Community' is a word that can be easily tossed about, but we recognize a community with these men which death and time do not dissolve. It is not a community of utility and mutual advantage; it is, rather, a community created by common history and shared vision. At a cultural moment when we are strongly inclined narcissistically to conceptualize ourselves apart from the past and separate from others, the cemetery witnesses to a deeper truth, one that challenges our almost compulsive tendency to absolutize the here and now.

For Christian believers our primary community, the one into which we and they have been inserted is, of course, the Mystical Body, that family of all those baptized, all those called by God's mysterious grace to be joined to Christ — sealed for resurrection and called to new life, those into whose heart the Spirit has been poured to transform them into the likeness of the Risen Lord. For those who hold to the ancient and enduring faith of the Church, this is no mere community of memory. As farfetched as it seems to many a modem mind, it is our firm conviction that these brothers are in truth *apud nos* ("among us"), living the risen life, which makes them, like the Risen Christ himself, not less, but more available to us, and we to them.

All the greater the need, then, for the cemetery, which is meant not so much to memorialize as to *witness to a belief* that lies at the heart of Christian faith. As Paul puts it squarely to the Corinthians: "If the dead are not raised, then Christ is not raised, and if Christ is not raised your faith is worthless. If our hopes in Christ are limited to this life only, we are the most pitiable of people" (I Cor 15, 16a, 19). A message that perhaps needs to be heard on university campuses today, where important questions are raised, clarity demanded, and new gospels proposed.

But besides witnessing to this belief through the cemetery renovation, we are making *an appeal*. We are looking to the lives of those who have gone before us for help in discerning our way *in the present*. We fully recognize that they are men of another time, many coming from other cultures, all facing specific challenges, and dealing with dilemmas different from our own. But precisely because they are so 'other' they may be able to awaken us to the otherness happening in our own day, with all the incoherence and specificity our own present moment is throwing up to us. What may emerge from a reflection on their lives is a wisdom our own moment needs.

In addition to the graves of presidents of Xavier, Fordham, Boston College, St. Peter's and Georgetown, the Fordham cemetery contains the graves of 48 Jesuit brothers. They were stonemasons, cooks, infirmarians, farmers, sacristans, carpenters. They were plumbers, tailors, receptionists, accountants. They cared for the garden, supervised the dining room, organized the clothes-room, and were in charge of the wine cellar. They repaired clocks and watches, played the organ and built the furniture. No buildings are named for them. No portrait of any of them adorns the halls of Xavier or Fordham or St. Peter's. All the more reason why their names and their example of humble, ordinary service should not be forgotten. It is not that the Jesuits who attracted public notice, who left literary legacies, who opened new schools and who founded parishes were less committed, less grounded in faith. Nor is to slight the daily battle of ordinary Jesuit teachers and preachers of those days  to inculcate learning and faith in their rough-hewn immigrant charges. But the special grace of the Brother's vocation is that it signals unambiguously what is at the core of the following of Christ, and what is the essence of our human excellence: that love incarnated in Jesus, which forgets itself in humble, everyday service. This is the love Dostoyevsky calls the "harsh and dreadful love," a love which is not done for applause, generally not much noticed.

The Jesuits' 34th General Congregation in 1995 identified certain attitudes, values and patterns of behavior which together form "the Jesuit way of proceeding." Based on the practice of St. Ignatius, the Congregation maintains that it belongs to our way of proceeding to bring "the counter-cultural gift of Christ to a world beguiled by self-centered human fulfillment, extravagance, and soft living, a world that prizes prestige, power, and self-sufficiency." How many of the dead Jesuits in the cemetery who committed their lives in ordinary, undramatic service, possessed that precious, unsettling gift in their own day!

That same Jesuit General Congregation insisted that "It is characteristic of our way of proceeding that we live with an operative freedom: open, adaptable, even eager for any mission that may be given to us" (#24). The Jesuits whose graves are in our cemetery were certainly men who understood that a Jesuit is one always available for mission. Almost every one of them had served in a number of parishes, schools, missions, from Maine to California. Many had left behind family and country to follow what they took to be God's call. The witness of these men offers to Jesuits and their colleagues a reminder that movement, disruption, change are not to be feared or avoided. As we strive to recognize and respond to the call of God in our lives, their examples warn us against becoming rigid and immobile, and inspire us to strive to remain ready and willing for new forms of discipleship, for new missions.

Moreover, there has never been a time when New York was not a city of immigrants, but at no time was the number of newcomers proportionally greater than in the period 1847-1889. It is not surprising, therefore, to find Jesuits back then committed to responding to the new immigrants' needs. Through their colleges, parishes and other ministries they helped the immigrants organize themselves for their own protection and advancement in the face of entrenched corruption and intolerance. And, if the immigrants' lot was not bad enough, these Jesuits reached out even further to the poor, the sick, the marginalized and the prisoners, who, as we learn from St. Ignatius' memoirs, were a special concern for him as well. The "option for the poor," much discussed, much misunderstood in recent years, has, in fact, been a constant feature in Jesuit ministry. Blackwells Island, with its Women's Lunatic Asylum, the Workhouse, the Almhouse, the Penitentiary, the City Hospital, was where Fr. Blumensaat spent the last 14 years of his life. He had been proceeded by Fr. Jaffré, the Island's first Catholic Chaplain, who died of typhoid fever after only one month in service there. Frs. Chopin, Pavarelli and Laufhuber followed him in that mission, and at the same cost. Frs. DeWolf, Petitdemange, and Prachensky would all served the unfortunate inmates of the prisons, asylums and hospitals of Wards Island and Randalls Island. Father Freeman took time away from his teaching and research at Fordham to serve as chaplain at St. Joseph's Institute for the Deaf.

In sum, the Jesuits buried at Fordham remind us that effective solidarity with and concerted labor for the newcomer, the unfortunate and the marginalized is not an option but rather a necessity for those who choose to be faithful to the legacy of those men. When Jesuits and their colleagues look for direction today, and seek to clarify their contemporary mission, it is once again the example of these men, which calls our attention to what is essential in our way of proceeding.

But the work these men began is anything but completed. There must still be schools and colleges, where faith and learning are understood as mutually complementary, where education is understood to be at the service of building character and as preparation for leadership in the community. The Word of God still must be preached coherently, faithfully, creatively, in a language and form which will move hearts to devotion and wills to action. Women and men still need to be accompanied in their quest for God in prayer. The life-giving sacraments of the Church must still be celebrated. And the poor, the neglected, the refugee, the immigrant must find a welcome. From their graves, they cry out: "Who will take up this mission? Who will now proceed as we did, in grateful love, in faith that endures to the end?"

Gerald R. Blaszczak. S.J.

# ENDNOTES

1. For more on this development, see C.J. Ligthart, *The Return of the Jesuits: Life of Jan Roothaan,* p. 259.

2. *WL,* Vol. 26, 266-67

3. Biographical sketches of Fr. Thébaud are offered in the first edition of the *Catholic Encyclopedia* (1911), the *New Catholic Encyclopedia* (1967), The *National Cyclopedia of American Biography* (1891-1984), and the *Dictionary of American Biography* (1961).

4. Many of the books in that early library are now in The St. John's Special Collection housed in the Archives and Special Collections of the Walsh Library.

5. The local curriculum was a major concern to the new faculty of the college and seminary. Changes needed to be made but made in such a way as to avoid fanfare. By the next year this was done by using Georgetown College's program as its model. Fr. Thébaud's visit to Georgetown was mentioned in the house diary; it was reported in greater detail in his *Forty Years in the United States of America,* p. 349.

6. The sites of the relief efforts were Pointe St. Charles and Griffintown, suburban areas near Montreal, according to Fr. A. Thébaud's memoirs, *Forty Years in the United States of America,* p. 221-222.

7. Two of the priests who ministered to the immigrants were already in Canada. One of them was the recently-ordained Martin Férard, the other was Remi Tellier (see his profile in the *Dictionary of [Canadian] Jesuit Biography*). The four Fathers who went directly from Fordham were: Irish-born Michael Driscol, Henri du Merle, Henry du Ranquet, and Charles Schianski.

Fr. Driscol did outstanding work with the immigrants but caught the infection and came close to death; afterwards he recovered and came back to Fordham. Later he was appointed pastor of St. Patrick's church in Montreal where he served the immigrants for several years. When he next retured to New York he was assigned to teach at the College of St. Francis Xavier in New York City. He became Rector-President of that institution in 1855.

Fr. Du Merle and Fr. Schianski both returned to Canada several years later and died there. Their deaths were attributed to infections they received while first working with the immigrants. Surely they were Fordham's first martyrs of charity. They were both honored when their remains were placed side-by-side in the crypt of what was later called Montreal's 'old Cathedral'. For their obituaries, see Appendix III.

8. This letter ended with a summary of the events of the past year at the new Jesuit College down in New York City; we cite that summary below in Chapter 9.

9. Pp. 232-236.

10. Fr. Larkin's official assignments in his last year (1858) were listed in the province Catalogue thus: spiritual Father and confessor for Jesuits, pastoral worker in the parish church, house consultor, and consultor to the French province's American Missions.

Biographical sketches of Fr. John Larkin may be found in the *Dictionary of [Canadian] Jesuit Biography* [1991], *the New Catholic Encyclopedia* (1967), *the*

*National Cyclopedia of American Biography (1984)*, and the *Dictionary of American Biography* (1961).

11. See also Fr. E. I. Devitt's "History of the Maryland-New York Province, College and Church of St. Francis Xavier" in the *Woodstock Letters*, 65, 1936, p. 192-195. Fr. Devitt provides details about many issues that the History of the House treats briefly.

12. The church basement was probably used in 1850, but the building wasn't completed until 1851; college classes began in November, 1850.

13. At that time the age for receiving First Communion was at least 12.

14. The Living Rosary was organized into cells; each cell had fifteen members who would recite a single particular decade each day; they also engaged in good works.

15. The Manhattan House of Detention; in the original Latin a rare typographical error called it *Fombs*.

16. A footnote in the Annals said of these numbers: "These are the numbers we received" but the province Catalogue says there were 30 in the community, 16 priests, 4 scholastics, and 10 Brothers. The Vice-Rector was Rev. Joseph Durthaller who was succeeded as Vice-Rector on July 31, 1863 by Rev. Joseph Loyzance, confirmed as Rector on Jan 1, 1865. He remained such until Sept. 5, 1870.

17. The "priest" was Rev. Henry Du Ranquet (1809-1891) whose residence for many years was in the Xavier community. He spent upwards of 24 years serving the religious needs of prisoners (his "favorite apostolate") and others at the Tombs, at Randalls Island and elsewhere. Venerated universally as a truly holy man, he overcame much anti-Catholic bias among administrators, physicians, and others and was regarded as the Apostle of the Prisoners. For decades he accompanied many condemned men, Catholic and non-Catholic, to their execution.

18. Because of the transfer of the Mission to the French Province of Champagne that December, this letter — like Letter XI in Chapter 6 — was published in the *Litterae Annuae Prov. Campaniae* under the title *NeoEboricense Collegium*.

19. Thus in the report; but the name used in fact was the Xavier Alumni Sodality, founded in 1863. Some of the later history of this association was reported in the first edition of the *Catholic Encyclopedia*, under "Catholic Club of New York." In 1871 The Xavier Alumni Sodality was reorganized and renamed as the Xavier Union to broaden its scope and include more social activities. In 1888 the name was changed again to the Catholic Club of the City of New York. Its growth was such that it purchased and built its own home and library at 120 Central Park South. For many years its membership was over 1,000. The club was not mentioned in later editions of the *Encyclopedia*.

20. The old cemetery also included a vault for members of the Rodrigue family. William Rodrigue was a Haitian-born architect who was hired by a dynamic Philadelphia pastor to build the new St. John's church in that city. That was the beginning of vast changes in William's life. For one thing, he married the pastor's sister in 1836. And when the pastor, John Hughes, became bishop of New York and needed an architect to build a seminary chapel and erect or enlarge buildings on Rose Hill, William Rodrigue and his wife Margaret followed him to New York and settled down there.

The seminary also included St. John's College and William taught drawing there at least from 1845 to 1855 (he may have begun earlier but in 1845 he was first recorded as a teacher of "drawing, penmanship, and civil engineering"). The family residence during most of William's college teaching tenure was in a structure he built (later known as the Rodrigue Cottage) on land retained by the bishop when he sold the college to the Jesuits.

We do not know when the first death occurred in the Rodrigue family. But it happened between 1847 when the Jesuits began to use the cemetery and 1887. The burial was probably discussed with the Jesuits and the decision was made that, due to their special circumstances, the particular individual who had died and other members of the family could be interred in the Jesuit cemetery. In 1887 Fr. Joseph Loyzance constructed a chart of those buried in the old cemetery. In the upper right hand of the chart a vault is listed as "Mr. Rodrigue vault, a woman and 3 children. When the other bodies were transferred to the new Fordham cemetery, the Rodrigue vault and its contents were moved to "Westchester Cemetery." Inquiries made in 1999 of the major Westchester cemeteries about the Rodrigue family re-burials from the Fordham cemetery produced only denials of such transfers. However, before 1890 St. Raymond's Cemetery was still in Westchester County (the annexation by the City took place in 1895) though the Fordham and some other areas were annexed by the City in 1874. It turned out that the "Westchester Cemetery" of the diary was the St. Raymond's Cemetery.

A report from St. Raymond's Cemetery states that a deed for a plot in Section 2, range 14, graves 1-4 was owned by John Rodrigue. Of the seven members of the Rodrigue family interred in those graves only three were reported as transferred from the Fordham Cemetery: James A. Rodrigue, aged 28 years; William Rodrigue, aged 67 years; and Margaret Rodrigue, aged 2 years. Clearly, there is variance between the Fordham vault notice (one woman; 3 children) and St. Raymond's records (2 men and one infant girl). Unfortunately, neither cemetery report provided the dates of the deaths of those individuals. Could it be that, in addition to the two infants and woman reported as not found, the remains of other members of the Rodrigue family are still resting in the New York Botanical Garden?

Carthy (*A Cathedral of Suitable Magnificence,* p. 166) reported that the Rodrigue family lived at least from 1854 to 1864 in the home of the Archbishop on the northwest corner of 36th Street and Madison Avenue; Mrs. Rodrigue, the Archbishop's sister, was probably the Archbishop's housekeeper. So, assuming that the family did not return to campus after the Archbishop's death in 1863, they probably lived on the seminary or college grounds from 1841 to 1854.

21. *WL* Vol. 19, 406. The obituary cited here identifies his Christian name as Arahilles; The *Liber Defunctorum* gives his country of birth as Spain. Those details are at variance with other sources about him but they are just some of the mysteries that envelope him. A final mystery is that he is not listed in the Index of the *Catalogus Defunctorum Societatis Iesu, 1814-1970,* the most authoritative source on Jesuit vital statistics in that time frame. Nevertheless, his name and

statistics *are* in the volume and can be found in Section 4, #180 — one of only two Jesuits in the whole world who died on the day he did.

22. The Fordham presidents were August Thébaud (president, 1846-1851; 1860-1863); John A. Larkin (president, 1851-1854); Edward Doucet (president, 1863-1864); Peter Tissot (acting president, 1865); William Moylan (president, 1865-1868); Patrick F. Dealy (president, 1882-1885).

Presidents of other institutions were: Peter Cassidy, St. Peter's College, Jersey City, NJ (1889-1891); , the College of St. Francis Xavier, NYC (1855-1860); David A. Merrick, Xavier College, NYC (1888-1891); Samuel Mulledy, Georgetown University, Washington, DC (1845); Jeremiah O'Connor, Boston College (1879-1884); William O'B. Pardow, the College of St. Francis Xavier, NYC (1891-1893); James Perron, Woodstock College and Seminary, Woodstock, MD (1875-1881); Nicolas Russo, Boston College, Boston, MA (acting president 1887-1888).

23. These documents in some few cases correct the inscriptions on the original cemetery tombstones and restore information that had to be omitted on the new granite markers because of space, e.g., the names of the village or town of their birth, so warmly recalled by many émigrées.

24. *WL, Vol.* 20, 149; 31, 128-132.

25. The tributes were published in *Historical Records and Studies*, VI, #2 (1913), 69-79.

26. *WL, 31*, 406-415.

27. *WL, 56*, p.178.

28. *Forty Years*, p. 245-6.

29. Vol. X, 130-151.

30. *WL, 20*, 149.

31. See the profile of Br. Hennen's life, in the *WL, 20*, 117-119.

32. Vol II, 163-171.

33. Dooley, p. 157.

34. Vol. X, 152-161.

35. Dooley, p. 146.

# APPENDIX I

## The *Liber Defunctorum* on Moving the Cemetery

The following details, translated from his longer account of the history of the cemetery's move, were written in Latin by Rev. Joseph Zwinge, S.J.

Mr. [George] Mulry, S.J., died at St. John's College, Fordham, on Oct. 1, 1889. And on the following day Fr. Scully, the Rector, summoned the house consultors to consider [questions about] the cemetery. There were three proposals to be considered, namely:

1) Buy a section (100 lots, at a cost $2,000 plus funeral expenses, $5 for digging a grave and about $60 for hearse, etc.) at St. Raymond's cemetery.

2) Make another cemetery on our property (either in the south east corner of the orchard, or part of the vineyard).

3) Bury our brethren at Manresa, West Park, which was recently established by the Provincial as a Jesuit residence.

[The consultors] were divided but Fr. Zwinge spoke in favor of the vineyard. Since nothing was decided, Mr. Mulry temporarily was placed in the St. Raymond's vault. Some of the older Fathers, specifically Fr. I. Daubresse, heard that the consultors were tending toward buying land in St. Raymond's and were saddened. When Fr. Daubresse complained to me about it, I made known their feelings to Fr. Doucet, one of the consultors. He, after reviewing the difficulties from the view of both religious piety and the costs involved, inclined toward having the cemetery here with us (*apud nos*). That position was indicated to Fr. Rector who thereafter sought to obtain permission of the Park Commissioners to open a new cemetery here.

A petition was made to the Health Board which sent an inspector to review the place. The inspector said it would be better to choose the vineyard rather than the orchard. Then Fr. Dealy was sent to the Board to place with them a formal petition and for an examination thereof. On November 15 we received a notification that permission was denied us to open a new cemetery because they had to deny that permission to other orders. Father Rector sent a friendly letter to the Health Board. The letter was complimentary to them but said that our case was different from the [other] case; our cemetery would not be in the city but in an almost rural area (*quasi in rure*).

Then a friendly emissary came [from the city] and it was decided that we could very probably obtain the permission if we ask the Park Board to allow us to remove the bodies from the cemetery in the Bronx Park, and then petition the Health Board for permission to bury those bodies in the proposed new cemetery in the vineyard.

Fr. Rector first obtained the permission from the Park Board and then petitioned the Health Board to bury our brethren in the new cemetery. And so on Jan. 9, 1890 we obtained this letter [from the Department of Public Parks and another one after it from the Health Department City of New York]:

City of New York,
Department of Public Parks,
36 Union Square.

Dec 20th 1889

Permission is hereby granted the Trustees of St. John's College, Fordham, to remove remains from their former burial-ground located in Bronx Park, under the supervision of the General Inspector &c., and subject to the rules and requirements of the Health Department.

[signature]
President D.P.P.

# Health Department City of New York,

### No. 301 Mott Street,

No. 6653    When issued    **Jan. 7, 1890.**

Permission is granted John Scully President of St. John's College to remove sixty bodies from the Bronx Park Cemetery, to St. John's College Cemetery at Fordham, New York. Provided the work be done during freezing weather, and under the supervision of the District Medical Sanitary Inspector.

☞ This Permit to be in force until revoked by this Board.

By Order of the Board.

[signature]
Secretary.

Therefore, once we obtained the permission, we began the project on Jan. 13 according to the plan proposed by Fr. Minister; on the same day the Medical Inspector, Dr. Parsons, of Kingsbridge, appeared and gave me instructions regarding the transfers. In the consultation we had on Jan. 14 it was decided to place [the graves of] the Fathers on the Gospel side of the chapel to be erected at the foot of the middle path, to place the Brothers on the Epistle side, to provide a tombstone for each one, and henceforth to bury those who die in order based [only] on the time of their death.

On Jan. 15, 1890 we began to dig a ditch which our undertaker advised us to make ourselves [not use others to do that work].

Jan. 20: Today I sought out the General Inspector in Lorillard's Mansion and showed him the document from the Park Department Board and he agreed to it.

Jan. 21, 1890: The job of digging out and removing the bodies from our [former] cemetery in the Bronx Park to our new cemetery has begun. We took out Fathers Maguire (who was buried in Kentucky and had been transferred here in a casket), Lebreton, Tomei, McDonnel, Ansault/Maréchal, Monroe, three Scholastics (Sauzeau, E. O'Connor, C. Quinn), Novice Scholastic McShea, Fathers Chopin, Dansdurand, Jaffré. We buried all of these again.

Jan. 22: Fathers Larkin, Gresselin, Pavarelli, Laufhuber, Mulledy, Foertsch, Fouché, Murphy, and Sorria we buried again. Fathers Foertsch and Mulledy no longer had their crosses [above their graves] in the old cemetery but we identified them from the chart made by Fr. Loyzance.

Jan. 23: We moved [the remains of] Fathers Tissot, Legoüais, Schemmel and DeLuynes. ... We moved Brothers Joset, Fauris, Proulx, Séné and Jarry ...

Jan. 25: Today we dug out [the bodies of] Fathers Pacciarini, Thébaud, and Thiry; in the case of Fr. Driscol and Fr. Fitzpatrick, only the bottom part of their caskets was intact and in both cases we placed their remains in large boxes. Fr. Fitzpatrick's vestments were clearly distinguishable.

So all the Fathers have been moved [as of] today.

Furthermore, we dug up the remains of Brothers Spalding, Lafferty, Crowe, MacNulty, Bacon, O'Connor, Vaughen, Doyle, and Shannon. However, though we labored at it for the whole day, we could not find [the body of] Br. Creeden.

In the caskets of Brothers Doyle and Shannon we found some remains of their habits.

Jan. 26: Today we removed the bodies of Brothers Rooney, Byrne, Cunningham, Stoecklin, Garvey, Alsberge, Vanrenterghan, Buckley, Ledoré, Brendle, Meyer.

The work of removing all our Brethren from the cemetery in the Bronx Park to our new cemetery took 5 days.

However, we did not find Br. Creeden's body although two men sought for him and worked for three days [on that task]. So we kept his place in the new cemetery, that is, we left vacant the first place in the first Brothers' row for him [and placed a memorial to him there].

On Jan. 20: The task of removing the bodies of the seminarians, students, and workers was started.

Jan. 21: This morning we transported from the cemetery vault [in St. Raymond's, Westchester] three bodies, namely, Br. Julius Macé, and Scholastics George Mulry and Arthur O'Leary. We placed them between the remains of Fr. Thiry and Fr. Perron.

In the afternoon the job of removing all the bodies from our cemetery and from St. Raymond's was completed.

In all we removed: 34 Fathers and Scholastics (and Fr. Perron, 35); Brothers, 26. Total: 60, with Fr. Perron, 61.

Then there were: 3 Seminarians; 12 students; 2 employees. So the total number [interred anew in 1890] was 77.

Jan. 27: I wrote a petition to the Vicar General for the blessing of the new cemetery. I received a rescript from him on the evening of Jan. 29, sending all the necessary faculties for blessing of the cemetery.

So that same night we erected a cross in the cemetery and [set] the hour for the ceremony at 9:00 A.M, on Jan. 30. But because of the bad weather the ceremony was delayed to 2:15 P.M.

EXPENSES OF REMOVAL

| | |
|---|---|
| Lumber for boxes | $59.78 |
| Carpenters' work | 48.00 |
| Carbolic acid @.70 per gal. | 35.00 |
| Workmen (9) | 72.25 |
| Cart (7 days) | 12.00 |
| Our workmen (5 for 4 days) | 30.00 |

Of these expenses, according to the decision of Fr. Provincial, Fordham College should pay 1/3, the College of St. Francis Xavier, 1/3, the college in Jersey City, 1/6, and St. Lawrence Residence, 1/6.

The [black wooden] crosses have been removed [from the cemetery] but not replaced above the graves. Moreover, the bodies of the Rodrigue family (Mrs. Rodrigue was the sister of Archbishop Hughes) were taken away by Mr. Rodrigue to the Westchester cemetery [St. Raymond's], at his own expense, in the last week of January.

The pathway was made of marble (marble chips from 2nd Div. Building and marble sand from quarry).

After many delays, finally on May 17, 1890, we ordered marble memorial stones and two columns from Vermont. But they were not brought here until Aug. 4. The stone-cutters began their work on Aug. 11. In the first week they did 10 tombstones; in the second week and part of the third they did the rest.

| | |
|---|---|
| Cost of all stonework @$3.10 | $221.30 |
| Columns | $40.00 |

Aug. 27: The two marble columns were put in their place at the cemetery entrance. On Aug. 28 the task of putting the tombstones in place was begun and finished on Aug. 29.

Expenses:

| | |
|---|---|
| For lettering | $401.20 |
| For rounding @ $6.66 | $26.30 |

Aug. 30: The work of putting the Jesuit tombstones in place was completed. That was done by the contractor of the new residences [Faculty wing in Dealy Hall].

Sept. 6: We put in place the tombstones of the seminarians and of 2 of the young boys. The stone for Hillenmeyer and Thompson we took from a foundation stone in the old cemetery.

All expenses for the materials and work (these expenses worked out for us by Myles Tierney, the contractor.)                                    $902.80

Add to them expenses we incurred in the beginning of the year, for digging out the bodies and for setting the statue in place [a footnote added reads: *statua nondum erecta est* (the statue has not yet been erected]

$301.03

Total Cost                                                              $1,203.83

# APPENDIX II

## The Honored Dead

This list included all those buried in the Fordham Jesuit Cemetery. The marker code after each name indicates their place in the post-1959 cemetery arrangment. found at the end of this list. An asterisk before a name indicated that a photo of the individual appears in Chapter 12.

Alsberge, Br. Charles [I-R-7]

Bacon, Br. Patrick [J-R-3]
Beaven, Bonaventure [A-6]
*Blumensaat, Fr. Herm. [F-R-6]
Brendle, Br. Charles [I-R-4]
Broderick, Fr. James [G-R-6]
Buckley, Br. John B. [I-R-6]
Byrne, Br. Malachy [C-L-2]
*Byrnes, Fr. Michael [G-L-2]

*Cardella, Fr. Philip [H-R-3]
*Cassidy, Fr. Peter [F-R-9]
Chester, Fr. John [I-L-1]
Chopin, Fr. Philip [B-R-11]
Connell, Mr. Thomas [E-R-8]
Conway, Fr. James[F-L-2]
Corbett, Mr. Michael[F-R-5]
Corrigan, Br. Patrick [H-R-10]
Crane, Mr. John [F-L-3]
Creeden, Br. Joseph [B-L-1]
Cremin, John [A-1]
Crowe, Br. Patrick [J-R-5]
Cunningham, Br. Bern [C-L-3]
Curray, Bernard [A-3]

Daly, Maurice [A-4]
Dandurand, Fr. Anat. [B-R-10]
*Dealy, Fr. Patrick [E-R-7]
DeLuynes, Fr. Chas. H. [C-R-13]
DePooter, Br. Fred. [D-L-3]
Desribes, Fr. Jos. [F-R-10] & p.180
DeWolf, Br. John B. [E-L-3]
Donovan, Br. William [H-R-6]
*Doucet, Fr. Edward [D-R-11] & p.179
Doyle, Br. James [H-R-9]

Doyle, Br. William [C-L-4]
Driscol, Fr. Michael [D-R-1]
Duquesnay, H. L. [A-8]
Dwyer, Br. James [I-L-2]

Ealy, Br. Martin [H-R-8]
Echeverria, Mr. Rom. [H-R-4]
Eddrington, H. M. [A-10]
Egan, Br. James [I-R-2]

*Fagan, Fr. James [G-R-8]
Farrell, Br. Patrick [D-L-2]
Fauris, Br. Francis [B-l-4]
Fennel, James [A-2]
Fernandez, John [A-9]
Fitzgerald, Br. James [G-R-7]
Fitzpatrick, Fr. John [D-R-2]
*Flynn, Fr. Michael [F-R-1]
Foertsch, Fr. George [C-R-4]
Fouché, Fr. Simon [C-R-5]
*Freeman, Fr. Thomas [J-L-2]

Galligan, Fr. John [F-R-4]
Garvey, Br. Jeremiah [I-R-9]
Gormley, Br. Thomas [E-R-10]
Gresselin, Fr. Chas. [B-R-12]

Hanrahan, Fr. Nich. [E-R-4]
Heindenreich, Fr. H. [E-R-5]
Hennen, Br. William [D-L-1]
Hillenmeyer, R. [A-13]
Hoefele, Br. Fridolin [H-L-1]

Jaffré Fr. John [B-R-9]
Jarry, Br. Michael [B-L-2]
Joset, Br. Fidelis [B-L-3]
*Jouin, Fr. Louis [F-R-3]

Kain, Br. Joseph [H-R-7]
Keating, Fr. Andrew [E-L-2]
Keon, Patrick [A-12]
Keys, Br. Michael [F-R-7]

Lafferty, Br. Neal [J-R-6
*Larkin, Fr. John A. [B-R-8]
*Laufhuber, Fr. Geo. [C-R-1]

Lebreton, Fr. Peter [B-R-2]
Ledoré Br. Philip [I-R-5]
*Legoüais, Fr. Thomas [C-R-11]

Macé, Br. Julius [D-R-6]
Mackey, Br. Henry W. [F-R-8]
Maguire, Fr. Eugene [B-R-1]
Maréchal, Fr. F. X. [B-R-6]
McDonnel, Fr. John [B-R-4]
McGovern, Fr. F. X. [H-R-5]
*McKinnon, Fr. Neil [J-L-3]
MacNulty, Br. Patrick [J-R-4]
McShea, Br. William [B-R-5]
*Merrick, Fr. David [I-L-3]
Meyer, Br. Conrad [I-R-3]
Monroe, Fr. Francis [C-R-8]
*Moylan, Fr. William [E-R-2]
Mulledy, Fr. Samuel [C-R-2]
*Mulry, Mr. George [D-R-7]
Murphy, Fr. Henry [C-R-6]

*Nash, Fr. Michael [H-L-2]

*O'Brien, Fr. Michael [G-R-9]
*O'Connor, Fr. Chas. [E-L-1]
O'Connor, Mr. Edward [C-R-3]
*O'Connor, Fr. Jerem. [E-R-3]
O'Connor, Br. William [J-R-2]
O'Lalor, Mr. Chas. [I-R-1]
O'Leary, Mr. Arthur [D-R-8]
O'Neill, Mr. Jeremiah [H-L-3]

Pacciarini, Fr. Basil [D-R-3]
Palacios, Louis [A-5]
*Pardow, Fr. Wm. O'B. [J-L-1]
Pavarelli, Fr. Joseph [B-R-13]
Pelletier, Fr. Alphon. [C-R-9]
Peña, Charles [A-12]
*Perron, Fr. James [D-R-9]
Petitdemange, Fr. Chas. [G-R-3]
*Prachensky, Fr. Jos. [E-R-1]
*Prendergast, Fr. John [F-R-2]
Proulx, Br. Joseph [J-R-9]

Quinn, Mr. Charles [C-R-7]

*Risler, Br. Emile [G-R-4]
Robertson, Fr. John [E-R-9]
Rochfort, Fr. Val. [G-L-1]
Rogers, Br. Michael [G-R-5]
*Ronayne, Fr. Maurice [F-L-1]
Rooney, Br. Patrick [C-L-1]
Ruiz, Antonias [A-7]
*Russo, Fr. Nicolas [H-R-2]

Sarria, Fr. Achilles p. 169
Sauzeau, Mr. John [B-R-7]
Schemmel, Fr. Seraph. [C-R-12]
Séné, Br. James [J-R-8]
Shanahan, Br. Edmund [G-R-1]
Shannon, Br. David [I-R-10]
Spalding, Br. Hilary [J-R-7]
Stoechlin, Br. Martin [H-R-1]

*Thébaud, Fr. August [D-R-4]
*Thiry, Fr. Theodore [D-R-5]
Thompson, George [A-13]
*Tissot, Fr. Peter [C-R-10]
Tomei, Fr. Michael X. [B-R-3]

*Van Rennselaer, Fr. H. [G-L-3]
Vaughen, Br. George [J-R-1]
Vaurenterghan, Br. D. [I-R-8]

Ward, Fr. Thomas [G-R-2]
Wellworth, Fr. J. [D-R-10] & p.178
Whyte, Fr. Richard 154 [E-R-6]

## THE POST-1959 FORDHAM CEMETERY

### BRICK WALL

3 2 1 (J)                              (J) 9 8 7 6 5 4 3 2 1

3 2 1 (I)                              (I) 10 9 8 7 6 5 4 3 2 1

TREE                                   TREE

3 2 1 (H)                              (H) 10 9 8 7 6 5 4 3 2 1

3 2 1 (G)                              (G) 9 8 7 6 5 4 3 2 1

3 2 1 (F)                              (F) 10 9 8 7 6 5 4 3 2 1

3 2 1 (E)                              (E) 10 9 8 7 6 5 4 3 2 1

3 2 1 (D)                              (D) 11 10 9 8 7 6 5 **4** 3 2 1

4 3 2 1 (C)                            (C) 13 12 11 10 9 8 7 6 5 4 3 2 1

4 3 2 1 (B)                            (B) 13 12 11 10 9 8 7 6 5 4 3 2 1

                                       (A) 13 12 11 10 9 8 7 6 5 4 3 2 1

                                       [Original stones for those in row (A)]

LEFT SIDE (L)                          (R) RIGHT SIDE

GATE

ROAD

To find a grave:

1. Choose any name from this Appendix, e.g. THÉBAUD, Fr. AUGUST.
2. Note the alphanumeric code after the name, in this case, [D-R-4]
3. D stands for row D.
4. R stands for the right side rather than the left (L)
5. 4 is the number of the grave on that side (see the bold number above).

# APPENDIX III

## Martyrs of Charity

### Rev. Henri Du Merle, S.J. and Rev. Charles Schianski, S.J.,

In 1846-47 both Fr. Du Merle and Fr. Schianski were among the pioneers assigned to Rose Hill. Fr. Du Merle's job that year was as Prefect of Discipline and Catechist for Students; Fr. Schianski's was to teach German while he also completing his fourth year of theology.

The following year they both worked in Canada helping Irish immigrants suffering from plagues of typhoid fever and cholera. After a brief revisit to Fordham, they returned north to work with the immigrants at great personal sacrifice and at personal risk as both of them succumbed to the illnesses of their parishioners. The bishop of Montreal recognized the value of the services of both of these Jesuits by allowing them to be interred and be together again in the crypt of his cathedral church [known today as 'the old cathedral'] where they lie in peace, side by side.

The documentary account of Fr. Du Merle's life is taken from the *Litterae Annuae, Provinciae Franciae, S.I.,* 1850-51. Fr. Schianski's account is taken from the *Litterae Annuae, Provinciae Franciae*, 1852-53.

### FR. HENRI DU MERLE

Born of a noble family on July 5, 1819 in the town of Chevray in the Diocese of Evreux, Father Henri du Merle entered the Society on September 7, 1839. He wonderfully exemplified the words of Proverbs: "Teach your son not to give up hope." For though as a young man his mother was very fearful about his future, he proved those fears baseless. To clarify this, here are the words of a devout Father who had been his teacher:

"I was deeply grieved by his premature death. Nevertheless I could not help but feel a certain joy reflecting that he died a martyr of charity. He had indeed to thank his mother in heaven because it was to her, and to her prayers, that he owed his salvation.

Most particularly, this fact must not be omitted in your obituary. This woman was in fact another Monica for another Augustine. Madame Du Merle was a woman remarkable for her natural qualities. She had given herself totally to God during a mission preached in her neighborhood around 1822. Since that time she lived only for her children for whose santification she unceasingly pleaded with God. Unfortunately, her dear Henry was not as pious as she would wish. This she told me herself.

When he was a young boy he was sent to our college at St. Acheul, where he remained until 1828. There he was taught by Fr. Bruneau who developed a liking for him because of his naturally good character. Although the child's conduct was not always admirable, Fr. Bruneau never ceased to expect him to turn out well. He frequently wrote to his mother to reassure her concerning the boy's future ....

After St. Acheul was closed, Henry was sent to Fribourg. There he was as unhappy as he had been been at St. Acheul. At the end of six months, he and some sixty others were dismissed. I know nothing about his stay in that house, except that there was a young man named Augustine there who was much persecuted; ... he died at the college with the reputation of being a saint. Henry used to tell me: 'I made him go through purgatory on earth, poor fellow. I was placed next to him in study hall and when he did not want to talk, I would kick him under the table.`

... I am telling you this so that you may better understand what I said in the beginning, that without the prayers of his mother, that child would have been lost. From 1828 to 1834 she had three Masses said for him each week.... There is more to be said about her: every day at four o'clock in the morning she would pray for him in the little chapel of her chateau.

After Fribourg he was sent to a college in Picardy. There . . . he joined up with the wild element and showed a very stubborn character. To tease his mother, he would frequently say that he would become either a priest or a soldier. At the end of rhetoric year, he almost seriously compromised the college. A vendor of small plaster statues came into the courtyeard. He was selling busts of [King] Louis Philippe. Du Merle took one, flung it into the mud beneath the house and then destroyed all the others with his feet. Then he immediately paid for the damage he had caused.

It was about this time that a noticeable change was taking place in him. He began to become more serious, to pray actively. Then God subjected him to a terrible trial: He made him pass, so to speak, through fire. He was of an intense nature; he now underwent strong temptations which he had to fight all day long. He fought with heroic persistence; but all this resulted in the poor boy's acting in strange and bizarre ways. People pitied the boy and sympathized with his mother.

With this background, when he entered the seminary of St. Sulpice and then left for America, people said to themselves, and I believe they never abandoned the idea, that he had to some degree lost his mind. He had trouble adjusting to the Sulpician seminary. In the beginning everything about the house displeased him. . . . His mother was in despair: her sole recourse was God. She greatly desired that he become a priest; but she found it very hard to think of him as a secular priest, alone, taking care of a parish .... Still, before her death, God did give her the consolation of seeing him, if not in religious life, at least as a man of solid virtue.

During her last illness she said that like St. Monica, she did not regret the approach of death because her dear Henry seemed at last to have chosen the correct path. It was he, courageous son, who was the one to tell his dear mother that she was about to die and he did not leave her until she had breathed her last. When I said the prayers for the dying, he made all the responses. This good woman died as one predestined for heaven.

After his mother's death, Henry returned to St. Sulpice. He was then 20 years old. In 1836 the late Bishop Bruté of Vincennes, Illinois, visited the seminary seeking young volunteers to help him in his mission to the Indians. Du Merle was among the first to volunteer, and left in spite of all opposition. The rest you know."

Hence, after losing his remarkable mother, he soon realized that he needed another. Two years later, he went from Vincennes to St. Mary's College where for a while he stayed as a helper, since no novitiate had yet been established. Then, under Father Gilles, he completed the two years of probation and was ordained.

In St. Mary's College and later in St. John's College in New York, for the most part he was prefect of discipline for the students. In this difficult and thankless task he showed both strength and dedication. But in 1847, when typhus was raging in the cities of Canada, Henry promptly volunteered and, when the superior of the Canadian mission summoned him and others of the same college, throughout the long vacation he gave himself to the care of those dying in hospitals. Then 9 priests and 13 nuns died but, by the gift of God, no Jesuit did. After the long vacation, our men returned to their work.

But after a year, Father Du Merle was again summoned to Montreal to stay in the residence founded for the Irish by the Sulpicians. There for three consecutive years he toiled day and night for the poor Irish, especially during an outbreak of cholera, till he finally contracted the deadly disease.

It happened at the start of summer, when the Irish poor migrated and typhus usually strikes, that Father Du Merle, a doctor and a hospital nun had been summoned to an ailing family. Soon, similarly stricken, all of them became ill; only the nun survived. The doctor died. And Father Du Merle humbly received Viaticum and other sacraments and, shortly after 5:00 A.M. on June 21, the feast of St. Aloysius, breathed forth his devoted soul to his Creator.

The bishop [Most Rev. Ignace Bourget] noted the special circumstance of that day, for thus he wrote to Father Rector:

"I still have not recovered from my surprise at the sad news you relayed to me and which I by no means expected. I had no idea that the good Father was ill or that death might carry him off. Your Society loses another martyr and the diocese an indefatigable worker. On his feast day, St. Aloysius Gonzaga wants him to share his glory, because he too, died of the plague. From the bottom of my heart I say: *Requiescat in pace* for him who so diligently took care of my sheep. Then I commend myself to him that he might procure for me what he already enjoys, the sight of the Good Shepherd who first gave his life for his sheep.

I think you did quite right to have asked that your beloved deceased be interred in the Cathedral Church: this is a privilege I would grant to very few. The Bishop's house received the first Jesuits who came to help this country, and the zeal of their priests conquered G.C.[?]. It is more than fitting that the church of that bishop be the tomb of those who die in combat and with arms in their hands. I wrote to the Vicar that High Mass should be sung for him as soon as possible."

The body of Father Henri Du Merle lies in the cathedral in the crypt reserved for priests, beneath the altar of the Blessed Virgin, to whom he had always been devoted. His funeral was attended by about 20 priests and 600 Irishmen who followed their custom of filing four by four. Even the hostile secular newspapers wrote favorably of his death and the reason for it.

Fr. Charles Schianski

It is with regret that we announce the death of Father Charles Schianski of the Society of Jesus. Father Schianski passed away in the evening of Friday, March 12, 1852, at age 45. He was born in Wipsau, Moravia, and received his primary education at Brun from the Benedictines, of whom, to the end of his life, he retained an affectionate memory. Leaving his native country for several years to travel abroad, he visited the major cities of Europe. A talented musician, he acquired in the course of these travels, the reputation of a distinguished performing artist. Despite his success as an artist, he felt that he was called to devote himself completely to God. With that aim in mind, after several years of study at the Roman College to improve his knowledge of philosophy, he entered the Jesuit novitiate at Rome. On the completion of his novitiate, he returned to the Austrian Province, to which he belonged, and spent three years at Innsbruck in the Tyrol studying theology. In 1846, his superiors gave him permission to come to the missions in America. Consequently, he came to the College at Fordham, near New York, to complete his study of theology and was ordained to the priesthood there in 1847.

He had scarcely been clothed with the sacred character of the priesthood when he saw a field worthy of his zeal opening up. Typhus was ravaging Montreal at that time, and, because of their devotion to its victims, part of the Catholic clergy of the city had fallen victim to the plague themselves. The Bishop of Montreal appealed to the Society of Jesus for help. Father Schianski was a priest and a Jesuit and, has a Jesuit ever hesitated to answer a call like that? Six Jesuits spontaneously volunteered their services. Fr. Schianski and the late Fr. Du Merle [+ 6-21-1851], whose loss we recently had occasion to mourn, were among them. They came to Montreal in July, 1847. The devoted service they rendered the unfortunate victims of the plague are still fresh in the memory of most of our readers.

Thanks to his mastery of several European languages, Father Schianski was able to preach with ease in French, English, German, and Italian. Obviously an extremely valuable acquisition for the diocese, Father Schianski, together with Father Tellier, was given charge of the chapel opened for the immigrants whom the plague had stranded on the river bank. Falling victim to typhus himself in January 1848, Father Schianski was fortunate enough to recover. Shortly after his recovery, he was able to bring together a small congregation to whom he ministered, at first in the chapel of the Grey Nuns, and, successively after that, in the church of the Recollet Fathers and in the chapel of St. Mary's College. A number of German Protestants also came there regularly to listen to his sermons.

For three years he was a member of the community in the residence which the Sulpician Fathers had made available to the Jesuits serving on the staff of St. Patrick's Church. Then, in 1851, at the time when St. Mary's College was opened, Father Schianski was appointed to the post of Master of Novices, a position which he held for the little that remained of his life.

On March fifth the signs of the illness which was to prove fatal made their first appearance. On the previous Sunday, Father Schianski had preached the usual French sermon in the chapel of St. Mary's College. At peace and fully confident in the merits of His Savior, Father Schianski waited quietly for the death whose coming he had long desired. He asked for and received the last sacraments on Friday, the twelfth day of the month. Shortly afterwards, at about eight o'clock in the evening, his soul left this world to appear before God and receive the reward the Lord has promised to His good and faithful servants. On Sunday morning, Father Schianski's mortal remains were buried in the crypt of the Cathedral, next to the body of Father DuMerle. There it will rest waiting for the resurrection of the blessed.

# APPENDIX IV

## Fr. Mulledy's Last Days

Documentation for the account given in Chapter 12 of Fr. Mulledy's last days comes from these three main sources, the first two of which are in the Fordham Archives: (1) An important letter from Fr. Thomas Gannon, the Jesuit provincial, to Fr. Zwinge; (2) the entry about Fr. Mulledy in the *Liber Defunctorum*; (3) references to him in Fr. Patrick Dooley's 1917 book, *Fifty Years in Yorkville*.

I. On August 14, 1890, Fr. T. J. Gannon, S.J., who at that time was the Jesuit Provincial and was twice the rector-president of Fordham, wrote the following letter to Fr. Zwinge, the Fr. Minister at Fordham:

"Dear Fr.Zwinge,

Fr. Samuel Mulledy was received the second time into the Society on Friday, Jan. 5th, 1866 & died Jan.8th. Fr. Joseph Loyzance then Rector of St. Francis X. had called upon Fr. Samuel Mulledy at 84th St. & heard his confession; he was quite sick and expressed a great desire to get his vows in the Society. Fr. Loyzance said that he would write and ask the Provincial of Maryland for the permission. [At that time New York was a mission of the Champagne province, and separate from the Jesuit Maryland province.]

Following are the exact words of Fr. Loyzance:

On Friday morning, Jan. 5th, 1866, I sent a telegram & received the answer of Fr. Paresche: 'I authorize you to receive the vows of Samuel Mulledy.' At once I went to Yorkville. At noon on Friday, the 5th of Jan. 1866, [Fr. Mulledy] read the formula of vows in the small refectory of St. Lawrence's old residence, kneeling down. Towards the middle of the formula, overpowered by the feeling, he added the words of the Maccabees: '*Corde magno et animo volenti* (heart generous and mind willing).' Stopped a little while and continued. After the vows we gave him the kiss of peace. He was ... delighted.

On the same day he wrote a letter to Archb. McCloskey letting him know the news and asking his Lordship to give St. Lawrence to the Jesuits.'

I got these exact details from Fr. Loyzance & trust that this will furnish you ... all the information you desire. They accord with the documents of our Archives.

In Xt.,

T. J. Gannon, S.J.

2. The life-summary of Fr. Mulledy in the *Liber Defunctorum* states:

"Fr. Samuel Mulledy was born on March 27, 1811 in [Hampshire County, West] Virginia. Formerly, he had been in the Society [entered Aug 29, 1831, and later left]. Lately pastor of the [diocesan] parish in Yorkville, he renewed his vows when close to death [Jan. 5], and died on Jan. 8, 1866 at Yorkville, at age 54 ... [This first section was in Latin like most of the other notices in the book; but it continues in English as follows.] Fr. Provincial says that the date of 2nd entrance has to be put on his headstone. [Also] *natus* 1811 instead of 1810. This is from letter of Fr. Ward, [the Fr. Socius, Assistant to the Provincial] from Frederick, May

23, 1890. Fr. Mulledy was rec'd into Soc the 2ⁿᵈ time by Fr. Jos. Loyzance by order of Fr. Paresce, Provincial of Maryland, January 5 in 1866, in presence of Fr. [Michael] Meagher. He made his vows, kneeling, in his small refectory in S. Lawrence's, E. 84ᵗʰ St.

3. Fr. Dooley's book quoted a letter that the Maryland provincial, Fr. A. M. Paresce, sent to his houses. It read in part: "... I granted his dying request. The news of his readmission filled him with so much joy and vigor, that, though in the agony of death, yet he sprang out of bed, and on his knees devoutly pronounced the Formula of the Simple Vows of the Society in the presence of the Rev. Joseph Loyzance, Rector of St. Francis Xavier's College, New York. Four days after, namely on the night of the 8ᵗʰ inst., he died a most saintly and edifying death, having also had the consolation of being assisted in his last moments by one of the Fathers of our Province [Rev. John Early, rector-president of Georgetown]."

Dooley regarded as doubtful a tradition that "Father Mulledy begged the Archbishop to entrust St. Lawrence's parish to the Jesuits" (p. 60). He regarded that transfer to be based on easier transportation for the Jesuits who were chaplains to city institutions in Blackwell's and other islands (p. 61-62), and to the Good Shepherd convent at 90ᵗʰ St. and the East River (p. 62-63). Those who disagree with Dooley's position can point to the fact about two months after Fr. Mulledy's death, on March 8, the Jesuits took over the parish. Furthermore, they wonder if Dooley was aware of Fr. Provincial Thomas Gannon's 1890 letter quoting Fr. Loyzance's assertion that Fr. Mulledy asked his Archbishop to give his church to the Jesuits, and Fr. Gannon's claim that province archives confirmed that account.

A final note about Fr. Mulledy pertains to his likeness. An effort in the usual likely sources proved fruitless. However, a verbal portrait may suffice. Its author was identified only as "one who was a youthful admirer of Fr. Mulledy" and is quoted from Dooley (p. 52):

"I cannot recall any person of the old days whose stride so resembled that of the seasoned military man. He was about 5 ft. 10 in. in height and weighed about 180 pounds, brown hair, piercing black or very dark brown eyes, large hands and feet, sharp voice, quick nervous action and alertness of movement that indicated the working of the mind that must always be doing something. When speaking at the altar he was keen, exhaustive, unimpassioned; this was his exterior; but to the writer, who knew him well, he was almost as sensitive as a child. Father Mulledy was a man of strong character and fixed opinions. I cannot recall that [he] made any effort to win popularity, but he was a worker to his fingers' ends."

# SELECTED REFERENCES

Burrows, Edwin G. and Wallace, Mike, *Gotham: A History of New York City to 1898* (New York: Oxford, 1998).

Campbell, Thomas J. "St. John's College, Fordham," *Historical Records and Studies*, III, 1903, 88.

Campbell, Thomas J. "Fordham University," *Woodstock Letters*, 45, 1916, 349.

Cassidy, Francis P. *Catholic College Foundations and Developments in the United States 1677-1850*, Catholic University of America Ph.D. dissertation, 1924.

*Catalogus Defunctorum Societatis Iesu, 1814-1970*, Rufo Mendizábal, editor. (Rome: Jesuit Curia, 1972). Provides vital statistics of Jesuits who died during 1814-1970.

*Catalogus Provinciae Franciae, 1847 -*. Paris.

*Catalogus Provinciae Marylandiae-NeoEboracensi, 1880 -*. New York.

*The College of St. Francis Xavier: A Memorial and a Retrospect, 1847-1897.*

*Connolly, Francis X.* "Fordham History," *The Centurian*, 1941, Fordham University Yearbook.

Corby, William. *Memoirs of Chaplain Life: Three Years with the Irish Brigade in the Army of the Potomac*, Lawrence F. Kohl, Ed. (New York, Fordham U. Press, 1992).

Cornell, Thomas C. "Catholic Beginnings in Yonkers," *Historical Records and Studies*, 36, 76-77.

Corrigan, Michael A. "Register of the Clergy Laboring in the Archdiocese of New York ... to 1885," *Historical Records and Studies*, 3-13 (1903-1913).

Curran, Francis X., "Archbishop Hughes and the Jesuits: Prologue to Fordham." *Woodstock Letters*, 97, #1 (1968) 5-56.

*Dictionary of Jesuit Biography: Ministry to English Canada*, (Toronto, Ontario: Canadian Institute of Jesuit Studies, 1991).

Dooley, Patrick J., S.J., *Fifty Years in Yorkville*. (New York: Parish House, 1917).

*Fordham College Monthly* (1882 -) for background articles on early Fordham history.

Hennessy, Thomas C., S.J., Ed., *Fordham, The Early Years*. (New York: Something More Publications [distributed by the Fordham U. Press], 1998).

Gannon, Robert I. *Up to the Present*. (Garden City, NY: Doubleday, 1967).

Garraghan, Gilbert J. "Fordham's Jesuit Beginnings," *Thought*, March, 1941, 17-39.

Garraghan, Gilbert J. *The Jesuits of the Middle United States*. 3 vols. (New York: The America Press, 1938).

*Historical Records and Studies*, 1901-. The U.S. Catholic Historical Society.

Klein, Christa R., *The Jesuits and Catholic boyhood in nineteenth-century New York City*. Ann Arbor, University Microfilms, 1980.

Melick, Harry C.W., *The Manor of Fordham and Its Founder* (New York: Fordham University Press, 1950)

Minister's *Diaries*, 1832-, St. Mary's, Kentucky, St. John's College, Fordham. FU

Archives. (First written in Latin, then in French, and later in English).

Mullaly, John, *The New Parks Beyond the Harlem.* New York: Record & Guide, 1887.

Mulry, Patrick. *My Brother, A Memoir.* Staten Island, Mission of Immaculate Virgin, 1891.

Nelligan, Francis J. "Father John Larkin, S.J., 1801-1858," *Canadian Messenger of the Sacred Heart,* 1957, 68, 37-43; 102-110; 181-187.

O'Connell, Marvin R., *Edward Sorin* (University of Notre Dame Press, 2001).

Owens, Sister M. Lilliana, "Simon Fouché, S.J.: Missionary, Educator, Spiritual Director," *WL,* 98 (1969), 425-434.

Schroth, Raymond A., S.J. *Fordham: A History and Memoir.* (Chicago: Loyola Press, 2002).

Shea, John Gilmary, (Ed.). *The Catholic Churches of New York City.* (New York: Goulding, 1878).

Shelley, Thomas J., *Dunwoodie*: *The History of St. Joseph's Seminary* (Westminster, MD: Christian Classics, 1993).

Somervogel, C. *Bibliotheque de la Compagnie de Jesus.* 12 vols. (Bruxelles: O. Schepens, 1890-1932).

Taaffe, Thomas G., *A History of St. John's College*, Fordham. (London: Burns & Oates, 1891).

Thébaud, August J. *Forty Years in the United States of America* (1839-1885) (1904); *Three-Quarters of a Century: A Retrospect.* (I, 1912); (II, 1913). Edited posthumously by Charles G. Herbermann. (New York: the U.S. Catholic Historical Society).

Webb, Ben J., *A Century of Catholicity in Kentucky* (Louisville, KY: Charles A. Rogers, 1884).

*Woodstock Letters.* For references to individuals see the 1951 Index to volumes 1-80 (1872-1951). Unless another source is noted, obituary quotations in this book are typically from the *Woodstock Letters* (in this book, *WL).*

# INDEX

**A**

Abbadie, Rev. Francis   16, 19, 33, 45
Adams, Rev. Joseph   54
Ahern, Maurice   157
Alsberg(e), Br. Charles   34, 40, 43, 45, 167
*Annual Letters*   65-67, 68, 105, 109, 113, 115, 122, 129, 149
*apud nos*   155, 259
Aquaviva, V. Rev. Claudio   249
Archbishop of Oregon (Norbert Blanchet)   15, 42
Ausley, Mr.   3

**B**

Bacon, Br. Patrick   167
Bailly, French theology of   28
Baxter, Br.   45-46
Beaven, Bonaventure   168
Bidwell, novice Thomas   36, 43
Bishop of Albany, Most Rev. John McCloskey   53
Bishop of Louisville, see Flaget, Bishop
Bishop of New York, see Hughes, Bishop
Bishop of Pittsburgh,   see O'Connor, Bishop
Bishop of Toronto,  Most Rev. Michael Power   56
Blackwells Island   133, 135, 145, 149, 168, 173, 208, 224, 243
Blanchet, Most Rev. Norbert   41, 42
Blasczcak, Rev. Gerald R. viii, 158, 251-254
Blessed Virgin Mary 53, 109, 133, 137, 152, *et passim*
Blumensaat, Rev. Hermann   168, 254
Bonfils, Rev. Robert  viii, 13
Bourget, Bishop Ignace 261
Boulanger, Rev. Clément   2-46, 60, 63, 64, 78, 119, 241
Bouvier, philosophy of   28
Brendle, Br. Charles   169
Broderick, Rev. James   169
Bronx Park   249
Brothers of Christian Doctrine   121
Brothers of St. Joseph   9, 25-29
Brownson, Orestes   81
Buckley, Br. John  B. 169
Burrows, Edwin G.   275
Byrne, Br. Malachy   170
Byrnes, Rev. Michael J.   170

# C

Cagnard, Rev. F.   35

Campbell, Rev. Thomas J.   51,   275

Cardella, Rev. Philip   171

Cases of Conscience   54 *et passim*

Cassidy, Francis P.   275

Cassidy, Rev. Peter   171

*Catalogus Defunctorum Societatis Iesu*   247, 275

Cemetery, chronology of   159-160

Cemetery, history of   155-159

Chabrat, Bishop Guy (Louisville)   22-23, 27, 32, 35

Charity commissioners   145, 147

Chauvet, Rev. Joseph   16, 17, 18, 24, 40, 45, 53

Chazelle, Rev. Peter   2, 7-8, 14, 17, 18, 20, 23, 114, 278

Chester, Rev. John   172

Choné, Rev.   John Peter   14, 16-18, 25, 30, 35, 37, 39, 41, 46

Chopin, Rev. Philip   173, 254

Civil War   122, 165

Cleanliness   26, 27

Connell, Mr. Thomas M.   174

Consolers of the Sacred Heart of Jesus 140

Converts, Ministry to   101, 104

Conway, Rev. James   174

Corbett, Mr. Michael 174

Corby, William   265

Corne, Br. Philip 44, 46, 59

Cornell, Thomas C.   275

Corrigan, Br. Patrick   175

Corrigan, Michael A.   265

Coté, Br.   58, 62

Coué, Rev. Eugene   24, 28, 31, 35, 38, 42, 43, 46,

Cox. Rev. Ignatius 157

Craigie, Br. F.   26

Crane, Mr. John T.   175

Creeden, Br. Joseph   59, 71, 155, 159, 162, 175

Cremin, John   176

Crowe, Br. Patrick   39, 54, 176

Cunningham, Br. Bernard   176

Curran, Rev. Francis X.   vi, 265

Curray, Bernard Francis   177


# D

Daly, Maurice 177

Dandurand, Rev. Anatoly 177

Daubresse, Rev. Isidore   29, 50, 53, 155, 172, 200, 248, 259

De Smet, Rev. Peter  2, 57

De Wolf, Rev. John B.  182
De Pooter, Br. Frederick  180
Dealy, Rev. Patrick Francis  36, 43, 54-61, 155, 178, 212, 258-259, 263-264
Debating Society  93
Delaune, Rev. Mr. Julian  9, 25, 29, 71
DeLuynes, Rev. Charles Hippolyte  52, 117, 119, 179
Department of Public Parks  259
DePooter, Br. Frederick  59
Desjacques, Martin  36, 43, 53
Desribes, Rev. Joseph  181
Devitt, Rev. E. I.  246
De Wolf, Rev. John  182, 254
d'Istia, Msgr. Stack  31
Documents, what they can tell  161-163
Dongan, Col. Thomas  v
Donigani, Rev.  33, 34, 37, 38
Donnelly, Terence  119
Donovan, Br. William  182
Dooley, Patrick  211, 258, 273-275
Doucet, Rev. Edward  24, 29, 33, 42, 52, 53, 66, 183, 258, 259, 264
Doyle, Br. James  184
Doyle, Br. William  184
Driscol, Rev. Michael  6-10, 26-27, 36, 60-62, 119-121, 130, 185, 255, 261
Du Merle, Rev. Henri  40, 42, 255, 269-271
Du Ranquet, Rev. Dominic  32
Du Ranquet, Rev. Henry  21, 39-41, 43-45, 62, 121, 255-256
Duquesnay, Henry Lemercier  186
Durthaller, Rev. Joseph  256
Dwyer, Br. James  186

E
Ealy, Br. Martin  186
Early, Rev. John  264
Echeverria, Mr. Romuald M.  187
Eddrington, Henry Malory  187
Egan, Br. James  187
Elizabeth and Walker Streets  117, 123
English Language  16, 17, 20, 28, 40, 56

F
Fagan, Rev. James  188
Farmer, Rev. Ferdinand  v
Farrell, Br. Patrick  188
Fauris, Br. Francis  189
Fennel, James Chrysostom  189
Fenwick, Bishop Benedict (Boston)  52

Férard, Martin 39, 41-46, 53, 56, 57, 59, 60, 62, 121, 255
Fernandez, John 189
Fire at St. Francis Xavier 17, 117-118, 123-124
Fitzgerald, Br. James 190
Fitzpatrick, Rev. John 190
Flaget, Bishop Benedict Joseph (Bardstown/Louisville) 6, 8, 14-15, 23, 25-9, 33, 66, 70, 179
Flynn, Rev. Michael 190
Foertsch, Rev. George 191
Fordham cemetery 155-244, 256-257, 259-268
Fordham Prep vii
Fouché, Rev. Simon 21, 191
Fournier, Rev. Nicholas 6, 36, 45
Freeman, Rev. Thomas 192, 254
Frémiot, Rev Nicolas 61
French and Irish in New York, 74
Fulton, Rev. Robert 50

**G**
Gaignon, Mme. 7
Galligan, Rev. John 193
Gallitzin, Prince Demetrius Augustine 37
Gannon, Rev. Robert I. 265
Gannon, Rev. Thomas 264
Gardiner, Br. 61
Gargain, Rev. 37
Garraghan, Rev. Gilbert J. 265
Garvey, Br. Jeremiah 39 54, 118, 120, 194
Gatti, Rev. Daniel J. viii
Gauthier, Br. 31
Georgetown 214, 255 *et passim*
Gilles, Rev. Vitalis 37, 40, 45, 53
Giraud, Charles (engineer/surveyor) 157
Glover, D. 119
Gockeln, Rev. William 6, 7, 10-11, 30, 37, 42, 46, 59
Gormley, Br. Thomas 194
Graves, Br. J. 42
Gresselin, Rev. Charles 195
Grimot, Rev. J. 24
Guidée, Rev. A. 19, 21

**H**
Hampston, James/Jobn/Augustine 36, 43, 54, 56, 57
Hanipaux, Rev. Joseph 14, 16, 17, 18, 28, 31, 36, 41, 45
Hanrahan, Rev. Nicholas 195
Harley, Rev. John B. 55

Harvey, Rev. Thomas  v
Haveques, Rev. Arsenius  54
Health Department, City of New York  249
Heindenreich, Rev. Hubert  196
Hennen, Br. William  7, 9-10, 166, 196-197, 248, 265
Hennessy, Rev. Thomas C.  v-viii, 275
Herbermann, Charles G.  51, 276
Hillenmeyer, Remigius  197
*Historia Domus*  45, 117
Hoefele, Br. Fridolin  197
Hollinger, Rev. Anthony  36, 39, 40, 43, 53
House of Corrections  135
Houses of Detention  144
Hudon, Rev. Henry  10, 20, 36, 42, 55
Hughes, John Bishop/Archbishop (of New York)  3, 14, 50, 55-56, 58-59, 61, 66, 73-74, 78, 84, 93-94, 96, 111, 118-120, 139, 146, 148-149, 214, 256
Hus, Rev. John-Baptist  3-9, 14, 20, 22-26, 30, 39, 66, 68, 93, 102

**I**
Irish Faith  74
Irish housemaids 125, 129
Ives, Dr. Levi Stillman  150

**J**
Jaffré, Rev. John  22-23, 41-42, 149, 198
Janvier, theology of  28
Jarry, Br. Michael  77, 198
Jennessaux, Br. Joseph  17, 38, 43-44, 60
Jogues, St. Isaac  v
Jordan, Rev. Julian [Lyons Provincial]  37, 39-40, 44, 45
Joset, Br. Fidelis  121, 199
Jouin, Rev. Louis  118. 120, 199
Jubilee  74-75, 130

**K**
Kain, Br. Joseph  201
Keating, Rev. Andrew P.  201
Keon, Patrick  202
Kessel, Joseph  162
Keys, Br. Michael  202
Klein, Christa R.  275
Know-Nothings  49
Kohler, Rev. August  20, 33, 36, 42-43, 46, 52, 58-59, 120
Kohlmann, Rev. Anthony  v

**L**

Lacoste, Br. A.  31, 36, 38, 42-43, 54
Lafferty, Br. Neal  202
Larkin, Rev. John A.  13, 44. 46, 66, 68, 113-130, 203, 248, 255, 276
Lasalle, Mr.  31
Laufhuber, Rev. George  203, 254
Law and religious instruction  131
Lebreton, Rev. Peter  44, 53, 60, 62, 118, 204, 261
Ledoré, Br. Philip  204
Legoüais, Rev. Thomas  59, 63, 96, 205
Leo XII, Pope, Bull of,  29
*Liber Defunctorum*  156, 162, 176, 184, 191, 203, 243, 247, 249, 263
Liberal Arts  92
Living Rosary  109, 128, 256
Loriquet, Rev. Jean-Nicolas  247
Loyzance, Rev. Joseph  246-247, 251, 257, 273-274
Lynch Building  134, 137

**M**

Macé, Br. Julius  82, 102, 205, 251, 266
Mackey, Br. Henry W.  206
MacNulty, Br. Patrick  209
Madame B.  19
Maguire, Rev. Eugene  159, 206, 261
Maillard, Rev.  34-35
Mainguy, Rev. John  20, 44
Maldonado, Rev. Francis  38, 39, 55, 119, 179
Maréchal, Rev. Francis X.  36, 208
Martin, Rev. Felix  14, 21, 24-25, 28-29, 31-38, 40-45, 54
McCloskey, Most Rev. John  53, 117, 123, 273
McDonnell, Rev. John  207
McElroy, Fr. John  32
McCool, Rev. Gerald A.  viii, 245-251
McGovern, Rev. Francis X.  208
McKinnon, Rev. Neil N.  208
McParland, Br. Felix  56
McShea, Br. William  210
Medical student  130
Menet, Rev. John Baptist  27, 36, 41, 45-46
Merrick, Rev. David A.  210, 248
Methodist director  146
Meyer, Br. Conrad  211
Mignard, Rev. Paul  21, 37, 43, 44, 57, 58, 60, 62
Minister's diary  5,  8, 10, 50, 52, 60, 63, 156, 161, 189, 245, 247
Ministry to Negroes  122, 133, 136
Ministry to priests  101, 104

Ministry to prisons   125, 136-137
Mission to Vermont   107-108
Monroe, Rev. Francis   212
Moylan, Rev. William   213
Mullaly, John   265
Mulledy, Rev. Samuel   214, 258, 273-274
Mulry, Mr. George A.   215
Mulry, Patrick   266
Murphy, Rev. Henry   216
Murphy, Rev. William Stack   10, 14, 44-45, 62, 68, 70, 247

**N**

Nash, Rev. Michael   42, 117, 217, 248
Nativitists   49
Nelligan, Francis J.   266
New York-Canada Mission   3
New York Botanical Gardens   vi

**O**

O'Brien,  Rev. Michael H.   218
O'Connell, Marvin R.   266
O'Connor, Bishop  Michael (Pittsburgh)
O'Connor, Br. William   221
O'Connor, Mr. Edward   220
O'Connor, Rev. Charles J.   219
O'Connor, Rev. Jeremiah   220, 258
O'Gorman, Mr. Richard   158
O'Hare, Rev. Joseph A.   iii-iv, viii, 158
O'Lalor, Mr. Charles H.   221
O'Leary, Mr. Arthur   221
O'Malley, Rev. John W.   viii-xii
O'Neill, Mr. Jeremiah   222
O'Reilly, Mr.
O'Reilly,  Rev. Patrick
Ouellet, Rev. Thomas   24, 28, 33, 36, 42, 52, 56, 63, 165
Owens, Sister M. Lilliana   266

**P**

Pacciarini, Rev. Basil   222
Palacios, Louis   222
Palko, Mr.   30
Paradise, Br. Nicolas P.
Pardow, Rev. William O'Brien   169, 223, 258
Paresce, Rev. Angelo M.   274
Parish Missions   139
Park Commissioners   249

Pavarelli, Rev. Joseph  224, 254
Pédelope, Rev. John  14, 16-17, 21, 36
Pelletier, Rev. Alphonse  225
Peña, Charles  225
Pernot, Rev. John B.  24, 43, 53, 59
Perron, Rev. James  160, 164, 225-227, 258
Petit, Rev. Nicolas  5, 9-13, 22, 32-34, 44, 53, 61-62,  68-72, 82, 105, 117,
    131-142
Petitdemange, Rev. Charles  227, 254
Pillon, Rev. A.  28
Point, Rev. Nicolas  14-45 *et passim*
Power, Bishop John/Michael (Toronto)  56
Prachensky, Rev. Joseph  228, 254
Prendergast, Rev. John B.  229
Protestants  142
Proulx, Br. Joseph  230


**Q**
Queen, Mr.  30
Quinn, Mr. Charles  230


**R**
R Rabillon, Rev. Ambrose  5
Randalls Island  91, 99, 135, 145, 147, 148, 151, 169, 227 *et passim*
Régnier, Rev. Augustine  19, 23, 33, 36, 42, 52, 58
Religious of the Sacred Heart  121, 141
Risler, Br. Émile  126, 231
Robertson, Rev. John  231
Rochfort, Rev. Valentine H.  231
Rodrigue Family  246-247
Rodrigue, William  49, 246-247
Rogers, Br. Michael  232
Ronayne, Rev. Maurice  50, 233
Rooney, Br. Patrick  234
Roothaan, Very Rev. Jan  2, 245
Rose Hill  26, 29
Rouillé, Br. Leo  43
Roy, Br. John  123
Rubillon, Very Rev. Ambrose  5, 13, 18, 35, 39,
Ruiz, Antonias  233
Russo, Rev. Nicolas  234, 248
Ryan, Rev. John  6, 7, 10, 11, 19, 27, 59-60, 62, 120-121


**S**
Saché, Fr. L.  20, 45
Sarria, Rev. Achilles P.  162-163

Sauzeau, Mr. John  234

Schemmel, Rev. Seraphim  235

Schianski, Rev. Charles  38-39, 43, 54, 58, 60-61, 165, 255, 271-272

Schneider, Rev. George  32

Schroth, Rev. Raymond A.  266

Sealy,  Rev. Robert  viii, 13

Séné, Br. James  235

Shanahan, Br. Edmund  236

Shannon, Br. David  236

Shea, John Gilmary  58, 61, 276

Shelley, Rev. Thomas J.  276

Sing-Sing  135

Sisters of Charity (French)  135

Sisters of Charity of Mt. St. Vincent  135, 147, 148

Sisters of the Good Shepherd  46

Sodalities  65,  109, 126, 128, 130, 132-134, 142 , 150. *et passim*

Soderini, Rev. Tiberius  38, 41, 54, 61-62, 123

Soller, Rev. Joseph  17, 40

Somervogel, C.  266

Spalding, Br. Hilary  237

Spalding, Bishop Martin    (Louisville) 6, 14, 15, 27-28, 251, 257

St. Francis Xavier  College and Parish 112-153, 245-246, 248, 252, 264-265

St. John's College 47-111, 117, 123, 245-249, 261, 265-266

St. John's Hall 49

St. Joseph's College, Bardstown  5

St. Joseph's Institute for the Deaf, 194

St. Joseph's Parish, Troy  49, 190

St. Lawrence O'Toole, parish of  49 *et passim*

St. Mary's College, Kentucky  5-46, 48, 68-70, 262

St. Peter's College  156, 164, 172, 196, 201, 209, 221, 258

St. Raymond's  Cemetery 155-159, 216, 247-252

St. Vincent de Paul, Society of  132

St. Vincent's Hospital, Benefit for  130

Stoechlin, Br. Martin  237

Stokes, Rev. Joseph  53, 59

Stratch,  Mr.  30


**T**

Taaffe, Thomas G.  266

Talence, De, Mr.  35

Tellier,  Rev. Remi  31-32, 34, 38, 40, 44, 46, 58-59, 94, 110, 121, 255, 272

Thébaud Hall  51

Thébaud, Rev. August J.  44, 46, 48-51, 238, 248, 255

Third Ave, # 77    48-51, 118, 124

Thiry, Rev. Theodore  238

Thompson, George  239

Tissot, Rev. Peter  43, 53, 240
Tombs  135, 144, 246
Tomei, Rev. Michael X.  241, 261
Tupin, Br. P.  17, 27

**U – V**
University degrees, power to grant  134
Vachon, Br. Francis  53, 58
Van de Velde, Rev. James  13-19, 24, 31, 37, 39, 40
Van Rennselaer, Rev. Henry  241
Vaughen, Br. George  242
Vaurenterghan, Br. Désiré  242
Verhagen, Rev. Peter  14, 24, 28
Verheyden, Rev. Peter  37-38, 43, 117
Véroneau, Br. John  36-38, 54
Vicar General  135

**W**
Wallace, Mike  275
Ward, Rev. Thomas  243
Wards Island  2, 145, 208, 228
Warner, Mr.
Webb, Ben J.  266
Wellworth, Rev. James  243
Welsh, Br.
Weniger, Rev. Francis X.  140
West Farms, Town of  11
Whyte, Rev. Richard J.  244
Wine at dinner, reasons for  26
Workman's Diary  (Br. W. Donovan) 161

**X-Z**
Xavier Alumni Sodality  212, 256
Zwinge, Rev. Joseph  157, 259